Virtual Reality Development for the Google Daydream

Virtual Reality Development for the Google Daydream

by Matthew Scarpino

For permission requests, write to the publisher, addressed "Attention – Permissions Coordinator," at the following address:

Quiller Technologies, LLC

12546 Melrose Circle

Fishers, IN 46038

www.quillertech.com

Printed in the United States of America

Publisher's Cataloging-in-Publication data

Author: Scarpino, Matthew

Title: Virtual Reality Development for the Google Daydream

Description: Guide to programming virtual reality applications for the Google Daydream

ISBN: 978-0-9973037-1-1

p. cm.

Table of Contents

Chapter 1

Introduction

At the Google I/O Conference in May 2016, Clay Bavor announced Google's new effort to bring virtual reality to Android smartphones. The project's name was Google Daydream and the release date was Fall 2016. As an Android fanatic and a virtual reality enthusiast, I bought a Google Pixel and a Daydream headset as soon as they became available.

Daydream improves on Google Cardboard by providing a wealth of VR capabilities including motion tracking, spatial audio, low motion-to-photon latency, and high-speed graphical rendering. The result is a user experience that is both visually and aurally immersive. As Clay Bavor put it, "when you nail those things, it just feels like you're there."

The presentation introduced the three ingredients of Daydream:

- **Android 7 improvements** — high-speed processing for graphical rendering
- **Headset and controller** — enable the user to interact with the environment
- **VR applications** — create a virtual world for users to enjoy

This book focuses on the last point. That is, this book explains how to write Daydream apps that provide users with the immersive experiences that they've come to expect from virtual reality. We'll also look at deploying these apps to the Google Play Store so that other Daydream users can share the experience.

In essence, a Daydream app is an Android app that accesses special VR capabilities. Don't be concerned if you've never written an Android app—the first few chapters walk through the fundamentals of Android coding. The primary programming langauge in this book is Java, but later chapters explain how to improve performance by writing native code (C/C++).

The goal of this chapter is to describe what Daydream development is all about and explain why you should drop whatever you're doing and learn it. But before getting into the technical details, I'd like to provide a brief account of virtual reality's development. This isn't a complete history, but it will clarify what makes the Google Daydream so revolutionary.

1.1 A Brief History of Virtual Reality

To appreciate the Google Daydream, it helps to take a step back and look at the evolution of virtual reality. Many historians attribute the first VR developments to painters of panoramic images and flight simulators, but I like to start with a science fiction story published in 1959.

1.1.1 Pygmalion's Spectacles

If we take fictional characters into account, then the inventor of virtual reality must be Professor Albert Ludwig of Stanley Weinbaum's 1959 short story, *Pygmalion's Spectacles.* The story's text is freely available at www.gutenberg.org/ebooks/22893.

The story begins with a philosphical discussion between Professor Ludwig and a worn-out businessman named Dan Burke. Burke laughs at the idea of virtual reality:

"Anybody can tell the difference between a picture and the real thing, or between a movie and life."

"But," whispered the other, "the realer the better, no? And if one could make a—a movie—very real indeed, what would you say then?"

"Nobody can, though."

The eyes glittered strangely again. "I can!" he whispered. "I did!"

To prove his point, Ludwig asks Burke to try his new invention—magic spectacles with chemicals that control the wearer's sensory input. As Burke puts them on, he becomes immersed in an idyllic forest world named Paracosma. Naturally, he falls madly in love with an elf named Galatea.

The next morning, Burke wakes up in a daze, unable to distinguish between reality and his life in Paracosma. When he runs into Prof. Ludwig again, he agrees that the professor had been right about virtual reality all along.

1.1.2 Morton Heilig

Putting aside science fiction, the father of modern virtual reality is Morton Heilig. In 1961, he filed a patent for the Sensorama, a single-person theater that uses stereoscopy, spatial audio, and body tilting to provide a fully-immersive cinematic experience. Figure 1.1 presents the drawing from Heilig's patent.

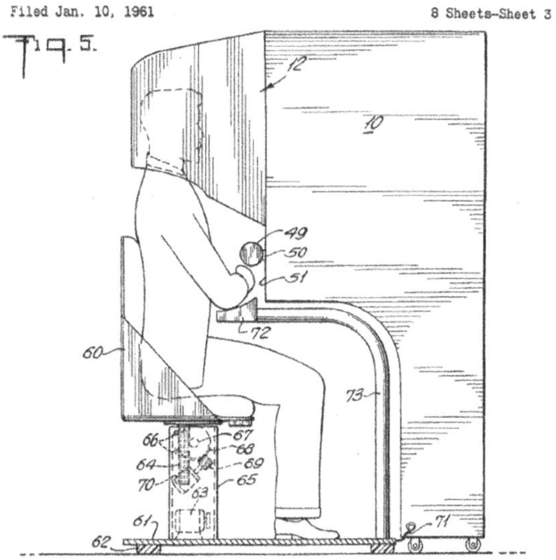

Figure 1.1 Heilig's Sensorama

Given the high cost of building the Sensorama, Heilig turned his attention to headsets. Figure 1.2 presents a drawing from Heilig's patent for his Telesphere Mask.

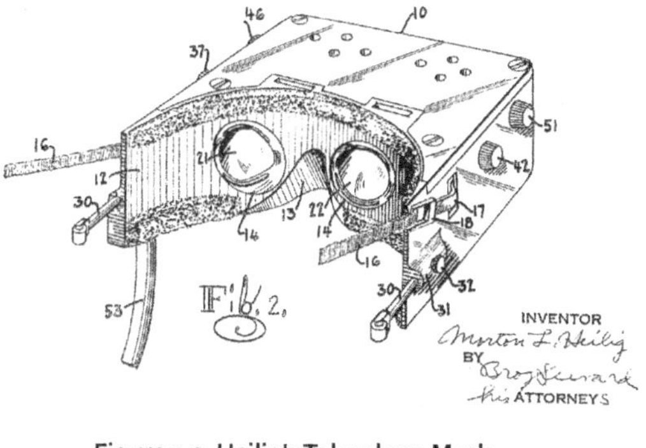

Figure 1.2 Heilig's Telesphere Mask

For owners of VR headsets, the Telesphere Mask depicted in Figure 1.2 should look familiar. Its goal was to enable viewers to watch television in three dimensions. The principle underlying its operation is *stereoscopy*.

Originally discovered in the 19th century, stereoscopy creates the illusion of depth by displaying two nearly-identical images—one for each eye. When a viewer's brain fuses the images, slight deviations are interpreted as differences in depth. Stereoscopy is employed in all modern VR headsets including the Google Daydream, and later chapters will explain how app developers can take advantage of this.

1.1.3 Incremental Improvements (1960 – 2010)

In the decades following the Telesphere Mask, scientists and engineers made many improvements to Heilig's design. None of the commercial products gained traction in the marketplace, but they laid the groundwork for the development of more advanced VR systems.

- In 1961, Philco engineers developed a headset that employed magnetic motion tracking to determine the headset's orientation. This is called *head tracking*, and became a common feature in all modern VR systems.
- In 1968, Ivan Sutherland and Bob Sproull connected a headset to a computer capable of drawing graphics in a stereoscopic display.
- In 1987, Jaron Lanier popularized the term "virtual reality" to represent his research into using graphical environments for education.
- In 1991, Jonathan Waldern launched the Virtuality Group, which created VR gaming machines whose headsets combined stereoscopic display, computer generated graphics, head tracking, and networking.
- In 1992, Silicon Graphics released the first version of OpenGL (Open Graphics Language) to serve as a specification for 3-D graphical programming.
- In 1993, Sega announced a VR headset for its Genesis gaming console. The headset featured head tracking, stereo sound, and a liquid crystal display (LCD) screen.
- In 1995, Nintendo released the Virtual Boy, a gaming console integrated within a VR headset. The headset featured stereoscopic graphics and head tracking.
- In 2003, a variant of OpenGL was released called OpenGL ES (OpenGL for Embedded Systems). This is the graphical rendering tool used by Android devices.

The importance of graphical processing can't be overstated. The public's desire for video games forced hardware vendors to release more powerful graphics cards with each passing year. This processing capability has enabled modern VR applications to provide the visual immersion that users have come to take for granted.

1.1.4 The Oculus Rift

In 2010, a technically-minded teenager named Palmer Luckey developed the first of a series of VR headsets. As he became more experienced, the headsets acquired features such as stereoscopic display and 270° field of view. With each new prototype, Palmer discussed his progress on a message forum for VR enthusiasts.

In 2012, Luckey created his sixth-generation VR headset, called the Rift. He announced a Kickstarter effort to provide kits that would allow developers to build their own systems. John Carmack, founder of id Software, championed Luckey's new system and demonstrated it at the 2012 Electronic Entertainment Expo.

After Carmack's demo, the Rift became a worldwide sensation. Up to that point, virtual reality had always been viewed as practically impossible. But with Luckey's hardware and Carmack's software, there was no denying that the day of VR had dawned.

The Rift was renamed the Oculus Rift, and Palmer Luckey formed a company, Oculus VR, to sell it. In 2014, Facebook purchased Oculus VR for three billion dollars.

The Oculus Rift has improved dramatically since the initial Kickstarter effort, and Figure 1.3 shows what the Consumer Version 1 (CV1) looks like. (Image provided by Samwalton9 under the Creative Commons License.)

Figure 1.3 The Oculus Rift CV1

To the rear, the headset's cord connects to a PC. The headset doesn't perform graphical rendering on its own, but receives graphical data from the computer's GPU. Because it's connected to a computer, the headset is called a *tethered* headset.

1.1.5 The Vive and PlayStation VR

In the wake of the Oculus Rift's phenomenal success, other companies rushed to join the virtual reality revolution. At the time of this writing, two of the most popular VR systems are the Vive, developed by HTC and Valve, and the PlayStation VR developed by Sony.

The Vive is similar to the Oculus Rift in that the headset is tethered to a PC. Unlike the Oculus Rift, the headset uses motion tracking to monitor the user's position. This makes it possible for applications to keep track of the user's movement in the virtual world. This capability is called *room-scale* virtual reality.

Sony's PlayStation VR (PSVR) headset is tethered to a PlayStation 4 console. Using head tracking, it allows the wearer to interact with the game environment. The headset provides many impressive features, including a 1920-by-1080 pixel display, stereoscopic 3-D rendering, and the ability to display graphics at up to 120 frames per second.

1.1.6 Google Cardboard

One of the most impressive features of modern smartphones is high-performance graphics. Ever since Android 1.0, Android phones have supported OpenGL ES for graphical rendering. The graphical processor units (GPUs) in these smartphones aren't as powerful as GPUs in desktop PCs, but every new generation produces GPUs that are faster and more powerful than those that preceded it.

In 2014, two Google engineers, David Coz and Damien Henry, developed Android apps capable of displaying VR-like graphics. To view the display, they created a viewer with glass lenses and a cardboard frame. Figure 1.4 shows what the viewer looks like. (Image provided by Evan Amos as public domain.)

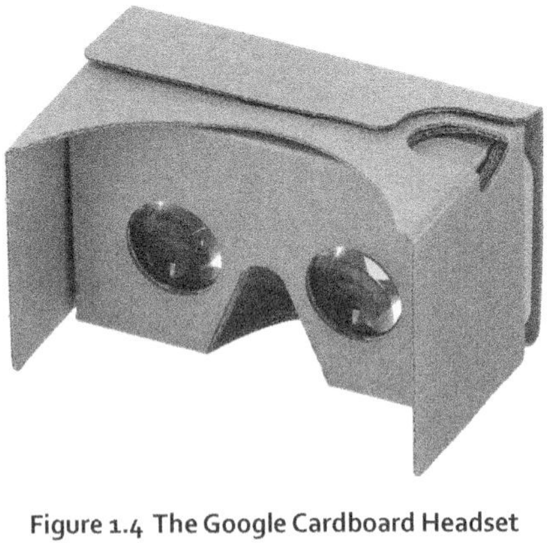

Figure 1.4 The Google Cardboard Headset

The side project gathered attention throughout the company, and at the 2014 Google I/O conference, the new Google Cardboard project was announced. Each attendee received a Cardboard viewer and Google released a software development kit (SDK) for developing Cardboard apps.

Google Cardboard acquired a wide following, with more than 5 million viewers shipped. But many consider the system a novelty instead of a viable VR platform. Two concerns are mediocre rendering performance and the lack of an external method of interacting with the virtual world, such as a joystick or controller.

1.1.7 Google Daydream

In 2016, Google made it clear that it was going to take virtual reality seriously. They announced the Daydream project and released the first Daydream-ready smartphones: the Pixel and the Pixel XL. To be Daydream-ready, a phone must meet a number of requirements, including the following:

1. At least two physical cores
2. Screen resolution of at least 1080p
3. Consistent graphical rendering at 60 frames per second
4. Wireless connectivity through Bluetooth LE 4.2
5. Sensors capable of reading the surface's temperature
6. Support for OpenGL ES 3.2

Any phone that meets these requirements should be able to execute Daydream apps reliably and at high performance. At the time of this writing, only the Pixel, Pixel XL, Moto Z, and Axon 7 meet the criteria.

A Daydream system encompasses more than just a powerful smartphone. The Daydream kit provides a headset that connects to the smartphone using near field communication (NFC) and a controller that connects using Bluetooth LE. In addition, the Android 7 operating system provides a new processing mode called VR Mode, which ensures high-speed processing for virtual reality applications.

To enable developers to write apps for the Daydream, Google has released a handful of different development kits. These are freely available for download, and the main site is https://developers.google.com/vr/daydream/overview.

This book focuses on two of these kits. The Google VR Software Development Kit (SDK) provides Java classes for Daydream development. The Google VR Native Development Kit (NDK) provides C/C++ libraries and files that make it possible to improve the performance of Daydream apps.

1.2 Overview of Daydream Development

The goal of this book is to explain how to code, deploy, and execute applications for the Google Daydream. A Daydream app is a special type of Android app, and to reach as wide an audience as possible, the first part of this book presents the fundamentals of coding Android apps. The second part discusses the classes in the Google VR SDK and the last part presents the features in the Google VR NDK.

At minimum, readers need to have a solid understanding of Java. To compile and run the example code, readers should have Android Studio installed on their development system. Of course, it would also help to have a connected Daydream-ready device.

1.2.1 Android Fundamentals

The first four chapters of this book explore Android topics that every Daydream developer should be familiar with. Chapter 2 introduces Android Studio, the most popular environment for developing Android applications. We'll look at project structure and the process of building Android application packages (APKs). The chapter also discusses Gradle, the build automation system used by Android Studio.

Chapters 3 through 5 present the basic classes involved in Android development. The discussion starts with the `Activity` and `View` classes, and proceeds further with the `TextView` and `ImageView` classes. The topic of resources is also critical, and we'll look at many different kinds of resources, including image resources, layout resources, and values resources.

1.2.2 The Google VR Software Development Kit

Chapters 6 through 13 discuss the first of Google's development kits: the Google VR SDK. This provides Java classes that enable Android apps to access virtual reality features. For example, the `GvrActivity` class represents an activity in a VR app, the `HeadTransform` class identifies the orientation of the headset, and the `Controller` class provides data about the Daydream controller.

When coding VR apps, most of the effort is put into creating the graphical environment. For Android devices, this means programming with OpenGL ES. Therefore, a large part of this discussion is devoted to explaining how to use OpenGL ES to perform graphical rendering. Topics in this discussion include the graphical pipeline, vertex shaders, fragment shaders, textures, transformations, depth testing, and the Blinn-Phong lighting model.

1.2.3 The Google VR Native Development Kit

The majority of Daydream apps, like the majority of Android apps, are coded only in Java. But if routines need to be executed at high speed, they can be coded as C/C++ functions. This makes many Java developers nervous, but when used properly, low-level access can dramatically improve an application's performance.

For this reason, Google provides the Google VR Native Development Kit. This contains C/C++ libraries and header files that make it possible to access VR capabilities in native code. One advantage is that applications can call OpenGL ES functions directly instead of using Java wrappers. Another advantage is that Daydream apps can access popular C/C++ toolsets like FreeType.

Chapters 14 through 16 discuss the Google VR NDK and demonstrate how it can be used. It's worth noting that, even with the NDK, all Daydream apps require Java code to define the overall activity. Also, because of the combination of Java and C/C++, applications require the Java Native Interface (JNI), which is difficult to work with.

1.2.4 Example Code

In my opinion, the best way to learn how to write code is to read code. For this reason, I've provided this book's example code in an archive at http://www.dreambookvr.com. This code is free and is available under the public domain.

If you unzip the archive, you'll see that it consists of an Android Studio project that contains multiple modules. Each module corresponds to an app discussed in a later chapter. Chapter 2 discusses the difference between projects and modules and explains how the example code is structured.

1.2.5 The Unity SDK and Unreal Engine SDK

In addition to the Google VR SDK and Google VR NDK, Google provides two more toolsets for Daydream development. The Google VR SDK for Unity makes it possible to adapt code written for the Unity 3D game engine into Daydream applications. Similarly, Daydream in Unreal makes it possible to access Daydream capabilities in code written for the Unreal Engine.

This book doesn't discuss either of these toolsets. However, many books are available that explain how to write code for Unity 3D and the Unreal Engine. There are also many resources online. Stack Overflow is particularly helpful, and questions related to Google VR can be found at http://stackoverflow.com/questions/tagged/google-vr.

1.3 Personal Note

My favorite game for the Daydream is *AFFECTED: The Manor* by Fallen Planet Studios. The gameplay involves exploring a haunted house and figuring out what terrible events have transpired.

This was my first horror game in virtual reality and I was amazed by how frightening it was. At one point, I walked into a room and the door slammed shut. The lights flickered and a gravelly voice whispered: *"Look behind you."*

If I'd played this on a PC with stereo speakers, the scene would be silly. But thanks to the Daydream's spatial audio projection, I really heard the voice come from behind me. And thanks to the Daydream's head tracking, that damned ghost knew exactly when I turned around...

This and other games have strengthened my belief that virtual reality is going to cause a revolution in entertainment. I predict that future VR apps will provide interactive movies, where users get to dodge bullets with James Bond and solve mysteries with Sherlock Holmes.

As I write this in February 2017, tethered VR systems like the Vive are more popular than untethered systems like the Daydream. But as smartphones become more powerful, I predict that users will prefer the freedom and convenience of untethered VR experiences. I sincerely hope that this book will enable you to create VR experiences of your own.

Chapter 2

Android Studio

Before you can understand Daydream development, you need to understand Android development. The goal of Android development is to combine a series of files into a special archive called an Android Application Package, or APK. An APK may contain hundreds or even thousands of files, including resources, manifests, libraries, assets, and Java class files.

Processing these files requires multiple complex tasks. Google provides utilities that run on the command line, but it's more convenient to click on toolbar items in an integrated development environment (IDE). Google's official IDE for Android development is Android Studio, which is the topic of this chapter.

The good news is that Android Studio is free, it runs on all common operating systems, and it provides a wealth of capabilities for Android development. These capabilities include full-featured editors, debuggers, and simulators. Also, its operation can be customized through plugins.

The bad news is that Android Studio is difficult to learn. Its project structure is different than that of other tools. To build projects, it relies on a management system named Gradle, which is based on a Java-like language named Groovy. You can use Android Studio without being an expert with Gradle or Groovy, but it helps to understand the basics.

The goal of this chapter is twofold. The first sections of the chapter explain how to obtain Android Studio and use it to build a project. The later sections explain how to download the example code for this book and access the code in Android Studio. Once you understand how the example code is structured, you'll be better able to understand the content of later chapters.

2.1 Installation and Setup

At the time of this writing, Android Studio can be freely downloaded from Google at https://developer.android.com/studio/index.html. The software is released under the Apache License 2.0, so it can be used without restriction for free and commercial software development.

This section starts by explaining how to install Android Studio. Then we'll walk through the process of creating a project.

2.1.1 Installing Android Studio

After downloading the Android Studio package, the next step is to run the setup executable. This launches a series of pre-installation dialogs, and on my Windows system, there are four dialogs in total:

1. Choose Components — Select the desired components to install. For this book, you'll need the **Android Studio** and **Android SDK** components.
2. License Agreement — Click **I Agree** to accept the Android SDK license, which contains the following requirement: "You agree that if you use the SDK to develop applications for general public users, you will protect the privacy and legal rights of those users."
3. Configuration Settings — Select directories to hold the desired components, including Android Studio (the IDE) and the Android SDK (the tools and libraries needed for Android development). Pay close attention to the location of the Android SDK.
4. Choose Start Menu Folder — Pick a start menu to contain the program's shortcuts.

The last dialog has a button called **Install**. When this is pressed, the setup executable configures and installs Android Studio. This may take a few minutes.

2.1.2 The Setup Wizard

When you run Android Studio for the first time, the setup wizard will present a series of dialogs that configure the application's properties:

1. In the **Welcome** dialog, click **Next** to proceed.
2. The **Install Type** dialog asks if you want to customize the IDE's components. Leave the radio button marked **Standard** selected and click **Next**.

3. The **Verify Settings** presents the configuration that Android Studio intends to use. If you want to make changes, click **Previous** and select a custom installation. If you're satisfied, click **Finish**.

2.1.3 Creating an Initial Project

After the setup wizard has installed the SDK's components, it will present a dialog for launching Android Studio. The first option is called **Start a new Android Studio project**. If you click on this, Android Studio will present the **New Project** dialog.

1. The first entry box asks for an application name that identifies the project. I recommend setting the domain name to **MyFirstProject**.
2. The next entry box asks for a domain address that identifies the organization creating the project. This is usually given as a fully-qualified domain name, and I recommend setting this to **me.example.com**.
3. Most of the projects in this book will make use of C/C++ code. Therefore, check the box named **Include C++ Support**.
4. The last box asks for a directory to hold the project's contents. I recommend choosing the default, which is a folder called **AndroidStudioProjects** in the user's home directory.

After filling out the dialog, click **Next**. The **Target Android Devices** dialog asks for information related to the target device. By default, the **Phone and Tablet** option is selected.

The example code in this book assumes that the target device is running at least Android 7.0. Therefore, set the minimum SDK version to API 24. Click **Next**.

The next dialog configures the initial content of the project. The three options are **No Activity**, **Basic Activity**, and **Empty Activity**. For now, the goal is to become acquainted with the application, so select **No Activity** and click **Next**.

The **Customize the Activity** dialog configures the project's activity. Leave the activity name set to `MainActivity` and the layout name at `activity_main`. Click **Next** to proceed.

The **Customize C++ Support** dialog configures how a project's C++ source code should be compiled. Most of this book focuses on Java, but starting with Chapter 14, projects will use C/C++ as well. Set the C++ standard to **C++11** and click **Finish**.

Android Studio will perform a series of tasks needed to create and configure the new project. When it's finished, the Android Studio IDE window will appear. The following section presents this window and explains how the IDE can be used.

2.2 Android Studio

Figure 2.1 shows what the Android Studio IDE looks like when it first starts up. If there are any errors about a missing NDK, don't be concerned.

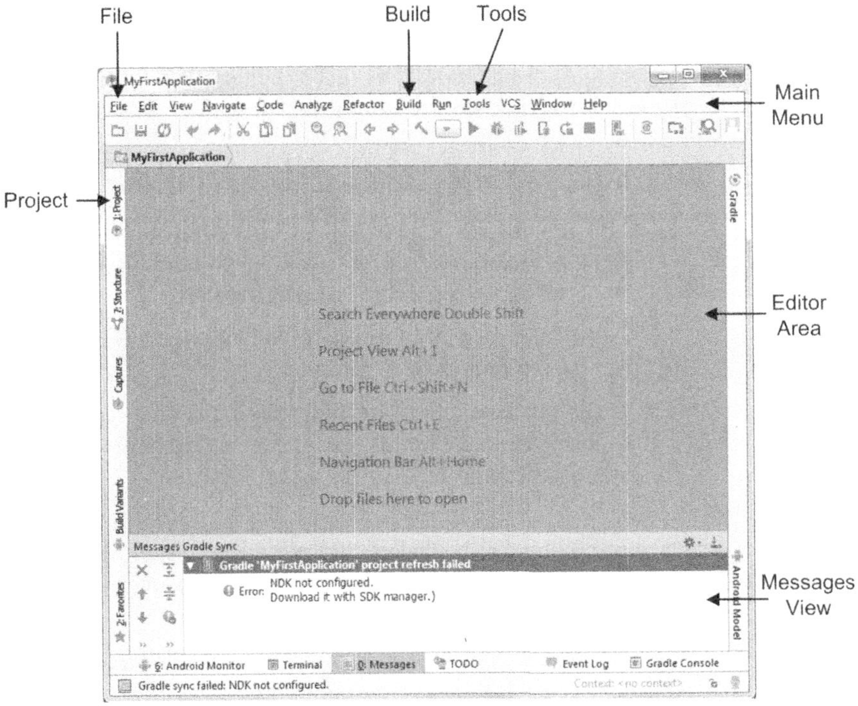

Figure 2.1 The Android Studio IDE

As in many applications, the main menu and toolbar are positioned on top. At the bottom, Android Studio has a messages view and a status bar. The rest of the application serves as an editing area. In addition, the IDE has tool entries placed all around the perimeter.

It would take an entire book to discuss all of Android Studio's features. To get started, you only need to be familiar with four aspects of the IDE:

1. The File menu — Creates new projects and configures the IDE's operation
2. The Build menu — Compiles a project's source code and constructs an APK
3. The Tools menu — Accesses tools that support Android development
4. The Project tool — Opens the Project Navigator

The Tools menu is particularly important because it provides access to the SDK Manager. The following discussion explains what this tool accomplishes. Then we'll examine the process of accessing a device connected to a Windows system.

2.2.1 The SDK Manager

The SDK Manager makes it possible to install or remove features from Android Studio. To access it, go to the main menu and select **Tools** > **Android** > **SDK Manager**. In the dialog that appears, select the **SDK Tools** tab in the upper center. Figure 2.2 illustrates what this looks like.

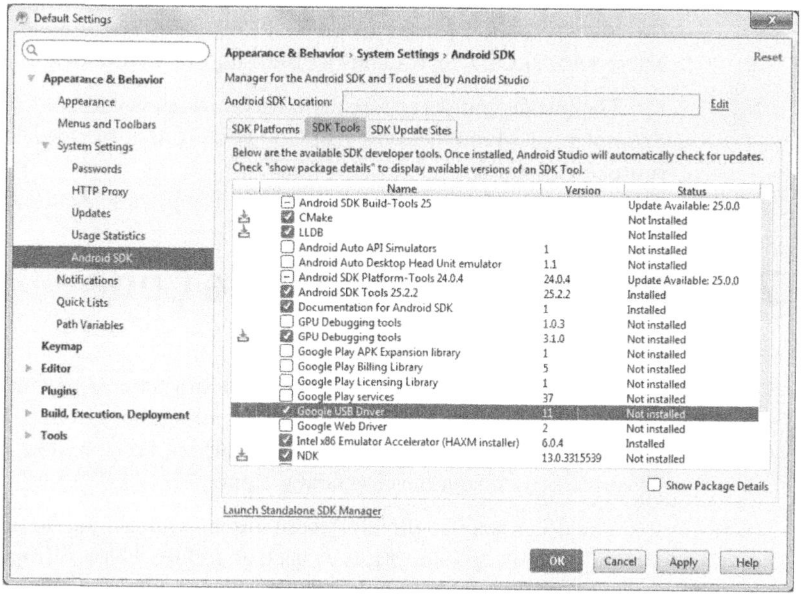

Figure 2.2 The SDK Manager

To build and analyze the code discussed in this book, you need to select and install components listed in the SDK Manager:

- NDK — The Native Development Kit contains the tools for C/C++ development
- CMake — Versatile tool for building C/C++ code
- LLDB — Low-level debugger makes it possible to debug processes on remote targets
- GPU Debugging Tools — Utilities for analyzing the graphics processor
- Google USB Driver (Windows only) — Provides access to connected devices

After clicking **OK**, accept the tool licenses and download the tools. All of the downloaded files will be stored in the directory of the Android SDK.

2.2.2 The Google USB Driver (Windows only)

Before proceeding further, it's important to make sure that Android Studio can recognize your device. If you haven't already, be sure to connect it to your development system. If you're using a Linux or Mac OS system, Android Studio should be able to access your device immediately.

On Windows systems, access to a connected device requires the Google USB Driver, which should have been downloaded through the SDK Manager. If this was downloaded, the driver files should be in the $ANDROID_SDK/extras/google/usb_driver directory, where $ANDROID_SDK identifies the Android SDK folder.

The installation procedure depends on which version of Windows you're using. For a complete set of instructions, visit Google's site at https://developer.android.com/studio/run/oem-usb.html.

2.3 Importing the Example Code

The main site for this book is www.dreambookvr.com. This site provides a link for downloading a zip file containing the book's example code. The file's name is dreambookvr.zip, and before proceeding further, I recommend that you download it and decompress it on your development system.

The decompressed directory contains an Android Studio project called DreamBookVR. To import this project, go to **File** > **New** > **Import Project...** in Android Studio's main menu. In the file navigator dialog, select the DreamBookVR directory and press OK.

After reading the project's content, Android Studio will display the modules that make up the project in the left pane. If the pane isn't initially visible, click the **1:Project** tab in the upper-left. Figure 2.3 shows what the tab looks like.

At this point, it's important to discuss terminology. In most IDEs, the files needed to create an application are contained in a top-level folder called a *project*. If you've ever used the Eclipse IDE, then you know that it organizes projects in a container called a *workspace*. If you're familiar with Microsoft's Visual Studio, then you know that it organizes projects in a container called a *solution*.

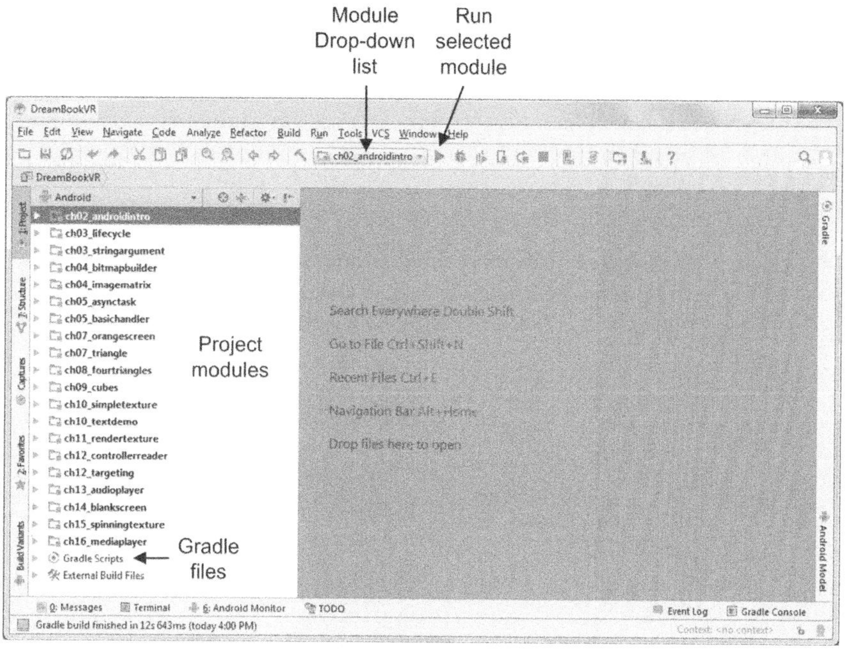

Figure 2.3 A Project and its Modules

In Android Studio, the terms are slightly reversed. Files related to a specific app are contained in a *module*. Modules are contained in a *project*. Android Studio displays one project at a time, and as illustrated in the figure, the DreamBookVR project contains an assortment of modules whose names start with a chapter number.

In the center of the toolbar, a drop-down list makes it possible to select one of the project's modules. This identifies the module that you intend to operate upon. For example, the toolbar item to the right of the drop-down list tells Android Studio to execute the selected module. Other module-specific operations include debugging, stopping, and running with code coverage.

In general, each module of a project corresponds to a single APK. The APK can be constructed using the items in the Build menu. The first entry, **Make Project**, builds every module in the project. The second entry, **Make Module**, builds only the module selected in the drop-down list.

In addition to listing the modules, the left pane has an entry called **Gradle Scripts**. If you expand this, you'll see a listing of files related to Gradle. These files determine how Android Studio builds APKs for modules. The next section discusses this important topic in detail.

2.4 Brief Introduction to Gradle

To build the modules of a project, Android Studio relies on Gradle. Gradle is a build automation system based on the Groovy programming language. You don't have to understand Groovy to use Gradle, but you should be familiar with Gradle before building projects with Android Studio.

Gradle builds are defined using a series of configuration files. A project's Gradle files can be accessed by expanding the **Gradle Scripts** entry below the list of modules. Figure 2.4 illustrates the list of Gradle files in the DreamBookVR project.

- Gradle Scripts
  - **build.gradle** (Project: DreamBookVR)
  - **build.gradle** (Module: ch02_androidintro)
  - **build.gradle** (Module: ch03_lifecycle)
  - **build.gradle** (Module: ch03_stringargument)
  - **build.gradle** (Module: ch04_bitmapbuilder)
  - **build.gradle** (Module: ch04_imagematrix)
  - **build.gradle** (Module: ch05_asynctask)
  - **build.gradle** (Module: ch05_basichandler)
  - **build.gradle** (Module: ch07_orangescreen)
  - **build.gradle** (Module: ch07_triangle)
  - **build.gradle** (Module: ch08_fourtriangles)
  - **build.gradle** (Module: ch09_cubes)
  - **build.gradle** (Module: ch10_simpletexture)
  - **build.gradle** (Module: ch10_textdemo)
  - **build.gradle** (Module: ch11_rendertexture)
  - **build.gradle** (Module: ch12_controllerreader)
  - **build.gradle** (Module: ch12_targeting)
  - **build.gradle** (Module: ch13_audioplayer)
  - **build.gradle** (Module: ch14_blankscreen)
  - **build.gradle** (Module: ch15_spinningtexture)
  - **build.gradle** (Module: ch16_mediaplayer)
  - **gradle-wrapper.properties** (Gradle Version)
  - **gradle.properties** (Project Properties)
  - **settings.gradle** (Project Settings)
  - **local.properties** (SDK Location)

Figure 2.4 Gradle Files in the DreamBookVR Project

Each file's purpose is identified by its name:

- build.gradle — Defines the build characteristics of the project or an individual module
- settings.gradle — Identifies the modules to be included in the project
- gradle-wrapper.properties — Configuration settings for the Gradle wrapper
- gradle.properties — Configuration settings for Gradle operation
- local.properties — Configuration settings for Android

As shown, every Gradle file's suffix is .gradle or .properties. A *.gradle file is formatted according to the Gradle standard. Properties files are simpler and each contains a list of *name=value* pairs.

For example, on my system, gradle.properties specifies the maximum amount of memory that should be allocated for Gradle's operation. This is set with the following *name=value* pair:

```
org.gradle.jvmargs=-Xmx1536m
```

The local.properties file defines characteristics that apply to Android processing. On my system, this contains two entries: `SDK.DIR` identifies the location of the Android software development kit (SDK) and `NDK.DIR` identifies the location of the Android native development kit (NDK).

The settings.gradle file is also simple to understand. This contains a series of `include` statements that identify which modules should be included in the project. For example, the following line states that the ch02_androidintro module should be included in the DreamBookVR project:

```
include ':ch02_androidintro'
```

Three of the `include` statements are commented out. As a result, the ch14_blankscreen, ch15_spinningtexture, and ch16_mediaplayer modules are not initially included in the project. This is because these modules require native libraries in order to compile properly. These libraries must be specially installed and Chapter 14 discusses the installation process in detail.

The build.gradle files are more important and more complex than the settings.gradle file. A full discussion of Gradle could take up an entire book, but I hope the next section will provide a solid background on the topic.

2.5 Build Files

Looking back at Figure 2.4, it's clear that most of the Gradle files in the DreamBookVR project are named build.gradle. The project contains one top-level build.gradle file and one build.gradle file for each module. This book refers to the first file as the *project build file* and the others as *module build files*.

Both types of build files employ the same general format, which contains a mixture of statements and blocks. Each block starts with a name and zero or more statements contained in curly braces:

```
task1 {
   ...
}

task2 {
   ...
}
```

To understand how Android Studio builds APKs from code, it's important to be familiar with the different types of blocks. This section discusses project build files first and then presents module build files.

2.5.1 The Project Build File

The project build file provides general information about building the project. To be specific, it identifies what dependencies are needed and how they can be obtained.

In the DreamBookVR project, most of the project build file consists of the basic commands that Android Studio generates for all projects. There are four blocks:

- `buildscript` — identifies repositories and dependencies for Gradle
- `allprojects` — identifies repositories and dependencies for every module in the project
- `task clean` — defines the operations that clean up the project after a build
- `task helloGradle` — demonstrates Gradle scripting

To build Android projects, Gradle needs a plugin called com.android.application. This is provided in a package called com.android.tools, which is not included in Android Studio. For this reason, the `buildscript` block identifies the plugin and specifies that it must be downloaded from https://bintray.com/bintray/jcenter.

The project build file identifies the required plugin and its download site by inserting two sub-blocks into buildscript: dependencies and repositories. A dependency is usually a file or plugin needed for the build process. A repository is a location that Gradle can access to obtain dependencies.

The following code shows what this looks like:

```
buildscript {

  repositories {
    jcenter()
  }

  dependencies {
    classpath 'com.android.tools.build:gradle:2.2.3'
  }

}
```

In this code, the jcenter() method provides Gradle with the URL of the jcenter website. Android Studio will download the plugin whenever the project is built or synced to the IDE.

While the buildscript block identifies dependencies required by Gradle, the allprojects block identifies dependencies required by the project's modules. For Android builds, both types of dependencies are provided from the same jcenter repository. The project build file specifies this with the following block:

```
allprojects {
  repositories {
    jcenter()
  }
}
```

The third block identifies actions to be performed when Android Studio cleans the project. This is accomplished by defining a task named clean:

```
task clean(type: Delete) {
  delete rootProject.buildDir
}
```

The clean process can be customized by inserting Gradle commands into this block. But the focus of this discussion isn't Gradle scripting. Instead, my goal is to make you sufficiently familiar with the build process so that you can read build files and configure them for your projects.

2.5.2 Module Build Files

Every module needs a build.gradle file to specify how its code should be compiled. It provides this build information in a block called `android`, which is defined by the com.android.application plugin mentioned earlier.

In an Android project, a module build file needs to perform three operations:

1. Load com.android.application with `apply plugin`.
2. Define the module's characteristics in an `android` block.
3. Specify the module's dependencies in a `dependencies` block.

Given these tasks, module build files usually have the following structure:

```
apply plugin: 'com.android.application'

android {
  ...
}

dependencies {
  ...
}
```

This discussion looks at the `android` and `dependencies` blocks. At the end of the discussion, I'll present the build.gradle file for the ch02_androidintro module.

The android Block

The `android` block contains Android-specific build options. In most modules, this block will contain the six elements listed in Table 2.1.

Table 2.1

Fundamental Elements of the android Block

Element	Description
`compileSdkVersion`	Level of the API that should be used to compile the module
`buildToolsVersion`	Version of the SDK tools that should be used in the build
`buildTypes`	Different build types, such as debug and release
`productFlavors`	Different product releases, such as free or paid

defaultConfig	Configuration of the default build variant
externalNativeBuild	Configuration settings for the native build

The `compileSdkVersion` and `buildToolsVersion` elements are straightforward. The first value sets the level of the API that should be used to compile the module's code and the second value sets the version of the tools that should perform the build. These values aren't packaged in the APK, so it's usually a good idea to set them to the highest versions available.

To understand the other `android` elements, you need to be familiar with three terms:

- build type — A configuration of the build process intended for a specific purpose. By default, Android Studio supports two build types: debug and release. Other types may be created for unit testing or simulation.
- product flavor — A customized version of the released app. Different flavors may be created for free apps versus paid apps or apps targeting different locales.
- build variant — A unique combination of a build type and product flavor.

In the `android` block, build types are configured in the `buildTypes` subblock and product flavors are configured in the `productFlavors` subblock. The modules in this book don't have product flavors, but each configures an aspect of the `release` build type. The following code shows what this looks like:

```
apply plugin: 'com.android.application'

android {
  compileSdkVersion ...
  buildToolsVersion ...
  defaultConfig {
    ...
  }
  buildTypes {
    release {
      minifyEnabled true
      proguardFiles getDefaultProguardFile('proguard-android.txt')
    }
  }
}
```

This build file specifies that release builds should be minified using ProGuard. ProGuard is a helpful utility contained in Android Studio, and a later section will discuss its operation and configuration.

The build file only defines a release build type, but Android Studio will create a debug type anyway. When you develop and test your app, the debug configuration will be selected by default. To select a different build variant, click the **Build Variants** tool in the lower-left of the IDE.

A build file can set characteristics for all build variants by adding a `defaultConfig` block to the `android` block. Table 2.2 lists seven common elements of this block.

Table 2.2

Common Elements of the defaultConfig Block

Element	Description
`minSdkVersion`	Minimum SDK version supported by the application
`targetSdkVersion`	The target SDK version
`versionCode`	Integer used to uniquely identify the app's version
`versionName`	String used to tell customers about the app's version
`applicationId`	String that uniquely identifies the application
`testApplicationId`	String that uniquely identifies the application for testing
`testInstrumentationRunner`	The tool used to run the app's unit tests

The `minSdkVersion` field tells the Google Play Store which devices can run the app. In other words, any device that doesn't support this minimum SDK will be blocked from executing the app. To ensure a large user base, it's important to keep this value as low as possible.

In contrast, `targetSdkVersion` identifies which SDK version is considered the desired version. This tells Android to apply features from that SDK to the app. For this reason, it's good to set the `targetSdkVersion` value as high as possible.

The `versionCode` and `versionName` fields don't relate to the Android SDK, but to the version of the app being created. `versionCode` is an integer that uniquely identifies the current version. The Google Play Store uses this value to keep track of different versions of the same app. This integer must increase with each new version, but it doesn't necessarily have to be incremented by 1.

`versionName` is a string that tells customers about the app's version. It's common to set this to *x.y.z*, where *x* is the major version, *y* is the minor version, and *z* is the revision number. Many organizations update the revision number to identify bug fixes, the minor version to identify new features, and the major number when the new version is incompatible with previous versions.

Every app has a string that uniquely identifies it on the Google Play Store and on installed devices. This is given by the `applicationId` field, which is usually set to the fully-qualified name of the package used to create the app.

Every deployable build variant of an app needs its own ID, and this can be set with `applicationId` or `applicationIdSuffix`. Similarly, if an app is used in a unit testing framework, a test ID can be set with the `testApplicationId` field.

The last entry in the table, `testInstrumentationRunner`, identifies the toolset to be used when unit testing the app. For this purpose, Android provides a test runner based on JUnit called `AndroidJUnitRunner`. To access this, build.gradle should set `testInstrumentationRunner` to `android.support.test.runner.AndroidJUnitRunner`.

Most Android apps are coded solely in Java. But as will be shown in Chapters 14 through 16, apps can also contain C and C++ code. This code is called *native code* because it executes outside of the Java Virtual Machine (JVM). If a module contains native code, the `android` block should have a block called `externalNativeBuild`. This tells Android how the native code should be compiled.

The dependencies Block

Just as the project build file identifies top-level dependencies, each module build file needs to identify the dependencies needed to build the module. These are given in the build file's `dependencies` block.

This block is frequently used to access classes of the Android Support Library. These frequently have names that end in `Compat`, such as `AppCompat`, `ContextCompat`, and `IntentCompat`. The following code shows how a module build file can access the `AppCompat` class of SDK version 25.1.1:

```
dependencies {
  compile 'com.android.support:appcompat-v7:25.1.1'
}
```

The `compile` keyword identifies that the dependency should be included when compiling the module. In contrast, the `apk` keyword identifies that the dependency should be included in the APK but not accessed in the compile step.

If a module depends on another, a dependency can be added to the `dependencies` block. For example, the following code states that `moduleb` should be accessed:

```
dependencies {
  compile project(":moduleb")
}
```

Example Module Build File

Now that you have a basic understanding of module build files, it helps to look at a practical example. Listing 2.1 presents the build.gradle file for the ch02_androidintro module.

Listing 2.1: ch02_androidintro/build.gradle

```
apply plugin: 'com.android.application'

android {
  compileSdkVersion 25
  buildToolsVersion "25.0.2"
  defaultConfig {
    applicationId "com.dreambookvr.ch02_androidintro"
    minSdkVersion 24
    targetSdkVersion 25
    versionCode 1
    versionName "1.0.0"
  }
  buildTypes {
    release {
      minifyEnabled true
      proguardFiles getDefaultProguardFile('proguard-android.txt')
    }
  }
}

dependencies {
    compile 'com.android.support:appcompat-v7:25.1.1'
}
```

At the time of this writing, the latest SDK version is 25, so the `compileSdkVersion` and `targetSdkVersion` fields are both set to `25`. The `minSdkVersion` field is set to `24` because this is the minimum version acceptable for Daydream applications.

This is the first release of the app, so the `versionCode` value is set to `1`. The Google Play Store uses this to uniquely identify the app's version. Similarly, the `applicationId` field sets the string that the store will use to uniquely identify the app.

The `buildTypes` block configures the release build to use ProGuard. The next section will explain what ProGuard accomplishes and how its operation can be configured.

The last block, `dependencies`, states that the `AppCompat` class of the Android Support Library should be compiled into the build.

Now that you understand how ch02_androidintro is intended to be built, I recommend that you build and run the module. To do this, select the module in the drop-down list and go to **Build** > **Make Module** in the menu. Then select **Run** > **'ch02_androidintro'** to deploy the APK to a connected device.

2.6 ProGuard

The size of the generated APK is a major concern for developers and users, and Google Play currently requires all APKs to be 100 MB or less. Android Studio makes it possible to reduce the size of APKs by providing access to ProGuard.

ProGuard analyzes the compiled code and removes unnecessary classes, fields, methods, and attributes. It also obfuscates the names of classes, fields, and methods, thereby providing a small amount of security against reverse engineering.

To enable this capability, a module's build file needs to configure ProGuard inside the `buildTypes` section. This configuration generally involves two parts:

1. `minifyEnabled` is set to `true` or `false`
2. `proguardFiles` identifies one or more files containing configuration rules

If `minifyEnabled` is set to `true`, ProGuard will analyze and shrink the module's code. If set to `false`, ProGuard will not shrink the code. Most of the modules in this book set `minifyEnabled` to `true`, but once modules start using native code, it's usually best not to shrink the code.

The tools/proguard directory of the Android SDK contains three text files:

- proguard-android.txt — Rules that configure ProGuard for Android modules
- proguard-android-optimize.txt — Like proguard-android.txt, but performs additional analysis to optimize the resulting bytecode
- proguard-project.txt — Instructions for enabling ProGuard for projects

To obtain the full path of one of these files, the build file must call `getDefaultProguardFile`. For example, the full path of proguard-android.txt can be obtained by calling `getDefaultProguardFile("proguard-android.txt")`.

A module's build file identifies ProGuard configuration files by following `proguardFiles` with the name of one or more files. As an example, the following code specifies that ProGuard should shrink the module's code and follow the rules given in proguard-android.txt.

```
release {
  minifyEnabled true
  proguardFiles getDefaultProguardFile("proguard-android.txt")
}
```

The `proguardFiles` block can identify multiple files, including those containing custom configuration rules. A full description of ProGuard configuration is beyond the scope of this discussion, but the manual is freely available online at https://www.guardsquare.com/en/proguard/manual.

2.7 Tasks

This section discusses an advanced topic that isn't necessary to know but may prove useful for those with complex build/test procedures. This is the topic of *tasks*, which are named operations to be executed by Gradle. Gradle tasks are conceptually similar to Ant tasks, but Gradle provides more flexibility.

To understand how tasks work, it helps to be familiar with the Gradle wrapper. This is a binary executable in the top-level project named gradlew. The purpose of this executable is to run Gradle tasks outside of Android Studio. Using the wrapper requires three steps:

1. Open a terminal utility.
2. Change to the top-level directory of the desired Gradle project. This directory must contain a file named build.gradle.
3. Enter `gradlew` followed by the name of a task defined in build.gradle.

In the DreamBookVR project, the top-level build.gradle file defines a task named `helloGradle`. To run the task using the Gradle wrapper, change to the project's top-level directory and enter the following command:

```
gradlew -q helloGradle
```

If you look at the build.gradle file, you'll see that the task is defined as follows:

```
task helloGradle {
  Set<Project> children = project.subprojects;
  for(Project child: children) {
    println child.name
  }
}
```

The `task` keyword identifies the block as a new task. Like Java methods or C/C++ functions, Gradle tasks are named blocks that contain statements inside curly braces. But Gradle tasks have many idiosyncratic characteristics to be aware of, including the following:

1. All tasks must be defined in files named build.gradle.
2. The commands in a Gradle task are statements in the Groovy programming language.
3. Groovy is based on Java, but doesn't use semicolons and doesn't surround method parameters with parentheses.
4. The term *module* is specific to Android Studio. In Gradle, modules are referred to as subprojects.
5. Every Gradle task can access the current `Project` object named `project`.

This last point is particularly important. Gradle's power stems from the ability to interact with a project and its files. To see how this can be accomplished, you need to be familiar with the `Project` class.

2.7.1 The Project Class

The `Project` class plays a central role in Gradle tasks. Its methods provide information about the project and make it possible to operate on the project's content. Table 2.3 lists twenty methods of the `Project` class and provides a description of each.

Table 2.3

Methods of the Project Class (Abridged)

Method	Description
`absoluteProjectPath(String path)`	Converts the argument to an absolute project path
`configure(Iterable objects, Action configureAction)`	Configures a collection of objects
`copy(Action<? super CopySpec> action)`	Copies selected files
`delete(Action<? super CopySpec> action)`	Deletes selected files
`exec(Action<? super ExecSpec> action)`	Executes an external command

`getAllprojects()`	Returns a set containing the project and its subprojects
`getAllTasks(boolean recursive)`	Returns a map containing the project's tasks and optionally the tasks of its subprojects
`getBuildDir()`	Returns the project's build directory
`getChildProjects()`	Returns a map containing the project's direct child projects
`getDepth()`	Returns the nesting level of the project in a multi-project hierarchy
`getName()`	Returns the project's name
`getParent()`	Returns the parent project, if available
`getPath()`	Returns the project's path
`getProjectDir()`	Returns the directory containing the project build file
`getRootDir()`	Returns the root directory of the project
`getRootProject()`	Returns the root project in the hierarchy
`getSubprojects()`	Returns a set containing the project's subprojects
`getTasks()`	Returns the project's tasks
`mkdir(Object path)`	Creates a new directory
`task(Map<String, ?> args, String name)`	Creates a new task and adds it to the project

One convenient aspect of Grade development is that an object's fields can be accessed directly. That is, instead of calling `get`*`XYZ`*`()`, the field can be accessed simply as *`XYZ`*. For example, a project's tasks can be accessed as `project.tasks` instead of `project.getTasks()`.

A task can iterate through Gradle collections using the same for loops available in Java. For example, the `helloGradle` task iterates through a project's subprojects (modules) and prints the name of each.

```
task helloGradle {
  Set<Project> children = project.subprojects;
  for(Project child: children) {
    println child.name;
  }
}
```

The copy, delete, and exec methods require CopySpec, DeleteSpec, and ExecSpec interfaces, respectively. But most tasks don't invoke the copy, delete, and exec methods. Instead, a task may set its type parameter to Copy, Delete, and Exec. The next discussion explores this further.

2.7.2 Copying and Deleting Files

Consider the following task, which copies the settings.gradle file to a directory called dstDir:

```
task copyFile(type: Copy) {
  from 'settings.gradle'
  into 'dstDir'
}
```

The from and into methods aren't available to ordinary tasks, but this task can invoke them because its type parameter is set to Copy. As a result, the underlying Task object implements the CopySpec interface, which provides a number of methods that include the following:

- from — identifies the file or directory of files to be copied
- into — identifies the directory to contain the transferred files
- exclude — identifies files to be excluded from the copy
- rename — renames files based on a regular expression

The DeleteSpec interface is similar to CopySpec. If a task's type is set to Delete, it can invoke the delete method provided by the DeleteSpec interface. As an example, the following code deletes the .gitignore file:

```
task deleteFile(type: Delete) {
  delete '.gitignore'
}
```

The DeleteSpec interface also provides a method named setFollowSymlinks. This accepts an argument that identifies whether symbolic links should be followed during the deletion operation. If set to true, the deletion process will delete each symbolic link and the file it references.

2.8 Summary

Once you've ascended the learning curve, Android Studio is a powerful tool for app development. With a few mouse clicks, you can build complex projects and deploy APKs to Android devices.

But ascending the learning curve requires time and effort. There's a vast array of toolbar items and windows, and the new terminology (modules, projects, dependencies, repositories, and so on) can be daunting for the uninitiated. This chapter hasn't explored all the capabilities of Android Studio, but I hope you've acquired enough familiarity to be able to create and build your own projects.

Android Studio relies on Gradle to manage the build process, which is configured using files named build.gradle. Most projects will have at least two types of build files. The first type of build file applies to the entire project and identifies general dependencies. The second type of build file applies to a module and identifies build characteristics for the module.

Android Studio accesses a Gradle plugin specifically for Android development. This is why the module build files contain an `android` block that receives Android-specific configuration. This configuration information includes the desired SDK version and the name and version of the APK to be generated.

The last section in this chapter explored the subject of tasks. A Gradle task is a named block of Groovy code in a build.gradle file. This can be executed outside of Android Studio using the Gradle wrapper (gradlew) and tasks can access projects by accessing methods of the `Project` class.

Chapter 3

Activities, Views, and Resources

From a programmer's perspective, an Android application is a combination of software components that work together to perform a task. Android supports four types of components and the most important of them is the *activity*. Activities define how an application appears to the user and how the application responds to the user's actions.

Each activity is represented by a subclass of the `Activity` class. Every example module in this book contains at least one activity, and the first sections of this chapter explain how activities are defined and how they can be created in code.

An activity controls an application's appearance by creating *views*. A view defines the content of a rectangle within the activity's screen. One view might provide a text label while another depicts an image. Every view is represented by a subclass of Android's `View` class, and the third section of this chapter examines this class in detail.

The last part of this chapter explores the topic of resources. A resource is an external data source (usually a file) that provides information required by the application. Android recognizes many different types of resources, including the following:

- **Layout resources** — Define the views of an activity and their arrangement
- **Image resources** — Images to be used in the activity and to serve as the application's icon
- **Value resources** — Text or numerical data used by the application

Before we explore the activities, views, and resources that make up an application, it's important to look at the application's manifest. This file, named AndroidManifest.xml, tells Android about the application's characteristics and the resources it provides.

3.1 The Android Manifest

The AndroidManifest.xml file gives Android the information it needs to run an application. If you want to understand what a project does and how it behaves, this is the first place to look.

In Android Studio projects, the manifest is located in the module's src/main directory. For example, Listing 3.1 presents the manifest of the ch02_androidintro module:

Listing 3.1: ch02_androidintro/src/main/AndroidManifest.xml

```
<?xml version="1.0" encoding="utf-8"?>
<manifest
  xmlns:android="http://schemas.android.com/apk/res/android"
  package="com.dreambookvr.ch02_androidintro">

  <!-- Describe the application -->
  <application
    android:allowBackup="true"
    android:icon="@mipmap/ic_launcher"
    android:label="@string/app_name"
    android:supportsRtl="true">

    <!-- Define the activity -->
    <activity
      android:name="IntroActivity"
      android:label="@string/app_name">

      <intent-filter>
        <action android:name="android.intent.action.MAIN"/>
        <category
          android:name="android.intent.category.LAUNCHER"/>
      </intent-filter>
    </activity>

  </application>
</manifest>
```

The `<manifest>` element provides top-level information about the application. This includes the name of the app's package, which serves as the app's unique identifier. After an app is published, the `package` field must remain constant.

Changes to a published app should be reflected by updating its version. An app's version can be set in AndroidManifest.xml, but in this book, versions are specified in the module's build.gradle file.

3.1.1 The Application Element

Every `<manifest>` element must contain an `<application>` element that defines the application's characteristics. These characteristics include the application's icon (`icon`), label (`label`), and required permissions (`permission`). It also specifies if and how the application's data should be backed up (`allowBackup`, `fullBackupOnly`, and `fullBackupContent`).

The `<application>` element may also contain a `theme` attribute that sets the application's overall style. A later chapter will introduce the style that Google provides for virtual reality apps.

3.1.2 The Activity Element

The `<application>` element contains a subelement for each of the application's components. In this case, the application contains one `Activity`, so `<application>` contains one `<activity>` subelement. All of the modules in this book consist of a single `Activity`.

Within an `<activity>` element, the `name` attribute is particularly important. This must be set to a subclass of Android's `Activity` class. In Listing 3.1, `name` is set to `IntroActivity`, which indicates that the application's central activity is defined by the `IntroActivity` class.

An `<activity>` element also accepts attributes that determine the behavior of the activity's window. The `resizeableActivity` attribute identifies if the window can be resized and `screenOrientation` identifies the desired orientation of the window (`landscape` or `portrait`). These properties are important in virtual reality apps, which should never be resized and should always be displayed in landscape orientation.

3.1.3 Intent and Intent Filters

The example `<activity>` element has a subelement called `<intent-filter>`. This book won't explore intents in detail. For VR apps, there are three points to know:

1. Intents are messages transmitted by the operating system (and other components) that launch components such as activities or services.
2. A component receives intents by configuring one or more intent filters.
3. If a component has an intent filter whose `action` is set to `action.MAIN` and whose `category` is set to `category.LAUNCHER`, it will be launched immediately after being deployed to the device.

As configured in the manifest, the `IntroActivity` has an intent filter that passes intents whose `action` is set to `action.MAIN` and whose `category` is set to `category.LAUNCHER`. This is why the activity executes immediately after being deployed to a device.

3.2 The Activity Class

The ch02_androidintro module contains a class called `IntroActivity`. This is a subclass of `Activity`, which means it defines the content of one screen of an Android device. If an application has multiple screens, it will need multiple `Activity` objects. Similarly, if a screen contains many graphical controls, all of them must be added to the same `Activity`.

The `Activity` class has more than 150 methods, and the most important of them respond to the changes in an activity's state. These are called *lifecycle methods* and the first part of this section discusses them in detail. The last part of the section presents the methods that configure an activity's appearance.

3.2.1 Lifecycle Methods

Once Android determines which component should respond to an intent, it will create an instance of the component's class. If the component is an activity, the new `Activity` instance will be made active and its screen will receive focus.

After an activity is launched, it undergoes a series of state changes. That is, the activity will be paused if the app loses focus, and it will be resumed if the app regains focus. If the user presses the back button, the activity will be destroyed.

Every activity has five possible states:

1. Created — Android has constructed an instance of the activity
2. Active — the activity's screen is executing
3. Paused — the user has paused the activity or shifted focus to another activity
4. Stopped — the user has halted the activity or it's no longer visible
5. Destroyed — Android has deallocated the activity

Figure 3.1 illustrates how an activity's state changes during the course of its usage. The gray boxes identify the lifecycle methods of the `Activity` class.

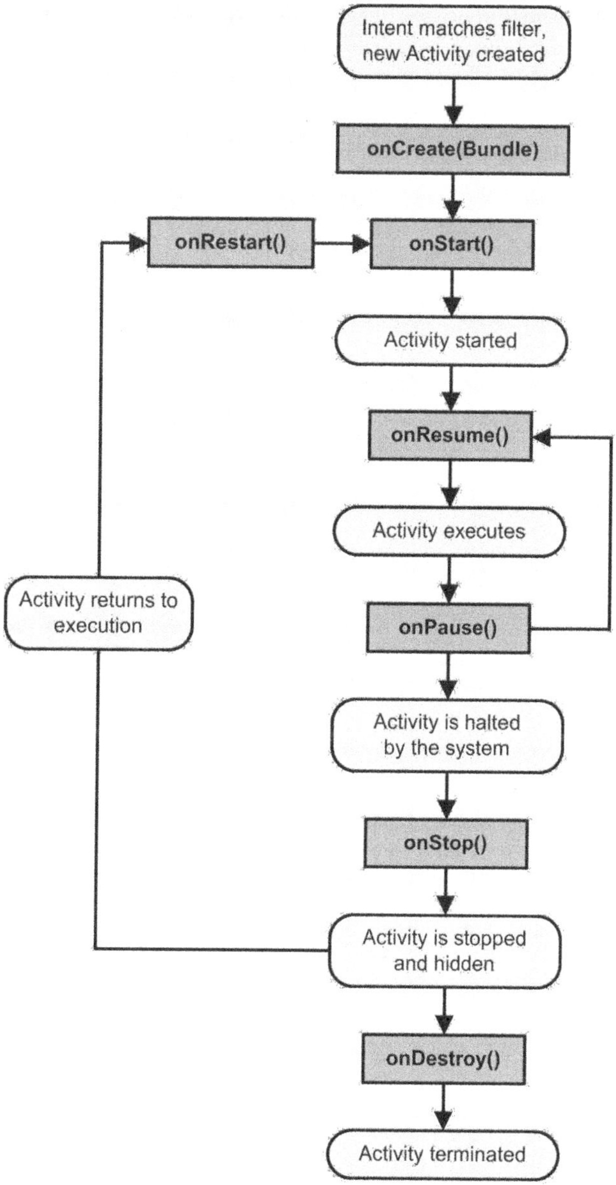

Figure 3.1 The Lifecycle of an Activity

Custom `Activity` subclasses usually don't implement all of the lifecycle methods, but most will provide code for `onCreate`. Table 3.1 lists `onCreate` and each of the lifecycle methods.

Table 3.1

Lifecycle Methods of the Activity Class

Lifecycle Method	Description
`onCreate(Bundle)`	Called after the activity is created. Commonly used to configure the screen's appearance and behavior.
`onStart()`	Called after onCreate() or when the user restarts the activity
`onRestart()`	Called when the user restarts an activity
`onResume()`	Called after onStart() or after the user unpauses the activity
`onPause()`	Called when the activity loses focus, but not visibility
`onStop()`	Called when the activity loses visibility
`onDestroy()`	Called when the activity's resources are deallocated

When invoked, each of these methods should call the corresponding method of the `Activity` superclass. That is, `onStart` should call `super.onStart`, `onResume` should call `super.onResume`, and so on. This is demonstrated in Listing 3.2, which presents the code in the `LifeCycleActivity` class of the ch03_lifecycle module.

Listing 3.2: ch03_lifecycleactivity/src/main/java/.../LifeCycleActivity.java

```
public class LifeCycleActivity extends Activity {

  TextView tv;

  // Called when the activity is created
  public void onCreate(Bundle savedInstanceState) {
    super.onCreate(savedInstanceState);
    tv = new TextView(this);
    tv.setText("Created");
    setContentView(tv);
  }

  // Called when the activity is started
  public void onStart() {
    super.onStart();
    tv.append("\nStarted");
  }
```

Listing 3.2: ch03_lifecycleActivity/app/src/main/java/.../LifeCycleActivity.java

```
  // Called when the activity is restarted
  public void onRestart() {
    super.onRestart();
    tv.append("\nRestarted");
  }

  // Called when the activity is resumed
  public void onResume() {
    super.onResume();
    tv.append("\nResumed");
  }

  // Called when the activity is paused
  public void onPause() {
    super.onPause();
    tv.append("\nPaused");
  }

  // Called when the activity is stopped
  public void onStop() {
    super.onStop();
    tv.append("\nStopped");
  }
}
```

Figure 3.2 displays the printed output on my Google Pixel.

Figure 3.2 Output of the ch03_lifecycle Module

When using lifecycle methods, it's important to remember when they're invoked relative to the associated event. `onStart`, `onResume`, and `onDestroy` are called before the corresponding event occurs. `onCreate`, `onStop`, `onPause`, and `onRestart` are called after the event occurs.

3.2.2 View Configuration

In Listing 3.2, the `onCreate` method of the `LifeCycleActivity` creates a `TextView`, sets its text, and then calls `setContentView`. `setContentView` is an important method to know because it determines the appearance of an activity's screen. In this book's code, every activity invokes `setContentView` inside the `onCreate` method.

To be precise, `setContentView` selects a view to serve as the activity's root view. This view defines the activity's overall appearance. A large part of this chapter and following chapters is devoted to the topic of views and the process of configuring their appearance and behavior.

In the `LifeCycleActivity`, `setContentView` is called with an instance of the `TextView` class, which is a subclass of `View`. This is one of three overloaded methods named `setContentView`. The full list is given as follows:

1. `setContentView(View view)` — Configures a screen's content based on a `View` object
2. `setContentView(View view, ViewGroup.LayoutParams params)` — Configures screen content according to a `View` object and layout parameters
3. `setContentView(int layoutResID)` — Configures screen content according to a layout resource

The first usage of `setContentView` is the simplest. But most Android apps rely on the third usage, which requires the ID of a layout resource. Later in this chapter, I'll explain what layout resources are and why they're so important.

In addition to setting the `View`, an `Activity` can retrieve a `View` by calling `findViewById`. The next section discusses the `View` class in detail.

3.3 The View Class

The `View` class is easy to understand. A `View` defines the appearance of a rectangle on the screen and each of its subclasses fills the rectangle with a different type of content. A `TextView` fills the rectangle with text, an `ImageView` fills the rectangle with an image, a `SurfaceView` fills the rectangle with graphics, and so on.

`View` has a vast number of subclasses, and on the following page, Figure 3.3 presents 25 of them. This book examines the classes shaded in gray. Chapter 4 presents the `TextView` and `ImageView` classes and Chapter 14 presents the `GLSurfaceView`, which plays a central role in graphical applications based on the native development kit (NDK).

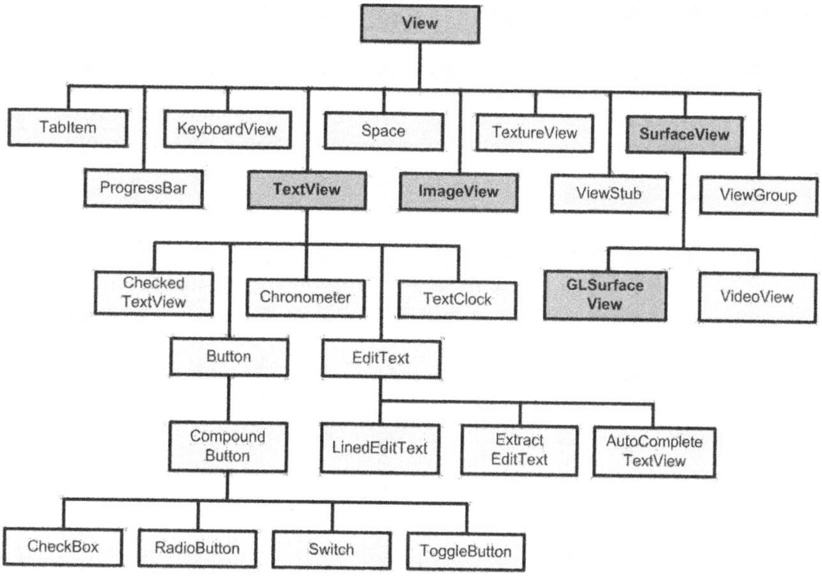

Figure 3.3 The View Class Hierarchy

One of the simplest `View` subclasses is `TextView`, which displays text. The following code creates a `TextView`, sets its text, and uses it to configure the appearance of the `BasicJavaActivity`:

```
public class BasicJavaActivity extends Activity {

  public void onCreate(Bundle savedInstanceState) {
    super.onCreate(savedInstanceState);
    TextView tv = new TextView(this);
    tv.setText("Hi there!");
    setContentView(tv);
  }
}
```

This code should be straightforward to understand. When the app is launched, Android creates an instance of `BasicJavaActivity`. Its `onCreate` method creates a `TextView` and then calls `setContentView` to assign the activity's appearance to the `TextView`.

This code is simple, but most Android apps don't create and configure views in code. Instead, they define views using special XML files called *layout resources*. This is the topic of the next section.

3.4 Layout Resources

A resource is an externalized data source that can be accessed by an application. The externalization is important because it ensures that different resources will be provided for different devices and locales. Resources are located in a module's src/main/res folder and each type of resource has a different subdirectory. A layout resource is an XML file in the src/main/res/layout folder.

A layout resource identifies the views of an activity and defines how they're arranged. It contains an XML element for each view and uses attributes to define properties such as the view's size and color.

Each view in a layout resource is represented by an XML element with the same name. For example, the following layout resource defines the same `TextView` as the one created in the preceding Java code:

```
<TextView
  xmlns:android="http://schemas.android.com/apk/res/android"
  android:layout_width="match_parent"
  android:layout_height="match_parent"
  android:text="Hi there!">
</TextView>
```

Layout resources are complex and their syntax is unintuitive. But many of the modules presented in this book use these resources to configure their views. The main goal of this section is to explain how to write layout resources. But first, I'd like to discuss why they're so helpful.

3.4.1 Rationale

As a devoted Java programmer, I initially coded all my views in Java. But as my applications became more complex, I started to appreciate the power of layout resources. For me, the chief advantage is that their hierarchical structure clearly reflects the activity's view hierarchy. That is, when I look at a layout resource, I can see the relationships among the views more clearly than when I look at Java code.

For others, the main advantage of using layout resources is that they isolate the application's appearance from its implementation in code. This *separation of concerns* makes it possible to change one aspect of the application without affecting the other. This allows designers to update the user interface without having to understand Java. For more information on this topic, I recommend that you search for "separation of concerns" or "model view controller" on the Internet.

3.4.2 Elements of Layout Resources

A layout resource, like any XML file, has a root element that contains other elements. The root element of a layout resource can be set to one of three types of values:

1. If the `Activity` contains one view, the top-level element is the name of the `View` subclass, such as `<TextView>`.
2. If the `Activity` contains multiple `Views`, the top-level element is `<ViewGroup>` or the name of a subclass of `<ViewGroup>`. This defines how the views are arranged.
3. If the objects in the `Activity` are intended to be merged into another layout, the top-level element can be set to `<merge>`.

Most Daydream apps consist of a single view, which is usually either a `GvrView` (introduced in Chapter 6) or a `GLSurfaceView` (introduced in Chapter 14). For this reason, every layout resource in this book has a root element and no child elements.

3.4.3 View Attributes

In a layout resource, a view's properties are configured using attributes. In XML, an attribute provides information about an element using a *name=value* pair. In a layout resource, each XML element is a `View` or a `View` subclass and the attributes configure the `View`'s characteristics.

Android-specific attributes must be preceded by the `android` prefix. In general, view attributes can be divided into four categories:

1. Dimensions — The height and width of the view's rectangle
2. Background — The view's background color or image
3. Padding — The border space that separates the view from siblings
4. Identifier — A name that uniquely identifies the view so that it can be accessed by an activity

The following discussion explores these categories. In each case, I'll present XML that demonstrates how the view attributes can be set.

Dimensions

A `View`'s maximum size is determined by its container. For the top-level `View`, the maximum amount of space is determined by the screen size. For a child `View`, the maximum space is determined by its parent.

A layout resource file can further constrain a `View`'s size by setting attributes for the view's element. Table 3.2 lists the attributes and methods that relate to a view's size.

Table 3.2
Size-Related Attributes and Methods

Attribute	Method	Description
`layout_width`	`setLayoutParams (ViewGroup. LayoutParams)`	Identifies how much of the container's width will be occupied by the view
`layout_height`	`setLayoutParams (ViewGroup. LayoutParams)`	Identifies how much of the container's height will be occupied by the view
`min_height`	--	Set minimum height
`min_width`	--	Set minimum width

The first two attributes, `layout_height` and `layout_width`, are particularly important because they're the only attributes required for every `View` element. The values of these attributes can be given in one of four ways:

- `match_parent` — Sets the `View`'s dimension equal to the parent's dimension (as large as possible)
- `wrap_content` — Makes the `View` just large enough to hold its content
- Numerical dimension — Identifies the `View`'s dimension using millimeters (`mm`), inches (`in`), points (`pt`), pixels (`px`), device-independent pixels (`dp`), or scale-independent pixels (`sp`).
- Dimension resource — Dimensions can be specified in a resource file in the project's res/values directory. These resources are discussed later in this chapter.

Most apps set `layout_height` and `layout_width` to one of the first two values. For example, suppose a `TextView` should occupy all of the available vertical space but only enough horizontal space to display its text. Its definition in a layout resource file could be given as follows:

```
...
  <TextView xmlns:android=
     "http://schemas.android.com/apk/res/android"
     android:layout_height="match_parent"
     android:layout_width="wrap_content"
  </TextView>
...
```

It's rare to set a `View`'s dimensions to specific values, but sometimes it's necessary. In this case, the choice of units is crucial. Table 3.3 lists the six units supported by Android.

Table 3.3

Dimension Units

Units	Name	Description
`in`	inches	--
`mm`	millimeters	--
`pt`	point	1/72 of an inch depending on the screen
`px`	pixels	Number of pixels on a screen
`dp`	density-independent pixels	Number of pixels relative to a 160 dpi screen
`sp`	scale-independent pixels	Number of pixels relative to a 160 dpi screen

The first four dimensions are easy to understand, which is a shame because they'll never be used in this book. Instead, all of the dimensions will be given in dp (density-independent pixels) or sp (scale-independent pixels).

If a dimension is given in dp, the actual pixel dimension will change depending on the density (dots per inch or dpi) of the device's screen. More precisely, the pixel dimension is computed by multiplying the dp dimension by a constant whose value depends on the device's density. Table 3.4 lists the multiplication factors for devices of different densities.

Table 3.4

Device Densities and Pixel Multipliers

Density	Multiplier	Designation
~120 dpi	0.75	ldpi
~160 dpi	1.0	mdpi
~240 dpi	1.5	hdpi
~320 dpi	2.0	xhdpi
~480 dpi	2.0 - 3.0	xxhdpi
~640 dpi	3.0 - 4.0	xxxhdpi

For example, the density of the Pixel places it in the xxhdpi category and the density of the Pixel XL is in the xxxhdpi category. On the Pixel, dimensions given in dp are multiplied by 2.6 to obtain pixel dimensions. On the Pixel XL, dimensions are multiplied by 3.5 to obtain pixel dimensions.

Android devices allow users to enlarge or shrink text to increase readability. Dimensions given in density-independent pixels don't take this scaling factor into account, so it's better to use scale-independent pixels, or sp. All font sizes in this book are given in sp.

The following equations clarify how dp and sp dimensions relate to pixel dimensions:

- pixels = dp * density_multiplier
- pixels = sp * density_multiplier * text_scaling

To tell Android which resource file to use, the files should be placed in folders whose names are followed by a hyphen and the density. That is, hdpi resource files should be placed in res/layout-hdpi and xhdpi resource files should be placed in res/layout-xhdpi.

Background

In addition to setting the size, a layout resource can specify a view's background. This is accomplished by setting the `background` attribute to a value that identifies a *drawable*. A drawable is a color or the name of a suitable image.

Color values are given by following the pound sign (#) with hexadecimal digits. These digits identify the color's components (red, green, blue, and alpha) and they can be arranged in one of four ways:

- `#RGB`
- `#ARGB`
- `#RRGGBB`
- `#AARRGGBB`

In the first two formats, the hexadecimal digits are doubled to form the actual color value. That is, `#408` produces the same color as `#440088` and `#8123` produces the same color as `#88112233`.

An example will show how the `background` attribute is used in practice. The following markup sets the view's background to a semi-transparent yellow:

```
<View
    android:layout_width="match_parent"
    android:layout_height="wrap_content"
    android:background="#80ffff00" >
</View>
```

The `alpha` attribute makes it possible to set the `View`'s transparency independently from its color. The attribute's value should be set to a floating-point value between 0.0 (completely transparent) and 1.0 (completely opaque).

As an example, the following markup defines a `View` that is 75% opaque.

```
<View
    android:layout_width="match_parent"
    android:layout_height="match_parent"
    android:alpha="0.75" >
</View>
```

To specify a background image for a view, the `background` attribute must identify an image file or an image resource. Chapter 4 provides an in-depth discussion of images and image views.

Padding

A `View` can be given an optional border region called *padding*. This is set with one of the five `padding` attributes. Table 3.5 lists them and provides a description of each.

Table 3.5

Padding-Related Attributes and Methods

Attribute	Method	Description
`padding`	`setPadding(int, int, int, int)`	Specify padding to be applied to the left, top, right, and bottom sides
`paddingLeft`	`setPadding(int, int, int, int)`	Specify padding along the left of the view
`paddingTop`	`setPadding(int, int, int, int)`	Specify padding along the top of the view
`paddingRight`	`setPadding(int, int, int, int)`	Specify padding along the right of the view
`paddingBottom`	`setPadding(int, int, int, int)`	Specify padding along the bottom of the view

These padding attributes accept values in the units listed in Table 3.3. That is, the following markup sets a `View`'s padding on the right side to 10 dp:

```
android:paddingRight="10dp"
```

If the padding attribute is associated with a single value, that border will be applied to all four sides of the view. For example, the following attribute adds a 50 dp border to every side:

```
android:padding="50dp"
```

Padding doesn't affect the activity's top-level view. For child views, the behavior of the padding changes depending on how the layout_height and layout_width attributes are set:

- If a layout attribute is set to match_parent, the padding will be subtracted from the View.
- If a layout attribute is set to wrap_parent or any value except match_parent, the padding will be added to the View.

Identifier

The id attribute provides a unique name for the View so that it can be accessed outside the resource file. Its form is given as follows:

```
android:id="@+id/<name>"
```

When this attribute is set, an Activity can access the View with the following code:

```
View v = findViewById(R.id.<name>);
```

This example makes use of the all-important R class, which makes it possible to access resources in Java code. The next discussion explores this topic further.

3.4.4 Layout Resources and the R Class

When the Android Asset Packaging Tool (aapt) constructs an APK for a project, it reads through the project's res folder and generates a Java file named R.java. This defines an R class whose inner classes identify resources using integer IDs. The name of each inner class is determined by the type of the corresponding resource.

An example will clarify how this works. In the ch02_androidintro module, the layout resource is res/layout/main_layout.xml. After the R.java file is generated, the R class contains an inner class such as the following:

```
public static final class layout {
   public static final int main_layout=0x7f030000;
}
```

With this in place, the application can access main_layout.xml through the integer `main_layout` defined in `R.layout`. The integer is the ID of the layout resource.

As discussed earlier, an `Activity` can configure its appearance by calling `setContentView` with the ID of a layout resource. In the ch02_androidintro module, this is accomplished with the following line of code:

```
setContentView(R.layout.main_layout);
```

In most of this example modules in this book, the layout resource is main_layout.xml. Therefore, you'll see this exact method called in many `Activity` classes.

3.5 Image Resources

If you look in the src/main/res directory of the ch02_androidintro module, you'll see that it contains five folders named mipmap-*density*, where *density* runs from mdpi to xxxhdpi. Each folder contains an image to serve as the app's icon for devices of the given density. For example, the Pixel XL is in the xxxhdpi category, so the device will display the image in the mipmap-xxxhdpi folder.

In the world of graphics programming, a *mipmap* is an image file that contains multiple images: a main image and smaller versions of the main image. This pyramidal structure is reflected in the word mipmap, where mip stands for *multum in parvo* (many in little). Mipmaps are popular in graphic applications because they allow graphics processors to access images of different densities as the user moves toward or away from an image.

An app identifies its icon by setting the `icon` attribute of the `<application>` in the AndroidManifest.xml file. The following markup shows what this looks like:

```
android:icon="@mipmap/ic_launcher"
```

This notation is important to understand. The manifest doesn't know the pixel density of the target, so it can't identify the folder containing the app's icon. Android understands that `@mipmap` refers to folders named mipmap-*density*, and the system will choose the appropriate folder when displaying the icon.

This `@` notation is frequently employed to identify resources. If a resource needs to access another resource, it will specify the target resource type using `@` notation.

Images placed in mipmap-*density* folders are intended to be used only as icons. If an image is intended to be used within the application, it should be placed in resource folders named drawable-*density*. The term *drawable* refers to Android's abstract `Drawable` class, which serves as a general abstraction for "something that can be drawn."

Android makes it possible to define drawables in many different ways. The simplest manner of defining a drawable is to provide a PNG or JPEG image file. Android also accepts shapes, which are defined by drawing commands in special XML files. Drawables can be defined in code using subclasses of the `Drawable` class. Chapter 4 goes into greater detail regarding the use of images and drawables in Android.

3.6 Values Resources

The simplest resource files identify basic values such as strings, numbers, colors, and boolean values. These resource files are referred to as *values resources* because they're stored in a module's src/main/res/values folder.

As explained earlier, Android creates integer IDs for a module's resources and places them in a generated class called `R`. `R` contains one or more inner classes, and identifier can be accessed as an integer field of one of these inner classes. For example, the layout resource file, main_layout.xml, can be accessed in code as `R.layout.main_layout`. `R` contains an inner class for each resource type, and because main_layout.xml is a layout resource, its inner class is `R.layout`.

Resources in one file can be accessed in other resource files using a slightly similar notation. This requires replacing `R.` with `@` and inserting a slash between the resource type and the resource name. That is, the XML identifier is given as follows:

```
@resource_type/resource_name
```

For example, to access main_layout.xml in another XML document, you'd refer to the layout as `@layout/main_layout` because `layout` is the resource type and `main_layout` is the resource ID.

If the resource being accessed is part of a different package, the resource type should be preceded by the package name and a colon. For example, if layout/main_layout.xml is located in a package named com.example.pkg, it could be accessed from a different package with the following identifier:

```
@com.example.pkg:layout/main_layout
```

It's uncommon to access layout resources inside other resource files, but it's very common to access string resources. This section discusses string resources first, and then introduces a variety of other resource types, including dimension resources, color resources, and integer resources.

3.6.1 String Resources

Traditional Java applications rely on properties files to externalize strings. This makes it easy to internationalize the application because different properties files can be used in different locales.

In Android projects, string resource files take the place of properties files. A string resource file uses XML to assign names to string values. As an example, Listing 3.3 presents the strings.xml file in the ch03_lifecycle module.

Listing 3.3: ch03_lifecycle/src/main/res/values/strings.xml

```
<resources>
  <string name="app_name">
    Ch03_LifeCycle
  </string>
</resources>
```

The format of a string resource is easy to understand. The base element, `<resources>`, contains one or more `<string>` subelements and each has an attribute called `name`. This attribute serves as an identifier for the element's body text. If this was translated into Java, the result might look like this:

```
String app_name = "Ch03_LifeCycle";
```

When the `R` class is generated, an inner class called `string` will be created from the string resource. On my system, this class is defined with the following code:

```
public static final class string {
  public static final int app_name=0x7f050000;
}
```

This definition makes it possible to access the string resource in Java and XML. In Java, it can be accessed in an `Activity` by using the `getResources` method followed by the `getString` method, which accepts an integer as the resource ID.

In XML, this string can be accessed as `@string/app_name`. For example, the project's manifest identifies the app's name by setting the `android:label` attribute in the following way:

```
android:label="@string/app_name"
```

This notation is frequently used in layout resources. For example, the following markup can be used inside a `<TextView>` element to set the view's text:

```
android:text="@string/app_name"
```

Backslashes and HTML

When using string resources, there are two important points to keep in mind:

1. Quotes — If a string resource contains quotes or apostrophes, the symbol must be preceded by a backslash or the string must be surrounded by double quotes.
2. HTML — String resources may use a limited set of formatting tags from HTML.

The first point is straightforward. Android delimits text using quotes and apostrophes, so these symbols must be specially identified within string resources. For example, the apostrophe in the following string will cause an error:

```
<string name="example">My application's name.</string>
```

This can be fixed by preceding the apostrophe with a backslash or by surrounding the entire text with double quotes. The following desfinitions are acceptable:

```
<string name="example">My application\'s name.</string>
<string name="example">"My application's name."</string>
```

String resources can use HTML tags to change how the text is displayed:

- `<i></i>` — Text contained in `<i>` and `</i>` will be displayed in italics
- `<b></b>` — Text contained in `<b>` and `</b>` will be displayed in boldface
- `<u></u>` — Text contained in `<u>` and `</u>` will be underlined

For example, the following string resource employs HTML tags to italicize one portion of text and underline another.

```
<string name="msg">Today\'s a <i>great</i> <u>day</u>!</string>
```

Printing Formatted Strings in an Activity

In many cases, a string may display dynamic content, such as a date or time. In this case, the string resource must be read and modified in Java, or more specifically, by an `Activity`. Accessing a string resource from an `Activity` is a two-step process:

1. Call `getResources`, which returns the current `Resources` object.
2. Call the `getString` method of the `Resources` object with the string's ID, such as `R.string.hello`.

After a string value is read, it can be formatted with the `String.format` method. That is, `String.format` accepts a string and a series of arguments, and returns a new, formatted string. For example, suppose the string `R.string.year_msg` is defined as follows:

```
<string name="year_msg">The year is %d.</string>
```

The following code accesses the string resource, reads the string, and calls `String.format` to insert the year variable:

```
Resources res = getResources();
String yearMsg = res.getString(R.string.year_msg);
String formattedMsg = String.format(yearMsg, year);
```

In this example, `%d` in `year_msg` serves as a placeholder for an integer. `year` is an integer, so `String.format` will replace `%d` with `year`'s value. Table 3.6 lists `%d` and other placeholders that represent data types.

Table 3.6

String Formatting Placeholders

Placeholder	Formatted Data Type
`%b`	Boolean
`%B`	Boolean (uppercase)
`%c`	Character

%C	Character (uppercase)
%s	String
%S	String (uppercase)
%d	Integer (decimal)
%o	Integer (octal)
%x	Integer (hexadecimal)
%X	Integer (hexadecimal - uppercase)
%f	Floating-point (decimal)
%e	Floating-point (exponential)
%E	Floating-point (exponential - uppercase)
%g	Floating-point (exponential or decimal, whichever is shorter)
%G	Floating-point (exponential or decimal - uppercase)
%a	Floating-point (hexadecimal)
%A	Floating-point (hexadecimal - uppercase)

The following examples demonstrate how `String.format` is used:

- `String.format("%S", "steve")` returns `STEVE`
- `String.format("%f", 246.8)` returns `246.8`
- `String.format("%e", 246.8)` returns `2.468000e+02`

Formatting Flags

String formatting can be further expanded by inserting flags between the placeholder's `%` and the letter denoting its data type. For example, if a comma is inserted between % and f, the returned string will have a comma separating groups of three digits. That is, if `%,f` refers to the value 5000.00, the resulting string will be `5,000.00`.

Table 3.7 lists all the flags recognized by `String.format`.

Table 3.7

String Formatting Flags

Flag	Data Type
#	Display hexadecimal values with `0x` and octal values with `0`
,	Places a comma between groups of three digits
' ' (space)	Places a leading space before nonnegative values

`+`	Always displays the value's sign (+ or -)
`(`	Places parentheses around negative values
`-N`	Follow with spaces until the width equals *N*
`0N`	Add leading zeros until the width equals *N*
`.N`	Add/remove digits until there are *N* digits after the decimal

The following examples demonstrate how these flags are used:

- `String.format("%,d", 1000000)` returns `1,000,000`
- `String.format("%+d", 1000000)` returns `+1000000`
- `String.format("*%-6s*", "Hi")` returns `*Hi    *`
- `String.format("%06d", 3)` returns `000003`
- `String.format("%06.2f", 3.50)` returns `003.50`

By default, floating-point values are displayed with six digits following the decimal point. In the last example, the `.2` flag tells `String.format` to display only two digits following the decimal. The `06` flag tells `String.format` to display the string with six characters, so zeros are prepended until the result is `003.50`.

Formatting Arguments

By default, `String.format` accesses arguments in the order they're given. But with numbered arguments, an argument's order can be set independently. A numbered argument is formed by inserting `N$` inside the placeholder where *N* is an index starting with 1. For example, `%3$s` specifies that the third argument should be read as a string.

In the ch03_stringargument module, strings.xml defines a string that contains three numbered arguments. This is shown in Listing 3.4.

Listing 3.4: ch03_stringargument/src/main/res/values/strings.xml

```
<resources>
  <string name="app_name">Ch03_StringFormat</string>
  <string name="msg">%2$s bought %1$d pens for $%3$.2f each.
  </string>
</resources>
```

Listing 3.5 presents the Java code that reads the string from the resource and formats it with three arguments.

Listing 3.5: ch03_stringargument/src/main/java/.../StringArgumentActivity.java

```
  // Access resources
  Resources res = getResources();
  String str = String.format(res.getString(R.string.msg),
      4, "John", 3.5);
  tv.setText(str);
...
```

Because `msg` contains numbered arguments, `String.format` displays the arguments in a different order than that in which they're given. As a result, the string displayed in the app will be `"John bought 4 pens for $3.50 each"`.

3.6.2 Dimension Resources

An earlier discussion explained how to set a `View`'s dimensions and the dimensions of its padding. So far, these dimensions have been specified with a number and a unit designation, which may be set to `in` (inches), `mm` (millimeters), `pt` (point), `px` (pixels), `dp` (density-independent pixels), or `sp` (scale-independent pixels).

Dimensions can also be defined in resource files. As with a string resource file, the top-level element is `<resources>`. Each dimension must be specified inside `<dimen>` and `</dimen>` tags and each must have a `name` attribute.

The following markup defines two dimension resources: one that defines a bitmap's width and one that defines the size of text:

```
<resources>
  <dimen name="bitmap_width">50dp</dimen>
  <dimen name="label_size">14sp</dimen>
</resources>
```

In Java code, these dimensions can be accessed by calling the `getDimension` method of the `Resources` class using the IDs of `R.dimen.bitmap_width` and `R.dimen.label_size`. In XML, they can be accessed as `@dimen/bitmap_width` and `@dimen/label_size`.

3.6.3 Color Resources

Color resources are ideal for development teams with artists who don't know how to program. Simply give the XML file to the artist, let him/her specify the colors, and put the updated file in the module's src/main/res/values directory.

A color resource is defined by a <color> element with a unique name attribute. As discussed earlier, a color's value is specified with a pound sign (#) followed by hexadecimal digits. The four accepted formats are #RGB, #ARGB, #RRGGBB, and #AARRGGBB.

As an example, the color yellow (255, 255, 0) could be given as #FF0, #FFF0, #FFFF00, or #FFFFFF00. The following markup shows how this can be written:

```
<resources>
  <color name="yellow">#FF0</color>
</resources>
```

In Java, this can be accessed by calling the getColor method of the Resources class with R.color.yellow. In XML, it can be accessed as @color/yellow.

3.6.4 Integer Resources

An integer resource is defined inside <integer> and </integer> tags, and each element must provide a name attribute. Negative integers must be preceded with a – sign. Nonnegative integers can have a + sign or no sign at all. For example, the following XML markup defines two integers named plus_twelve and minus_twelve.

```
<resources>
  <integer name="plus_twelve">+12</integer>
  <integer name="minus_twelve">-12</integer>
</resources>
```

To access the first integer in Java, call Resources.getInteger with the identifier R.integer.plus_twelve. To access the resource in an XML file, use the designation @color/plus_twelve.

3.6.5 Boolean Resources

Boolean resources are similar to integer resources, but the containing element is <bool> and the specified value must be true or false. These resources are particularly helpful when saving locale-specific configuration settings. The following markup defines a boolean resource named left_to_right.

```
<resources>
  <bool name="left_to_right">false</bool>
</resources>
```

In Java, this value can be accessed by calling the `getBoolean` method of the `Resources` class with the `R.bool.left_to_right` ID. It can be accessed in XML with `@bool/left_to_right`.

3.6.6 Integer Array Resources

Suppose you want a resource file to hold the ages of students in a classroom. Rather than create multiple single-integer resources, you can create one resource that contains an array of integers. These resources can be defined with `<integer-array>` elements that contain an `<item>` element for each integer in the array.

The following markup defines an array containing the initial values of the Fibonacci series. Note that the `<integer-array>` element requires a `name` attribute but the `<item>` elements don't have any attributes.

```
<resources>
  <integer-array name="fibonacci">
    <item>0</item>
    <item>1</item>
    <item>1</item>
    <item>2</item>
    <item>3</item>
  </integer-array>
</resources>
```

The primary advantage of using these resources is that they can be accessed as `int` arrays instead of `int`s. In Java, the array can be accessed by calling the `getIntArray` method of the `Resources` class using `R.array.fibonacci` as the ID. In XML, it can be accessed as `@array/fibonacci`.

3.6.7 ID Resources

In some applications, an `Activity` may need to assign a global identifier to a widget (such as a button or dialog box) that other classes can access. In this case, it's necessary to create an ID resource, assign it to the widget, and then access the widget through the ID.

ID resources are defined inside an `<item>` element that requires two attributes: `type` and `name`. The `type` attribute must be set to `id` and the `name` must be unique. The following markup defines an ID resource for a button.

```
<resources>
  <item type="id" name="close_button"/>
</resources>
```

With this definition, the ID can be referenced in Java as `R.id.close_button`. It can be accessed inside XML with `@id/close_button`.

3.7 Summary

Whether you're coding a Daydream app or a regular Android app, the first class you need to be concerned with is the `Activity` class. This defines the appearance and behavior of one screen of the application. As an activity's state changes, the application invokes the corresponding lifecycle methods of the `Activity`. The `onCreate` method is particularly important, and most applications perform their initialization and configuration in this method.

An activity's external characteristics, such as its name, icon, and label, are set in the application's manifest. This XML file is named AndroidManifest.xml and it can always be found in the module's src/main directory. In addition to describing properties of activities, the manifest also defines characteristics that relate to the entire application, such as desired permissions and required features.

To define its appearance, an `Activity` calls its `setContentView` method with a `View` instance or an identifier that represents a `View` instance. A view defines the content of a rectangle in an activity's screen, and Android provides many different types of views. Simple views present text or images, but later chapters will explain how to create views that display the results of 3-D graphical rendering.

An application can access external data using resources, which are files in the module's src/main/res directory. A layout resource defines the arrangement of views in an activity, and each XML element corresponds to a different view. Other types of resources include image resources and values resources.

Chapter 4

Text Views and Image Views

Most of this book is focused on three-dimensional graphical rendering, but every Android developer should be familiar with two basic types of views: text views and image views. These are the building blocks of Android user interfaces.

As its name implies, a text view displays text. If a virtual reality app needs to display a warning related to low battery or unsupported features, the text view is the simplest view to use. Similarly, apps may need to print text using transparent overlays, and text views are ideal for this purpose. Each text view is represented by a `TextView` instance, and the first part of this chapter explains how to create and configure `TextViews` in code.

Images play a central role in virtual reality development. As Chapter 10 will make clear, virtual reality apps use image data to apply textures to the surfaces of graphical models. Android provides many capabilities for loading and modifying images, and the second section of this chapter explains how applications can access and display image data through `ImageViews`.

The third section presents Android's `Drawable` interface. `Drawables` are abstract graphics, and by using the `Drawable` interface, applications can create graphics programmatically. This can be helpful for applications that need to draw two-dimensional shapes on top of three-dimensional rendering surfaces.

The last section of this chapter explores the topic of bitmaps, which make it possible to access image data at a low level. As later chapters will show, bitmaps serve as the bridge between an application's image resources and the textures used in virtual reality scenes. In code, bitmaps are represented by instances of the `Bitmap` class, which provides many methods for storing and manipulating image data.

4.1 Text Views

`TextView` is one of the most prominent subclasses of `View` and it's also the easiest to understand. If you've coded user interfaces with other APIs, you're probably familiar with *labels*—rectangular boxes that display text. This is how a `TextView` works. Its subclasses augment this behavior with different capabilities and behaviors.

Chapter 3 presented layout attributes and methods that make it possible to configure the appearance of `Views`. All of these apply to `TextViews`, but Android also provides attributes and methods specifically for `TextViews`. Table 4.1 lists many of them and provides a description of each.

Table 4.1

TextView Attributes and Methods (Abridged)

Attribute	Method	Description
`text, bufferType`	`setText(CharSequence, TextView.BufferType)`	Sets text to be displayed
`textColor`	`setTextColor(int)`	Sets the color of text
`textSize`	`setTextSize(int,float)`	Sets size of text
`fontFamily`	`setTypeface(Typeface)`	Sets the font of the text
`typeface`	`setTypeface(Typeface)`	Sets the text's typeface: normal, sans, serif, or monospace
`textStyle`	`setTypeface(Typeface)`	Sets the text's style: bold, italic, or bolditalic
`gravity`	`setGravity(int)`	Specifies text alignment
`textAllCaps`	`setAllCaps(boolean)`	Specifies whether the text should be printed in uppercase
`cursorVisible`	`setCursorVisible(boolean)`	Specifies whether the cursor should be displayed
`selectAllOnFocus`	`setSelectAllOnFocus(boolean)`	Select all of the text when the TextView receives focus
`height`	`setHeight(int)`	Specifies the height of the TextView
`width`	`setWidth(int)`	Specifies the width of the TextView
`ems`	`setEms(int)`	Specifies the width of the TextView in ems

lines	setLines(int)	Specifies the number of lines of text in the TextView
maxLines	setMaxLines(int)	Specifies the maximum number of lines of text in the TextView
minLines	setMinLines(int)	Specifies the minimum number of lines of text in the TextView
lineSpacing Multiple	setLineSpacing (float, float)	Define line spacing as a multiple of the line height
lineSpacing Extra	setLineSpacing (float, float)	Define additional spacing for each line

The attributes and methods in this table can be divided into three categories:

- Text configuration — set text properties such as color, font, and alignment
- Geometry — define the size of the `TextView`
- Line configuration — specify how many lines of text should be displayed, the spacing between lines, and whether text should wrap to new lines

This section discusses the attributes in each of these three categories. In each case, we'll examine what the attribute accomplishes and how it can be set in a layout resource.

4.1.1 Text Configuration

Of the attributes listed in Table 4.1, `text` is the most important because it sets the text to be displayed in the `TextView`. In a layout resource, this can be provided as a string contained in double quotes or as string resource.

For example, in the following `TextView` definition, the layout resource sets the text equal to a string resource called `message`:

```
<TextView
   ...
   android:text="@string/message" >
</TextView>
```

As explained in Chapter 3, this view's text will be determined by a `<string>` element in the module's src/main/res/strings.xml file. To be specific, it will be set to the element whose `name` attribute is `message`.

Text Size

To set the size of text in a `TextView`, an application must provide two pieces of information: the desired size and the units of measurement. Chapter 3 presented the six measurement units supported by Android: inches (`in`), millimeters (`mm`), points (`pt`), pixels (`px`), density-independent pixels (`dp`), and scale-independent pixels (`sp`).

In a layout resource, the `size` attribute of a `TextView` must be set equal to the desired size followed by one of these abbreviations. For example, the following markup configures a `TextView` whose size is set to 30 scale-independent pixels:

```
<TextView
    ...
    android:textSize="30sp" >
</TextView>
```

As discussed in the previous chapter, scale-independent pixels are the recommended units for text sizes. This is because they can be easily scaled to the user's preference.

In Java, the size of text in a `TextView` can be configured with `setTextSize`. This accepts two arguments: the desired size of the text and the units of measurement.

Font and Style

As of Android 16, Android applications can access multiple fonts, including Roboto, Noto Serif, and Droid Sans Mono. In a layout resource, the choice of fonts is determined by the `typeface` attribute, which can be set to `sans` (Roboto), `serif` (Noto Serif), or `monospace` (Droid Sans Mono). For example, the following markup sets the `TextView`'s font to Droid Sans Mono:

```
<TextView
    ...
    android:typeface="monospace" >
</TextView>
```

Android fonts can be printed in regular face, italics, boldface, or a combination of italics and boldface. This choice is determined by the `textStyle` attribute, which can be set to `normal`, `bold`, `italic`, or `bold|italic`.

The following markup shows how this works. The layout resource sets the `TextView`'s font to Roboto Sans and its style to `bold|italic`.

```
<TextView
    ...
    android:text="This is printed in bold, italicized Roboto Sans."
    android:textSize="30sp"
    android:typeface="sans"
    android:textStyle="bold|italic"
</TextView>
```

Figure 4.1 displays the resulting text, along with that of italicized Noto Serif and Droid Sans Mono.

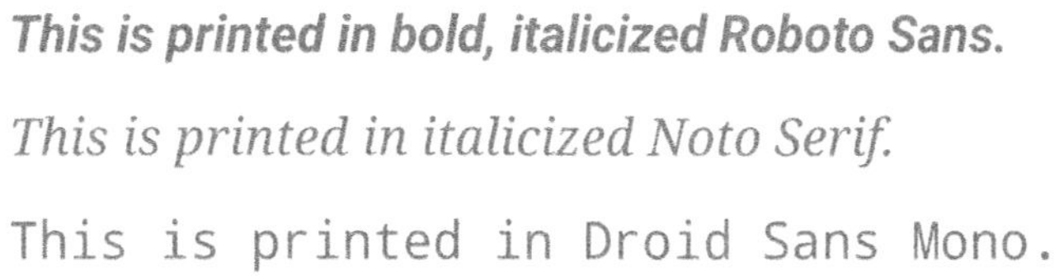

Figure 4.1 Android Fonts and Text Styles

Google provides many more fonts than those described here. The full list can be found by looking through Android's fonts.xml file.

Alignment

In the Android API, a view's horizontal and vertical alignment is called its *gravity*. For this reason, the attribute in a `TextView`'s layout resource that defines its text alignment is named `gravity`. This can be set to one of the values listed in Table 4.2.

Table 4.2

Gravity Attribute Values

Attribute	Description
`fill`	Expand to fill in the horizontal and vertical directions
`fill_horizontal`	Expand to fill in the horizontal direction
`fill_vertical`	Expand to fill in the vertical direction
`start`	Set the position to the start of its container
`center`	Set the position to the center
`end`	Set the position to the end of its container
`left`	Set the horizontal position to the left

`center_horizontal`	Set the horizontal position to the center
`right`	Set the horizontal position to the right
`top`	Set the vertical position to the top
`center_vertical`	Set the vertical position to the center
`bottom`	Set the vertical position to the bottom
`clip_vertical`	Horizontally clips the edges of the object to the container
`clip_horizontal`	Vertically clips the edges of the object to the container

These attributes are straightforward to understand. The following markup configures the text to be centered in the vertical axis and right-justified in the horizontal axis:

```
<TextView
   ...
   android:gravity="center_vertical|right"
</TextView>
```

4.1.2 TextView Geometry

Chapter 3 discussed the `layout_width` and `layout_height` attributes, which tell the layout engine how much space to allocate for a view. But these attributes don't necessarily set the view's actual dimensions. For this purpose, `TextView` provides the attributes `width` and `height`.

It's generally unwise to set a view's exact size. It's better to define a minimum size so that the text will always be displayed or a maximum size so that the `TextView` won't occupy too much space. `TextView` provides attributes for this purpose such as `maxWidth`, `maxHeight`, `minWidth`, and `minHeight`.

These attributes accept dimensions in pixels, but `TextView` also lets you set width in *ems*. Ems are used when a dimension should change relative to the size of the text. 1em has the same size as the current text, so a measurement of 1.5em is 1.5 times as large as the current text. A measurement of .75em is three-quarters as large as the current text.

The `ems` attribute sets the width of the `TextView` in ems. The following markup uses this method to set the width to be twice the size of the current text:

```
ems="2.0"
```

As with regular width and height, `TextView` provides `maxEms` for setting the maximum width in ems and `minEms` for setting the minimum width.

4.1.3 Configuring Lines of Text

If a text buffer's length exceeds the available horizontal space, Android will display the text on multiple lines. The `TextView` class provides attributes related to these lines and the most important is `lines`, which sets the number of lines that should be displayed. If this is set to 1, the text will be always displayed on one line. The attributes `maxLines` and `minLines` set the maximum and minimum number of lines.

In addition to setting the number of lines, `TextView` provides two attributes that control the spacing between adjacent lines. These are given as:

1. `lineSpacingMultiple` — a multiple of the current line spacing
2. `lineSpacingExtra` — additional spacing between adjacent lines

Both attributes accept floating-point values. The following example configures the `TextView`'s lines to be double-spaced with an additional spacing of 3.0 scale-independent pixels between lines.

```
<TextView
   ...
   android:lineSpacingMultiple="2.0"
   android:lineSpacingExtra="3.0sp"
</TextView>
```

In Java, line spacing can be configured with the `setLineSpacing` method, which accepts line spacing parameters. For example, calling `setLineSpacing(2.0, 3.0)` will set the view's lines to be double-spaced because the first argument sets the spacing to be twice the text size. In addition, the spacing between lines is increased by 3.0 because of the second argument.

4.2 Image Views

An `ImageView` is a rectangular region that contains graphic content (not necessarily an image). Like a `TextView`, it can be defined in an XML-based resource file or in Java.

In a layout resource file, `ImageView`s are configured with `<ImageView>` elements. This accepts the same attributes as regular `View`s, including `layout_width` and `layout_height`. In addition, Android provides attributes specifically for `ImageView`s. Table 4.3 lists seven of them and their corresponding Java methods.

Table 4.3

ImageView Attributes and Methods (Abridged)

Attribute	Method	Description
`src`	`setImageResource (int)`	Sets the content of the ImageView to the Drawable resource
`adjust ViewBounds`	`setAdjustView Bounds(boolean)`	Specifies whether the view's dimensions should be altered to maintain the aspect ratio of its content
`maxWidth`	`setMaxWidth(int)`	Sets the view's maximum width
`maxHeight`	`setMaxHeight(int)`	Sets the view's maximum height
`cropToPadding`	`setCropToPadding (boolean)`	Specifies whether the view's size should be limited to its padding region
`scaleType`	`setScaleType (ImageView.ScaleType)`	Identifies how the content should be scaled to fit inside the view
`tint`	`setColorFilter(int, PorterDuff.Mode)`	Sets the view's overall color

NOTE If an `ImageView`'s content can't be displayed, Android will print a string description in its place. This can be set with the `contentDescription` attribute inherited from the `View` class.

None of these attributes are required, but the first, `src`, is the most important. This identifies the content of the `ImageView`. Just as a `TextView` displays text, an `ImageView` displays a `Drawable`. I'll explain what `Drawable`s are later in this chapter. For now, all you need to know is that a `Drawable` represents an abstract graphic. It could be an image, a color, a drawing, or any other type of visual resource. Drawables can be defined as resources in a project's res/drawable directory, and these resources can be accessed in code as `R.drawable.`*`name`* and in XML as `@drawable/`*`name`*.

For example, the following markup defines an `ImageView` that occupies all of the available space, sets its content equal to a resource named `drawable/smiley`, and sets its description to a resource named `string/description`.

```
<ImageView
  android:layout_width="match_parent"
  android:layout_height="match_parent"
  android:src="@drawable/smiley"
  android:contentDescription="@string/description"
/>
```

The following code creates the same ImageView in a Java activity:

```
iv.setImageResource(R.drawable.smiley);
iv.setContentDescription(
    getResources().getString(R.string.description));
```

Most of the attributes in Table 4.3 relate to the size of the Drawable inside the ImageView. By default, if the two sizes aren't the same, the Drawable will be stretched or shrunk to fit the view region. If adjustViewBounds is set to true, the view's region will be constrained so that the Drawable's aspect ratio remains constant. Similarly, maximumWidth and maximumHeight configure the view's maximum dimensions.

4.2.1 Scaling

If an ImageView and its content have different sizes, the scale type identifies how the Drawable should be transformed. In a layout resource, this is given by the scaleType attribute of the <ImageView> element. In Java, this is identified by the argument of setScaleType, which accepts a value of ImageView.ScaleType. Table 4.4 lists the attribute values and the possible values of ImageView.ScaleType.

Table 4.4

ScaleType Values

Layout Attribute	ImageView. ScaleType	Description
fitCenter	FIT_CENTER	Scales Drawable to take up at least one dimension, positions Drawable in center
fitStart	FIT_START	Scales Drawable to take up at least one dimension, positions Drawable in upper left
fitEnd	FIT_END	Scales Drawable to take up at least one dimension, positions Drawable in lower right
fitXY	FIT_XY	Scales Drawable to occupy entire parent area
center	CENTER	Positions Drawable in center, no scaling
centerCrop	CENTER_CROP	Scales Drawable until both dimensions are greater than or equal to the parent's dimension
centerInside	CENTER_INSIDE	Scales Drawable until both dimensions are less than or equal to the parent's dimension
matrix	MATRIX	Transforms Drawable according to a transformation matrix

The default scale type is `fitCenter`, which centers the `Drawable` and increases or decreases its size to occupy at least one of the parent's dimensions. `fitStart` and `fitEnd` perform similar scaling, but position the `Drawable` in the upper left or the lower right.

`fitXY` scales the `Drawable` to occupy all of the parent's space—it's the only scale type that changes the image's aspect ratio. This is shown in Figure 4.2.

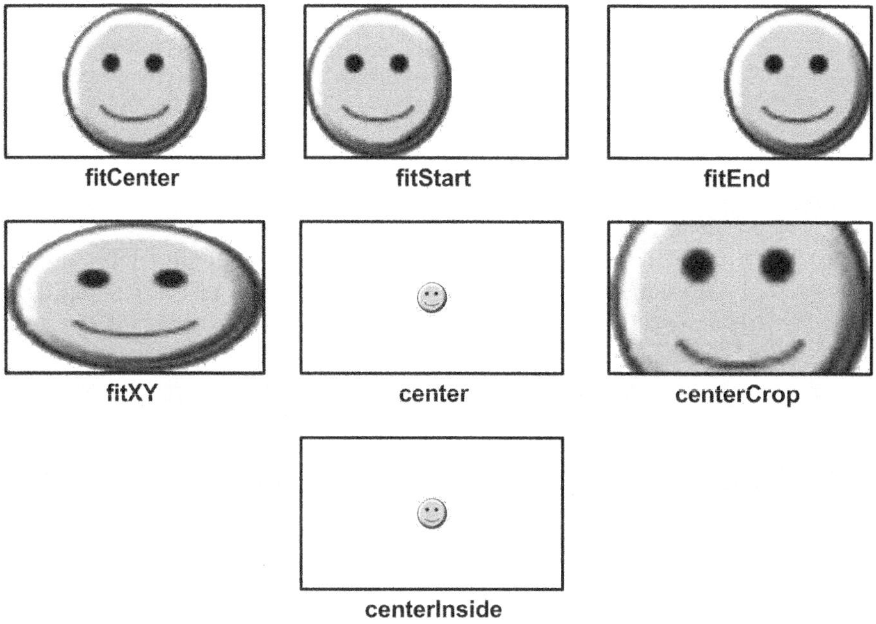

Figure 4.2 ImageView Scale Types

If the scale type is set to `center`, the `Drawable` will be positioned in the center but it won't be scaled. `centerCrop` is similar, but uniformly scales the `Drawable` until both of its dimensions are greater than or equal to the parent's. `centerInside` scales the `Drawable` until both dimensions are less than or equal to the parent's.

4.2.2 Transforming Images

If the `scaleType` attribute is set to `matrix`, the `Drawable` will be transformed according to the matrix associated with the `ImageView`. This makes it possible to perform general transformations such as translation, rotation, and/or scaling.

The method `setImageMatrix` configures the matrix for an `ImageView`. This accepts a `Matrix` object, which represents a 3x3 transformation matrix. By default, it's set equal to an identity matrix (1 on the matrix diagonal, 0 off the diagonal).

The elements of the matrix can be set directly with `setValues(float[])`, which copies an array of nine `float`s into the matrix. Alternatively, the matrix values can be set by calling methods that perform transformations. Table 4.5 lists these methods and describes their operations.

Table 4.5

Transformation Methods of the Matrix Class

Method	Description
`preRotate(float degrees)/` `postRotate(float degrees)`	Rotates the image before/after the current transformation
`preScale(float scale)/` `postScale(float scale)`	Scales the image before/after the current transformation
`preSkew(float skew)/` `postSkew(float skew)`	Skews the image before/after the current transformation
`preTranslate(float dx, float dy)/` `postTranslate(float dx, float dy)`	Translates the image before/after the current transformation

These methods are straightforward and the ch04_imagematrix module demonstates how they're used in practice. This application displays an `ImageView` whose matrix rotates an image by 45 degrees and then translates it by 200 pixels in the x-direction and 100 pixels in the y-direction. Figure 4.3 shows what the result looks like.

Figure 4.3 Matrix Transformation

When performing multiple transformations, order is important. As shown in Listing 4.1, the code in ch04_imagematrix calls `preTranslate` followed by `preRotate`. When a method starting with `pre-` is called, its operation will be performed before the others. In this case, the rotation is performed before the translation.

For transformation methods starting with `post-`, the result is reversed. That is, if `postTranslate` is followed by `postRotate`, `postRotate` will be performed last.

Listing 4.1: ch04_imagematrix/src/main/java/.../ImageMatrixActivity.java

```
public class ImageMatrixActivity extends Activity {

  protected void onCreate(Bundle savedInstanceState) {
    super.onCreate(savedInstanceState);

    // Create and configure the Matrix
    Matrix m = new Matrix();
    m.preTranslate(200.0f, 100.0f);
    m.preRotate(45.0f);

    // Create the ImageView
    ImageView iv = new ImageView(this);
    iv.setImageResource(R.drawable.smiley);
    iv.setScaleType(ScaleType.MATRIX);
    iv.setImageMatrix(m);

    setContentView(iv);
  }
}
```

This code defines the image's transformation by creating a `Matrix` object and calling its methods. Then it accesses an `ImageView` and sets its content to the drawable whose ID is `R.drawable.smiley`. In this case, the drawable is given as a PNG file in the project's res/drawable folder. But drawables are much more versatile than that, and the following section discusses the topic in detail.

4.3 Drawables

A `Drawable` is an abstract graphic. A `Drawable` might depict an image or a shape, or it might be as simple as a color. As stated in the Android documentation, "the `Drawable` class provides a generic API for dealing with an underlying visual resource that may take a variety of forms."

`Drawable`s serve as the content of `ImageView`s, but any view can insert a `Drawable` as its background. This is made possible through the `setBackground(Drawable)` and `setBackgroundResource(int)` methods of the `View` class.

`Drawable` is an abstract class with a wide range of subclasses. Figure 4.4 illustrates a large part of its class hierarchy. The four boxes shaded in gray identify the classes that will be discussed in this section: `Drawable`, `ColorDrawable`, `GradientDrawable`, and `BitmapDrawable`.

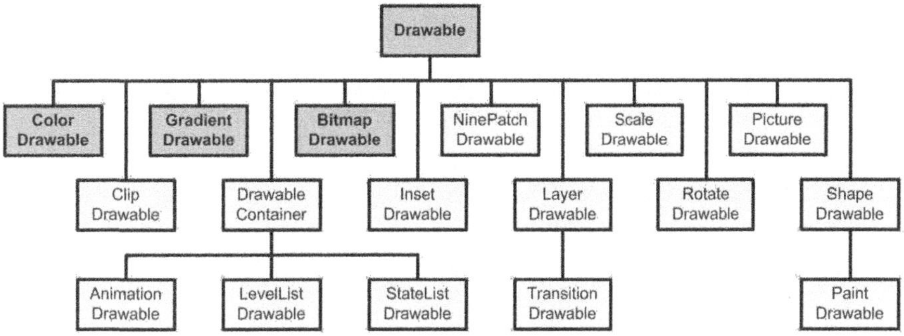

Figure 4.4 Drawable Class Hierarchy (Abridged)

`Drawable`s are frequently defined with resource files, but the format of the resource file depends on which subclass of `Drawable` is being defined. That is, the format of a `RotateDrawable` resource is markedly different than the format of a `BitmapDrawable` resource. In fact, `RotateDrawable`s are defined with XML files and `BitmapDrawable`s (usually) aren't.

Despite the significant differences between its subclasses, the `Drawable` class provides many methods that are available to all `Drawable`s. Two of the most important `Drawable` methods are:

- `createFromPath(String)` — Creates a `Drawable` from a file
- `setBounds(int left, int top, int right, int bottom)` — sets coordinates for the `Drawable`'s boundaries

The `createFromPath` method reads the content of an image file and returns a `Drawable`. This method accepts three types of files: *.png, *.jpg, and *.gif.

For example, suppose that the example.png is located in the images directory. The following code returns a `Drawable` from this file:

```
Drawable.createFromPath("images/example.png");
```

The `setBounds` method specifies the the `Drawable`'s boundaries. It accepts the coordinates of the upper-left corner (left, top) first, followed by the coordinates of the bottom-right corner (right, bottom).

In addition to these methods, the `Drawable` class makes it possible to assign levels, states, and callback methods. It also provides many methods for configuration animation. These capabilities are beyond the scope of this book.

4.3.1 ColorDrawable

The simplest `Drawable` subclass is `ColorDrawable`. As its name implies, this displays a single color. Its format must be given as 0xAARRGGBB and this can be set through the `ColorDrawable` constructor or its `setColor` method.

For example, the following code associates an `ImageView` with a light green `ColorDrawable`:

```
ImageView view = (ImageView)this.findViewById(R.id.iv);
view.setImageDrawable(new ColorDrawable(0xff88ff88));
```

`ColorDrawables` can also be defined in layout resources. If the `src` attribute of an `<ImageView>` element is set to a color value, an appropriate `ColorDrawable` will be created for the `ImageView`. This is shown in the following markup, which defines an `ImageView` similar to the one defined in Java:

```
<ImageView
  android:layout_width="match_parent"
  android:layout_height="match_parent"
  android:src="@color.light_green">
</ImageView>
```

This refers to a color resource defined in res/values/colors.xml, given as follows:

```
<resources>
  <color name="light_green">#0f0</color>
</resources>
```

4.3.2 GradientDrawable

`GradientDrawables` are slightly more involved than `ColorDrawables`. They depict color that changes gradually from one boundary to another. The `ColorDrawable` constructor accepts two arguments:

- the orientation of the gradient (TOP_BOTTOM, BOTTOM_TOP, LEFT_RIGHT, RIGHT_LEFT, BL_TR, BR_TL, TL_BR, or TR_BL)
- an array of colors to be depicted

The best way to understand this is through an example. The following code creates a rainbow-colored GradientDrawable that proceeds from the top-right corner (TR) to the bottom-left (BL). Then it associates the Drawable with an ImageView.

```
int colorArray[] = new int[]{Color.RED, 0xffff7f00,
    Color.YELLOW, Color.GREEN, Color.BLUE,
    0xff4B0082, 0xff8f00ff};

GradientDrawable gd = new GradientDrawable(
    GradientDrawable.Orientation.BL_TR, colorArray);

imageView.setImageDrawable(gd);
```

GradientDrawables can be defined inside XML files in the project's res/drawable directory. The top-level XML element is <shape> and the gradient is defined inside a <gradient> subelement. This accepts a number of attributes, but three are particularly important:

- startColor — the initial color of the gradient
- endColor — the final color of the gradient
- angle — the gradient's direction

The value of angle is given in degrees. If angle is set to 0, the gradient proceeds from left to right, and if set to 90, the gradient proceeds from bottom to top. The following markup defines a GradientDrawable that starts with red on the top and proceeds to green on the bottom:

```
<shape>
  <gradient
    android:angle="270"
    android:startColor="#f00"
    android:endColor="#0f0" />
</shape>
```

Similar <shape> elements can be used to define ShapeDrawable resources. These represent custom shapes composed of lines, circles, rectangles, and text.

4.4 Bitmaps

Just as a `GradientDrawable` depicts colors in a one-dimensional array, a `BitmapDrawable` depicts colors in a two-dimensional array called a bitmap. Of the many subclasses of `Drawable`, `BitmapDrawable` is probably the most commonly used.

4.4.1 BitmapDrawable Resources

Earlier, we looked at the ch04_imagematrix module, which demonstrates how images can be transformed. The module's res/drawable folder contains a file called smiley.png. This is the first resource file we've encountered that isn't an XML file. The application creates a `Drawable` representing the image—a `BitmapDrawable`. This can be accessed in Java or XML like a regular `Drawable`.

Android prefers PNG (Portable Native Graphics) files as images, but JPEG (Joint Photographic Experts Group) files and GIF (Graphics Interchange Format) files are also accepted. As long as valid *.png, *.jpg, *.jpeg, or *.gif files are placed in the project's drawable directory, Android will create `BitmapDrawables`.

As discussed in Chapter 3, the modules in this book store icons in folders named mipmap-*density*, where *density* identifies a pixel density category (hdpi, xhdpi, xxhdpi, and so on). It's a good idea to store image files in similarly named directories named drawable-*density*, such as drawable-hdpi, drawable-xhdpi, and drawable-xxhdpi.

4.4.2 The BitmapDrawable Class

In code, a `BitmapDrawable` can be created from a bitmap file, a `Bitmap` object, or an `InputStream`. To ensure proper density, the constructor should include a reference to the current `Resources` object. This is shown in the following code, which creates a new `BitmapDrawable` from an image file:

```
Resources res = getResources();
BitmapDrawable bd = new BitmapDrawable(res, "example.png");
imageView.setImageDrawable(bd);
```

Most of the methods of the `BitmapDrawable` class are similar to those we've seen earlier. But there are new methods that control how and where the `Drawable` is displayed:

- `setGravity` — controls the `Drawable`'s alignment. This accepts the same values as discussed for the `TextView`.

- `setTargetDensity` — identifies the density (in dpi) at which the image should be displayed. Must be given as an integer.
- `setTileModeX/setTileModeY/setTileModeXY` — controls how the image is repeated inside the view

If the bitmap is smaller than the drawable, the extra space in the drawable's area will be left empty by default. This behavior can be changed through tiling. Tiling sets the colors of the pixels outside the bitmap equal to colors inside the bitmap.

4.4.3 The Bitmap Class

For developers of games and similar graphical applications, creating `BitmapDrawables` from resource files isn't sufficient. For best performance, applications use multiple threads to create graphics programmatically. This requires a thorough understanding of the `Bitmap` class.

A `Bitmap` serves as intermediate storage between pixel data and the `Drawable` displayed in the view. The methods of this class can be divided into four categories:

1. Create an empty `Bitmap` with a given size and format
2. Provide information about the `Bitmap`
3. Modify the content of the `Bitmap`
4. Transfer the `Bitmap`'s content to a new file or stream

This discussion presents each of these categories. At the end of the discussion, we'll look at an application that demonstrates how these methods are called.

Bitmap Creation Methods

Table 4.6 lists the methods that create empty `Bitmap`s. Most have the same name, `createBitmap`, but have different configuration parameters.

Table 4.6

Creation Methods of the Bitmap Class

Method	Description
`createBitmap(int w, int h, Bitmap.Config fmg)`	Creates an empty Bitmap with the given width, height, and format

`createBitmap(DisplayMetrics dm, int w, int h, Bitmap.Config fmt)`	Creates an empty Bitmap with the given width, height, and format
`createBitmap(int[] colors, int w, int h, Bitmap.Config fmt)`	Creates a Bitmap with the given initial data, width, height, and format
`createBitmap(DisplayMetrics dm, int[] colors, int w, int h, Bitmap.Config fmt)`	Creates a Bitmap with the given initial data, width, height, and format
`createBitmap(int[] colors, int offset, int stride, int w, int h, Bitmap.Config fmt)`	Creates a Bitmap with the given initial data, offset, stride, width, height, and format
`createBitmap(DisplayMetrics dm, int[] colors, int offset, int stride, int w, int h, Bitmap.Config format)`	Creates a Bitmap with the given initial data, offset, stride, width, height, and format
`createBitmap(Bitmap src)`	Creates a clone of the source Bitmap
`createBitmap(Bitmap src, int x, int y, int w, int h)`	Creates a Bitmap from a portion of an existing Bitmap
`createBitmap(Bitmap src, int x, int y, int w, int h, Matrix m, boolean filter)`	Creates a Bitmap from a portion of an existing Bitmap, transformed by the given matrix
`createScaledBitmap(Bitmap src, int dstWidth, int dstHeight, boolean filter)`	Creates a Bitmap from an existing Bitmap. This content is scaled to the given width and height.

Many of these methods accept a `Bitmap.Config` that identifies the format of the bitmap's pixels. This can be set to one of three values:

- `ARGB_8888` — Each pixel contains four bytes: alpha, red, green, and blue
- `RGB_565` — Each pixel contains two bytes: five bits for the red channel, six bits for the green channel, and five bits for the blue channel
- `ALPHA_8` — Each pixel contains one byte. This is frequently employed for grayscale image data and image masks.

For example, the following code creates an empty 400-by-200 `Bitmap` whose pixels are formatted with `ARGB_8888`:

```
DisplayMetrics m = new DisplayMetrics();
getWindowManager().getDefaultDisplay().getMetrics(m);
bm = Bitmap.createBitmap(m, 400, 200, Config.ARGB_8888);
```

In this code, the first parameter of `createBitmap` is a `DisplayMetrics` object. This identifies the screen's size and density so that the bitmap can be scaled appropriately.

Bitmap Information Methods

The second category of methods provide information about the `Bitmap`, such as its dimensions (`getWidth` and `getHeight`), color content (`getPixel`), and density (`getDensity`).

For example, the following code obtains the color of the first pixel as an `int`:

```
Bitmap bm = BitmapFactory.decodeFile("example.png");
int color = bm.getPixel(0, 0);
```

The `getPixels` method is more involved. This returns an array of `int`s representing pixels at a given offset. Its signature is given as follows:

```
void getPixels(int[] pixels, int offset, int stride,
               int x, int y, int width, int height)
```

In addition, `getByteCount` returns the minimum number of bytes needed to store the bitmap's pixels.

Bitmap Modification Methods

By default, every new `Bitmap` is immutable, which means its content can't be modified. Therefore, the following code will produce an error:

```
Bitmap bm = BitmapFactory.decodeFile("example.png");
bm.setPixel(10, 10, Color.BLACK);
```

There are two ways to create a mutable `Bitmap`:

- Use one of the `BitmapFactory` methods with the `BitmapFactory.Options` object configured with the `inMutable` field set to `true`.
- Call the `copy` method of the `Bitmap` class with the second argument set to true.

The `copy` method creates a clone of a `Bitmap`, and if the second argument is `true`, the new copy will be mutable. If a `Bitmap` is mutable, the methods `setPixel` and `setPixels` make it possible to modify the bitmap's color content. The signatures of these methods are given as follows:

- `setPixel(int x, int y, int color)`
- `setPixels(int[] pixels, int offset, int stride, int x, int y, int width, int height)`

In addition, the bitmap's density and alpha content can be modified with the `setDensity` and `setHasAlpha` methods. These methods can be called for mutable and immutable `Bitmap`s.

Bitmap Storage Methods

The last category of `Bitmap` methods involves converting or storing the bitmap's color data. Two particularly helpful methods in this category are `compress` and `copyToBuffer`:

1. `compress(Bitmap.CompressFormat format, int quality, OutputStream stream)`
2. `copyPixelsToBuffer(Buffer dst)`

The `compress` method compresses the bitmap's data according to the `Bitmap.CompressFormat` value, which can be `JPEG`, `PNG`, or `WEBP`. The `OutputStream` can be directed to a file, and this is shown in the following code:

```
File file = "image.jpg"
FileOutputStream outStream = new FileOutputStream(file);
bitmap.compress(Bitmap.CompressFormat.JPEG, 10, outStream);
```

The second argument sets the quality of the compression and ranges from 0 (low-quality, small size) to 100 (high-quality, large size). If the format is set to `Bitmap.CompressFormat.JPEG`, this quality value won't be used.

The `copyPixelsToBuffer` method writes the bitmap data to a `Buffer` object. Provided by the Java NIO (New I/O) package, the `Buffer` class makes it possible to access memory efficiently using low-level operations.

`Buffer` objects are particularly important when working with Android's Native Development Kit (NDK) or other high-performance computing tools. Normally, data must be copied from the Java application to native C/C++ functions. But if the application stores its data in `Buffer`s, it can be directly accessed by the NDK. Chapter 7 will provide a thorough discussion of the `Buffer` class and its subclasses.

4.4.4 The BitmapFactory Class

In general, there are two ways to create a `Bitmap`. An uninitialized `Bitmap` can be obtained by calling one of the `createBitmap` methods of the `Bitmap` class. To construct a `Bitmap` from existing data, you need a method from the `BitmapFactory` class.

To be specific, the `BitmapFactory` methods create `Bitmap`s from five different types of data: byte arrays, files, file descriptors, resources, and streams. Table 4.7 lists each of the class's methods and provides a description of its purpose.

Table 4.7

BitmapFactory Methods

Method	Description
`decodeByteArray(byte[], int, int)`	Creates a Bitmap from the byte array with the given offset and length
`decodeByteArray(byte[], int, int, BitmapFactory.Options)`	Creates a Bitmap from the byte array with the given offset, length, and options
`decodeFile(String)`	Creates a Bitmap from the file with the given path
`decodeFile(String, BitmapFactory.Options)`	Creates a Bitmap from the file with the given path and options
`decodeFileDescriptor( FileDescriptor)`	Creates a Bitmap from the file with the given file descriptor
`decodeFileDescriptor( FileDescriptor, Rect, BitmapFactory.Options)`	Creates a Bitmap from the file with the given file descriptor, padding, and options
`decodeResource(Resources, int)`	Creates a Bitmap from the resource with the given identifier
`decodeResource(Resources, int, BitmapFactory.Options)`	Creates a Bitmap from the resource with the given identifier and options
`decodeStream(InputStream)`	Creates a Bitmap from the given InputStream
`decodeStream(InputStream, Rect, options)`	Creates a Bitmap from the given InputStream with the given padding and options
`decodeResourceStream(Resources, TypedValue, InputStream, Rect, BitmapFactory.Options)`	Creates a Bitmap from the InputStream with the given value, padding, and options

Each of these methods is static and each returns a new `Bitmap` object. As an example, the following code creates a `Bitmap` from an image file named example.png.

```
Bitmap bm = BitmapFactory.decodeFile("example.png");
```

Many of the listed methods accept as their final argument an optional `BitmapFactory.Options` object. This contains fields that represent the bitmap's properties. Table 4.8 lists most of these configuration fields.

Table 4.8

Configuration Fields of BitmapFactory.Options (Abridged)

Field	Value Type	Description
`inBitmap`	`Bitmap`	Bitmap to reuse (clone) in place of the source data (if possible)
`inPreferredConfig`	`Bitmap.Config`	The pixel format of the returned Bitmap (Bitmap.Config will be discussed shortly)
`inSampleSize`	`int`	For a value > 1, tells decoder to subsample the pixels to produce a smaller bitmap
`inMutable`	`boolean`	Specifies whether the returned Bitmap will be mutable or immutable
`inDensity`	`int`	Pixel density of the returned Bitmap
`inScreenDensity`	`int`	Pixel density of the screen
`inTargetDensity`	`int`	Pixel density of the Bitmap in the given application
`inTempStorage`	`byte[]`	Temporary storage for use in the decoding process
`inScaled`	`boolean`	Specifies whether the Bitmap's scaling should be determined by inTargetDensity or the Android graphics system
`inJustDecodeBounds`	`boolean`	Specifies whether the method should return null and set the option's fields (false by default)
`outWidth`	`int`	Pixel width of the returned Bitmap
`outHeight`	`int`	Pixel height of the returned Bitmap
`outMimeType`	`String`	MIME type of the decoded data

As shown, some of the fields start with `in` and some start with `out`. The `out` fields aren't set by the user, but are initialized as the method executes. If the `inJustDecodeBounds` field is set to true, the `decode` method will return null and its effect will be limited to setting the `outWidth` and `outHeight` fields. The following code shows how this works.

```
// Configure bitmap options
BitmapFactory.Options opts = new BitmapFactory.Options();
opts.inJustDecodeBounds = true;

// Create the bitmap
Bitmap bm = BitmapFactory.decodeFile("example.png", opts);
int width = opts.outWidth;
int height = opts.outHeight;
```

Code like this is particularly helpful when an application needs to determine an image's size and density before processing the image.

When dealing with large files, `inSampleSize` becomes useful because it reduces the number of pixels in the bitmap. For example, if this field is set to 2, the output `Bitmap` contains every other pixel from the input data.

> **NOTE** Android expects `inSampleSize` to be set to a power of 2. If a different value is given, Android will round to the nearest power of 2.

The `inPreferredConfig` specifies a `Bitmap.Config` value that sets the desired pixel format for the decoded `Bitmap`. This accepts the same three values as the `Bitmap` creation methods: `ARGB_8888`, `RGB_565`, and `ALPHA_8`.

The ch04_bitmapbuilder module demonstrates how the `Bitmap`, `BitmapFactory`, and `BitmapFactory.Options` classes are used in practice. Listing 4.2 presents the full code for BitmapBuilderActivity.java.

Listing 4.2: ch04_bitmapbuilder/src/main/java/.../BitmapBuilderActivity.java

```
public class BitmapBuilderActivity extends Activity {

  // Called when the activity is created
  protected void onCreate(Bundle savedInstanceState) {
    super.onCreate(savedInstanceState);

    // Configure bitmap creation options
    BitmapFactory.Options opts = new BitmapFactory.Options();
    opts.inMutable = true;
```

```
    // Create bitmap
    Bitmap bm = BitmapFactory.decodeResource(getResources(),
      R.drawable.smiley, opts);

    // Draw border around bitmap
    int w = bm.getWidth();
    int h = bm.getHeight();
    int borderColor = 0xffff0000;

    for(int i=0; i<w; i++) {
      bm.setPixel(i, 0, borderColor);
      bm.setPixel(i, h-1, borderColor);
    }

    for(int i=0; i<h; i++) {
      bm.setPixel(0, i, borderColor);
      bm.setPixel(w-1, i, borderColor);
    }

    // Create the ImageView
    ImageView iv = new ImageView(this);
    iv.setImageBitmap(bm);
    setContentView(iv);
  }
}
```

This activity's processing is performed in four steps:

1. Configure a `BitmapFactory.Options` object to ensure high-quality encoding instead of high-speed coding and set the resulting `Bitmap` to be mutable.
2. Invoke `BitmapFactory.decode` to create a `Bitmap` from a resource file.
3. Set the bitmap's border to red by calling `setPixel`.
4. Make the `Bitmap` the content of the activity's view.

Like earlier examples, this code displays the `BitmapDrawable` by associating it with a view. Another way is to call the `draw` method of `BitmapDrawable`. This accepts a `Canvas` that depicts the `Drawable` at the bounds specified by `setBounds`.

4.5 Summary

Text and images are crucial in all Android apps, from basic GUIs to full virtual reality apps. For this reason, this chapter has focused on the `TextView` and `ImageView` classes.

A `TextView` is a rectangular region that displays text. Android provides a number of ways to configure the text's properties, including its size, font, alignment (gravity), and color. Remember that, unless there's a good reason, it's better to configure views with layout resources than Java code.

`ImageView`s are similar to `TextView`s, but they display graphics. To be precise, every `ImageView` displays the content of a `Drawable`. A `Drawable` is an abstract graphic that can be created from an image file or from different types of resources. This chapter explained how resources can be used to create `ColorDrawable`s and `GradientDrawable`s.

The last part of this chapter discussed bitmaps. A `BitmapDrawable` is a drawable created from an image's pixel data, and it's one of the most common types of drawables used in Android applications. The discussion also touched on the `Bitmap` class, which contains the low-level pixel data from an image. `Bitmap`s play an important role in virtual reality applications, and Chapter 10 will explain how applications create textures from `Bitmap`s.

Chapter 5

Threads, Handlers, and AsyncTasks

Up to this point, every application presented in this book has performed its operations in a single thread of execution. This is called the *main thread* or the *UI thread*. The main thread is ideal for simple operations or updating the user interface, but it's not suitable for long-running operations. For example, if an application needs to read position data from the Daydream controller, it shouldn't halt the user interface while the data becomes available.

The solution is to create new threads and use them to execute long-running operations. This methodology, called *concurrency*, is particularly important in VR development because graphical rendering is always performed in a separate thread. Threads are also necessary when an application needs to read data from the Daydream controller.

The Android API provides the same basic classes and interfaces for concurrency as in traditional Java. The `Thread` class has a wide range of methods for configuring child threads. Even simpler, the `Runnable` interface provides a single method, `run`. The first part of this chapter provides a brief review of these structures.

The next part of the chapter looks at Android features that facilitate data transfer between threads. A `Handler` associated with one thread can receive data from other threads. This data is packaged into structures called `Message`s. An application can access a thread's message queue using special iterators called `Looper`s.

The last part of the chapter discusses an Android-specific concurrency class called the `AsyncTask`. This is a wrapper of the `Thread` class that makes it easy for a child thread to update the UI thread. It also enables the application to display the progress of the long-running tasks in child threads.

5.1 Threads and Runnables

If you've programmed Java for any length of time, you're probably familiar with the `Thread` class and the `Runnable` interface. But just in case you're unclear, this section provides a quick review.

5.1.1 Threads

The `Thread` class makes it straightforward to execute code in a separate thread. At minimum, its usage consists of three steps:

1. Create a subclass of `Thread`.
2. Add code to the subclass's `run` method.
3. Execute the new thread by calling the `start` method of the `Thread` subclass.

When the `start` method is invoked, the code inside `run` will be executed concurrently with the application's main thread. The following `Activity` code provides a high-level idea of how this works:

```
public class TestActivity extends Activity {

  class TestThread extends Thread {
    public void run() {
        ...
    }
  }

  public void onCreate(Bundle b) {
    TestThread t = new TestThread();
    t.start();
  }
}
```

When `onCreate` calls `t.start`, the code inside the thread's `run` method will execute concurrently with the rest of the code inside `onCreate`.

Every thread is assigned an integer value to serve as its ID. Also, a `Thread` subclass may be passed a string in its constructor to serve as its name. A thread's ID can be obtained through `getId` and its name can be obtained through `getName`. Table 5.1 lists these and other basic methods of the `Thread` class.

Table 5.1

Basic Thread Methods

Method	Description
`void run()`	Contains code to be executed when the thread is launched
`void start()`	Launches the thread, executing the code inside the run method
`long getId()`	Returns the ID of the current thread
`String getName()` `void setName(String)`	Returns/sets the thread's name
`int getPriority()` `void setPriority(int)`	Returns/sets the thread's priority
`bool isDaemon()` `void setDaemon(bool)`	Returns/sets the thread's status as a daemon thread
`static Thread currentThread()`	Returns the current thread
`static void sleep(int millisec)` `static void sleep(int millisec, int nanosec)`	Forces the thread to halt its processing for the given amount of time

Each `Thread` has a priority that identifies how much preference it should receive. This is given as an integer ranging from 10 (`Thread.MAX_PRIORITY`) to 1 (`Thread.MIN_PRIORITY`), and the default priority is 5. In theory, `Thread`s with higher priority will receive greater access to resources than lower-priority `Thread`s. But don't take this too seriously—Android considers it to be more of a recommendation than a hard requirement.

`Thread`s can be divided into two classes: user threads and daemon threads. The application's main thread is a user thread, and by default, every `Thread` created in a user thread is a user thread. The Dalvik JVM won't exit until every user thread has completed its processing.

`setDaemon` converts a user thread to a daemon thread, and by default, every `Thread` created in a daemon thread is a daemon thread. The main difference between daemons and user threads is that, when the JVM exits, it doesn't wait for daemon threads. In general, daemons are used to perform background tasks that don't tie up important resources.

The last method in Table 5.1 is `sleep`. This tells the current thread to halt its computation for a given length of time. The second `sleep` method accepts nanoseconds as the second argument, but the JVM's timing really isn't precise. As stated in Android's documentation, "the `Thread` may sleep more or less than requested."

5.1.2 Join and Interrupt Methods

At some point, a parent thread may need to wait until its child threads complete their processing. This wait-until-completion process is referred to as *joining*. When called from the main thread, `join` forces a parent thread to wait until the named thread completes its operation. The following code shows how this works.

```
TestThread t = new TestThread("Testing");
t.start();
...          // Continue processing while thread executes
t.join();    // Wait for TestThread to complete
...          // Perform processing
```

If a child thread becomes trapped in an infinite loop and the main thread executes `join`, the main thread can end up waiting forever. For this reason, `join` can be followed by one or two parameters that identify how long the calling thread should wait. Table 5.2 lists the three overloaded join methods of the `Thread` class.

Table 5.2

Join and Interrupt Methods

Method	Description

`join()`
`join(int millisec)`
`join(int millisec, int nanosec)`
	Halts the calling thread until the specified thread completes its processing or the specified amount of time elapses

`interrupt()`	Sends an interrupt request to the thread
`interrupted()`	Identifies whether the current thread has been interrupted

If a thread needs to halt the processing of another thread, there are no `stop` or `suspend` methods available. Instead, the `interrupt` method sends a request to the `Thread` asking it to halt. If the `Thread` is sleeping or waiting for access to a resource, it will receive this request as an `InterruptedException`.

5.1.3 The Runnable Interface

The `Thread` class provides a number of capabilities for concurrent execution, but many applications don't need features like priority, joining, and interruption. For these applications, the `Runnable` interface is ideal.

The purpose of the Runnable interface is simple—to specify code that should be executed in a separate thread. This code must be provided in the Runnable's run method, which accepts no arguments and has no return value.

Because Runnable is an interface, a class can implement Runnable while extending another class. This is shown in the following code, in which ThreadActivity subclasses Activity and implements Runnable.

```
public class TestActivity extends Activity implements Runnable {

  public void onCreate(Bundle b) {
    ...
    TestThread t = new Thread(this);
    t.start();
    ...
  }

  void run() {
    ...
  }
}
```

An important difference between a Runnable and a Thread is that a Runnable's operation can't be launched by calling start. But as shown in the code above, a Thread can be created from a Runnable and then launched with start.

The Android API provides another mechanism for launching Runnables. This involves objects called Handlers and the following section discusses them in detail.

5.2 Communicating Between Threads

The join method forces one thread to wait for another, but it doesn't allow the threads to communicate in any way. In regular Java, threads talk to one another through synchronized variables. In Android, inter-thread communication is made possible by Handlers.

A Handler is an object associated with a thread that is capable of receiving data from other threads. If the Handler is associated with the main thread, also called the UI thread, it can use the incoming data to update the user interface. A Handler's incoming data is provided in the form of Message objects. This section explains Handlers and Messages and shows how they're used in code.

5.2.1 Overview

Suppose an Android application needs to send two variables from a child thread to the main thread. This can be performed in four steps:

1. The child thread creates a `Message` using the main thread's `Handler`.
2. The child thread sets the `Message`'s data to the two variables.
3. The child thread sends the `Message` to the main thread's `Handler`.
4. When the main thread's `Handler` receives the `Message`, `handleMessage` is called automatically. This executes in the main thread, so `handleMessage` can use data from the child thread to update the user interface.

Listing 5.1 gives an idea how this works. In this case, the code in the child thread (given in the `run` method) creates a `Message` whose data contains two integers. The main thread reads the two values from the `Message` and prints them in the user interface.

Listing 5.1: ch05_basichandler/src/main/java/.../BasicHandlerActivity.java

```
public class BasicHandlerActivity extends Activity
            implements Runnable {

  // Configure Handler to display message content
  static class MsgHandler extends Handler {
    final TextView textView;

    MsgHandler(TextView view) {textView = view;}

    public void handleMessage(Message msg) {
      String str = "Arg1: " + msg.arg1 +
          "\nArg2: " + msg.arg2;
      textView.setText(str);
    }
  }
  private MsgHandler handler;

  public void onCreate(Bundle b) {
    super.onCreate(b);
    setContentView(R.layout.main_layout);
    TextView tv = (TextView)findViewById(R.id.tv);

    // Create and launch the thread
    handler = new MsgHandler(tv);
    Thread t = new Thread(this);
    t.start();
  }
```

Listing 5.1: ch05_basichandler/src/main/java/.../BasicHandlerActivity.java

```
  public void run() {

    // Create and configure a new Message
    Message msg = Message.obtain(handler);
    msg.arg1 = 21;
    msg.arg2 = 37;

    // Send Message to handler
    handler.sendMessage(msg);
  }
}
```

This example is straightforward to understand. The child thread creates a `Message` with two arguments and sends it to the main thread's `Handler`. The `Handler` receives the `Message` and uses the data to update the user interface.

This example demonstrates the interaction between `Message`s and `Handler`s, but there's more to these classes than the example presents. The following subsections go into greater depth.

5.2.2 The Message Class

A `Message` is a simple object that contains general data and a reference to the intended recipient. A `Message` may contain multiple types of data, including the following:

- The `Handler` that will receive the `Message`. This can be set with `setHandler` and retrieved with `getHandler`.
- (Optional) An integer that identifies the `Message`'s type. This can be accessed through the `what` field.
- (Optional) Two general-purpose integers. They can be accessed through the `arg1` and `arg2` fields.
- (Optional) A general-purpose `Object`. This can be accessed through the `obj` field or the `getData`/`setData` methods.
- (Optional) A `Runnable` to be executed by the target `Handler`'s thread. It can be set with `obtain` and retrieved with `getCallback`.

`arg1` and `arg2` are public, so they can be accessed directly. In contrast, the target `Handler` is private, and can only be accessed using the `getHandler` and `setHandler` methods.

The `what` field identifies the `Message`'s type. This is defined by the user and many applications set `what` equal to a value in an enumerated type. For example, suppose that an application has two types of `Messages` identified by the values `CONTROL` and `BULK`. The following code shows how a `Handler` can use the `what` field to determine how a `Message` should be processed:

```
static public enum Channel {CONTROL, BULK};

static class MsgHandler extends Handler {

  public void handleMessage(Message msg) {

    switch(msg.what) {
    case CONTROL:
      ...
      break;
    case BULK:
      ...
      break;
    }
  }
}
```

The code in Listing 5.1 transferred two integers from the child thread to the parent thread by setting the `arg1` and `arg2` fields of the `Message` object. To allow for larger data payloads, the `Message` provides an `obj` field that can be set to a general `Object`. For example, the following line sets a `Message`'s data equal to a `String`:

```
msg.obj = new String("Example object");
```

A `Message`'s data can also be accessed with `getData` and `setData`, but these methods return/accept `Bundles` instead of `Objects`. A `Bundle` is a general-purpose map from strings to different primitive types or arrays of primitives. As an example, the following code sets a `Message`'s data to a `Bundle` containing a `float` and an `int`:

```
Bundle b = new Bundle();
b.putFloat("PI", 3.14159f);
b.putInt("NUM_PLANETS", 8);
msg.setData(b);
```

The `Message` class implements the `Parcelable` interface. This means the `Message` can flatten itself with the `writeToParcel` method and describe its constituent data with `describeContents`.

The Obtain Method

The `Message` class provides a zero-argument constructor but the Android API documentation recommends using the static method `obtain` instead. There are eight overloaded methods available:

- `obtain()` — returns a new `Message`
- `obtain(Handler h)` — returns a new `Message` that targets the `Handler`
- `obtain(Handler h, int what)` — returns a new `Message` that targets the `Handler` and sets its type
- `obtain(Handler h, int what, int arg1, int arg2)` — returns a new `Message` that targets the `Handler` and sets its type and two integer arguments
- `obtain(Handler h, int what, Object obj)` — returns a new `Message` that targets the `Handler` and sets its type and general data
- `obtain(Handler h, int what, int arg1, int arg2, Object obj)` — returns a new `Message` that targets the `Handler` and sets its type, integer arguments, and general data
- `obtain(Message m)` — returns a copy of an existing `Message`
- `obtain(Handler h, Runnable callback)` — returns a new `Message` that targets the `Handler` and tells the `Handler` to execute the specified `Runnable`

Each of these configures the new `Message` with a different set of arguments. For example, the following code creates a new `Message` with a `Handler`, type, and two integer arguments:

```
Message msg = Message.obtain(handler, BULK, 22, 33);
```

The last `obtain` method accepts a `Runnable` as its last parameter. To see how this `Runnable` works, it's important to have a deeper understanding of the `Handler` class. I'll discuss this next.

Messages and Runnables

In most apps I've looked at, `Message`s store integers or `Bundle`s. But `Message`s can also deliver `Runnable`s to `Handler`s. When the `Handler` receives the `Runnable`, it will execute it in the `Handler`'s thread instead of calling `handleMessage`.

The only way to set a `Runnable` for a `Message` is through the `obtain` method. For example, the following code creates a `Message` with a `Runnable` that does nothing.

```
Message m = Message.obtain(handler, new Runnable() {
  public void run() { ... }
});
```

When the `Handler` receives this `Message`, it will execute the `Runnable`. `handleMessage` will not be called.

If the `Handler` is associated with the main thread, the `Message`'s `Runnable` will be executed as part of the main thread. Therefore, the `Runnable` can update the user interface using the same methods as the `Handler`.

5.2.3 Loopers and MessageQueues

In Listing 5.1, the application creates a `Handler` to allow the child thread to access the main thread. But what about communicating in the reverse direction? You might expect that the following code will work in a child thread:

```
public void run() {

  Handler handler = new Handler() {

    public void handleMessage(Message msg) {
      ...process message...
    }
  }
}
```

This code produces an inscrutable runtime error: `Can't create handler inside thread that has not called Looper.prepare()`. What's a `Looper`? What does its `prepare` method do? These are important questions and the goal of this discussion is to answer them.

By default, child threads can't receive `Messages`. So it makes sense that they can't create `Handlers`. For a child thread to receive `Messages`, it needs two objects: a `Looper` and a `MessageQueue`.

As the name implies, a `MessageQueue` is a queue (first-in, first-out) of `Messages` associated with a `Thread`. A `Looper` is essentially an iterator that cycles through the `Messages` in a `MessageQueue`. Every thread can access one `Looper/MessageQueue` pair at most.

This discussion introduces the `Looper` class and many of its important methods. But first, I'd like to present an analogy that I've found helpful. Like all good analogies, it involves pizza.

Loopers, MessageQueues, and Pizza

When I was seventeen, I spent one summer working as a cook in a pizza restaurant. It was my first job and it tended to be stressful. Sometimes orders came from the waiters and waitresses and sometimes they came over the telephone. Naturally, everyone wanted their pizzas to be cooked quickly and accurately.

The restaurant organized the incoming orders with a long metal panel. When a new order came in, the waiter/waitress/operator wrote it on a slip and stuck it to the left of the other slips on the board. I always worked on the rightmost slips first, and when I finished a pizza, I'd throw away the rightmost slip and move the other orders forward. This wasn't a high-tech system, but thanks to customer satisfaction or untimely death, I never heard any complaints.

I didn't think this job would have any use in my later life, but it made the concepts of `Looper`s and `MessageQueue`s simpler to understand. In my analogy, the participants in the restaurant are like threads. Each order slip is similar to a `Message` and the collection of slips resemble a thread's `MessageQueue`. The `Looper` is similar to the metal panel on which the orders were placed. As a thread processes a `Message`, the `Looper` removes it from the queue and moves the rest of the `Message`s forward. This should make sense given the FIFO (First-In, First-Out) nature of queues in general.

This analogy has a number of shortcomings and the foremost of them involves processing order. In my restaurant, orders are always processed in a FIFO manner. But the `Handler` class has methods that can place `Message`s in positions other than the back of the `MessageQueue`.

The Looper Class

Android's `Looper` class is similar to the `Iterator` interface in regular Java. `Iterator`s are commonly used in loops similar to the following:

```
Iterator itr = list.iterator();

while(itr.hasNext()) {
   ... // Process element
}
```

`Looper`s are more mysterious and don't interact with the `MessageQueue` directly. In fact, my applications rarely access `Looper` objects and instead rely on two static methods: `prepare` and `loop`. The following code shows how they can be used in a thread's `run` method.

```
public void run() {

    // Create the Looper and MessageQueue
    Looper.prepare();

    Handler handler = new Handler() {

        public void handleMessage(Message msg) {
            ...process current message...
        }
    }

    // Update the current Message
    Looper.loop();
}
```

The prepare method creates a Looper for the thread. The Looper constructor creates a new MessageQueue for the thread. With these objects created, the application can create a Handler and receive Messages.

A Handler only processes one Message at a time. Therefore, its handleMessage method only processes the topmost Message of its Thread's MessageQueue. When Looper.loop is called, the next Message on the MessageQueue becomes the current Message. The next time the Handler's handleMessage is invoked, it will process this new Message.

If a run method is coded in the manner shown above, the thread's operation will be limited to message processing. To break out of the loop, the quit method of the Looper class must be called. This isn't a static method, so it requires access to the current thread's Looper object. This is provided by the static myLooper method and the following code shows how it can be used.

```
Looper mLooper = Looper.myLooper();
mLooper.quit();
```

Or more simply:

```
Looper.myLooper().quit();
```

Similar methods, myThread and myQueue, return the current Thread and its MessageQueue. The Looper associated with the main thread can be obtained by calling Looper.getMainLooper().

5.2.4 The Handler Class

So far, the discussion of the `Handler` class has focused on two important roles: delivering `Messages` with `sendMessage` and processing `Messages` with `handleMessage`. These are important functions, but `Handlers` are capable of serving additional roles:

1. Creating and accessing `Messages`
2. Sending `Messages`
3. Processing `Messages`
4. Launching `Runnables`
5. Removing `Messages` and `Runnables`

The following discussion presents each of these tasks and the corresponding methods of the `Handler` class used to perform them.

Creating and Accessing Messages

Earlier, I presented the many `obtain` methods of the `Message` class and the manner in which they create new `Messages`. The `Handler` class provides `obtainMessage` methods that accept the same arguments and work in the same way. For example, these two lines accomplish the same results:

```
Message m = Message.obtain(handler, BULK, 22, 33);
Message m = Handler.obtainMessage(handler, BULK, 22, 33);
```

Each `obtainMessage` method serves its purpose by calling the corresponding `obtain` method. Therefore, the example code in this book will create new `Messsages` by calling `obtain`.

In addition to creating new `Messages`, the `Handler` class has three methods that provide information about existing `Messages`. Their signatures are given as follows:

- `hasMessages(int what)` — returns a boolean identifying if any pending `Messages` have the given `what` value
- `hasMessages(int what, Object obj)` — returns a boolean identifying if any pending `Messages` have the given `what` value and the given data
- `getMessageName(Message)` — returns a string containing the class name of the `Message`'s callback or the `Message`'s `what` value in hexadecimal

The first two methods make it possible to check whether upcoming `Messages` meet the given criteria. The last method can be replaced by calling `Message.getCallback` or checking `Message.what`.

Sending and Processing Messages

The code in Listing 5.1 calls `sendMessage` to transfer a `Message` from the child thread to the main thread's `Handler`. This is only one of many `Handler` methods capable of sending `Messages`. Table 5.3 lists all of them.

Table 5.3

Handler Methods for Sending Messages

Method	Description
`sendMessage(Message)`	Places a Message at the end of the queue
`sendMessageAtFrontOfQueue(Message)`	Places a Message at the front of the queue
`sendMessageAtTime(Message, long)`	Places a Message in the queue after all pending messages before the specified time in ms
`sendMessageDelayed(Message, long)`	Places a Message in the queue after all pending messages before the specified time in ms plus the current time
`sendEmptyMessage(int)`	Sends a Message with the given what value
`sendEmptyMessageAtTime(int, long)`	Sends a Message with the given what value to be processed after all pending messages before the specified time in ms
`sendEmptyMessageDelayed(int, long)`	Sends a Message with the given what value to be processed after all pending messages before the specified time in ms plus the current time

`sendMessageAtTime` and `sendMessageDelayed` both accept a time value given in milliseconds. The difference is that the time in `sendMessageAtTime` is an absolute time and the time in `sendMessageDelayed` is a delay time that starts from the point at which all pending messages have been processed.

The last three methods send empty messages. These don't accept a `Message` instance, but instead accept an integer that identifies the message's `what` field.

Processing Messages

As discussed earlier, a Message may contain a Runnable instead of data. This Runnable is referred to as the Message's *callback*. When a Handler receives a Message with a callback, it executes the Runnable instead of invoking its handleMessage method. This Runnable executes in the Handler's thread, so if the Handler is associated with the main thread, the Runnable can update the user interface.

This can be confusing, so it helps to look at the Android source code. When Looper.loop executes, the Looper calls the Handler's dispatchMessage method to process the current Message on the queue. The code for dispatchMessage (slightly modified for clarity) is given as follows:

```
public void dispatchMessage(Message msg) {

  // Run the callback if present
  if (msg.callback != null)
    message.callback.run();

  else {
    if (mCallback != null) {

      // Invoke the callback's handleMessage
      if (mCallback.handleMessage(msg)) {
        return;
      }
    }

    // Invoke the handler's handleMessage
    handleMessage(msg);
  }
}
```

If the Message has a callback, dispatchMessage calls its run method and never calls handleMessage. If the Message doesn't have a callback, one of two things will happen. If mCallback isn't null, its handleMessage method will be called to process the Message. If mCallback is null, the Handler's handleMessage method will be called instead.

mCallback is a class that implements the Handler.Callback interface. This interface requires a single method, handleMessage, which accepts a Message argument. This interface is provided so that Message-handling classes don't have to be subclasses of Handler.

To associate a Handler.Callback with a Handler, the Handler's constructor must be called with the Handler.Callback. This is shown in the following code.

```
public class TestClass implements Handler.Callback {
  public boolean handleMessage(Message msg) {
    return false;
  }
}

// Create a new handler for TestClass
TestClass tc = new TestClass();
Handler handler = new Handler(tc);
```

TestClass implements Handler.Callback and provides code for the handleMessage method. When handler receives a Message without a callback, dispatchMessage will call the handleMessage of the TestClass. Many applications make the top-level Activity implement Handler.Callback and use similar code to process messages.

Posting Runnables

The Handler class provides a number of methods that create Messages with Runnables and place them in the Handler's MessageQueue. This process is called *posting* and Table 5.4 lists each of the methods that perform this operation.

Table 5.4

Handler Methods for Launching Runnables

Method	Description
post(Runnable)	Places a Message containing the Runnable at the end of the queue
postAtFrontOfQueue(Runnable)	Places a Message containing the Runnable at the front of the queue
postAtTime(Runnable, long)	Places a Message containing the Runnable in the queue after all pending messages before the specified time in ms
postDelayed(Runnable, long)	Places a Message in the queue after all pending messages before the specified time in ms plus the current time

These post methods enable child threads to execute Runnables in the UI thread. The following code gives an idea of how this works. A child Thread accesses a Handler and calls post to execute a Runnable in the main thread.

```
// Create the child thread
Thread t = new Thread(new Runnable() {

  public void run () {

    // Perform long-running task
    processLongOperation();

    // Post a runnable that updates the user interface
    handler.post(new Runnable() {

      public void run () {
        updateUserInterface();
      }
    });
  }
});
```

This method of updating the UI from a child thread may seem unnecessarily complicated. To simplify matters, Android provides `AsyncTask`s, which will be discussed in the next section.

Removing Messages and Runnables

The last set of `Handler` methods remove messages and callbacks from the `Handler`. Table 5.5 lists them and provides a description of each.

Table 5.5

Handler Methods for Removing Messages and Runnables

Method	Description
`removeMessages(int)`	Remove all Messages with the specified value for what
`removeMessages(int, Object)`	Remove all Messages with the specified value for what and the specified data object
`removeCallbacks(Runnable)`	Remove every Message with the specified Runnable as its callback
`removeCallbacksAndMessages(Object)`	Remove all Messages and callbacks with the specified data object

As shown, there is no method to remove all `Message`s from a `Handler`. At minimum, the `Handler` has to provide the `what` value of the `Message`s to be removed.

5.3 AsyncTasks

To simplify concurrent programming, Android provides its own class called `AsyncTask`. `AsyncTask`s are similar to `Thread`s in that they contain code to be executed outside of the UI thread. Unlike `Thread`s, they can update the UI thread without dealing with `Handler`s or `Message`s. Table 5.6 lists differences between `Thread`s and `AsyncTask`s.

Table 5.6

Differences Between Threads and AsyncTasks

Thread Characteristics	AsyncTask Characteristics
Launched by invoking the start method, which doesn't accept any arguments	Launched by invoking the execute method, which accepts a variable number of arguments
Executes code from one method (run)	Executes code from multiple methods
Requires Handlers/Messages to communicate with UI thread	Can communicate with UI threads without Handlers or Messages
Available on all Java-compliant devices	Only available on Android devices
Can be used for short and long operations	Only suitable for short operations

The last entry is important. Android's documentation makes it clear that `AsyncTask`s should only be used for short operations that update the UI. In this case, "short" means "a few seconds at the most."

An `AsyncTask`'s operation can be configured by providing code for up to four protected methods:

1. `onPreExecute()` — executes in the UI thread, configures the task
2. `doInBackground(Params... params)` — executes in a separate thread, performs the task's operation
3. `onProgressUpdate(Progress... progress)` — executes in the UI thread while the task completes, provides progress update
4. `onPostExecute()` — executes in the UI thread after the task is completed, updates the UI with the processed data

Of these, only `doInBackground` is required. The arguments of this method are provided by the UI thread, which invokes the `AsyncTask` by calling `execute`. The following code provides a simple `AsyncTask` that updates a `TextView` named `tv`.

```
class ExampleAsyncTask extends AsyncTask<Void, Void, Void> {
  StringBuilder sb;

  protected void onPreExecute() {
    sb = new StringBuilder();
    tv.append("Just about to start the task.\n");
  }

  protected Void doInBackground(Void... params) {
    sb.append("Working on the task in a separate thread.\n");
    return null;
  }

  protected void onPostExecute(Void result) {
    sb.append("Task finished.");
    tv.append(sb.toString());
  }
}
```

An application can launch the task by creating an `ExampleAsyncTask` instance and calling its `execute` method.

```
ExampleAsyncTask task = new ExampleAsyncTask();
task.execute();
```

In the preceding definition of `ExampleAsyncTask`, it's important to see that the class has three generic types. All `AsyncTask`s use similar generics, and the three types determine the types of values processed in the `AsyncTask`. Android's documentation refers to these three types as `Params`, `Progress`, and `Result`:

- `Params` — The type of data passed to `doInBackground`
- `Progress` — The type of data passed to `onProgressUpdate`
- `Result` — The type of data returned by `doInBackground` and received by `onPostExecute`

As with all Java generics, these can't be set to primitive types like `int`, `float`, or `void`. Wrapper types must be used instead, such as `Integer`, `Float`, and `Void`. In the preceding definition, all three types were set to `Void`, which means that `doInBackground` and `onProgressUpdate` don't receive or provide data.

If the `Params` generic of an `AsyncTask` is set to something other than `Void`, the data must be provided by the `execute` method. For example, if `Params` is set to `String`, the application could invoke the `AsyncTask` with `execute("Message")` or `execute("Hello")`.

5.4 Example Application – AsyncTask Demo

The code in the ch05_asynctask module provides a more interesting example of how AsyncTasks can be used. In this case, the task uses the Sieve of Eratosthenes algorithm to find all the prime numbers less than N.

More specifically, the application's operation consists of five steps:

1. The application creates an instance of an AsyncTask named PrimeFinder and calls its execute method with a floating-point value.
2. Before the AsyncTask starts its computation, its onPreExecute method constructs a StringBuilder and updates the UI.
3. The doInBackground method receives the application's float, rounds it to an integer, and finds the primes less than or equal to the integer.
4. The doInBackground method calls publishProgress with a String message. The AsyncTask's onProgressUpdate method receives the message and displays it in the UI.
5. When doInBackground has completed, it returns an integer identifying the number of primes. The AsyncTask's onPostExecute method receives this result and updates the UI.

The doInBackground method receives a float, so the AsyncTask's first generic type should be a Float. It provides progress updates using a String, so the second generic type should be a String. The return value of doInBackground is an integer, so the last generic type should be an Integer. These types are reflected in the declaration of the PrimeFinder class:

```
class PrimeFinder extends AsyncTask<Float, String, Integer>
```

Listing 5.2 presents the code for the AsyncTaskActivity in the ch05_asynctask module. It's important to see that doInBackground is the only method that executes in a separate thread. The rest of the AsyncTask's methods are able to access the activity's TextView.

doInBackground can't access the UI directly, but it can send data to publishProgress, which causes onProgressUpdate to execute. In general, doInBackground calls publishProgress with a number that identifies how far it has progressed in its computation. onProgressUpdate can use this value to update the UI, which may involve printing status messages or updating a progress bar.

Listing 5.2: ch05_asynctask/src/main/java/.../AsyncTaskActivity.java

```
public class AsyncTaskActivity extends Activity {
  private TextView tv;

  private class PrimeFinder extends
    AsyncTask<Float, String, Integer> {
    StringBuilder sb;

    @Override
    protected void onPreExecute() {
      sb = new StringBuilder();
      tv.append("Starting the task.\n");
    }

    @Override
    protected Integer doInBackground(Float... nums) {
      int N = Math.round(nums[0]);
      int knownPrime, count = 0;
      boolean almostDone = false;

      // Initial label
      sb.append("Primes less than ").append(N).append(": ");

      // Default value is false - assume every number is prime
      boolean[] isComposite = new boolean[N + 1];
      isComposite[1] = true;

      // Find composite numbers
      for(int i=2; i<=N; i++) {

        // Check whether the value has been marked
        if(!isComposite[i]) {
          count++;
          sb.append(i).append(", ");
          knownPrime = 2;
          while(i * knownPrime <= N) {
            isComposite[i * knownPrime] = true;
            knownPrime++;
          }
        }

        // Provide a progress message
        if((i > N/2) && !almostDone) {
          publishProgress("Almost done!\n");
          almostDone = true;
        }
      }
```

Listing 5.2: ch05_asynctask/src/main/java/.../AsyncTaskActivity.java

```
      // Remove last two characters
      int len = sb.length();
      sb.delete(len-2, len-1);
      return count;
    }

    @Override
    protected void onProgressUpdate(String... progress) {
      tv.append(progress[0]);
    }

    @Override
    protected void onPostExecute(Integer result) {
      sb.append("\nThere are ").append(result).
        append(" primes in total.");
      tv.append(sb.toString());
    }
  }

  public void onCreate(Bundle b) {
    super.onCreate(b);
    setContentView(R.layout.main_layout);
    tv = (TextView)findViewById(R.id.tv);

    // Create and launch the thread
    PrimeFinder primeFinder = new PrimeFinder();
    primeFinder.execute(500.0f);
  }
}
```

AsyncTasks are particularly helpful in applications that need to perform network operations. If an application attempts to access the network in the UI thread, a NetworkOnMainThreadException will result. For this reason, it's better to perform short-term network operations in AsyncTasks.

An application can cancel a task by calling the AsyncTask's cancel method. This accepts a boolean that identifies whether the thread executing the task should be interrupted. cancel returns a boolean that identifies whether the task was successfully cancelled.

When cancel is called, the onCancelled method will be invoked instead of onPostExecute after the completion of doInBackground. An application can check on the task's cancellation state by calling isCancelled.

5.5 Summary

Concurrency is a major concern in virtual reality applications. Not only is graphical rendering performed in a child thread, but the application receives data from the Daydream controller in another child thread. Later chapters will explain how this multithreaded processing can be implemented.

This chapter has discussed the basics of Java concurrency. The first section briefly reviewed the `Thread` class and the `Runnable` interface. Because of the simplicity, I prefer to use the `Runnable` interface whenever possible.

To facilitate inter-thread communication, Android provides `Handler`s and `Message`s. A handler is like a post office box. Once it's created in the main thread, child threads can use it to receive data. This data must be packaged in structures called `Message`s.

For concurrent operations lasting less than a few seconds, I recommend using `AsyncTask`s. An `AsyncTask` is a wrapper of the `Thread` class that provides three methods to be executed at different stages. By using these methods, an application can update the UI with data from a child thread without needing `Handler`s and `Message`s.

Chapter 6

Introduction to Google VR Development

With this chapter, we put aside general Android development and start looking at coding virtual reality applications. To be specific, we're going to look at the classes and interfaces provided by the Google VR software development kit (SDK).

The first section explains how to obtain the SDK and explores its file hierarchy. The most important files are the Android archives (AARs) that contain classes and features required for VR development. This discussion explains how Gradle builds can be configured to access these classes.

Most of the chapter is devoted to examining four data structures provided by the Google VR SDK:

- `GvrActivity` — The activity class specifically suited for VR development
- `GvrView` — The view that manages the appearance of the `GvrActivity`
- `StereoRenderer` — An interface whose methods are called during the rendering process
- `AndroidCompat` — A support class whose methods enable and disable features required by VR applications

The chapter ends with a basic application that demonstrates how these structures work together. But this application doesn't perform any graphical rendering. To understand how applications add graphics to VR apps, you need to be familiar with OpenGL ES, which is the topic of Chapter 7.

6.1 The Google VR SDK

At the time of this writing, the basic Android API doesn't provide the classes needed to develop Google VR apps. The classes must be obtained separately, and the current download site is https://developers.google.com/vr/android/download.

This site tells developers to obtain the SDK by cloning the project's GitHub repository, which is located at https://github.com/googlevr/gvr-android-sdk.git. This requires installing the Git version control system and executing the following command:

```
git clone https://github.com/googlevr/gvr-android-sdk.git
```

When the download is finished, the gvr-android-git directory will contain five subdirectories:

- apks — APK files for support projects
- assets — Example panorama and video files
- gradle — Gradle build files
- libraries — Android archive (AAR) files that contain the SDK's classes
- samples — Sample Google VR code

For this book, only the libraries directory is important. The files in this directory provide the classes required to compile virtual reality apps for the Google Daydream.

If you look through the build.gradle file in the gvr-android-git directory, you'll see that it defines a task named `extractNdk`. This extracts the files needed for native VR development. A proper introduction to the Google VR Native Development Kit (NDK) will have to wait until Chapter 14.

6.1.1 AAR Files

Working with Google VR projects in Android Studio is like working with regular projects. The only difference is that Android Studio needs to know how to access the classes in the Google VR SDK. These classes are contained in the seven *.aar files in the SDK's libraries directory.

AAR stands for Android archive, and each AAR contains Android-specific classes and features. At the time of this writing, these archives have version 1.30.0. Table 6.1 lists each AAR and its content.

Table 6.1
AAR Files and Their Classes

AAR File	Contained Classes
sdk-audio-1.30.0.aar	`GvrAudioEngine`
sdk-base-1.30.0.aar	`AndroidCompat, Constants, Distortion, Eye, FieldOfView, GvrActivity, GvrView, GvrViewerParams, HeadMountedDisplay, HeadMountedDisplayManager, HeadTransform, ScreenParams, Viewport`
sdk-common-1.30.0.aar	`Google VR resources`
sdk-commonwidget-1.30.0.aar	`VrWidgetView, VrEventListener`
sdk-controller-1.30.0.aar	`Controller, ControllerManager`
sdk-panowidget-1.30.0.aar	`VrPanoramaView, VrPanoramaEventListener`
sdk-videowidget-1.30.0.aar	`VrVideoView, VrVideoEventListener`

Each AAR file defines a Java package whose name starts with com.google.vr.sdk.*. For example, `GvrView` is in the com.google.vr.sdk.base package and `VrVideoView` is in the com.google.vr.sdk.video package.

6.1.2 Building Google VR Modules in Android Studio

If a module's code relies on Google VR classes, its build.gradle file needs to tell Android Studio where to find the corresponding AAR file. You can directly copy AAR files to a folder in the module, but it's easier to access the AAR files through the jcenter repository discussed in Chapter 2.

To access AAR files from the repository, the module build file needs to add `compile` commands to the `dependencies` block. For example, the following block includes the sdk-base-1.30.0.aar and sdk-common-1.30.0.aar files in the module's build:

```
dependencies {
  compile 'com.google.vr:sdk-audio:1.30.0'
  compile 'com.google.vr:sdk-base:1.30.0'
}
```

You'll find similar `compile` statements in the build file of every module from Chapter 7 to Chapter 13. Keep in mind that the version number must be updated as Google releases newer versions of the SDK.

6.2 Fundamentals of Google VR Development

From a developer's viewpoint, a Google VR app is an Android app that accesses classes of the Google VR SDK. Most of these apps can be divided into two categories:

1. Apps that display Google VR widgets, which consist of the `VrVideoView` or `VrPanoramaView`
2. Apps that perform three-dimensional rendering

The vast majority of VR apps, including games, fall into the second category. For this reason, this and the following chapters focus primarily on 3-D rendering. The `VrVideoView` and `VrPanoramaView` classes will be discussed in Chapter 13.

In addition to accessing Google VR classes, VR projects need to configure the project's manifest to support VR operations. If the app performs 3-D rendering, the central activity will be a `GvrActivity` and the central view will be a `GvrView`. This section looks at each of these topics.

But first, it's important to make sure that the Daydream app is installed on your target device. This can be freely downloaded and installed from the Google Play Store. The Daydream app provides a central environment, called Daydream Home, that displays and launches VR applications.

Installing the Daydream app installs Google VR Services, which manages the overall operation of VR apps. This is necessary to link the device to the Daydream headset and it provides the software needed to receive data from the Daydream controller.

6.2.1 Android Manifest

A module's manifest must be specifically configured to support Daydream operations. There are five properties to be concerned with:

1. Hardware features — The target device must have the features needed to execute Daydream apps.
2. Window behavior — Daydream apps always occupy the entire window, always execute in landscape orientation, and cannot be resized.
3. Style — The Google VR SDK provides a specific theme for VR applications.
4. VR Mode — The device's VR mode should be enabled when the application runs.
5. Category — The Google VR SDK provides a category specifically for launching VR applications for the Daydream.

Hardware Features

Before executing an application, Android checks to see if the target hardware supports the app's required features. An app states its requirements by adding `<uses-feature>` elements to the `<manifest>` element in AndroidManifest.xml.

Daydream apps require a particular set of features. A target device must be able to execute OpenGL ES 3.2, must have an accelerometer and gyroscope, and must support Google's VR mode. These requirements can be expressed in a module's manifest with the following markup:

```
<uses-feature android:glEsVersion="0x00030002"
  android:required="true" />

<uses-feature android:name="android.hardware.sensor.accelerometer"
  android:required="true"/>

<uses-feature android:name="android.hardware.sensor.gyroscope"
  android:required="true"/>

<uses-feature android:name="android.software.vr.mode"
  android:required="true"/>

<uses-feature android:name="android.hardware.vr.high_performance"
  android:required="true"/>
```

The value of the `android:glEsVersion` attribute identifies the minimum version of OpenGL ES that the device must support. The high 16 bits of the value set the major number of the version and the low 16 bits set the minor number. For Daydream apps, the minimum OpenGL ES version is 3.2, so the value is `0x00030002`.

VR Mode is a special processing mode optimized for low-latency graphical rendering. If an app is only intended for the Daydream, `android:required` should be set to `true`. If an app is intended for Daydream and Cardboard, the attribute can be set to `false`.

Window Behavior

When a graphical Daydream app executes, its window is expected to behave in a specific manner. That is, the app must run in landscape mode and must occupy the entire window. Daydream apps cannot be resized.

This behavior can be configured in the manifest by adding attributes (`configChanges`, `screenOrientation`, and `resizeableActivity`) to the app's primary `<activity>` element. The following markup shows what this looks like:

```
<activity
    android:name="..."
    android:label="..."
    android:configChanges="orientation|keyboardHidden|screenSize"
    android:screenOrientation="landscape"
    android:resizeableActivity="false">
    ...
</activity>
```

The `configChanges` attribute identifies the configuration aspects that should be determined by the activity. In this case, the activity will control its orientation and screen size. The keyboard will remain hidden.

The `screenOrientation` attribute indicates that the app only runs in landscape mode. The `resizeableActivity` attribute indicates that the app can't be resized.

Style

If you unzip sdk-common-1.30.0.aar, you'll see that its res folder contains a wide range of resources for VR applications. The values.xml file contains the following definition:

```
<style name="VrActivityTheme"
  parent="@android:style/Theme.Black.NoTitleBar">

  <item name="android:windowFullscreen">true</item>
  <item name="android:windowAnimationStyle">@null</item>
  <item name="android:windowActionBar">false</item>
  <item name="android:windowDisablePreview">true</item>
  <item name="android:windowContentOverlay">@null</item>
</style>
```

This style defines characteristics expected of a VR app, including fullscreen operation and disabled preview. Google strongly recommends that VR apps use this style, and this can be set by adding a `theme` attribute to the `<application>` element in a module's manifest. The following markup shows what this looks like:

```
<application
  ...
  android:theme="@style/VrActivityTheme">
  ...
</application>
```

Chapter 2 didn't cover style resources, but this notation (`@style/`*`resource_name`*) uniquely identifies a style defined in values.xml.

VR Mode

Google introduced VR Mode in Android 7.0 to support virtual reality applications. This processing mode provides three advantages:

- VR apps can access an exclusive CPU core
- VR apps can take advantage of head tracking and stereoscopic processing
- Low-latency graphical rendering

An application can take advantage of VR mode by setting the `enableVrMode` attribute in the `<activity>` element. This doesn't accept a `true/false` value, but requires the name of the software component that launches VR mode. This can be accessed through the `gvr_vr_mode_component` string in the values.xml file of sdk-common-1.30.0.aar. The following markup shows how this can be set:

```
<activity
  ...
  android:enableVrMode="@string/gvr_vr_mode_component">
  ...
</activity>
```

VR Mode isn't a requirement for Daydream apps and VR apps can run without it. But apps perform significantly better when this mode is enabled.

Category

Chapter 2 briefly mentioned intent filters, which specify the conditions for launching an activity. Android provides a specific intent category for Daydream apps named `com.google.intent.category.DAYDREAM`. Setting this category ensures that the app will be accessible through Daydream Home. The following markup shows how the intent filter can be set:

```
<intent-filter>
  <action android:name="android.intent.action.MAIN" />
  <category android:name="android.intent.category.LAUNCHER" />
  <category android:name="com.google.intent.category.DAYDREAM" />
</intent-filter>
```

Android also supports a category for launching Cardboard apps named `com.google.intent.category.CARDBOARD`. If an app is intended to execute for Daydream and Cardboard, both categories should be included in `<intent-filter>`.

6.2.2 GvrActivity

If a Google VR app needs to perform graphical rendering, the first class to know is `GvrActivity`. This provides access to VR-specific features including controller access and head tracking. As a subclass of `Activity`, this provides regular lifecycle methods such as `onCreate` and `onResume`.

The `GvrActivity` class also defines four methods that are specific to VR development. Table 6.2 lists them and provides a description of each.

Table 6.2

GvrActivity Methods

Method	Description
`setGvrView(GvrView gvrView)`	Associates the activity with a View specifically configured for VR applications
`setGvrView(GvrView gvrView, boolean enableVrModeFallbacks)`	Associates the activity with a View specifically configured for VR applications
`getGvrView()`	Returns the associated GvrView
`onCardboardTrigger()`	Called when the Cardboard trigger is pulled

Unlike regular activities, a `GvrActivity` expects that its content will be defined by a particular type of view called a `GvrView`. This can be associated with the activity using the `setGvrView` method. Like the `setContentView` method discussed in Chapter 3, this ensures that the view will be notified when the activity's state changes.

As discussed earlier, devices can access a special high-performance mode called VR mode. This processing mode is only available if Google VR Services is running on the device, and if `setGvrView` is called with the `enableVrModeFallbacks` argument set to `true`, the application will ask the user to install or enable Google VR Services if it's not already running.

The last method in the table, `onCardboardTrigger`, is called if the device is linked to a Google Cardboard headset and the headset's trigger is pulled. This book focuses exclusively on Daydream development, so this isn't a concern.

6.2.3 GvrView

The primary purpose of a `GvrView` is to display the results of graphical rendering. If an application doesn't need to render graphics, it may be better to instantiate a regular `Activity` with a regular `View`.

The `GvrView` class is a subclass of `View` and can access all the methods discussed in Chapter 3. It also has methods of its own, and they can be divided into five categories:

- graphical configuration — configures how the view's graphics should be rendered
- head tracking — provides access to the display
- screen/viewer parameters — accesses the state of the screen and viewer
- vision — configures visual properties
- event handling — responds to external events

This subsection presents the methods in these categories. The methods in the first category are particularly important.

Graphical Configuration

High-performance graphical rendering is critically important to virtual reality applications. Table 6.3 lists the seven methods of `GvrView` that configure how the view's rendering is performed.

Table 6.3

Graphical Configuration Methods of GvrView

Method	Description
`setEGLContextClientVersion( int version)`	Sets the desired major version of EGL
`setEGLConfigChooser( int redBits, int greenBits, int blueBits, int alphaBits, int depthBits, int stencilBits)`	Specifies how many bits should be used for the RGBA components in the color buffer and the values in the depth and stencil buffers
`getAsyncReprojectionEnabled()`	Identifies if asynchronous reprojection is enabled
`setAsyncReprojectionEnabled( boolean enabled)`	Enables or disables asynchronous reprojection
`setRenderer( GvrView.StereoRenderer rend)`	Specifies a GvrView.StereoRenderer to manage the application's rendering
`setRenderer( GvrView.Renderer rend)`	Specifies a GvrView.Renderer to manage the application's rendering
`queueEvent(Runnable r)`	Enables the view to execute operations in the renderer's thread

EGL is an initialism, not an acronym, and it refers to the Khronos Native Platform Graphics Interface. For Android devices, EGL serves as a bridge between OpenGL ES and the native display. A device that supports a recent version of EGL will be able to render graphics using a recent version of OpenGL ES.

`setEGLContextClientVersion` identifies the version of OpenGL ES that the application intends to use. To run Daydream apps, a rendering device must support at least OpenGL ES 3.2. But the argument of `setEGLContextClientVersion` is an integer, so in this book's example code, the argument will be set to `3`.

`setEGLConfigChooser` identifies what components should be present in the rendered pixels and how many bits each component should occupy. For example, the following code specifies that each pixel should contain red, green, blue, and alpha components and that each component should occupy eight bits:

```
setEGLConfigChooser(8, 8, 8, 8, 0, 0);
```

The `depthBits` and `stencilBits` arguments of `setEGLConfigChooser` become important when the application needs to perform depth and/or stencil testing. Chapter 11 will explain how to configure and use depth testing.

Motion-to-photon latency refers to the time needed to render a frame after the viewer moves his/her head. If the delay is too high, the viewer may experience nausea. To reduce latency, many devices transform existing frames to account for the viewer's motion. If this is performed in a separate thread, the process is called *asynchronous reprojection*. Not all devices support this, but if it's available, calling `setAsyncReprojectionEnabled` with the argument set to true will tell the device to use asynchronous reprojection whenever necessary.

A `GvrView` doesn't manage its graphical rendering directly. Instead, it calls `setRenderer` to delegate the responsibility to a `GvrView.StereoRenderer` or a `GvrView.Renderer`. The difference between them is that a `StereoRenderer` handles stereoscopic rendering automatically and a `Renderer` doesn't.

Stereoscopic rendering refers to creating the illusion of depth by rendering two slightly different images, one for each eye. This is a complex process, so Google recommends rendering graphics with the `StereoRenderer`. For this reason, every SDK-based project in this book relies on a `StereoRenderer`. If an app needs low-level control, it's recommended to render graphics with the Native Development Kit (NDK), which will be discussed in Chapter 14.

Whether the `GvrView` uses a `StereoRenderer` or a `Renderer`, graphical rendering will always be performed in a separate thread. This makes it difficult for a `GvrView` to communicate with its renderer. Communication can be accomplished using the `queueEvent` method, which accepts a `Runnable`.

As discussed in Chapter 5, a `Runnable` defines an operation to be carried out in a separate thread. In this case, the `Runnable`'s operation is performed in the rendering thread. `queueEvent` is frequently called in response to an external event, and its `Runnable` invokes a method that tells the renderer to respond.

Head Tracking

One feature that differentiates VR apps from other graphical apps is that the graphical content changes as the device moves. Applications can access the device's orientation using sensors, but the `GvrView` simplifies the process by automatically keeping track of the headset's orientation. This is called *head tracking* and Table 6.4 lists five of the methods involved.

Table 6.4

Head Tracking Methods of GvrView

Method	Description
`getHeadMountedDisplay()`	Returns the view's head mounted display
`setNeckModelEnabled( boolean enabled)`	Identifies whether head tracking should take the neck model into account
`getNeckModelFactor()`	Returns the neck model factor
`setNeckModelFactor(float factor)`	Identifies the extent to which head tracking should take the neck model into account
`recenterHeadTracker()`	Sets the viewing origin to the current position/orientation of the display (Deprecated for Daydream apps)

An application can access the device's physical parameters by obtaining the `HeadMountedDisplay` returned by `getHeadMountedDisplay`. But there's no need to access this object because its methods, such as `getGvrViewerParams`, can be invoked directly through the `GvrView`. These methods will be discussed shortly.

As Chapter 8 will make clear, coordinates and rotations are vitally important. To model the viewer's rotation, an application can enable a neck model that accounts for the distance between the viewer's eyes and his/her neck, which is the real axis of rotation.

The `setNeckModelEnabled` method specifies whether the neck model should be taken into account. `setNeckModelFactor` accepts a number between 0.0 and 1.0 that identifies the extent to which the neck model should be used. A value of 0.0 disables the model and a value of 1.0 completely activates the model.

The last method, `recenterHeadTracker`, resets the head tracking so that the current headset orientation represents the initial state. This is only available for Cardboard apps. On Daydream apps, recentering is handled automatically.

Screen/Viewer Parameters

The `GvrView` class has three methods that provide information about the screen of the target device. Table 6.5 lists these methods and provides a description of each.

Table 6.5

GvrView Methods that Access Screen/Viewer Parameters

Method	Description
`getScreenParams()`	Provides information about the display screen
`getGvrViewerParams()`	Provides information about the viewer's state
`updateGvrViewerParams( GvrViewerParams params)`	Configures aspects of the viewer's state

It's important to see the difference between the `ScreenParams` returned by `getScreenParams` and the `GvrViewerParams` returned by `getGvrViewerParams`. The `ScreenParams` provides the screen's dimensions and the `GvrViewerParams` provides the viewer's physical parameters.

The `ScreenParams` object provides five pairs of methods that access the dimensions of the viewing screen:

- `getWidth/setWidth` — the screen width in pixels
- `getWidthMeters/setWidthMeters` — the screen width in meters
- `getHeight/setHeight` — the screen height in pixels
- `getHeightMeters/setHeightMeters` — the screen height in meters
- `getBorderSizeMeters/setBorderSizeMeters` — size of the border surrounding the screen in meters

The `GvrViewerParams` provides methods that access physical characteristics of the viewer and the viewing environment. Table 6.6 lists 16 of these methods.

Table 6.6

Viewer Parameter Methods of GvrViewerParams

Method	Description
`getDistortion()`	Distortion object that provides information about the headset's distortion
`getLeftEyeMaxFov()`	FieldOfView object that provides information about the viewing region
`getHasMagnet()/ setHasMagnet(boolean magnet)`	Whether the headset has a magnet to interface the phone
`getInterLensDistance()/ setInterLensDistance(float ild)`	Distance between the headset's lenses in meters
`getModel()/ setModel(String model)`	Name of the headset model
`getVendor()/ setVendor(String vendor)`	Name of the headset's vendor
`getVerticalAlignment()/ setVerticalAlignment( GvrViewerParams.VerticalAlignment)`	The strategy for aligning the phone display with regard to the lenses (top, center, or bottom)
`getVerticalDistanceToLensCenter() setVerticalDistanceToLensCenter( float distance)`	Vertical distance from the display's edge to the center of the lens in meters
`toString()`	String containing the viewer's parameters
`toUri()`	URI containing the viewer's parameters

Many of these methods are straightforward. The Daydream viewer doesn't have a magnet, so `getHasMagnet` will always return false.

Parameters involving distortion and lens distance become important when the application needs to control how stereo rendering is performed. But for most applications, this information is unnecessary.

The screen/viewer parameters do not include the viewer's position or angular orientation. This is provided by the `Eye` object, which will be discussed later in the chapter.

Vision

The `GvrView` class provides six methods related to how the user views the app. Table 6.7 lists them and provides a description of each.

Table 6.7
Vision Methods of GvrView

Method	Description
`getDistortionCorrectionEnabled()`	Identifies whether the device is correcting images for distortion
`setDistortionCorrectionEnabled( boolean enabled)`	Specifies whether the device should correct for distortion
`getStereoModeEnabled()`	Identifies if the device is producing stereoscopic images
`setStereoModeEnabled( boolean enabled)`	Specifies whether the device should produce stereoscopic images
`setTransitionViewEnabled( boolean enabled)`	Specifies whether the app should produce a dialog telling the user to place their phone in the viewer
`getInterpupillaryDistance()`	Returns the distance between the headset's pupils in meters

Without correction, the displayed image will appear distorted when viewed through the headset's lenses. But if distortion correction is enabled, the renderer will apply an inverse distortion transformation that reduces the effect. This is enabled by default, but can be disabled by calling `setDistortionCorrectionEnabled` with a value of `false`.

Another way to turn off distortion correction is to disable stereo mode. Stereo mode refers to the usage of stereo rendering and distortion correction. This is enabled by default, but it can be disabled by calling `setStereoModeEnabled` with a value of `false`.

By default, if a user attempts to run a VR app without placing the phone in a viewer, the app won't respond. But if `setTransitionViewEnabled` is called with a value of `true`, the device will present a notification message.

The last method in the table identifies the distance between the headset's lenses in meters. This distance, called the interpupillary distance or IPD, is used when performing stereo rendering.

Event Handling

Table 6.8 presents the last set of `GvrView` methods, which respond to events. The first two events are generated by the view's activity and the last three events are generated by the device.

Table 6.8

Event Handling Methods of GvrView

Method	Description
`onPause()`	The activity has been paused
`onResume()`	The activity has been resumed
`setOnCloseButtonListener( Runnable listener)`	Sets code to run when the close button is pressed
`setOnTransitionViewDoneListener( Runnable listener)`	Sets code to run when the transition view dialog is finished
`setOnCardboardTriggerListener( Runnable listener)`	Sets code to run when the Cardboard's magnet is

The `onPause` and `onResume` methods are similar to the activity's `onPause` and `onResume` methods discussed in Chapter 3. That is, they're called when the view's activity is paused and resumed.

By default, if the user clicks the close button, a Daydream app is expected to terminate its activity and return to the Android home launcher. The `setOnCloseButtonListener` method makes it possible to customize the process by assigning a `Runnable` to execute.

If the `setTransitionViewEnabled` method is invoked with a value of `true`, the app will prompt the user to place their phone into the viewer if it's not there. The `setOnTransitionViewDoneListener` method assigns a `Runnable` to execute after the prompt has been completed.

The last method, `setOnCardboardTriggerListener`, assigns a `Runnable` to execute when the user adjusts the magnet on the Cardboard headset.

6.3 The StereoRenderer Interface

The `GvrView`'s `setRenderer` method assigns an object to handle the view's graphical rendering. The argument must implement the `GvrView.StereoRenderer` interface or the `GvrView.Renderer` interface.

The `StereoRenderer` interface is simpler to work with because the app doesn't need to manage the process of stereo rendering. The SDK examples in this book all rely on the `StereoRenderer`, but when we get to Chapter 14, I'll explain how to implement stereo rendering at a low level using the NDK.

I'll refer to the class that implements the `StereoRenderer` interface as the *renderer class* or just the *renderer*. To implement the interface, this class must implement each of the methods listed in Table 6.9.

Table 6.9

StereoRenderer Methods

Method	Description
`onSurfaceCreated( EGLConfig config)`	Called when the rendering surface is initialized
`onSurfaceChanged( int width, int height)`	Called when the surface is resized
`onNewFrame( HeadTransform headTransform)`	Called just before a new frame is drawn
`onDrawEye(Eye eye)`	Called to draw the scene after head tracking
`onFinishFrame(Viewport viewport)`	Called before a frame is finished
`onRendererShutdown()`	Called just before the renderer's thread is shut down

The first two methods are easy to understand. `onSurfaceCreated` is called when the rendering surface is created or recreated. For this reason, many apps initialize their data structures in this method. The `EGLConfig` provided in `onSurfaceCreated` doesn't appear to serve any useful purpose.

`onSurfaceChanged` is called whenever the window's dimensions change. Daydream apps can't be resized, so this method isn't called frequently in VR applications. However, every app calls this method when the window is first displayed. Therefore, this method is guaranteed to execute at least once.

To understand `onNewFrame` and `onDrawEye`, it's important to keep in mind that the goal of stereo rendering is to produce two images: one for each eye. These images are combined into a single frame.

`onNewFrame` is called when the application needs to render a new frame. It provides a `HeadTransform` that identifies the headset's position and orientation. Applications can use this transform to determine where the user is looking.

To render the scene properly, it's not enough to know how the headset is oriented. The application needs to account for the angle of each eye. For this reason, `onDrawEye` is called twice after each call of `onNewFrame`. This method provides an `Eye` object that identifies the orientation of the corresponding eye. Chapter 9 discusses the methods of the `Eye` class and shows how they can be used in graphical rendering.

If an application needs to make any finishing touches to the frame, such as adding an overlay, it can insert the code in the onFinishFrame method. This is called after both invocations of onDrawEye, but before the frame is displayed.

As mentioned earlier, the renderer's operations are performed in a child thread. The last method in Table 6.9, onRendererShutdown, is called before the renderer's thread is terminated. This allows the renderer to free any resources that it allocated during the rendering process.

6.4 Example Application – Empty Screen

The ch06_emptyscreen module doesn't draw anything, but it demonstrates how GvrActivity and GvrView instances work together. It also illustrates the basic structure of Daydream modules used in this and later chapters.

To understand this module, the first place to look is the manifest. Listing 6.1 presents the module's AndroidManifest.xml file:

Listing 6.1: ch06_emptyscreen/src/main/AndroidManifest.xml

```
<manifest
  xmlns:android="http://schemas.android.com/apk/res/android"
  package="com.dreambookvr.ch06_emptyscreen">

  <uses-feature android:glEsVersion="0x00030002"
    android:required="true" />
  <uses-feature
    android:name="android.hardware.sensor.accelerometer"
    android:required="true"/>
  <uses-feature android:name="android.hardware.sensor.gyroscope"
    android:required="true"/>
  <uses-feature android:name="android.software.vr.mode"
    android:required="true"/>
  <uses-feature
    android:name="android.hardware.vr.high_performance"
    android:required="true"/>

    <application
        android:allowBackup="true"
        android:icon="@mipmap/ic_launcher"
        android:label="@string/app_name"
        android:supportsRtl="true"
        android:theme="@style/VrActivityTheme">
```

Listing 6.1: ch06_emptyscreen/src/main/AndroidManifest.xml

```
    <activity
      android:name="EmptyScreenActivity"
      android:label="@string/app_name"
      android:screenOrientation="landscape"
      android:configChanges=
        "orientation|keyboardHidden|screenSize"
      android:resizeableActivity="false"
      android:enableVrMode="@string/gvr_vr_mode_component">

      <intent-filter>
        <action android:name="android.intent.action.MAIN" />
        <category
          android:name="android.intent.category.LAUNCHER" />
        <category
          android:name="com.google.intent.category.DAYDREAM" />
      </intent-filter>

    </activity>
  </application>
</manifest>
```

As discussed earlier, the `<uses-feature>` elements identify features that every target device must support. These features include OpenGL ES 3.2 support, accelerometer and gyroscope sensors, and VR Mode operation.

In the `<application>` element, the theme attribute sets the application's style to the `VrActivityTheme`. This ensures that the application will occupy the full window, and will be displayed without the navigation bar and without any preview image.

The `<activity>` element further configures the window's behavior. The `configChanges` attribute indicates that the application's orientation and screen size should be determined by the activity. The `resizeableActivity` attribute specifies that the activity can't be resized and the `screenOrientation` attribute specifies that the application should only be displayed in landscape mode. The `enableVrMode` attribute indicates that the application can run in VR Mode.

The `<intent-filter>` element contains an entry that indicates that the activity is intended for the Daydream. With this set, the Daydream Home environment will be able to access the activity.

In the `<activity>` element, the name attribute indicates that the primary activity class is `EmptyScreenActivity`. As with most activities, the code is primarily contained in the `onCreate` method. Listing 6.2 presents the code.

Listing 6.2: ch06_emptyscreen/src/main/java/.../EmptyScreenActivity.java

```
public class EmptyScreenActivity extends GvrActivity {

  public void onCreate(Bundle savedInstanceState) {
    super.onCreate(savedInstanceState);

    // Set the window properties
    setImmersiveSticky();
    getWindow().getDecorView()
        .setOnSystemUiVisibilityChangeListener(
            new View.OnSystemUiVisibilityChangeListener() {
              public void onSystemUiVisibilityChange(int vis) {
                if ((vis & View.SYSTEM_UI_FLAG_FULLSCREEN)==0) {
                  setImmersiveSticky();
                }
              }
            });

    // Enable VR mode
    AndroidCompat.setVrModeEnabled(this, true);

    // Access and configure the Google VR view
    setContentView(R.layout.main_layout);
    GvrView gvrView = (GvrView) findViewById(R.id.gvr_view);
    gvrView.setEGLContextClientVersion(3);
    gvrView.setEGLConfigChooser(8, 8, 8, 8, 0, 0);
    gvrView.setStereoModeEnabled(true);
    gvrView.setRenderer(new EmptyScreenRenderer());
    setGvrView(gvrView);

    // Set sustained performance mode
    if (gvrView.setAsyncReprojectionEnabled(true)) {
      AndroidCompat.setSustainedPerformanceMode(this, true);
    }
  }

  private void setImmersiveSticky() {
    getWindow()
        .getDecorView()
        .setSystemUiVisibility(
            View.SYSTEM_UI_FLAG_LAYOUT_STABLE
                | View.SYSTEM_UI_FLAG_LAYOUT_HIDE_NAVIGATION
                | View.SYSTEM_UI_FLAG_LAYOUT_FULLSCREEN
                | View.SYSTEM_UI_FLAG_HIDE_NAVIGATION
                | View.SYSTEM_UI_FLAG_FULLSCREEN
                | View.SYSTEM_UI_FLAG_IMMERSIVE_STICKY);
  }
}
```

Most of the code in this class is concerned with the window's behavior. That is, the activity calls `setImmersiveSticky` to ensure that its window will occupy the entire screen and that the navigation bar will be hidden. The activity also creates an event handler that calls `setImmersiveSticky` when the system's visibility changes.

This repeated call of `setImmersiveSticky` may seem excessive, but until I used this code, the Daydream review team rejected my application because the navigation bar wasn't properly hidden. Chapter 17 discusses this and similar requirements needed to deploy apps to the Google Play Store as official Daydream apps.

After configuring the window, the activity's operation is straightforward. It enables VR mode by calling the `setVrEnabled` method of the `AndroidCompat` class. This support class provides methods related to enabling/disabling device capabilities, and if the device supports asynchronous reprojection, the activity invokes `AndroidCompat`'s `setSustainedPerformanceMode` method.

The activity relies on a `GvrView` to set the content of its window. It configures a number of aspects of the view, including its EGL version, the content of the view's pixels, and the stereo mode. The activity also creates a new `EmptyScreenRenderer` and associates it with the `GvrView`.

In later chapters, we'll see that the renderer class contains more code than the activity class. But in this simple example, the methods of `EmptyScreenRenderer` (which implements the `StereoRenderer` interface) are empty. Listing 6.3 makes this clear.

Listing 6.3: ch06_emptyscreen/src/main/java/.../EmptyScreenRenderer.java

```
class EmptyScreenRenderer implements StereoRenderer {

  @Override
  public void onSurfaceCreated(EGLConfig config) {}

  @Override
  public void onSurfaceChanged(int width, int height) {}

  @Override
  public void onDrawEye(Eye eye) {}

  @Override
  public void onNewFrame(HeadTransform headTransform) {}

  @Override
  public void onFinishFrame(Viewport viewport) {}

  @Override
  public void onRendererShutdown() {}
}
```

These methods are empty, so the renderer doesn't draw anything in the `GvrView`. As a result, when you execute the application, the entire screen will be black.

To add content to the `StereoRenderer`, the application needs to access the graphical capabilities of OpenGL ES. The next chapter introduces this important topic.

6.5 Summary

Apps written using the Google VR SDK are like regular Android apps, but there are a number of details to keep track of, including VR mode, stereo mode, asynchronous projection, and EGL configuration. Thankfully, once you've written one VR app for the Daydream, other apps will have essentially the same configuration code.

For graphical apps, the central data structures to know are `GvrActivity`, `GvrView`, and `StereoRenderer`. The `GvrActivity` configures a `GvrView` to define the content of its window and the `GvrView` delegates the actual drawing to a class implementing the `StereoRenderer` interface. Again, once you've coded one `GvrActivity` subclass, you'll be able to use the code in other VR applications with minor modification.

The hard part of coding VR applications involves adding code to the `StereoRenderer`. Its methods are called at different points in the rendering process, and it's crucial to understand that, in stereo mode, scenes are always drawn twice—once for each eye. Therefore, for each call to `onNewFrame`, the `onDrawEye` method will be called twice.

The `StereoRenderer` in this chapter's example application didn't draw anything. But that will change in the following chapters. Before you can perform graphical rendering in a `StereoRenderer`, you need to be familiar with OpenGL ES, and this will be discussed in Chapter 7.

Chapter 7

Graphics Development with OpenGL ES

The last chapter explained how the `GvrActivity`, `GvrView`, and `StereoRenderer` work together in Daydream applications. This chapter introduces the process of drawing graphics in the `GvrView`. This involves calling OpenGL ES methods inside the `StereoRenderer`'s methods.

For readers who haven't worked with OpenGL ES before, the first section of this chapter provides a high-level overview of what the toolset accomplishes. I'll explain how the graphical rendering pipeline converts the vertices of a 3-D model into pixels on a screen. I'll also discuss the fascinating topic of textures.

When coding graphical applications in Java, it's important to be aware of two points. First, Java classes access OpenGL ES 3.2 functions through methods of a wrapper class named `GLES32`. Second, the methods of `GLES32` don't accept data provided in Java arrays. Instead, graphical data must be stored in Java NIO buffers. The third section of this chapter explains what NIO buffers are and demonstrates how they can be accessed in code.

NIO buffers are particularly helpful when an application needs to pass data to routines executing on the GPU. These GPU-specific routines are called shaders, and an application can pass two types of data to shaders: attribute data and uniform data. The fourth section of this chapter discusses the topic of shaders and explains how an application can package attribute data.

To demonstrate the overall process of graphical rendering, this chapter provides an example module that draws a two-dimensional triangle. This shows how NIO buffers are created and used by `GLES32` methods. It also illustrates how an application can pass data to shaders executing on the GPU.

7.1 Overview of OpenGL ES Development

The "ES" in OpenGL ES stands for *Embedded Systems* and the OpenGL ES 3.2 spec defines how graphical applications can be written for compliant systems such as Android devices. If you look through the spec, you'll see that the API defines a wide range of functions and constants based on C/C++. Accessing C/C++ functions in Java is usually difficult because of the Java Native Interface (JNI), which is discussed in Chapter 14.

To simplify development, Android provides a static wrapper class named `GLES32`. The methods and constants of this class have the same names and purposes as those defined in the OpenGL ES 3.2 spec. For example, the `glBufferData` method of `GLES32` performs the same operation as OpenGL's `glBufferData` function and accepts similar arguments.

`GLES32` provides hundreds of methods, and though you don't need to know all of them, you should be familiar with a significant portion of them. This chapter introduces many fundamental methods of this class and later chapters will elaborate further.

The goal of this section is to provide a high-level overview of what the `GLES32` methods are intended to accomplish. To start with, I'll discuss the process of converting vertices to pixels.

7.1.1 From Vertices to Pixels

Put simply, the purpose of graphical rendering is to convert points in space to pixels on a screen. The points in space are called *vertices*, and in addition to specifying the coordinates of each vertex, an application can provide additional information such as colors, texture coordinates, and normal vector components. This per-vertex data is collectively referred to as *attribute data*.

The `GLES32` class provides a number of important functions named `glDraw*`, including `glDrawArrays` and `glDrawElements`. When one of these functions executes, the rendering engine starts processing attribute data. As the rendering is performed, the engine will generate an array of pixels that depict the scene in two dimensions.

The sequence of steps needed to convert vertices to pixels is called a *rendering pipeline* or a *graphical pipeline*. In the early days of graphical programming, this pipeline was *fixed*. This means that, after the graphical data was sent to the GPU, developers had no way to configure how pixels were generated.

Modern graphical processors support *programmable pipelines*. In these pipelines, some stages of the pipeline can be configured with special code. In Figure 7.1, the programmable stages are colored in gray.

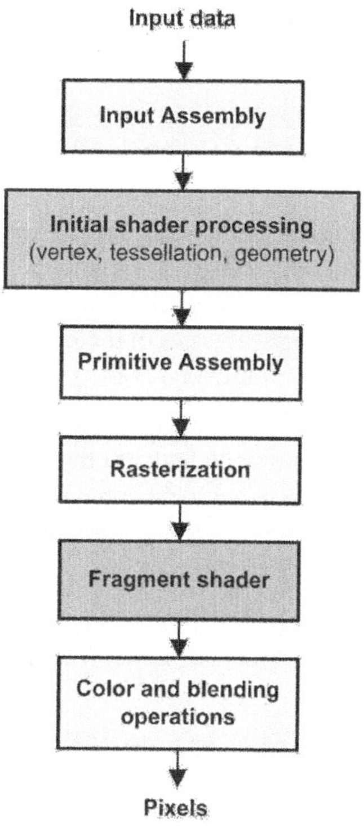

Figure 7.1 OpenGL ES Graphical Pipeline (Simplified)

The special programs executed in the programmable stages are called *shaders*. OpenGL ES 3.2 supports five different types of shaders, but this book will only be concerned with two types: vertex shaders and fragment shaders. Chapter 8 explains what these shaders accomplish and how they can be coded.

After the initial vertex processing, the pipeline assembles vertices into simple shapes called *primitives*. These may include points, lines, or triangles. An application specifies the desired primitive type by setting an argument in the `glDraw*` method. The last section of this chapter presents the different types of primitives and explains how they can be configured.

After the vertices have been combined into primitives, the next step is rasterization. This process breaks each primitive down to an array of discrete elements called fragments. Fragments are conceptually similar to pixels, but while pixels only have colors and (x, y) coordinates, fragments have colors, (x, y) coordinates, and *depth*.

Depth processing is vitally important in 3-D applications. To see why, consider two simple primitives, Triangle A and Triangle B. If Triangle A is larger than Triangle B and completely blocks Triangle B from view, the fragments generated from Triangle A will have lower depth values than those generated from Triangle B. Therefore, when the fragments are converted to pixels, the pixels of Triangle A will be displayed instead of the pixels of Triangle B.

The fragment shader stage receives the fragments produced by rasterization. This shader executes once for each fragment and can customize the fragment's color and depth. Many fragment shaders use lighting algorithms to set the fragment's color depending on the positions of light sources in the model. Chapter 8 discusses how fragment shaders work and Chapter 9 introduces the popular Blinn-Phong lighting model.

The last stage of the pipeline performs final operations on the processed fragments. Possible operations include depth testing, stencil testing, and blending. Depth and stencil testing will be discussed in Chapter 11. Blending refers to the process of combining the fragment's color with that of the surrounding buffer.

When the last stage has completed, the result will be a two-dimensional array of pixels. These pixels are stored in a special memory region called a *framebuffer*, and Chapter 11 explains how framebuffers can be accessed in code.

7.1.2 Uniforms, Textures, and Sampling

As mentioned earlier, attribute data, which includes vertex coordinates, changes from vertex to vertex. Data that remains constant between vertices is referred to as *uniform data*. For example, if an entire sphere is colored red, the color red is called a uniform because it remains constant for every vertex in the sphere.

Simple graphical applications may assign colors to vertices, but complex applications, such as games, usually associate an object's surface with the pixels of an image. For example, an application may associate a rectangle with the pixels of flag.png or a circle with the pixels of smiley.png.

The image data to be applied to the model is stored in data structures called *textures*. A texture is a uniform that remains constant over the vertices in an object. To apply a texture to an object, each of the object's vertices must be associated with a point in the texture. These texture coordinates change from vertex to vertex, so they are part of the application's attribute data.

The pixels in a texture are called *texels* and the process of selecting a texel from a texture is called sampling. An application can customize the sampling process in a number of ways, and Chapter 10 will provide a thorough discussion of the topic.

7.2 Example Application – Orange Screen

Rather than list the methods of the GLES32 class, it's better to look at a simple example. The ch07_orangescreen module demonstrates how GLES32 methods can be accessed and called in a StereoRenderer.

As its name implies, the ch07_orangescreen app fills the display with an orange color. To accomplish this, it performs three steps:

1. The OrangeScreenActivity accesses the GvrView in the layout resource and assigns its renderer to an OrangeScreenRenderer.
2. When the rendering surface is created, the OrangeScreenRenderer calls glClearColor to identify the desired background color.
3. As each new frame is drawn, the OrangeScreenRenderer calls glClear to fill the region with the background color.

The module's OrangeScreenActivity class is nearly identical to the EmptyScreenActivity class discussed in Chapter 6. But the OrangeScreenRenderer invokes two GLES32 methods. Listing 7.1 presents the code.

Listing 7.1: ch07_orangescreen/src/main/java/.../OrangeScreenRenderer.java

```
class OrangeScreenRenderer implements StereoRenderer {

  @Override
  public void onSurfaceCreated(EGLConfig config) {

    // Set the region's background color and line width
    GLES32.glClearColor(1.0f, 0.5f, 0.0f, 1.0f);
  }

  @Override
  public void onNewFrame(HeadTransform headTransform) {

    // Fill the rendering region with the background color
    GLES32.glClear(GLES32.GL_COLOR_BUFFER_BIT);
  }

  public void onDrawEye(Eye eye) {}
  public void onSurfaceChanged(int width, int height) {}
  public void onFinishFrame(Viewport viewport) {}
  public void onRendererShutdown() {}
}
```

If you look at Android's documentation on the `GLES32` class, you'll see that it's a subclass of `GLES31`, which is a subclass of `GLES30`, which is a subclass of `GLES20`. Each of these classes represents a different version of OpenGL ES, and each new version can access all the methods and constants of preceding versions.

The code in this class calls two methods of the `GLES32` object:

- `glClearColor(float r, float g, float b, float a)` — Sets a color to serve as the region's background color
- `glClear(int bit)` — Fills the region with its assigned background color

The `onSurfaceCreated` method will be invoked before the first frame is drawn. This means that `glClearColor` will set the background color before `onNewFrame` fills the region with the desired color.

The component values provided in `glClearColor` must be set between 0.0 and 1.0. In this code, the RGB values are set to 1.0, 0.5, and 0.0 to produce an orange color. The last component, called the alpha component, identifies the color's opacity. In this case, the alpha value is 1.0, so the color is fully opaque.

7.3 Packaging Data with Java NIO

If I want to send a lamp to someone, I can't just hand the lamp to a shipping company. I need to place the lamp in a standard package, affix a label with information, and hand the labeled package to the shippers.

Similarly, Android applications can't just pass Java arrays to `GLES32` methods. Graphical data must be packaged in Java NIO (Non-blocking I/O) buffers. This section explains the basics of NIO storage, but if you're already familiar with the topic, feel free to skip this discussion.

7.3.1 Overview

Java applications execute in a Java Virtual Machine (JVM), so they generally don't run as quickly as applications coded in a low-level language. To improve performance, Java 1.4 introduced classes that access memory using the same high-speed routines employed by low-level applications. These classes form the Java NIO toolset.

Every NIO class serves as a container of primitive data. They all extend from the `Buffer` class, and Figure 7.2 illustrates the inheritance hierarchy.

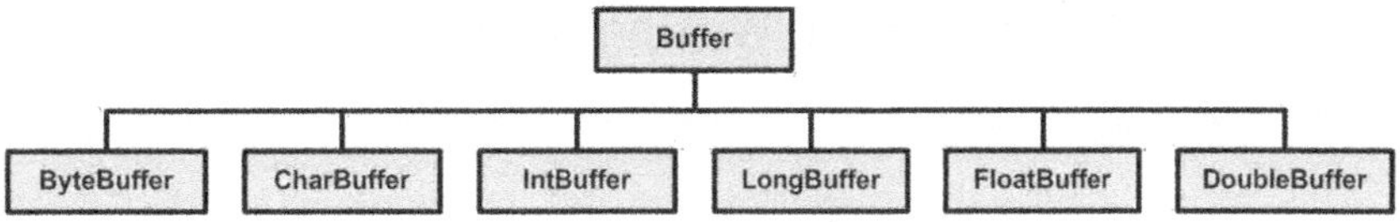

Figure 7.2 NIO Buffer Classes

These classes become particularly important when an application needs to transfer data between Java and C/C++ routines. Chapter 14, which introduces the Java Native Interface (JNI), discusses this topic in detail. For now, the discussion focuses on creating NIO buffers and accessing their data.

7.3.2 Direct NIO Buffers

There are many ways to create NIO buffers, but not all of them are suitable for graphical applications. Android-GLES applications require *direct* NIO buffers. As stated in the Javadoc, "Given a direct byte buffer, the Java virtual machine will make a best effort to perform native I/O operations directly upon it." In other words, if an NIO buffer is direct, its data can (in theory) be readily accessed by C/C++ code.

The process of creating a direct NIO buffer consists of three steps:

1. Call `ByteBuffer.allocateDirect` with the number of bytes to be stored in the buffer. This returns a new `ByteBuffer` object.
2. Call the `ByteBuffer`'s `order` method to set the order of the buffer's bytes to the byte order of the underlying platform.
3. Call the `ByteBuffer`'s `as`*`XYZ`*`Buffer` method, where *`XYZ`*`Buffer` identifies the desired type of NIO buffer, such as `FloatBuffer` or `IntBuffer`.

For example, the following code creates a `FloatBuffer` capable of holding 64 `float`s:

```
ByteBuffer tempBuffer = ByteBuffer.allocateDirect(64 * 4);
tempBuffer.order(ByteOrder.nativeOrder());
FloatBuffer floatBuffer = tempBuffer.asFloatBuffer();
```

A `float` occupies four bytes, so the argument of `ByteBuffer.allocateDirect` is multiplied by 4. If the buffer was intended to hold 16 `double`s, the argument would be set to `16 * 8` because each `double` occupies eight bytes.

7.3.3 Reading and Writing Data

NIO buffers are similar to arrays in that they contain multiple elements of the same type. Unlike arrays, an element in an NIO buffer can't be selected by index. Instead, each NIO buffer has a value called a *position* that identifies where data can be written to and read from.

When a buffer is created, the position's value is 0. When N elements are written to the buffer or read from the buffer, the new position will equal N. If called without an argument, the `position()` method returns the current value of the buffer's position. If called with an argument, `position(N)` sets the position's value to `N`. Table 7.1 lists both `position` methods and other methods related to accessing NIO buffers.

Table 7.1

Methods for Accessing NIO Buffers

Method	Description
`position()`	Returns the buffer's current position
`position(int pos)`	Sets the buffer's position
`rewind()`	Sets the buffer's position to the start (0)
`put(`*type* `val)`	Stores a value of the given type in the buffer
`put(`*type*`[] arr)`	Stores an array of values in the buffer
`put(`*type*`[] arr, int offset, int len)`	Stores an array of len values in the buffer starting with the value whose index equals offset
`get()`	Returns a value of the buffer's type
`get(`*type*`[] arr)`	Reads values from the buffer and places them in the array
`put(`*type*`[] arr, int offset, int len)`	Reads len values from the buffer and places them in the array, starting with offset

In this table, *`type`* identifies the type of element stored by the buffer. That is, *`type`* will be a `float` for `FloatBuffers`, an `int` for `IntBuffers`, and so on.

An example will clarify how these methods are used. The following code initializes an array of six `floats`, creates a direct `FloatBuffer`, stores the array data in the `FloatBuffer`, and reads three of its values into a second array:

```
// Initialize data
float[] firstArray = {1.0f, 2.0f, 3.0f, 4.0f, 5.0f, 6.0f};
float[] secondArray = new float[3];
```

```
// Create and configure ByteBuffer
ByteBuffer tempBuffer =
  ByteBuffer.allocateDirect(firstArray.length * 4);
tempBuffer.order(ByteOrder.nativeOrder());
FloatBuffer floatBuffer = tempBuffer.asFloatBuffer();

// Insert and extract array data
floatBuffer.put(firstArray);
floatBuffer.rewind();
floatBuffer.get(secondArray);
```

The most common type of NIO buffer used in Android-GLES applications is the `FloatBuffer`. This is because coordinates and colors are usually provided as floating point values.

7.4 Vertex Data and Attributes

An earlier section introduced the topic of shaders, which are functions that perform graphical operations on the GPU. Chapter 8 will discuss the topic of shader coding. For now, the goal is to understand how to pass data to the first shader, which processes vertices received by the GPU. This is called the vertex shader.

A vertex shader can receive two types of information:

1. Attribute data — data that changes from vertex to vertex, may include coordinates and normal vectors
2. Uniform data — data that remains constant over a set of vertices, may include colors (if the vertices have the same color) and transformation matrices (which will be discussed in Chapter 8)

This section focuses on storing attribute data and passing it to vertex shaders. Uniform data is optional, and will be discussed in Chapter 8.

7.4.1 Storing Attribute Data

An example will help clarify how attribute data works. Suppose an application needs to draw a two-dimensional triangle whose points have different colors (red, green, and blue). Figure 7.3 illustrates the coordinates and colors of the triangle's vertices.

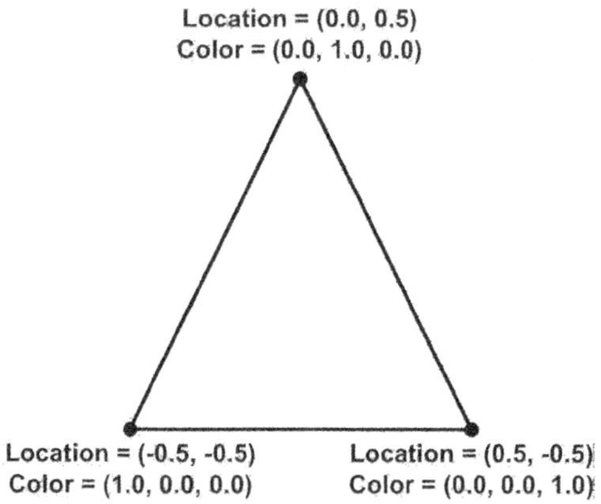

Figure 7.3 Simple Attribute Data

To draw this triangle, the GPU needs to know the coordinates and colors of each vertex. These properties change from vertex to vertex, so this is attribute data. The following code shows how this data can be stored in separate arrays:

```
float[] vertexCoords = {
 -0.5f,  0.0f,
  0.0f,  0.5f,
  0.5f,  0.0f};

float[] vertexColors = {
  1.0f, 0.0f, 0.0f,
  0.0f, 1.0f, 0.0f,
  0.0f, 0.0f, 1.0f};
```

Another method is to combine the coordinates and colors into one large array:

```
float[] vertexData = {
  -0.5f, 0.0f, 1.0f, 0.0f, 0.0f,    // First vertex
   0.0f, 0.5f, 0.0f, 1.0f, 0.0f,    // Second vertex
   0.5f, 0.0f, 0.0f, 0.0f, 1.0f};   // Third vertex
```

The second array contains the coordinates of the first vertex followed by the color of the first vertex. This is followed by the attribute data for the second vertex and the attribute data for the third vertex. Because the data for each vertex is combined together, this process is called *interleaving*. In general, this provides better performance than using separate arrays, and all the example code in this book will use interleaving to store attribute data.

In an ideal world, the application would be able to send `vertexData` to the GPU and the shader would automatically know which values represent coordinates and which represent color components. But in the real world, this information needs to be carefully identified. The following discussion explains how this is accomplished.

7.4.2 Associating Shader Variables with Attribute Data

Shaders access input data through special C variables. The nature of a variable's declaration identifies if it provides attribute data or uniform data. If the application has been coded correctly, the GPU will know which portions of the attribute data correspond to each variable.

An example will clarify how this works. The following code presents a vertex shader with two input variables: one named `in_coords` and one named `in_color`.

```
in vec2 in_coords;
in vec3 in_color;

out vec3 new_color;

void main() {
  ...
}
```

Don't be concerned about the strange-looking data types (`vec2` and `vec3`) or the `in`/`out` modifiers. Chapter 8 will make this clear. For now, it's important to see that one portion of the attribute data (the `vertexData` array discussed earlier) needs to be associated with the `in_coords` variable and the other portion needs to be associated with the `in_color` variable.

Shader variables that receive values from attribute data are called *attributes*. In this case, we can say that the shader has two attributes named `in_coords` and `in_color`. Each attribute has an index that identifies its position among the shader's attributes: the index of `in_coords` is 0 and the index of `in_color` is 1.

In code, the process of associating attribute data with a shader's attribute requires calling three `GLES32` methods:

1. Call `glGetAttribLocation` to obtain the attribute's index.
2. Call `glEnableVertexAttribArray` with the index to specify which attribute is being associated with data.
3. Call `glVertexAttribPointer` to associate a portion of the attribute data with the specified attribute.

The first two methods are simple. glGetAttribLocation accepts the name of an attribute and returns its index. glEnableVertexAttribArray accepts an attribute's index and returns void. The following code shows how these functions can be called:

```
int coordIndex = glGetAttribLocation(program, "in_coords");

glEnableVertexAttribArray(coordIndex);
```

The glVertexAttribPointer method is more complicated, but it's one of the most important GLES32 functions to know. Its signature is given as follows:

```
glVertexAttribPointer(int index, int size, int type,
                      boolean normalized, int stride,
                      Buffer data)
```

The first argument identifies an attribute's index and the last argument provides the NIO buffer that contains the attribute data. The other arguments identify which portion of the buffer's data should be associated with the attribute.

As mentioned earlier, the elements in an NIO buffer always have the same type. The type argument of glVertexAttribPointer must identify this data type, and may be set to GL_BYTE, GL_UNSIGNED_BYTE, GL_SHORT, GL_UNSIGNED_SHORT, GL_INT, GL_UNSIGNED_INT, GL_FLOAT, or GL_DOUBLE.

The normalized argument identifies whether the data needs to be normalized. This should be set to true if signed integers should be mapped between -1 and 1 and unsigned integers should be mapped between 0 and 1. For floating-point types (GL_FLOAT and GL_DOUBLE), this can be set to false.

The size argument identifies how many elements should be accessed from the attribute data at a time. For the vertices of the triangle discussed earlier, coordinates are provided in pairs, so size would be set to 2. The triangle's colors are provided in triples, so size would be set to 3.

The stride argument identifies how many *bytes* separate one group of attribute values from the next group. For the triangle, each vertex's data occupies five floats: two for coordinates and three for the colors. This means the first set of coordinates is five floats away from the second set, which is five floats away from the third set. A float occupies four bytes, so for both attributes, stride should be set to 5 * 4 = 20.

The following code shows how these methods can be used. It starts by storing the data in the vertexData array into a FloatBuffer. Then it associates portions of the buffer's data with attributes named in_coords and in_color.

```
// Create an NIO buffer to hold attribute data
ByteBuffer tempBuffer =
  ByteBuffer.allocateDirect(vertexData.length * 4);
tempBuffer.order(ByteOrder.nativeOrder());
FloatBuffer vertexBuffer = tempBuffer.asFloatBuffer();
vertexBuffer.put(vertexData);

// Associate coordinate data with in_coords
vertexBuffer.rewind();
int coordIndex = GLES32.glGetAttribLocation(program, "in_coords");
GLES32.glEnableVertexAttribArray(coordIndex);
GLES32.glVertexAttribPointer(coordIndex, 2,
  GLES32.GL_FLOAT, false, 20, vertexBuffer);

// Associate coordinate data with in_colors
vertexBuffer.position(2);
int colorIndex = GLES32.glGetAttribLocation(program, "in_color");
GLES32.glEnableVertexAttribArray(colorIndex);
GLES32.glVertexAttribPointer(colorIndex, 3,
  GLES32.GL_FLOAT, false, 20, vertexBuffer);
```

When looking at this code, it's important to see how `vertexBuffer`'s position is set. The `rewind` method sets its position to `0`. This means that `glVertexAttribPointer` will associate the first two `float`s in the buffer with the first `in_coords` attribute.

Later, the `position` method sets the buffer's position to `2`. This prepares the buffer so that the second call to `glVertexAttribPointer` associates the third, fourth, and fifth `float`s with the `in_color` attribute.

This code tells the GPU where to find vertex data in the `FloatBuffer`, but it doesn't tell the GPU how many vertices should be drawn. That is the responsibility of the `glDraw*` method, which will be discussed at the end of the chapter.

7.5 Example Application – Triangle

This chapter has discussed a number of topics, from graphical rendering to Java NIO to `GLES32` methods. To demonstrate how it all works together, the ch07_triangle module draws the triangle illustrated in Figure 7.3.

The `TriangleRenderer` class manages the drawing process. That is, it writes the `vertexData` array data to the `vertexBuffer`, associates the data in `vertexBuffer` with the `in_coords` and `in_color` attributes, and calls `glDrawArrays` to tell the GPU to draw the triangle. Listing 7.2 presents the `TriangleRenderer` code.

Listing 7.2: ch07_triangle/src/main/java/.../TriangleRenderer.java

```
class TriangleRenderer implements StereoRenderer {

  private static final String VERTEX_SHADER = "triangle.vert";
  private static final String FRAGMENT_SHADER = "triangle.frag";

  private Context context;
  private int coordIndex, colorIndex;
  private FloatBuffer vertexBuffer;

  private static final float[] vertexData = {
    -0.5f, -0.5f, 1.0f, 0.0f, 0.0f,   // First vertex
     0.0f,  0.5f, 0.0f, 1.0f, 0.0f,   // Second vertex
     0.5f, -0.5f, 0.0f, 0.0f, 1.0f};  // Third vertex

  TriangleRenderer(Context ctx) {
    context = ctx;

    // Store attribute data in an NIO buffer
    ByteBuffer tempBuffer =
        ByteBuffer.allocateDirect(vertexData.length * 4);
    tempBuffer.order(ByteOrder.nativeOrder());
    vertexBuffer = tempBuffer.asFloatBuffer();
    vertexBuffer.put(vertexData);
    vertexBuffer.rewind();
  }

  public void onSurfaceCreated(EGLConfig config) {

    // Set the region's background color and line width
    GLES32.glClearColor(1.0f, 1.0f, 1.0f, 1.0f);
    GLES32.glLineWidth(10);

    // Read and compile vertex shader
    int vertDescriptor =
      GLES32.glCreateShader(GLES32.GL_VERTEX_SHADER);
    String vertFile =
      ShaderUtils.readFile(context, VERTEX_SHADER);
    GLES32.glShaderSource(vertDescriptor, vertFile);
    ShaderUtils.compileShader(vertDescriptor);

    // Read and compile fragment shader
    int fragDescriptor =
      GLES32.glCreateShader(GLES32.GL_FRAGMENT_SHADER);
    String fragFile =
      ShaderUtils.readFile(context, FRAGMENT_SHADER);
    GLES32.glShaderSource(fragDescriptor, fragFile);
    ShaderUtils.compileShader(fragDescriptor);
```

Listing 7.2: ch07_triangle/src/main/java/.../TriangleRenderer.java (Continued)

```
    // Create program and bind attributes
    int program = GLES32.glCreateProgram();
    GLES32.glAttachShader(program, vertDescriptor);
    GLES32.glAttachShader(program, fragDescriptor);

    // Link and use program
    ShaderUtils.linkProgram(program);
    GLES32.glUseProgram(program);

    // Determine the indices of the shader variables
    coordIndex =
      GLES32.glGetAttribLocation(program, "in_coords");
    colorIndex =
      GLES32.glGetAttribLocation(program, "in_color");
  }

  public void onNewFrame(HeadTransform headTransform) {

    // Fill the rendering region with the background color
    GLES32.glClear(GLES32.GL_COLOR_BUFFER_BIT);

    // Associate coordinate data with in_coords
    vertexBuffer.rewind();
    GLES32.glEnableVertexAttribArray(coordIndex);
    GLES32.glVertexAttribPointer(coordIndex, 2,
        GLES32.GL_FLOAT, false, 20, vertexBuffer);

    // Associate color data with in_colors
    vertexBuffer.position(2);
    GLES32.glEnableVertexAttribArray(colorIndex);
    GLES32.glVertexAttribPointer(colorIndex, 3,
        GLES32.GL_FLOAT, false, 20, vertexBuffer);

    // Draw the triangle
    GLES32.glDrawArrays(GLES32.GL_LINE_LOOP, 0, 3);
  }

  public void onDrawEye(Eye eye) {}

  public void onSurfaceChanged(int width, int height) {}

  public void onFinishFrame(Viewport viewport) {}

  public void onRendererShutdown() {}
}
```

The class's constructor stores the attribute data in a `FloatBuffer` and the `onSurfaceCreated` method compiles and links the two shaders. An explanation of shader processing will have to wait until Chapter 8. At the end of `onSurfaceCreated`, the method obtains the indices for the two shader attributes, `in_coords` and `in_color`.

The `onDrawFrame` method starts by clearing the region with the background color. Then it associates the `FloatBuffer`'s data with the `in_coords` and `in_color` attributes. The last line of the method calls `glDrawArrays`, which will be discussed in the following section.

The code in the ch07_triangle module is easy to understand but it's inefficient. This is because the `onDrawFrame` method performs so much work. With every frame, it accesses the `FloatBuffer` and associates the shader's attributes with data.

Ideally, the application would transfer its data to the GPU once and access that data for its drawing operations. This can be accomplished using vertex buffer objects (VBOs), and Chapter 11 will explain how they work.

One last point. Because the drawing is so simple, the `TriangleActivity` class sets the stereo mode to `false`. This tells the application not to redraw the model for each eye. This is why the renderer's `onDrawEye` method is left empty.

7.6 Drawing Primitives

To grasp how the ch07_triangle application works, it's important to understand the `glDrawArrays` method called at the end of `onDrawFrame`:

```
glDrawArrays(int mode, int firstVertex, int numVertices)
```

The second argument, `firstVertex`, identifies the index of the first vertex to be drawn. The last argument, `numVertices`, tells the renderer how many vertices should be drawn, starting from `firstVertex`. For our triangle, `firstVertex` is 0 and `numVertices` is 3.

The first argument of `glDrawArrays` identifies the type of primitives that should be assembled from the vertices. As discussed earlier, an OpenGL primitive is a basic shape from which a graphical model can be constructed. The `mode` argument can be set to one of twelve values:

- `GL_POINTS` — Each vertex is drawn as an individual point
- `GL_LINES` — Each pair of vertices form a distinct line
- `GL_LINE_STRIP` — Each vertex is part of a line connected to its successive vertex

- GL_LINE_LOOP — Similar to GL_LINES, but a line is drawn from the last vertex to the first
- GL_LINES_ADJACENCY — Similar to GL_LINES, but each endpoint has an adjacent vertex that can be accessed by a geometry shader
- GL_LINE_STRIP_ADJACENCY — Similar to GL_LINE_STRIP, but each endpoint has an adjacent vertex that can be accessed by a geometry shader
- GL_TRIANGLES — Each set of three vertices forms a separate triangle
- GL_TRIANGLE_STRIP — Forms a triangle with first three vertices and each succeeding vertex forms a triangle with the two preceding it
- GL_TRIANGLE_FAN — Forms a triangle with first three vertices and each succeeding pair of vertices form a triangle with first vertex
- GL_TRIANGLES_ADJACENCY — Similar to GL_TRIANGLES, but each endpoint has an adjacent vertex that can be accessed by a geometry shader
- GL_TRIANGLE_STRIP_ADJACENCY — Similar to GL_TRIANGLE_STRIP, but each endpoint has an adjacent vertex that can be accessed by a geometry shader
- GL_PATCHES — Group of vertices whose characteristics are determined by a tessellation control shader

These values tell OpenGL how to connect the vertices whose attributes are stored within the active array. On the following page, Figure 7.4 illustrates six of the different drawing modes. Each case presents six vertices ordered from v_0 to v_5.

The simplest modes are GL_POINTS, GL_LINES, and GL_TRIANGLES. When these are set, each primitive is drawn separately, without connections to others. For example, if GL_LINES is set, each pair of vertices is drawn as a separate line. If GL_TRIANGLES is set, each triple of vertices forms a separate triangle.

GL_LINE_STRIP and GL_TRIANGLE_STRIP create interconnected primitives from each successive vertex. If GL_LINE_STRIP is set, the renderer simply draws a line from the first vertex to the second, from the second to the third, from the third to the fourth, and so on. If GL_TRIANGLE_STRIP is set, then each successive vertex forms a triangle with the two vertices preceding it. For example, if there are four vertices, v_0 to v_3, this mode will cause two triangles to be drawn: v_0–v_1–v_2 and v_1–v_2–v_3.

Five of these modes are only useful when optional shaders are inserted in the graphical pipeline. The four modes involving adjacency, such as GL_LINES_ADJACENCY, require that a geometry shader process adjacent vertices. Similarly, the GL_PATCHES mode can only be specified when a tessellation control shader is available to establish order among the vertices. This book will not discuss geometry shaders or tessellation control shaders.

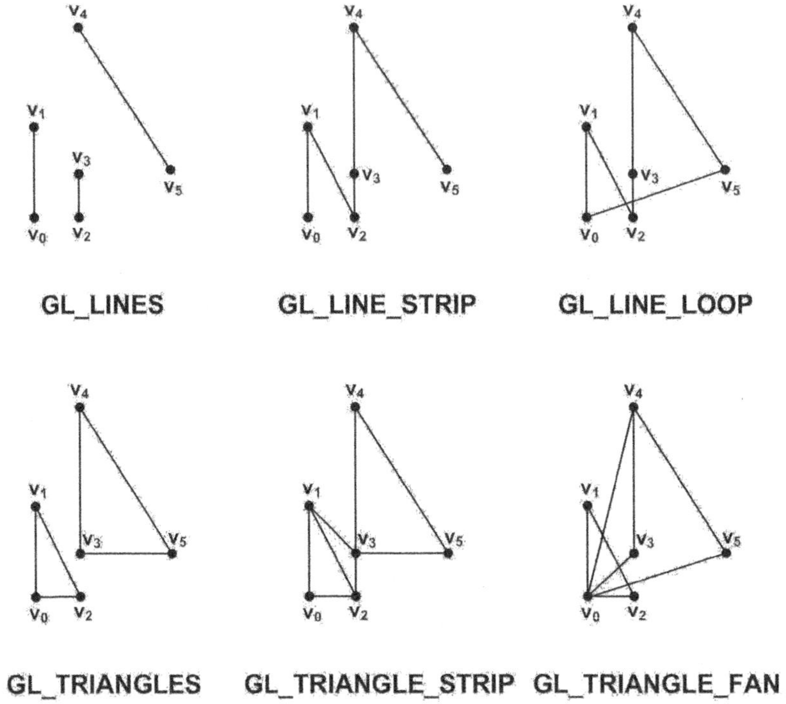

Figure 7.4 OpenGL Primitive Modes

For the triangle drawn by the ch07_triangle application, the primitive mode is set to `GL_LINE_LOOP`. This ensures that a line will be drawn from the third vertex back to the first. If the mode is set to `GL_LINE_STRIP`, this last line won't be drawn.

OpenGL used to support quadrilateral primitives, but those have been deprecated. Therefore, if an application needs to draw surfaces, the surfaces must be drawn as collections of triangles. For this reason, the most common primitive modes in virtual reality applications are `GL_TRIANGLES` and `GL_TRIANGLE_STRIP`. Later chapters will demonstrate how these modes are used in practice.

This discussion has introduced the `glDrawArrays` method, which simply draws a succession of vertices. This is one of many `glDraw*` methods provided by the `GLES32` class. As an example, Chapter 8 draws its graphics by calling `glDrawArraysInstanced`, which draws multiple instances of the same set of vertices. Similarly, Chapter 9 introduces `glDrawElements`, which draws vertices in a sequence determined by a set of index values.

7.7 Summary

Learning OpenGL can be difficult because there are so many factors to take into account, including attributes, uniforms, shaders, and textures. Accessing OpenGL in Java is even harder because a mechanism is needed to bridge Java and the underlying C/C++ routines. Thankfully, Android provides the `GLES32` class, whose methods correspond to the functions of the OpenGL ES 3.2 specification.

The methods of `GLES32` accept Java primitives, such as `int`s and `float`s. But if an application needs to provide a block of graphical data, such as vertex coordinates, a Java array won't be sufficient. The data must be placed in Java NIO buffers, or more specifically, direct NIO buffers. These buffers can be a pain to work with, but they guarantee high-performance data transfer between the application and the GPU.

In general, the data passed to the GPU can be divided into two types: attribute data and uniform data. Attribute data changes from vertex to vertex while uniform data remains constant for multiple vertices. Vertex shaders access attribute data through attribute variables. This chapter explained how to store attribute data in NIO buffers and associate portions of a buffer with a shader's variables.

The last section of the chapter discussed the `glDrawArrays` method, which is one of many `glDraw*` methods provided by `GLES32` for launching the rendering process. In the example code, `glDrawArrays` was called to draw line primitives between three points. Later chapters will draw different primitives and employ different `glDraw*` methods.

Chapter 8

Shaders and Uniform Data

This chapter goes further in discussing shaders and how applications can pass data to them. The chapter starts by introducing the OpenGL Shader Language, GLSL, which is the programming language of OpenGL ES shaders. The discussion explores vertex shaders and fragment shaders, and explains what they accomplish and how they can be coded.

After shaders are written, the next step is to combine them into programs. The process is straightforward—the application obtains a descriptor for each shader, compiles the shader code, and links the shader code into a program. After a program has been linked and made active, it can be passed to the GPU to configure its pipeline.

As discussed in Chapter 7, uniform data is data passed to the GPU that remains constant between vertices. This chapter explains how applications can store uniform data in NIO buffers and pass the data to vertex shaders and fragment shaders. In many respects, the process is similar to that of passing attribute data to the GPU.

One important type of uniform data is transformation matrices. These matrices are passed to the vertex shader, which uses matrix-vector multiplication to translate, rotate, and/or scale the vertex coordinates. The mathematics behind generating these matrices is complex, but thankfully, the Android API provides a `Matrix` class whose methods simplify the process.

The last part of the chapter demonstrates how applications generate transformation matrices and pass them to a vertex shader as uniform data. This application also shows how OpenGL ES makes it possible to draw multiple instances of a graphic. This is called *instanced rendering*, and it's useful when an application needs to draw copies of an object in different positions.

8.1 The OpenGL Shading Language (GLSL)

Chapter 7 provided an overview of the GPU's graphical pipeline, which behaves like an assembly line. Some stages are programmable, which means their operations are determined by shaders. In OpenGL ES applications, shaders are written in the OpenGL Shading Language, or GLSL. The GLSL specification defines six types of shaders, but this book only discusses two: vertex shaders and fragment shaders.

GLSL is a variant of the C programming language and supports much of the C syntax, including variable declarations and function definitions. As in a C program, a shader's execution starts with a function named `main`. Unlike a C program, a shader can't contain `#include` statements, pointers, or any kind of string handling.

Outside the `main` function, shaders can declare variables that receive data from the application running on the CPU. Chapter 7 introduced the functions that provide attribute data to shaders. The end of this chapter presents the functions that provide uniform data.

When coding shaders for OpenGL ES 3.2, there are two important points to know:

1. At the time of this writing, every shader file must start with "`#version 300 es`". Otherwise, the system will return an invalid version error.
2. If an attribute variable brings data into the shader, its declaration must be preceded by `in`. If the variable provides data to another shader, its declaration must be preceded by `out`. This is a major change from earlier versions of GLSL, which used `attribute` and `varying` modifiers.

The following example shows how shaders are structured. This shader receives an input vector named `in_var` and produces an output vector named `out_var`.

```
#version 300 es

in vec4 in_var;
out vec4 out_var;

void main(void) {
  out_var = in_var * 2;
}
```

Shaders can access specially-named variables called *built-in variables*. For example, vertex shaders can access built-in variables containing vertex coordinates and fragment shaders can access built-in variables containing pixel colors.

8.1.1 Data Types

In the preceding example, in_var and out_var are declared as vec4, which indicates that they're both vectors containing four values. Table 8.1 lists vec4 and other data types for vectors and matrices. GLSL also provides data types related to samplers and images, and they'll be discussed in Chapter 10.

Table 8.1

Data Types Available in GLSL Shaders (Abridged)

Data Type	Description
bool/int/uint/float	Scalars such as booleans, integers, unsigned integers, and floats
bvec2/bvec3/bvec4	Vectors containing 2/3/4 boolean values
ivec2/ivec3/ivec4	Vectors containing 2/3/4 signed integers
uvec2/uvec3/uvec4	Vectors containing 2/3/4 unsigned integers
vec2/vec3/vec4	Vectors containing 2/3/4 single-precision floating-point values
mat2/mat3/mat4	Square matrices containing 2-by-2, 3-by-3, or 4-by-4 single-precision floating-point values
mat2x3/mat2x4/mat3x2/ mat3x4/mat4x2/mat4x3	Rectangular matrices containing single-precision floating-point values

Many of these vector/matrix types identify their content with prefixes: i for integer, d for double-precision, and so on. If a vector or matrix type doesn't have a prefix, it contains single-precision floating-point values. For example, a vec4 contains four floats and a mat3 contains nine floats in a 3-by-3 matrix.

The syntax used to initialize a vector or matrix is similar to that used to create a Java object. For example, the following code uses the uvec3 constructor to initialize a vector containing three unsigned integers:

```
uvec3 ex_vec = uvec3(1, 2, 3);
```

Vectors can be used to initialize other vectors, as in the following code:

```
vec2 two_vec = vec2(0.3, 0.4);

vec3 three_vec = vec3(0.2, two_vec);
```

The following code uses the `mat2` constructor to intialize a 2-by-2 matrix:

```
mat2 ex_mat = mat2(1.0, 2.0, 3.0, 4.0);
```

When initializing a matrix, the values are interpreted in *column-major order*. That is, if a matrix has N rows, the first N values will form the first column, the next N values will form the second column, and so on.

Individual elements of vectors and matrices can be accessed using regular array syntax. For example, the third element of `my_vec` can be accessed as `my_vec[2]`. If `my_mat` is a matrix, `my_mat[3]` is a vector containing the elements of the matrix's fourth *column*. `my_mat[3][2]` is the element in the matrix's third row and fourth column.

Like the members of a Java object, the elements of a GLSL vector can be accessed using dot notation. In this case, each field is a letter that can be taken from three groups of four letters each:

- `x`, `y`, `z`, `w` — used with vertex coordinates
- `r`, `g`, `b`, `a` — used with color components
- `s`, t, `p`, `q` — used with texture coordinates

When accessing elements with dot notation, order is important. If `my_vec` is a vector with four elements, the first element can be accessed with `my_vec.x`, the second with `my_vec.y`, and so on.

8.1.2 Operators and Functions

GLSL supports the same basic operators as C, including `+`, `-`, `*`, and `/`. They can be used with scalars, vectors, and matrices. But when operating on vectors and matrices, there are three points to be aware of:

1. If one operand is a scalar and the other is a vector or matrix, the operation will be performed on each element of the vector or matrix.
2. If both operands are vectors or matrices of the same size, addition, subtraction, and division will be performed component-wise.
3. If two vectors of the same size are multiplied with `*`, their elements are multiplied component-wise and placed in the resulting vector. For vector-matrix multiplication or matrix-matrix multiplication, `*` produces a result according to linear algebra.

In addition to supporting basic arithmetic, GLSL provides five built-in math functions. Table 8.2 lists them all, using `vec` for vector types and `mat` for matrix types.

Table 8.2
Built-In Math Functions

Function	Description
`mat matrixCompMult (mat x, mat y)`	Multiplies input matrices component-wise
`mat outerProduct (vec x, vec y)`	Returns the outer product of two vectors
`mat transpose(mat x)`	Returns the transpose of a matrix
`mat inverse(mat x)`	Returns the inverse of a square matrix
`float determinant(mat x)`	Returns the determinant of a square matrix

When multiplying matrices, it's important to understand the difference between the * operator and `matrixCompMult`. The * operator performs traditional matrix-matrix multiplication, so if `matA` has dimensions m-by-n and `matB` has dimensions n-by-p, `matA * matB` will have dimensions m-by-p. In contrast, `matrixCompMult` multiplies matrices component-wise. This means both operands must have the same dimensions and the resulting matrix will have the same dimensions as its operands.

The `transpose`, `determinant`, and `inverse` functions each accept one matrix. `determinant` returns a `float` that serves as the matrix's characteristic value. In two dimensions, this is the area of the region bounded by the two vectors that form the matrix. In three dimensions, this is the volume of the region bounded by the three vectors that form the matrix.

The GLSL spec provides a full description of the operators and functions available for shaders. This can be downloaded from http://www.opengl.org/documentation/glsl.

8.2 Vertex Shaders

The first type of shader executed in the graphical pipeline is the vertex shader. This executes once for each vertex in the model and receives input data from the host application. This input data may include vertex coordinates, colors, texture coordinates, and normal vectors.

A vertex shader can't add or remove vertices, but it can change their characteristics, such as their coordinates or colors. For example, if an application needs to display a model from a given angle, the vertex shader can update the coordinates of its vertices. It can also change a vertex's normal vectors to alter the way light reflects from the point.

At minimum, a vertex shader needs to set the position of each vertex it processes. It accomplishes this by providing a value for a built-in variable called `gl_Position`. This is a `vec4`, so the shader needs to provide four `float`s to assign a vertex's position.

An example will clarify how this works. Suppose a vertex shader has an input variable named `in_vec` that receives attribute data from the host. If that data contains vertex coordinates, a simple vertex shader can pass the coordinate data to `gl_Position` with the following code:

```
in vec4 in_vec;

void main() {
  gl_Position = in_vec;
}
```

This may seem trivial, but if `gl_Position` isn't set properly, the renderer won't know where to place the model's vertices.

Most vertex shaders do more than just set a vertex's output coordinates equal to its input coordinates. Vertex shaders frequently employ matrix-vector multiplication to update vertices' positions. If coded correctly, a matrix can rotate, move, or scale a model's vertices. These operations are collectively called *transformations* and their corresponding matrices are called transformation matrices.

For example, the following shader rotates each vertex by 45° in the x-y plane:

```
in vec4 in_vec;

void main() {

  /* Define the rotation matrix */
  mat3x3 rot_matrix = mat3x3(0.707, 0.707, 0.000,
                            -0.707, 0.707, 0.000,
                             0.000, 0.000, 1.000;

  /* Transform the input coordinates */
  vec3 coords = rot_matrix * in_vec;

  /* Set the vertex's position */
  gl_Position = vec4(coords, 1.0);
}
```

Vertex shaders can access two helpful built-in variables that provide input:

- `gl_VertexID` — index of the vertex received by the shader
- `gl_InstanceID` — index of the instance being drawn

`gl_VertexID` makes it possible to process vertices differently according to their position in the rendering sequence. `gl_InstanceID` becomes important for applications that perform *instanced rendering*, or just *instancing*. This involves drawing multiple instances of an object, but processing each differently according to its instance index. The advantage of instanced rendering is that an application can draw multiple copies of an object but only transfer the object's vertex data once.

An app can perform instanced rendering by calling `glDrawArraysInstanced`. The example code presented at the end of this chapter demonstrates how this method is used in practice.

The vertex shader is the only shader that can receive attribute data from the application. Therefore, if the host application wants to assign colors to vertices, it needs to send color data to the vertex shader. The vertex shader can pass this data to later shaders by declaring output variables.

To ensure that an output variable from the vertex shader will be linked to an input variable of a later shader, the two variables must have the same name and type. In the following code, the linker will understand that the `vert_colors` variable from the vertex shader should be passed to the `vert_colors` variable in the fragment shader:

```
/* Declared in the vertex shader */
out vec3 vert_colors;

/* Declared in the fragment shader */
in vec3 vert_colors;
```

In addition to receiving attribute data, a vertex shader can also receive data that remains constant from vertex to vertex. This is called uniform data, and a later section will explain how uniform variables are declared and how to pass them to shaders.

8.3 Fragment Shaders

After the vertex shader completes its execution, the renderer needs to convert the model's three-dimensional primitives into an array of two-dimensional elements. As mentioned in Chapter 7, this conversion process is called rasterization.

The elements produced by rasterization aren't the final pixels displayed by the renderer. These candidate pixels are called *fragments*. Like a pixel, a fragment has a position (x, y) and a color. Unlike a pixel, a fragment also has depth. Later in the rendering process, a depth test can be used to test which fragments should be displayed as pixels. Depth configuration and testing will be discussed in Chapter 9.

Just as a vertex shader executes once for each vertex, a fragment shader executes once for each fragment. The shader can't change a fragment's position or access other fragments, but it can serve multiple roles, including the following:

- Apply texture data
- Configure lighting — identify how light reflects from the model
- Set the fragment's depth
- Bump-mapping — add roughness to an image
- Additional effects such as fog and shadow

At minimum, a fragment shader's purpose is to accept an input fragment and set the color of the output fragment. The renderer will use this to determine the final color of the corresponding pixel.

Some of these roles will be discussed in later chapters. For now, the discussion focuses on coding a fragment shader. In particular, we'll look at how the fragment shader assigns the output color and accesses built-in variables.

8.3.1 Setting the Output Color

GLSL used to provide a built-in variable called `gl_FragColor` to hold a fragment's output color, but that's no longer supported. Instead, a fragment shader can declare any variable to store the fragment's output color so long as it meets two criteria:

1. Its type must be `vec4`.
2. It must be an output variable (preceded with `out`).

For example, in the ch07_triangle module from the previous chapter, the fragment shader receives the input color in a `vec3` called `in_color`. It uses this to set the output fragment's color, which is given in a `vec4` called `out_color`.

```
in vec3 in_color;
out vec4 out_color;

void main() {
  out_color = vec4(in_color, 1.0);
}
```

Chapter 9 presents a more complex method of determining a fragment's color. This method, called Blinn-Phong lighting, uses the normal vector at the given fragment to determine how the output fragment's color should be set.

8.3.2 Built-in Variables

Every fragment shader can access a set of input/output variables that represent different aspects of the input/output fragments. Table 8.3 lists each of these built-in variables and identifies the type of each.

Table 8.3

Built-In Variables for Fragment Shaders (Abridged)

Variable	Dir	Type	Description
gl_FragCoord	in	vec4	The fragment's location in the window
gl_PrimitiveID	in	int	Index of the primitive being rendered
gl_PointCoord	in	vec2	The fragment's location relative to its point primitive
gl_FrontFacing	in	bool	Whether the fragment was generated by the front face of its primitive
gl_Layer	in	int	Index of the layer being rendered
gl_FragDepth	out	float	Depth of the output fragment

The first variable, `gl_FragCoord`, identifies the coordinates of the fragment inside the window. The third value provides the depth of the input fragment and the fourth value is necessary to display models in perspective.

The `gl_PrimitiveID` variable displays the index of the current primitive being drawn. As an example, the following code changes the fragment's color according to its primitive index:

```
out vec4 out_color;
vec3 base_color;
void main() {
  base_color = vec3(0.1, 0.1, 0.1);
  out_color = vec4(base_color * gl_PrimitiveID, 1.0);
}
```

If the fragment's primitive is a point, `gl_PointCoord` identifies the location of the fragment relative to the point. If the fragment's primitive faces the front of the viewing area, `gl_FrontFacing` will be set to true. Otherwise, it will be false.

A fragment shader can't change the position of a fragment, but it can change the fragment's depth through the `gl_FragDepth` variable. If this isn't set, the depth of the output fragment will be set equal to the depth of the input fragment.

8.4 Shaders and Programs

Now that you're familiar with shaders, it's important to know how to pass them to the device for processing. This entails five steps:

1. Read the text of each shader file into a string.
2. Compile the shader text with `glCompileShader`. Optionally, access the compiler's output with `glGetShaderInfoLog`.
3. If the shader compiles successfully, call `glAttachShader` to associate its descriptor to a program object.
4. After all the shaders have been successfully attached to a program, call `glLinkProgram` to link the compiled code into the program. Access the linker's output with `glGetProgramiv`.
5. Only one program can be active at a time, so call `glUseProgram` to identify which program should be active.

The goal of this section is to explain and demonstrate how these steps can be accomplished. Ideally, Steps 1–4 can be performed once at the start of the application. Step 5 should be performed only when needed.

8.4.1 Accessing Shader Files

It's customary to place code for each shader type in its own file. These are simple text files, and Android provides two general methods of accessing text files:

1. Place the files in the module's res/raw directory. Each file can be accessed through the `R.raw.`*`filename`* identifier. One disadvantange is that developers can't create subdirectories of res/raw.
2. Place the files in the project's assets directory. The advantage of this is that subdirectories can be created. The disadvantage is that accessing files requires obtaining the context's `AssetManager`, which takes more time than calling the context's `getResources` method with a resource ID.

The example code in this book adopts the second option. This is because shader files usually have the same names but different suffixes. To be specific, vertex shader files commonly end in .vert and fragment shader files end in .frag. If similarly-named files are placed in res/raw, they will be assigned identical resource IDs, making them indistinguishable.

Most of the example modules in this book have a class named `ShaderUtils`. The static methods in this class perform operations related to shaders and shader files. The `readFile` method receives a `Context` and a filename, and accesses the shader text with the following code:

```
try {
  InputStream input = context.getAssets().open(fileName);
  BufferedReader buf =
    new BufferedReader(new InputStreamReader(input));
  ...
  input.close();
} catch (IOException e) {
  e.printStackTrace();
}
```

The `getAssets` method returns the context's `AssetManager`. This provides an `open` method that returns an `InputStream` for the asset, and a `close` method that closes the `AssetManager`.

8.4.2 Compiling Shader Code

After the application has read the text in a shader file, the next step is to compile it. In OpenGL ES, shader compilation takes place at runtime. The advantage of this is that applications don't have to deal with intermediate build files. The disadvantage is that compilation can take a significant amount of time.

Before shader code can be compiled, it must be associated with a numeric descriptor. This requires two steps:

- Call `glCreateShader` with a constant that identifies the shader's type. This returns an integer to serve as the shader's descriptor.
- Call `glShaderSource` with the shader's descriptor and the shader code. This creates the association between the descriptor and the code.

In the first step, vertex shaders are identified by `GL_VERTEX_SHADER` and fragment shaders are identified by `GL_FRAGMENT_SHADER`. As an example, the following code obtains a descriptor for a fragment shader and associates it with a `String` named `fragShaderCode`. This `String` contains the content of a fragment shader file.

```
int fragDescriptor =
  GLES32.glCreateShader(GLES32.GL_FRAGMENT_SHADER);

GLES32.glShaderSource(fragDescriptor, fragShaderCode);
```

After associating the shader code with a descriptor, an application can compile the code by calling `glCompileShader` with the descriptor. Then the application can check if a compile error occured by calling `glGetShaderiv`.

The method's signature is given as follows:

```
glGetShaderiv(int shaderDesc, int name, int[] params, int offset)
```

The first argument identifies the shader's descriptor and the second identifies the type of information being sought. To obtain messages from the compiler, this should be set to `GL_COMPILE_STATUS`. The third argument contains the compiler status, and if the compile completed successfully, the first element of the array will be set to `GL_TRUE`.

If a compile error occurred, the application can access the error message by calling `glGetShaderInfoLog` with the shader's descriptor. This returns a `String` containing the error message.

The following code demonstrates how `glCompileShader`, `glGetShaderiv`, and `glGetShaderInfoLog` can be used in practice. This code attempts to compile the fragment shader identified by `fragDescriptor`:

```
GLES32.glCompileShader(fragDescriptor);

// Determine if the compile succeeded
int[] result = new int[1];
GLES32.glGetShaderiv(fragDescriptor, GLES32.GL_COMPILE_STATUS,
                     result, 0);

// If the compile failed, print the message to the log
if(result[0] == GLES32.GL_FALSE) {
  Log.v(TAG, GLES32.glGetShaderInfoLog(fragDescriptor));
}
```

The `glGetShaderiv` method can provide more information than just compile status. If the second argument is set to `GL_SHADER_SOURCE_LENGTH`, it provides the number of characters in the shader source code. If the second argument is set to `GL_SHADER_TYPE`, it provides the constant identifying the shader's type.

8.4.3 Programs

In OpenGL parlance, a program is a data object that contains the compiled results of the application's shaders. When the application starts, the program is passed to the GPU to configure the graphical processing pipeline.

In general, working with a program involves four steps:

1. Call `glCreateProgram` to create the program. This returns an integer that serves as the program's descriptor.
2. For each compiled shader, call `glAttachShader` to associate it with the program.
3. Call `glLinkProgram` to link all the shader code into the program.
4. Call `glUseProgram` to make the program part of the current rendering state.

These methods are easy to understand. To demonstrate this, the following code creates a program, attaches two shader descriptors, and links the shader code.

```
int program = GLES32.glCreateProgram();
GLES32.glAttachShader(program, vertDescriptor);
GLES32.glAttachShader(program, fragDescriptor);
GLES32.glLinkProgram(program);
```

An application can check the link operation's status by calling `glGetProgramiv`. This accepts the same arguments as the `glGetShaderiv` method discussed earlier. The only significant difference is that the second argument must be set to `GL_LINK_STATUS` instead of `GL_COMPILE_STATUS`.

If the link operation failed, the application can obtain the error message by calling `glGetProgramInfoLog`. This accepts the program's descriptor and returns a `String` containing the error message. The following code demonstrates how `glGetProgramiv` and `glGetProgramInfoLog` can be used:

```
// Check the link status
int[] result = new int[1];
GLES32.glGetProgramiv(program, GLES32.GL_LINK_STATUS, result, 0);

// Log the error message
if(result[0] == GLES32.GL_FALSE) {
  Log.v(TAG, GLES32.glGetProgramInfoLog(program));
}
```

An application can create multiple programs, but only one can be active at any time. This active program will be delivered to the GPU to configure the graphical pipeline. To make a program active, an application needs to call `glUseProgram` with the program's descriptor. An application can recompile the program's code and attach new shaders, but the content of the active program won't be changed until `glLinkProgram` is called.

8.5 Transformations and Uniform Data

Suppose that an app needs to rotate an object over time, perhaps due to animation. Mathematically, this can be accomplished by multiplying the object's coordinates by a special type of transformation matrix called a rotation matrix.

If a vertex shader receives this matrix, it can perform the matrix-vector multiplication needed to update the object's vertices. That is, it multiplies the coordinates of each vertex by the same matrix. Because the matrix remains constant between vertices, it should be provided as uniform data. If the name of the 4-by-4 matrix variable is `rot_matrix`, it can be declared in the vertex shader with the following code:

```
uniform mat4 rot_matrix;
```

The `uniform` modifier identifies the variable as uniform data, which means it won't change from vertex to vertex. It also can't be changed by the shader. Uniform variables are always read-only.

This section starts by explaining how applications can generate the matrices needed to transform vertices. Then we'll look at the code needed to pass uniform data to the shader. The last section of the chapter will demonstrate how transformation matrices can be generated and used in practical code.

8.5.1 Transformation Matrices

When we say that a vertex is being transformed, we mean that its coordinates may be changing in three ways:

- translation — shifting the vertex's position
- rotation — rotating the vertex through an angle about an axis
- scaling — moving the vertex toward or away from the origin

Mathematically, these transformations are represented by matrices. When a vertex's coordinates are multipled by a transformation matrix, its position is changed accordingly.

Many books discuss the mathematics underlying vertex transformations. They explain how the nature of the transformation determines the elements of the matrix, and explain the difference between matrices for translation, rotation, and scaling. This book doesn't delve into linear algebra, but focuses instead on generating these matrices using methods of Android's `Matrix` class.

The Matrix Class

Android provides at least two `Matrix` classes: one in the android.graphics package and one in android.opengl. This discussion focuses on the `Matrix` class in android.opengl. This provides a set of static functions, each ending in the letter `M`, that operate on 4-by-4 matrices stored in `float` arrays.

Table 8.4 lists six `Matrix` methods related to transformations. Chapter 9 will present other `Matrix` methods that involve three-dimensional projection.

Table 8.4

Transformation Methods of the Matrix Class

Methods	Description
`setIdentityM(float[] mat, int offset)`	Initializes the matrix to the identity matrix
`setRotateM(float[] mat, int offset, float angle, float x, float y, float z)`	Initializes the matrix to a rotation matrix that rotates by the given angle about the axis (x, y, z)
`translateM(float[] mat, int offset, float x, float y, float z)`	Translate matrix by (x, y, z)
`rotateM(float[] mat, int offset, float angle, float x, float y, float z)`	Rotate matrix by the given angle about the axis (x, y, z)
`scaleM(float[] mat, int offset, float x, float y, float z)`	Scale the matrix by factors x, y, and z
`multiplyMM(float[] result, int resultOffset, float[] matA, int offsetA, float[] matB, int offsetB)`	Multiply two matrices and store the result in a third

In each of these functions, the first argument is an array containing `float` values and the second argument is an offset into the array. The offset is helpful when multiple matrices are stored in the same array.

An identity matrix is a matrix whose diagonal elements equal 1 and whose off-diagonal elements equal 0. When a vertex's coordinates are multiplied by an identity matrix, the values of the coordinates remain constant. For this reason, we say that an identity matrix performs an identity transformation. The `setIdentityM` method initializes the input `float` array with columns of a 4-by-4 identity matrix.

Similarly, `setRotateM` initializes the `float` array with columns of a 4-by-4 rotation matrix. The `angle` argument identifies the number of degrees in the rotation angle, and if this value is positive, the rotation will be counter-clockwise. If `angle` is negative, the rotation will be clockwise. The last three arguments identify the axis of rotation.

For example, the following code initializes `mat` with a matrix that rotates vertices 40° counterclockwise about the z-axis, whose components are given as (0, 0, 1):

```
setRotateM(mat, 0, 40.0f, 0.0f, 0.0f, 1.0f);
```

Combining Transformations

The next three methods in the table—`translateM`, `rotateM`, and `scaleM`—modify an existing matrix to perform an additional transformation. If the matrix is an identity matrix, the function's transformation will be the only transformation.

For example, the following code initializes `matrix` as an identity matrix and then configures it to translate vertices by 0.2 in the x-direction and 0.3 in the y-direction:

```
Matrix.setIdentityM(matrix, 0);
Matrix.translateM(matrix, 0, 0.2f, 0.3f, 0.0f);
```

If a matrix was already configured to perform one or more transformations, the function will combine its transformation with the existing transformations. To see what I mean, consider the following code:

```
Matrix.setIdentityM(matrix, 0);
Matrix.translateM(matrix, 0, 0.2f, 0.3f, 0.0f);
Matrix.rotateM(matrix, 0, 40.0f, 0.0f, 0.0f, 1.0f);
```

It should be clear that this code configures `matrix` to perform a translation and a rotation. What isn't clear is the order in which the two transformations are performed. As it turns out, the rotation is performed *first* and the translation is performed *second*. Therefore, when performing multiple transformations, keep in mind that the first function's transformation will be performed last.

Another way to combine transformations is to multiply their matrices. This is made possible by the `multiplyMM` method. For example, the following code multiplies `matA` and `matB` and stores the result in `matC`.

```
Matrix.multiplyMM(matC, 0, matA, 0, matB, 0);
```

The order of the input matrices is important. The transformation of the first matrix will be performed *after* the transformation of the second matrix. Therefore, if `matA` performs translation and `matB` performs rotation, `matC` will perform rotation first and translation second.

8.5.2 Passing Uniforms to Shaders

After the transformation matrices are generated, the next step is to pass them to a shader. These matrices are usually passed as uniforms. and a shader can access this data using variable declarations that start with the `uniform` modifier. The following declaration shows what this looks like:

```
uniform mat4 trans_matrix;
```

The process of transferring uniform data to a shader is similar to that of transferring attribute data. There are two steps involved:

1. Call `glGetUniformLocation` with the name of the uniform variable. This returns an integer that identifies the uniform's location.
2. Call `glUniform*` or `glUniformMatrix*` to associate data with the uniform variable.

As discussed in Chapter 7, the integer associated with an attribute variable is called its *index*. The integer associated with a uniform variable is called its *location*. The reason for this difference is that attribute variables can *only* be declared in a vertex shader, so the index identifies a variable's position in the sequence. Uniform variables can be accessed by every shader in a program, so the value returned by `glGetUniformLocation` doesn't necessarily identify its order within any particular shader.

For example, the following code returns the location of the `trans_matrix` variable presented above:

```
int transLocation =
  GLES32.glGetUniformLocation(program, "trans_matrix");
```

A uniform may have different types of data associated with it. For this reason, OpenGL ES provides many methods that create the association. `glUniform*` associates a uniform with a scalar or vector value and `glUniformMatrix*` associates a uniform with a matrix value. Both methods have many variants available and Table 8.5 lists 25 of them.

Table 8.5

Methods for Setting Uniform Data (Abridged)

Method	Description
`glUniform1i(int location, int x)`	Associate an integer with the uniform variable at the given location
`glUniform1f(int location, float x)`	Associate a float with the uniform variable at the given location
`glUniform1iv(int location, int count, IntBuffer vec)`	Associate integer data with the given uniform int array
`glUniform1fv(int location, int count, FloatBuffer vec)`	Associate float data with the given uniform float array
`glUniform2i(int location, int x, int y)`	Associate two integers with the uniform ivec2 variable at the given location
`glUniform2f(int location, float x, float y)`	Associate two floats with the uniform vec2 variable at the given location
`glUniform2iv(int location, int count, IntBuffer vec)`	Associate integer data with the given uniform ivec2 array
`glUniform2fv(int location, int count, FloatBuffer vec)`	Associate float data with the given uniform vec2 array
`glUniform3i(int location, int x, int y, int z)`	Associate three integers with the uniform ivec3 variable at the location
`glUniform3f(int location, float x, float y, float z)`	Associate three floats with the uniform vec3 variable at the given location
`glUniform3iv(int location, int count, IntBuffer vec)`	Associate integer data with the given uniform ivec3 array
`glUniform3fv(int location, int count, FloatBuffer vec)`	Associate a float vector with the given uniform vec3 array
`glUniform4i(int location, int x, int y, int z, int w)`	Associate three integers with the uniform ivec4 variable at the location
`glUniform3f(int location, float x, float y, float z, float w)`	Associate three floats with the uniform vec4 variable at the given location
`glUniform4iv(int location, int count, IntBuffer vec)`	Associate integer data with the given uniform ivec4 array
`glUniform4fv(int location, int count, FloatBuffer vec)`	Associate float data with the given uniform vec4 array

`glUniformMatrix2fv(int location, int count, boolean transpose, FloatBuffer buff)`	Associate float data with the given uniform mat2 or mat2 array
`glUniformMatrix3fv(int location, int count, boolean transpose, FloatBuffer buff)`	Associate float data with the given uniform mat3 or mat3 array
`glUniformMatrix4fv(int location, int count, boolean transpose, FloatBuffer buff)`	Associate float data with the given uniform mat4 or mat4 array
`glUniformMatrix2x3fv(int location, int count, boolean transpose, FloatBuffer buff)`	Associate float data with the given uniform mat2x3 or mat2x3 array
`glUniformMatrix2x4fv(int location, int count, boolean transpose, FloatBuffer buff)`	Associate float data with the given uniform mat2x4 or mat2x4 array
`glUniformMatrix3x2fv(int location, int count, boolean transpose, FloatBuffer buff)`	Associate float data with the given uniform mat3x2 or mat3x2 array
`glUniformMatrix3x4fv(int location, int count, boolean transpose, FloatBuffer buff)`	Associate float data with the given uniform mat3x4 or mat3x4 array
`glUniformMatrix4x2fv(int location, int count, boolean transpose, FloatBuffer buff)`	Associate float data with the given uniform mat4x2 or mat4x2 array
`glUniformMatrix4x3fv(int location, int count, boolean transpose, FloatBuffer buff)`	Associate float data with the given uniform mat4x3 or mat4x3 array

The `GLES32` class provides many more variants of `glUniform*` and `glUniformMatrix*` than those listed in the table. Each method that accepts an NIO buffer, such as `IntBuffer` and `FloatBuffer`, will also accept a primitive array, such as an `int[]` or `float[]`, followed by an offset into the array.

An example will demonstrate this. The following methods both associate a 4-by-4 floating-point matrix with the uniform variable whose location is 2:

```
glUniformMatrix4fv(2, 1, false, matrixBuffer);
glUniformMatrix4fv(2, 1, false, matrixArray, 0);
```

The third argument indicates that the matrix should be transferred to the device in its column-major order. If this is set to `true`, the matrix will be transposed beforehand.

The second argument, `count`, indicates that only one matrix in the shader should be associated with the data. If the shader variable is an array of matrices, `count` can be set to a larger value to associate the data with multiple matrices.

This `count` argument is present in all methods whose names end in `v`. These methods make it possible to associate data with array variables in the shader. For example, suppose the shader contains the following declaration:

```
uniform vec3[4] colors;
```

The following code associates the data in `colorBuffer` with all of the elements in the shader's `colors` array:

```
int loc = GLES32.glGetUniformLocation(program, "colors");

GLES32.glUniform3fv(loc, 1, false, colorBuffer);
```

In a `glUniform*` method, the end of the method name identifies the size of the shader variable to be affected, the type of the variable's elements, and whether the method is intended to associate data with an array variable. If the name is `glUniformXYZ`, the following conclusions can be drawn:

- If *X* is 1, the method associates data with a scalar variable or scalar array. If *X* is greater than 1, the method associates data with a vector variable or vector array.
- If *Y* is `f`, the shader variable contains one or more `float`s. If *Y* is `i`, the shader variable contains one or more `int`s. Though not listed in the table, *Y* may also be set to `ui`, which indicates that the shader variable contains unsigned integers.
- If *Z* is set to `v`, the method is intended to associate data with an array variable in the shader. The method has a `count` argument that identifies how many elements of the target array should be affected. If *Z* isn't set, the method associates data with a single element in the shader.

Let's look at a second example. The following code associates an integer named `index` with a shader variable named `ind`:

```
int loc = GLES32.glGetUniformLocation(program, "ind");

GLES32.glUniform1i(loc, 1, false, index);
```

Because `glUniform*` and `glUniformMatrix*` associate host data with the GPU, it's important to invoke them only when necessary.

8.6 Example Application – Four Triangles

The ch08_fourtriangles module has a lot in common with the ch07_triangle module presented in the last chapter. But it demonstrates four new capabilities:

- Generating a transformation matrix using the `Matrix` class
- Obtaining the location of a uniform variable
- Passing uniform data to a shader
- Instanced rendering

The last point, instanced rendering, involves drawing multiple copies of an object while only sending one set of vertices to the GPU. In this case, the application draws four copies of a triangle. Figure 8.1 shows what this looks like:

Figure 8.1 The ch08_fourtriangles Module

The application generates a 4-by-4 matrix that rotates points by 15°. The vertex shader receives the rotation matrix and uses it to update the coordinates of each vertex. Listing 8.1 presents the vertex shader's code.

The shader starts by multiplying the incoming vertices by `rot_matrix`. This uniform variable is a 4-by-4 floating-point matrix whose values are provided by the host application.

Listing 8.1: ch08_fourtriangles/src/main/assets/fourtriangles.vert

```
#version 300 es

in  vec2 in_coords;
in  vec3 in_color;
out vec3 new_color;

// Uniform variable - rotation matrix
uniform mat4 rot_matrix;

vec2 offset[4] = vec2[4] (
  vec2(-0.5, -0.5), vec2(-0.5, 0.5),
  vec2(0.5, -0.5), vec2(0.5, 0.5));

void main(void) {

  // Rotate the incoming vertex
  vec4 new_coords = rot_matrix * vec4(in_coords, 0.0, 1.0);

  // Apply the offset based on the instance
  new_coords.xy += offset[gl_InstanceID];

  // Set the output coordinates and color
  gl_Position = new_coords;
  new_color = in_color;
}
```

After rotating the input coordinates, the shader applies an offset. The offset depends on the built-in `gl_InstanceID` variable, which identifies which of the four instances is being drawn. The shader uses this as an index into the `offset` array and adds the array element to the coordinates.

The last line in the vertex shader sets the output variable, `new_color`, equal to the input variable, `in_color`. The fragment shader receives `new_color` and uses it to set the color of the outgoing fragment. Listing 8.2 presents the code for the fragment shader.

Listing 8.2: ch08_fourtriangles/src/main/assets/fourtriangles.frag

```
#version 300 es

in  vec3 new_color;
out vec4 out_color;
void main() {
  out_color = vec4(new_color, 1.0);
}
```

This fragment shader is trivially simple, but fragment shaders can perform sophisticated operations to compute fragment colors. Chapter 9 will explain how fragment shaders can assign colors using the Blinn-Phong lighting model.

8.6.1 The FourTrianglesRenderer Class

To handle its rendering, the `FourTrianglesActivity` creates and configures a `FourTrianglesRenderer`. This accesses the `GLES32` object to draw its triangles and Listing 8.3 presents the code.

Listing 8.3: ch08_fourtriangles/src/main/java/.../FourTrianglesRenderer.java

```
class FourTrianglesRenderer
  implements GvrView.StereoRenderer {

  private static final String VERTEX_SHADER =
    "fourtriangles.vert";

  private static final String FRAGMENT_SHADER =
    "fourtriangles.frag";

  private Context context;
  private int coordIndex, colorIndex, rotMatrixLocation;
  private FloatBuffer vertexBuffer, matrixBuffer;

  // Vertex data
  private static final float[] vertexData = {
    -0.1f, -0.0866f, 1.0f, 0.0f, 0.0f,    // First vertex
     0.0f,  0.0866f, 0.0f, 1.0f, 0.0f,    // Second vertex
     0.1f, -0.0866f, 0.0f, 0.0f, 1.0f};   // Third vertex

  FourTrianglesRenderer(Context ctx) {
    context = ctx;

    // Initialize rotation matrix
    float[] rotMatrix = new float[16];
    Matrix.setRotateM(rotMatrix, 0, 15.0f, 0.0f, 0.0f, 1.0f);

    // Store attribute data in an NIO buffer
    ByteBuffer tempBuffer =
      ByteBuffer.allocateDirect(vertexData.length * 4);
    tempBuffer.order(ByteOrder.nativeOrder());
    vertexBuffer = tempBuffer.asFloatBuffer();
    vertexBuffer.put(vertexData);
    vertexBuffer.rewind();
```

Listing 8.3: ch08_fourtriangles/src/main/java/.../FourTrianglesRenderer.java (Continued)

```
    // Store uniform data in an NIO buffer
    tempBuffer =
        ByteBuffer.allocateDirect(rotMatrix.length * 4);
    tempBuffer.order(ByteOrder.nativeOrder());
    matrixBuffer = tempBuffer.asFloatBuffer();
    matrixBuffer.put(rotMatrix);
    matrixBuffer.rewind();
  }

  public void onSurfaceCreated(EGLConfig config) {

    // Set the region's background color and line width
    GLES32.glClearColor(1.0f, 1.0f, 1.0f, 1.0f);
    GLES32.glLineWidth(10);

    // Read and compile vertex shader
    int vertDescriptor =
      GLES32.glCreateShader(GLES32.GL_VERTEX_SHADER);
    String vertFile =
      ShaderUtils.readFile(context, VERTEX_SHADER);
    GLES32.glShaderSource(vertDescriptor, vertFile);
    ShaderUtils.compileShader(vertDescriptor);

    // Read and compile fragment shader
    int fragDescriptor =
      GLES32.glCreateShader(GLES32.GL_FRAGMENT_SHADER);
    String fragFile =
      ShaderUtils.readFile(context, FRAGMENT_SHADER);
    GLES32.glShaderSource(fragDescriptor, fragFile);
    ShaderUtils.compileShader(fragDescriptor);

    // Create program and bind attributes
    int program = GLES32.glCreateProgram();
    GLES32.glAttachShader(program, vertDescriptor);
    GLES32.glAttachShader(program, fragDescriptor);

    // Link and use program
    ShaderUtils.linkProgram(program);
    GLES32.glUseProgram(program);

    // Obtain the location of the uniform variable
    coordIndex =
      GLES32.glGetAttribLocation(program, "in_coords");
    colorIndex = GLES32.glGetAttribLocation(program, "in_color");
    rotMatrixLocation =
      GLES32.glGetUniformLocation(program, "rot_matrix");
  }
```

Listing 8.3: ch08_fourtriangles/src/main/java/.../FourTrianglesRenderer.java (Continued)

```
  public void onNewFrame(HeadTransform headTransform) {

    // Fill the rendering region with the background color
    GLES32.glClear(GLES32.GL_COLOR_BUFFER_BIT);

    // Associate coordinate data with in_coords
    vertexBuffer.rewind();
    GLES32.glEnableVertexAttribArray(coordIndex);
    GLES32.glVertexAttribPointer(coordIndex, 2,
        GLES32.GL_FLOAT, false, 20, vertexBuffer);

    // Associate color data with in_colors
    vertexBuffer.position(2);
    GLES32.glEnableVertexAttribArray(colorIndex);
    GLES32.glVertexAttribPointer(colorIndex, 3,
        GLES32.GL_FLOAT, false, 20, vertexBuffer);

    // Associate rotation matrix with rot_matrix
    GLES32.glUniformMatrix4fv(rotMatrixLocation,
      1, false, matrixBuffer);

    // Draw four triangle instances
    GLES32.glDrawArraysInstanced(GLES32.GL_LINE_LOOP, 0, 3, 4);
  }

  @Override
  public void onDrawEye(Eye eye) {}

  @Override
  public void onSurfaceChanged(int width, int height) {}

  @Override
  public void onFinishFrame(Viewport viewport) {}

  @Override
  public void onRendererShutdown() {}
}
```

The renderer's constructor is essentially similar to that of the `TriangleRenderer` discussed in Chapter 7. The main difference is that the constructor creates and initializes a `FloatBuffer` to hold the rotation matrix to be passed to the vertex shader.

The matrix is initially stored as a 16-element `float` array. The constructor invokes `Matrix.setRotateM` to generate values of a rotation matrix that rotates vertices by 15°. After generating the matrix, the constructor creates a direct `FloatBuffer`, writes the matrix data to the buffer, and then rewinds the buffer.

The onSurfaceCreated method handles the initial shader processing. It starts by obtaining a descriptor for the vertex shader, reading the shader's code, associating the descriptor with the code, and compiling the code. Then it performs the same operations on the fragment shader.

After compiling the shaders, onSurfaceCreated creates a program object and attaches both shader descriptors to the program. Then it links the program and makes it active. To simplify the code, the method accesses a helper class called ShaderUtils, which will be presented shortly.

The onNewFrame method associates attribute data in vertexBuffer with the shader variables named in_coords and in_color. Then it calls glUniformMatrix4fv to associate the rotation matrix in matrixBuffer with the location of the corresponding uniform variable.

The last method called in onNewFrame is glDrawArraysInstanced, which launches the drawing process. This is similar to the glDrawArrays method discussed in Chapter 7, but it tells the renderer to draw multiple instances of the object. Its signature is as follows:

```
glDrawArraysInstanced(int mode, int firstVertex, int vertexCount,
                      int instanceCount)
```

As with glDrawArrays, the first argument identifies the type of primitive that should be drawn and the second identifies the index of the first vertex. It's important not to confuse the third and fourth arguments. vertexCount sets the number of vertices to be drawn and instanceCount sets the number of instances. In Listing 8.3, vertexCount is set to 3 because each triangle has three vertices. instanceCount is set to 4 because the application should draw four instances of the triangle.

8.6.2 The ShaderUtils Class

Listing 8.4 presents the code of the project's ShaderUtils class. This provides three static methods that perform operations related to shaders and programs:

1. readFile — reads the shader file in the project's assets directory and returns a String containing its text
2. compileShader — compiles the shader, and in the event of an error, prints error messages to the log
3. linkProgram — links the program's code, and in the event of an error, prints error messages to the log

Listing 8.4: ch08_fourtriangles/src/main/java/.../ShaderUtils.java

```
class ShaderUtils {

  private static final String TAG = "FourTriangles";

  static String readFile(Context context, String fileName) {

    // Read file
    String line;
    StringBuilder sb = new StringBuilder();

    try {

      // Open the asset file with the given name
      InputStream input = context.getAssets().open(fileName);
      BufferedReader buf =
        new BufferedReader(new InputStreamReader(input));

      // Combine the lines of text into the StringBuilder
      while((line = buf.readLine()) != null){
        sb.append(line).append("\n");
      }

      // Close the input stream
      input.close();
    } catch (IOException e) {
      e.printStackTrace();
    }
    return sb.toString();
  }

  static void compileShader(int shader) {
    int[] result = new int[1];

    // Compile shader code
    GLES32.glCompileShader(shader);

    // Obtain the result of the compile operation
    GLES32.glGetShaderiv(shader, GLES32.GL_COMPILE_STATUS,
      result, 0);
    if(result[0] == GLES32.GL_FALSE) {

      // Log the compiler's message
      Log.v(TAG, GLES32.glGetShaderInfoLog(shader));
      System.exit(1);
    }
  }
```

Listing 8.4: ch08_fourtriangles/src/main/java/.../ShaderUtils.java (Continued)

```
  static void linkProgram(int program) {
    int[] result = new int[1];

    GLES32.glLinkProgram(program);
    GLES32.glGetProgramiv(program, GLES32.GL_LINK_STATUS,
      result, 0);
    if(result[0] == GLES32.GL_FALSE) {
      Log.v(TAG, GLES32.glGetProgramInfoLog(program));
      System.exit(1);
    }
  }
}
```

This class will be used throughout this book's example code. Therefore, it's a good idea to have a basic understanding of its methods and what they accomplish.

The `readFile` method receives the project's `Context` and uses it to access the project's `AssetManager`. It calls the manager's `open` method to obtain an `InputStream` for the shader file and then uses a `BufferedReader` to read each line of the file. Afterward, it closes the `InputStream`.

The Java NIO package has recently been updated to provide methods that efficiently extract text from files. But at the time of this writing, these methods aren't available in the Android SDK.

The `compileShader` and `linkProgram` methods are similar in structure. Both perform an operation, check for an error, and print the error message to the log if an error occurred. The `compileShader` method invokes `glCompileShader`, `glGetShaderiv`, and `glGetShaderInfoLog`. The `linkProgram` method invokes `glLinkProgram`, `glGetProgramiv`, and `glGetProgramInfoLog`.

8.7 Summary

Chapter 7 explained how applications can pass attribute data (vertex coordinates, colors, and so on) to shaders running on the GPU. This chapter has progressed further and discussed how applications can pass uniform data to shaders.

During the course of the discussion, the chapter explored the important subject of shader coding. Shaders are coded in GLSL, which is similar to C in many respects. But GLSL provides a wide range of data types and built-in variables specifically for graphical processing.

Every graphical application discussed in this book contains two types of shaders: vertex shaders and fragment shaders. The primary job of a vertex shader is to set the coordinates of the model's vertices. The primary job of a fragment shader is to set the color of each fragment. Both types of shaders use the same programming language and have the same general structure, but they can access different types of built-in variables.

When coding graphical applications, it's important to know how to rotate, translate, and scale the vertices in the model. These operations are collectively referred to as transformations, and they can be performed mathematically using matrix-vector multiplication. Android's `Matrix` class provides static methods for generating and manipulating transformation matrices and the example code demonstrated how these methods can be used in practice.

Chapter 9

Rendering Objects in Three Dimensions

So far, all of the example applications discussed in this book have displayed graphics in two dimensions. But 2-D applications are no fun. To be immersive, a Daydream app needs to create a three-dimensional world with lighting and color. The goal of this chapter is to present a series of topics that bridge the gap between 2-D and 3-D development.

To ensure that objects will be drawn in perspective, three-dimensional applications require additional vertex transformations than those discussed in preceding chapters. In particular, an application needs to perform a view transformation, which accounts for the viewer's position and orientation, and a projection transformation, which accounts for the properties of the viewing volume. The first section of this chapter explains the theory behind these transformations.

Nothing creates the illusion of reality like seeing light reflected off of objects in the model. The mathematics underlying computer-generated illumination is difficult, but the Blinn-Phong Model has proven reliable in many applications. This chapter introduces this model and presents a fragment shader that shows how it can be implemented in practice.

Another major concern in 3-D application development is depth. If one object is closer to the viewer than another, the first object should appear larger than the second. If the first object overlaps the second, its pixels should be drawn on top of the pixels of the second object. This may seem obvious, but depth testing is an important topic and this chapter explains how to customize the depth testing process.

The last section of the chapter presents a Daydream application that displays cubes in three-dimensional space. This application incorporates Blinn-Phong lighting, view and projection transformations, and custom depth testing. The module's code should serve as an excellent starting point for those planning to develop VR apps for the Daydream.

9.1 Transformations and Head Tracking

As discussed in Chapter 8, the methods of the `Matrix` class make it possible to translate, rotate, and scale coordinates. For 2-D applications, these operations are the only transformations you need to know about. But if an application needs to render objects in three dimensions, the vertex transformation process becomes more complex.

To be specific, the application needs to be concerned with two factors: the viewer's location/orientation and the shape of the three-dimensional volume containing the model. To take these factors into account, the application needs to perform additional transformations. This means generating and applying new transformation matrices.

In a regular application, these transformations are determined by the developer. But in a virtual reality application, they're determined by the user, or more precisely, the orientation of the user's headset. This section will explain how an application can access the headset's data. But first, I'd like to discuss the important topic of coordinate systems.

9.1.1 Transformation Coordinate Systems

Modern 3-D applications transform an object's vertices multiple times before drawing the object in the rendering region. To keep track of the different transformations, developers use specific terms to refer to the object's coordinates at each stage. Terms differ slightly between sources, but the most common terms are as follows:

- *object coordinates* — initial coordinates given relative to the object's origin
- *world coordinates* — the object's coordinates after being placed in the rendering volume (world), given relative to the volume's origin
- *eye coordinates* — the object's coordinates after the viewer's location and orientation have been set
- *clip coordinates* — the object's final coordinates after the viewing region has been defined

To obtain clip coordinates for an object, an application needs to perform at least three transformations. The *model transformation* converts object coordinates to world coordinates, the *view transformation* converts world coordinates to eye coordinates, and the *projection transformation* converts eye coordinates to clip coordinates.

Model transformations are the easiest to work with. These consist of the basic translations, rotations, and scaling operations needed to set the object's initial position and orientation. If an object's new origin should be (–5.0, –4.0, –3.0), the transformation will be a simple translation that adds (–5.0, –4.0, –3.0) to each of the model's vertices.

Chapter 8 introduced the methods of the `Matrix` class that perform these simple transformations. The matrix that performs the model transformation is referred to as the *model matrix.*

There is one important point to be aware of. By convention, the direction into the rendering volume is given as the *negative* z-direction. Therefore, if Object A's origin is moved to (0, 0, –5) and Object B's origin is moved to (0, 0, –10), Object B will appear further away than Object A.

9.1.2 View Transformation

After the model's objects have been placed in their positions, the next step is to define how the model will be viewed. This is accomplished through the view transformation, which converts the world coordinates of each vertex to eye coordinates. Mathematically, this transformation is represented by a matrix called the *view matrix.*

In a Google VR app, obtaining the view matrix involves two steps:

1. Initialize the view matrix as each new frame is drawn.
2. Update the view matrix to account for the user's position/orientation.

This discussion presents the code needed to implement both steps. The ch09_cubes module presented at the end of the chapter demonstrates how these steps are performed in an application.

Initializing the View Matrix

As discussed in Chapter 6, a `StereoRenderer` calls `onNewFrame` just before each new frame is drawn. When this is called, the application needs to reset the view matrix. That is, it needs to configure the view matrix so that it reflects the position and orientation of the user's Daydream headset.

This initial configuration can be accomplished by calling the `setLookAtM` method of the `Matrix` class. The method's signature is given as follows:

```
setLookAtM(float[] matrix, int offset,
  float eyeX, float eyeY, float eyeZ,
  float centerX, float centerY, float centerZ,
  float upX, float upY, float upZ)
```

Like the `Matrix` methods discussed in Chapter 8, the first argument of `setLookAtM` is a `float` array that will contain the output matrix. The second argument is the index of the first element of the array to hold the 4-by-4 matrix computed by the method.

The last nine arguments provide information about the viewer's location, the target of the viewer's observation, and the viewer's orientation:

- eyeX, eyeY, eyeZ — coordinates of the viewer's location
- centerX, centerY, centerZ — coordinates of where the viewer is looking
- upX, upY, upZ — vector that identifies the viewer's "up" direction

An example will clarify how this method can be called. Suppose the viewer should be placed at (5.0, 4.0, 3.0) and oriented to look at the point (0.0, 3.0, –3.0). If the viewer's up-direction is the positive y-axis (0.0, 1.0, 0.0), the required matrix can be generated with the following code:

```
setLookAtM(matrix, 0, 5.0f, 4.0f, 3.0f, 0.0f, 3.0f, -3.0f,
  0.0f, 1.0f, 0.0f)
```

Google's example code establishes a convention that will be adopted throughout this book. This convention places the viewer at (0.0, 0.0, 0.01) and orients the viewer to look down the z-axis (0.0, 0.0, 1.0). The viewer's up-direction is always the positive y-axis, so the initial view matrix will be obtained with the following code:

```
Matrix.setLookAtM(viewMatrix, 0, 0.0f, 0.0f, 0.01f,
  0.0f, 0.0f, 0.0f, 0.0f, 1.0f, 0.0f);
```

For this chapter, initializing the view matrix is the only operation performed in the onNewFrame method. However, the HeadTransform provided by the method is very helpful and can be used to determine what object the viewer is looking at.

Updating the View Matrix with Eye Data

When drawing a frame, it's not enough to know the headset's position and orientation. The application needs to take into account the orientations of the user's eyes. This information is contained in the Eye object provided by the onDrawEye method of the StereoRenderer.

The most important method of the Eye class is getEyeView. This doesn't accept any arguments, and returns a float array containing a 4-by-4 matrix that can be used to update the view matrix.

The updating process consists of pre-multiplying the view matrix with the result of getEyeView. Chapter 8 explained how the multiplyMM method of the Matrix class can be used to multiply matrices. The following code demonstrates how this can be used:

```
public void onNewFrame(HeadTransform headTransform) {

  // Initialize the view matrix
  Matrix.setLookAtM(initMatrix, 0, 0.0f, 0.0f, 0.01f,
    0.0f, 0.0f, 0.0f, 0.0f, 1.0f, 0.0f);
}

public void onDrawEye(Eye eye) {

  ...
  Matrix.multiplyMM(viewMatrix, 0,
    eye.getEyeView(), 0, initMatrix, 0);
}
```

In this code, the initial matrix and result matrix have different names because `multiplyMM` returns undefined results if the result matrix overlaps one of the input matrices.

Applications frequently combine the model matrix and the view matrix to form a matrix called the *modelview matrix*. This matrix performs the model transformation first and the view transformation second.

For example, if the model matrix is given as `modelMatrix` and the view matrix is given as `viewMatrix`, the following code will determine the modelview matrix:

```
Matrix.multiplyMM(modelViewMatrix, 0, viewMatrix, 0,
                  modelMatrix, 0);
```

Matrix multiplication isn't commutative, which means A*B doesn't equal B*A. When multiplying matrices, it's important to make sure they're in the correct order.

9.1.3 Projection Transformation

After positioning the model's vertices and setting the viewer's position and direction, the next step is to define the volume containing the model. This is called the application's *viewing region*, and in most cases, it has one of two shapes:

- A three-dimensional box whose opposite faces have the same size
- A volume whose front face is smaller than its rear face. This is frequently called a truncated pyramid or *frustum*.

Setting the shape of the viewing region is important because it determines how objects in the model will be displayed. Figure 9.1 shows what the two shapes look like.

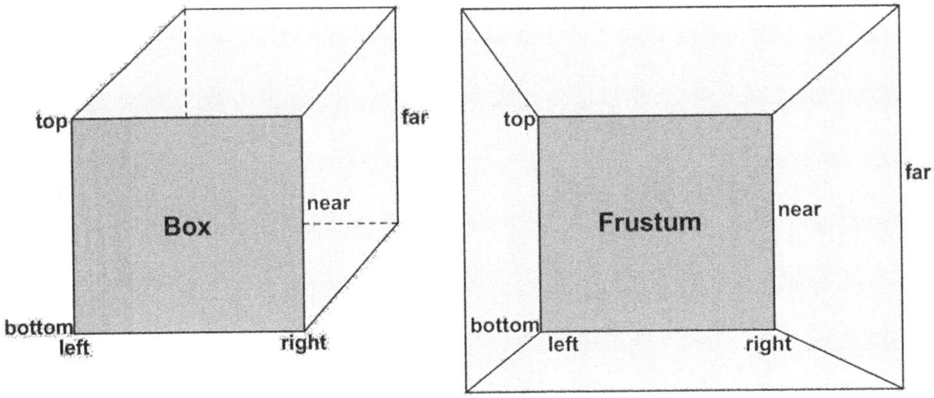

Figure 9.1 Viewing Regions

The primary difference between the two involves the perception of depth. If objects are placed in the box-like volume, their displayed size will remain constant regardless of their depth. If objects are placed in a frustum, near objects will be displayed larger than far objects.

In other words, objects in a frustum resemble objects in the real world. Because VR apps are expected to resemble reality as closely as possible, this book will only be concerned with frustum-shaped volumes.

When we say that an object is "placed in a volume," what we're really saying is that the object's vertices are transformed relative to the volume. This transformation is called *projection*. A matrix that performs projection is called a *projection matrix*.

If a projection transforms objects so that they appear smaller as they get further away, it's called a perspective projection. The `Matrix` class provides two static methods, `frustumM` and `perspectiveM`, that provide matrices for perspective projections. In regular OpenGL ES apps, these are the methods to know.

But a Google VR app can obtain a projection matrix through the `Eye` object provided by `onDrawEye`. This has a method called `getPerspective`, which returns a `float` array containing the 4-by-4 matrix to perform the perspective projection.The signature of `getPerspective` is given as follows:

```
getPerspective(float near, float far)
```

The two arguments set the z-values of the frustum's near face and far face. In other words, `getPerspective` won't let you set the frustum's vertical and horizontal dimensions, but you can identify the range of the frustum's depth.

In keeping with Google's convention, the VR apps in this book position the frustum's near plane at z = 0.1 and the far plane at z = 100.0. The following code obtains the perspective matrix to be applied:

```
float[] projMatrix = eye.getPerspective(0.1f, 100.0f);
```

The product of a model matrix, view matrix, and projection matrix is called the model-view-projection matrix, or the MVP matrix. This transforms coordinates from object coordinates to clip coordinates.

In general, it's a good idea to use the perspective matrix provided by `getPerspective`. But applications can customize the frustum's shape by calling the `getFov` method of the `Eye` object. This returns a `FieldOfView` object whose methods make it possible to read and set the half-angles of the frustum's field of view. Table 9.1 lists ten of these methods. Note that all angle measures are given in degrees.

Table 9.1

FieldOfView Methods

Method	Description
`getLeft()/ setLeft(float left)`	Access the left field of view half-angle
`getRight()/ setRight(float right)`	Access the right field of view half-angle
`getBottom()/ setBottom(float bottom)`	Access the bottom field of view half-angle
`getTop()/ setTop(float left)`	Access the top field of view half-angle
`setAngles( float left, float right, float bottom, float top)`	Set the left, right, bottom, and top field of view half-angles
`toPerspectiveMatrix( float near, float far, float[] perspective, int offset)`	Generate a matrix to perform the projection transformation with the frustum whose half-angles have been configured

To configure the frustum's shape, an application needs to call one or more of the `set`*XYZ* methods listed in the table. Then it can generate the projection matrix by calling `toPerspectiveMatrix`. The elements of the 4-by-4 matrix will be stored in the `float` array identified by the method's third argument.

9.2 Polygon Culling

The ch07_triangle and ch08_fourtriangles applications both combined vertices into lines by setting the primitive mode to GL_LINE_LOOP. But to display solid shapes, most VR apps combine vertices into triangles using modes like GL_TRIANGLES, GL_TRIANGLE_STRIP, and GL_TRIANGLE_FAN. It's not uncommon for graphical models in VR apps to contain millions of triangles.

But not all of the triangles will be visible to the viewer at the same time. To improve performance, an application can tell the renderer which triangles should be rendered and which should be discarded. This discarding process is called *polygon culling*. To configure this operation, an application needs to perform three steps:

1. Enable polygon cullling by calling glEnable with GL_CULL_FACE.
2. Call glFrontFace with a value that identifies which vertex orientation corresponds to a front-facing triangle.
3. Call glCullFace to identify whether front-facing triangles should be culled, rear-facing triangles should be culled, or all triangles should be culled.

In the second step, the argument of glFrontFace can be set to GL_CW or GL_CCW. The default value is GL_CCW, which means that every triangle whose vertices are oriented in a counterclockwise manner will be considered a front-facing triangle. If the argument is set to GL_CW, every triangle whose vertices are oriented in a clockwise manner will be considered a front-facing triangle.

In the third step, glCullFace identifies which triangles should be discarded. The argument of this function can be set to one of four values:

- GL_FRONT — Discard front-facing polygons
- GL_BACK — Discard back-facing polygons
- GL_FRONT_AND_BACK — Discard all polygons

As an example, the following code tells the renderer to discard all triangles whose vertices are oriented in a clockwise manner:

```
glEnable(GL_CULL_FACE);
glFrontFace(GL_CW);
glCullFace(GL_FRONT);
```

It's important to note that polygon culling only discards triangle primitives. Lines and points are not affected.

9.3 Lighting Models

To draw a three-dimensional scene, it isn't enough to have three-dimensional vertices in a three-dimensional rendering volume. To create the illusion of depth, objects need to reflect light based on their positions relative to a light source.

Many models have been developed to determine how light should reflect from an object's surface. This section looks at two popular models: the Phong Model and the Blinn-Phong Model. Both models involve three general steps:

1. Create one or more light sources. Pass this information to shaders as uniforms.
2. For each vertex in the model, find the vector perpendicular to the surface. This is called the normal vector. This should also be passed to shaders.
3. Using the information provided by Steps 1 and 2, the fragment shader computes a fragment's color using the lighting model.

This discussion presents the theory behind the Phong Model and the Blinn-Phong Model. The ch09_cubes module discussed at the end of the chapter presents a fragment shader that implements the Blinn-Phong Model.

9.3.1 The Phong Lighting Model

In 1973, a Ph.D dissertation by Bui Tuong Phong described a new method of modeling light reflected from objects in a computer-generated model. This model splits light into three components:

- ambient component — background illumination that travels in all directions
- diffuse component — light that travels in one direction
- specular component — light that travels in one direction and particularly affects the point on the object closest to the light source

Phong's model presents a formula for determining the illumination at a given point. $I = I_a + I_d + I_s$, where I_s is the ambient component of the light source, I_d is the diffuse component, and I_s is the specular component. I_a applies equally to every point in the model, so you can think of it as the base lighting of a scene.

To compute the diffuse component, the fragment shader needs to know the normal vector at the given point. If the normal vector and the light vector (the vector from the light source to the point on the surface) have the same direction, I_d will be significant. If the two vectors are perpendicular, I_d will be zero.

Using math terminology, we say that I_d is proportional to $N \cdot L$, where N is the normal vector at the surface point and L is the vector from the point to the light source. Figure 9.2 depicts the relationship between these vectors.

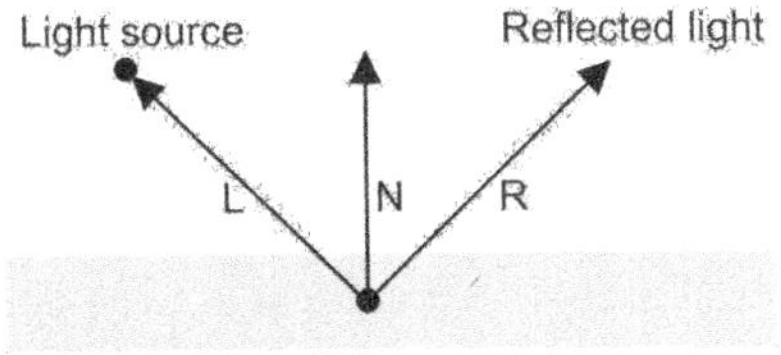

Figure 9.2 Light Vectors and the Normal Vector

Computing the specular component of light is more difficult because it relates to how *shiny* the object is. To develop an expression for specular reflection, Phong made two important observations.

1. The shinier a surface is, the more concentrated the brightness is around points of greatest reflectivity.
2. The shine perceived by the viewer depends on the angle of the viewer to the light reflected from the point.

Taking these observations into account, Phong derived an expression for specular illumination: I_s is proportional to $(V \cdot R)^n$, where V is the vector from the point to the viewer, R is the vector of light reflected at the point, and n represents the surface's reflectivity at the point. For shiny surfaces, n will be large and I_s will be concentrated around points where $V \cdot R$ is high. Figure 9.3 illustrates how these vectors are related:

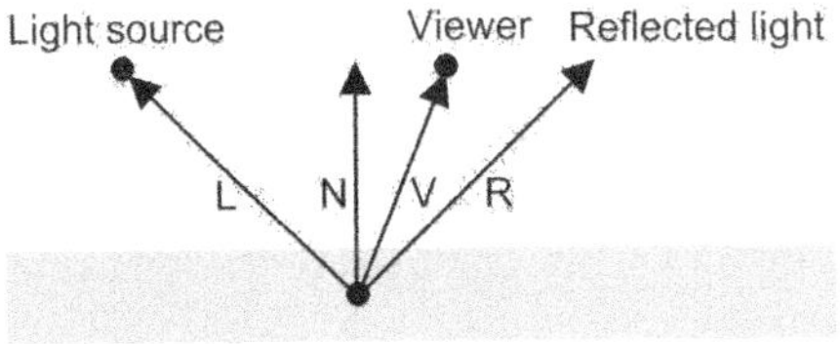

Figure 9.3 Vectors Involved in Specular Illumination for Phong Shading

The R vector in Figure 9.3 has the same meaning as the R vector in Figure 9.2. Therefore, using vector projection, R can be obtained in terms of L and N:

$$R = 2(N \cdot L)N - L$$

Summing the expressions for the three light components, the Phong model presents the following equation for the total illumination for a fragment:

$$I = k_a + k_d(N \cdot L) + k_s(V \cdot R)^n$$

In this equation, k_a, k_d, and k_s are constants identifying the basic intensities of ambient, diffuse, and specular illumination. They're not mathematically derived, but must be selected by the developer or artist to obtain suitable lighting properties.

9.3.2 The Blinn-Phong Model

The Phong model provides a good approximation to real-world lighting, but there are two important concerns. First, the model produces unaccepable results when V and R are separated by 90° or more. Second, computing $V \cdot R$ is unnecessarily complicated.

To resolve these issues, Jim Blinn changed the model so that I_s equals $(N \cdot H)^{n'}$, where H is the vector halfway between L and V and n' is a new value for the surface's reflectivity. Figure 9.4 shows how these vectors are related.

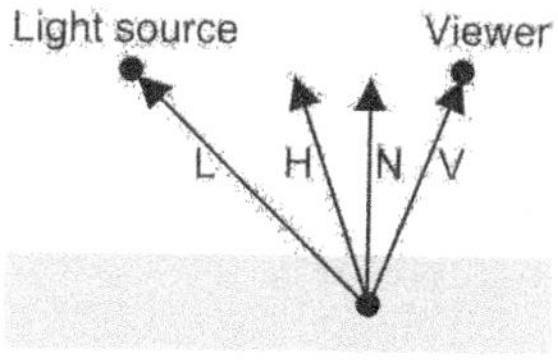

Figure 9.4 Vectors Involved in Specular Illumination for Blinn-Phong Shading

N and H are closer to one another than V and R. To make sure the result approximates that of the Phong model, many applications increase the exponent of $N \cdot H$. It's common to set the new exponent, n', equal to four times the old exponent, n.

Replacing $(V \cdot R)^n$ with $(N \cdot H)^{n'}$, the Blinn-Phong model produces the following equation for the illumination of a fragment:

$$I = k_a + k_d(N \cdot L) + k_s(N \cdot H)^{n'}$$

The discussion at the end of this chapter presents code that demonstrates how a fragment shader can determine a fragment's color using Blinn-Phong illumination.

9.4 Depth Testing

Chapter 8 explained how fragment shaders can assign depth values to fragments using the `gl_Depth` variable. If the shader doesn't assign a value, each fragment's depth will be determined by the z-coordinate of the corresponding point in the primitive.

The GPU stores a depth value for each (x, y) location in the viewport. After each fragment shader execution, the GPU compares the fragment's depth to the depth value at the fragment's location. If the fragment's depth is lower, the fragment's color will be stored. If the fragment's depth is greater than or equal, it will be discarded. This process is called *z-culling*, and it ensures that near objects are drawn on top of far objects.

OpenGL ES applications can also execute a custom depth test. This compares each fragment's depth to values in a memory location called a *depth buffer*. The nature of the comparison and the values in the depth buffer can be controlled in code.

To configure a custom depth test, an application needs to perform at least five steps:

1. When configuring the `GvrView`, set the fifth argument of `setEGLConfigChooser` to the number of bits to be stored for each depth buffer value.
2. In the renderer's code, enable depth testing by calling `glEnable` with `GL_DEPTH_TEST`.
3. Identify the comparison to be performed by calling `glDepthFunc`.
4. Set an initial value for the depth buffer by calling `glClearDepthf` with a value between 0.0 and 1.0.
5. Fill the depth buffer with the initial value by calling `glClear` with the `GL_DEPTH_BUFFER_BIT` bit set.

In the first step, each depth buffer value should occupy at least 16 bits. Sizes of 24 and 32 bits provide better precision, but they may not be supported on mobile devices.

As an example, the following code specifies that each RGBA component should occupy 8 bits and each depth buffer value should occupy 16 bits:

```
setEGLConfigChooser(8, 8, 8, 8, 16, 0);
```

In the third step, `glDepthFunc` accepts a value that identifies how fragment values should be compared with the values in the depth buffer. Table 9.2 lists the eight possible values and describes the nature of the comparison. If the comparison fails, the fragment will be discarded.

Table 9.2

Depth Comparison Identifiers for glDepthFunc

Identifiers	Description
GL_ALWAYS	Always passes
GL_NEVER	Never passes
GL_LESS	Passes if the fragment depth is less than the buffer value
GL_LEQUAL	Passes if the fragment depth is less than or equal to the buffer value
GL_EQUAL	Passes if the fragment depth is equal to the buffer value
GL_NOTEQUAL	Passes if the fragment depth is not equal to the buffer value
GL_GEQUAL	Passes if the fragment depth is greater than or equal to the buffer value
GL_GREATER	Passes if the fragment depth is greater than the buffer value

In the fourth step, `glClearDepthf` accepts a value between 0.0 and 1.0 that identifies the initial value of every point in the depth buffer. But the depth buffer's values aren't updated until `glClear` is called with `GL_DEPTH_BUFFER_BIT`.

The depth buffer is similar to the color buffer, whose values are updated when `glClear` is called with `GL_COLOR_BUFFER_BIT`. In fact, both buffers' values are usually set with the same call to `glClear`.

An example will demonstrate how depth testing can be configured. The following code enables the depth buffer and configures the test to discard fragments whose depth is equal to or less than 0.75:

```
GLES32.glEnable(GLES32.GL_DEPTH_TEST);

GLES32.glDepthFunc(GLES32.GL_LESS);

GLES32.glClearDepthf(0.75f);

GLES32.glClear(GLES32.GL_COLOR_BUFFER_BIT |
               GLES32.GL_DEPTH_BUFFER_BIT);
```

In this code, `glClear` fills the color buffer with the color set by `glClearColor` and fills the depth buffer with the color set by `glClearDepthf`. The example project in the next section will use similar code for its depth test.

In addition to updating the depth buffer with `glClear`, OpenGL ES makes it possible to write images to the depth buffer. But that topic lies beyond the scope of this discussion.

9.5 Example Application – Cubes

The ch09_cubes module demonstrates how three-dimensional rendering can be performed in a Daydream application. It creates a frustum-shaped viewing region and draws three instances of a cube inside of it. It also configures a depth test that discards all of the vertices from the third cube. Figure 9.5 shows what the model looks like before and after the depth test.

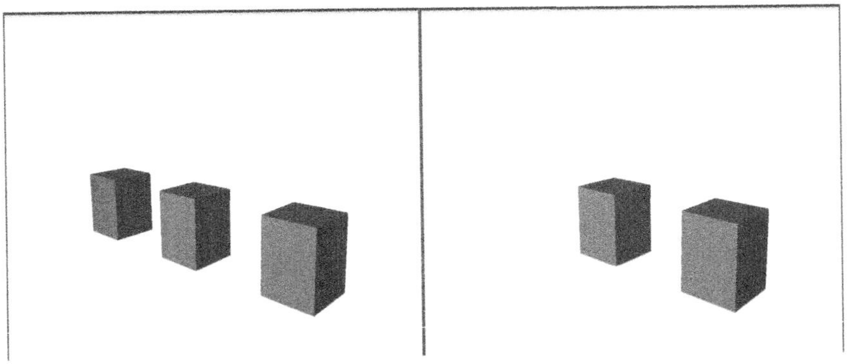

Figure 9.5 The ch09_cubes Module Before and After Depth Testing

Like the ch08_fourtriangles application from the preceding chapter, the application generates matrix data with the `Matrix` class and passes attribute/uniform data to shaders. But the ch09_cubes application has five important characteristics that make it markedly different:

1. It creates a view matrix using `Matrix.setLookAtM` and a projection matrix using `Matrix.perspectiveM`.
2. The fragment shader uses Blinn-Phong shading to illuminate the model.
3. It culls polygons based on how their vertices are oriented.
4. It enables a depth buffer and configures a depth test that discards vertices.
5. It calls `glDrawElementsInstanced` to execute the rendering process.

The following discussion will explore the first four items and show how they're implemented in the ch09_cubes code. The fifth item is more involved, and will be discussed in the last section of the chapter.

9.5.1 Vertex Data

Before getting into the functions and shaders, I'd like to discuss the application's vertex data. The cube has six faces and each face has four vertices. Each vertex has a location, a color, and a normal vector that identifies the direction perpendicular to its face. This is illustrated in Figure 9.6.

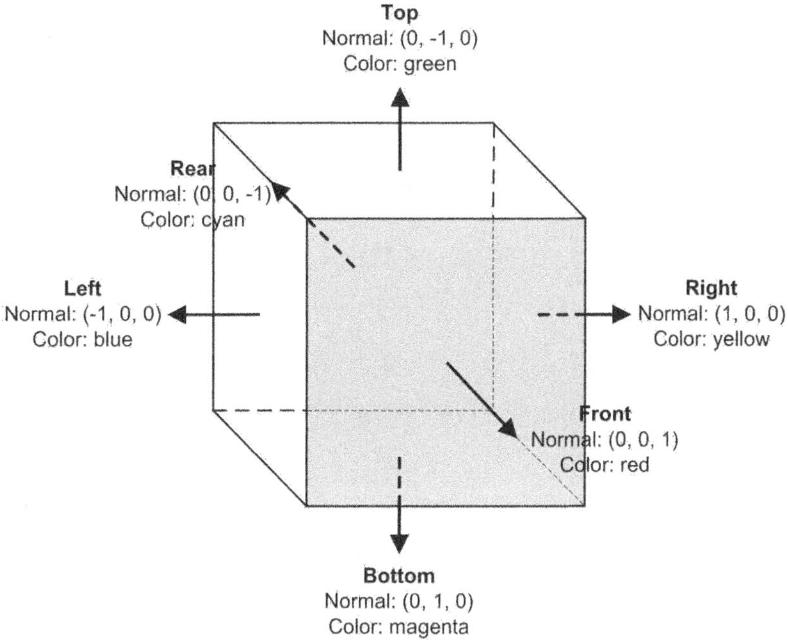

Figure 9.6 Coordinates, Colors, and Normal Vectors in the ch09_cubes Module

In code, each vertex requires nine `floats`: three for x-y-z coordinates, three for RGB color components, and three for normal vector components. Therefore, the `vertexData` array contains 9 * 4 * 6 = 216 `floats`. To make this clear, the following code defines the vertices in the cube's left face:

```
private static final float[] vertexData = {
  // Left face
  -1.0f, -1.0f, -1.0f,  0.0f,  0.0f,  0.8f, -1.0f,  0.0f,  0.0f,
  -1.0f,  1.0f, -1.0f,  0.0f,  0.0f,  0.8f, -1.0f,  0.0f,  0.0f,
  -1.0f,  1.0f,  1.0f,  0.0f,  0.0f,  0.8f, -1.0f,  0.0f,  0.0f,
  -1.0f, -1.0f,  1.0f,  0.0f,  0.0f,  0.8f, -1.0f,  0.0f,  0.0f,
```

Each line contains the (x, y, z) coordinates of a vertex followed by its RGB color components and its normal vector components. The `vertexData` array is stored in a `FloatBuffer` which is associated with the `in_coords`, `in_colors`, and `in_normals` variables of the vertex shader.

It's important to understand that the vertices aren't drawn in the order in which they're stored in the `vertexData` array. Instead, the application reads values from another buffer called an index buffer. I'll explain how that works shortly.

9.5.2 Transformation Matrices

To transform the model's vertices, the ch09_cubes application multiplies each vertex by three matrices—one that places the vertex in its desired position, one that positions the viewer, and one that defines the overall viewing region. Figure 9.7 depicts the viewing region and shows how the cubes and viewer are positioned inside of it.

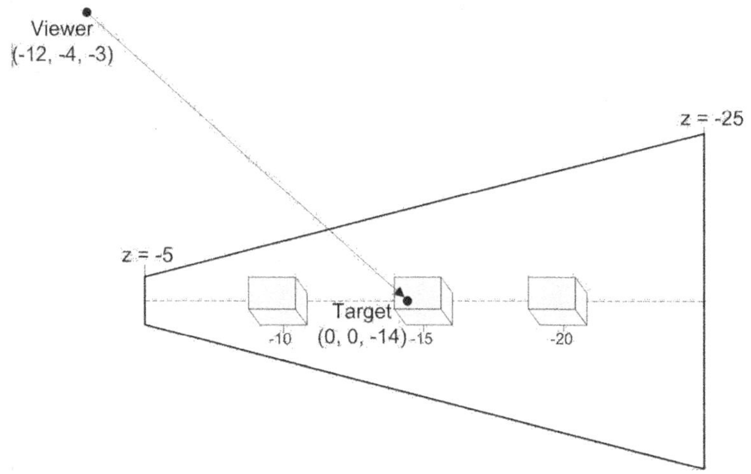

Figure 9.7 Viewer and Cubes in the Viewing Region

To obtain this result, the application generates three matrices: the model matrix, the view matrix, and the projection matrix. An earlier section explained what these matrices are intended to accomplish. The following discussion shows how these matrices are generated in the ch09_cubes project.

The Model Matrix

The model matrix is the simplest of the three vertices. As illustrated in Figure 9.7, the first cube should be positioned so that its center is located at (0, 0, –10). In object coordinates, the cube's center is (0, 0, 0), so the model matrix needs to translate its vertices ten units in the –z direction.

This can be accomplished with the `translateM` method of the `Matrix` class. In the following code, `translateM` provides a 4-by-4 matrix that translates vertices ten units in the –z direction.

```
Matrix.translateM(mvpMatrices, 0, 0.0f, 0.0f, -10.0f);
```

The resulting values are stored in the `float` array named `mvpMatrices`. This array will also hold elements of the view matrix and the projection matrix.

The View Matrix

As shown in Figure 9.7, the viewer is placed at (–12, –4, –3) and is oriented to look at the point (0, 0, –14). The viewer's positive vertical direction should be set to (0, 1, 0).

The matrix that sets the viewer's position and viewing direction is called the view matrix. In the ch09_cubes module, this is obtained with the static `setLookAtM` method of the `Matrix` class:

```
Matrix.setLookAtM(mvpMatrices, 16, -9.0f, 4.0f, -3.0f,
                  0.0f, 0.0f, -14.0f, 0.0f, 1.0f, 0.0f);
```

The elements of the view matrix are stored in the same `mvpMatices` mentioned earlier. The `offset` argument is set to 16 to place these elements immediately after the elements of the model matrix.

The Projection Matrix

The application configures its viewing region so that objects far from the origin are displayed at a smaller size than objects located near the origin. This requires creating the frustum-shaped viewing region depicted in Figure 9.7.

The matrix that positions vertices inside of this viewing region is called the projection matrix. The ch09_cubes application generates the elements of this matrix by calling the `perspectiveM` method of the `Matrix` class.

```
Matrix.perspectiveM(mvpMatrices, 32, 40.0f, 1.33f,
                                     5.0f, 25.0f);
```

The first argument defines the field-of-view in the y-direction. In this case, the vertical field of view should be set to ±20°, so the first argument is set to `40`.

The second argument identifies the ratio of the region's width to its height. This aspect ratio is commonly set to 4:3, so the argument is set to `1.33`.

The third and fourth arguments define the planes that bound the viewing region in the z-direction. Even though the arguments have positive values, the actual coordinates of the planes are negative. That is, the near clipping plane is located at $z = -5$ and the far clipping plane is located at $z = -25$.

9.5.3 The Vertex Shader

After generating the model, view, and projection matrices, the host calls `glUniformMatrix4fv` to associate them with a uniform variable in the vertex shader. The vertex shader accesses the matrices through its `mvp_matrices` array.

Listing 9.1 presents the code for the vertex shader of the ch09_cubes module. This performs six operations:

1. Multiply each incoming vertex by the model matrix. This converts the vertex's object coordinates to world coordinates.
2. Translate vertices in the second instance by 5 units in the –z direction and vertices in the third instance by 10 units in the –z direction.
3. Multiply each vertex by the view matrix. This converts world coordinates to eye coordinates.
4. Determine the vector from the vertex to the viewer's location. The fragment shader will use this to compute the specular component of surrounding light.
5. Multiply each vertex by the projection matrix. This converts eye coordinates to clip coordinates.
6. Determine the direction from the vertex to the light source. The fragment shader will use this vector to compute the diffuse component of surrounding light.

The vertex shader passes four variables to the fragment shader. `out_color` identifies the color associated with the vertex, `out_normal` identifies the vector perpendicular to the surface at the vertex, `out_viewer_direction` identifies the direction from the vertex to the viewer, and `out_light_direction` identifies the direction from the vertex to the light source.

Listing 9.1: ch09_cubes/src/main/assets/cubes.vert

```
/* Attribute data */
in vec3 in_coords;
in vec3 in_color;
in vec3 in_normal;

/* Uniform data */
uniform mat4 mvp_matrices[3];
uniform vec3 viewer_pos;
uniform vec3 light_pos;

/* Passed to the fragment shader */
out vec3 new_color;
out vec3 new_normal;
out vec3 new_viewer_direction;
out vec3 new_light_direction;

void main() {

  /* Apply the model transformation */
  vec4 world_coords =
    mvp_matrices[0] * vec4(in_coords, 1.0);

  /* Translate the second and third instances */
  world_coords.z = world_coords.z -
                     (float(gl_InstanceID) * 5.0f);

  /* Apply the view transformation */
  vec4 eye_coords =
    mvp_matrices[1] * world_coords;

  /* Determine the direction to the viewer */
  new_viewer_direction =
    normalize(viewer_pos - eye_coords.xyz);

  /* Apply the projection transformation */
  vec4 clip_coords =
    mvp_matrices[2] * eye_coords;

  /* Determine the direction to the light source */
  new_light_direction =
    normalize(light_pos - clip_coords.xyz);

  /* Set output variables */
  new_color = in_color;
  new_normal = in_normal;
  gl_Position = clip_coords;
}
```

9.5.4 Blinn-Phong Shading

Unlike the fragment shader in the ch08_fourtriangles module, the fragment shader in the ch09_cubes module performs a great deal of computation. To compute the fragment's color, the shader receives four variables from the vertex shader: the base color, a normal vector, and vectors to the viewer and the light source.

It also receives uniform data from the host application. This includes the components of the scene's illumination (ambient, diffuse, and specular), and the shininess to serve as the exponent of the specular component.

Using this information and the Blinn-Phong shading model, the shader determines how the fragment should be illuminated. This involves five steps:

1. Compute $N \cdot L$, where N is the normal vector and L is the direction of light
2. Compute H, the vector halfway between L and V, the direction to the viewer
3. Compute $(N \cdot H)^{n'}$, where n' is the shininess of the surface.
4. Using the results of Steps 1-3, add together the the components of the ambient, diffuse, and specular light.
5. Take the average of the computed light components and the color provided by the vertex shader.

The code in Listing 9.2 shows how the fragment shader performs these tasks. In much of the computation, the possible results may exceed 1.0, which is the maximum floating-point value of a color component. For this reason, the `clamp` function is frequently employed to hold the value between 0.0 and 1.0.

For the second step, the shader adds the vectors representing the direction to the light source (L) and the direction to the viewer (V). Then it calls `normalize` to ensure that the vector's length will be set to 1.0. If a vector's only purpose is to identify a direction, it's called a direction vector and its length must be normalized to 1.0.

After adding the ambient, diffuse, and specular components, the fragment shader blends the sum with the color received from the vertex shader. In this way, the shader lightens or darkens the color of the original surface.

Because every surface is flat, a fragment's normal vector will always equal that of the vertices that bound the corresponding primitive. But for general surfaces, fragment shaders must compute a normal vector for each fragment. This frequently involves interpolating among the normal vectors associated with nearby vertices. It can also be accomplished by taking the cross product of vectors that identify the change in the surface in different directions.

Listing 9.2: ch09_cubes/src/main/assets/cubes.frag

```
in vec3 new_color;
in vec3 new_normal;
in vec3 new_viewer_direction;
in vec3 new_light_direction;

/* Uniform data */
uniform vec3 light_params[3];
uniform float shininess;

/* Output color */
out vec4 out_color;

void main() {

  /* Step 1: Compute N . L */
  float n_dot_l = dot(new_normal, new_light_direction);

  /* Step 2: Compute H, the vector between L and V */
  vec3 half_vector =
    normalize(new_light_direction + new_viewer_direction);

  /* Step 3: Compute (N . H)^n' */
  float blinn = dot(new_normal, half_vector);
  blinn = clamp(blinn, 0.0f, 1.0f);
  blinn = pow(blinn, shininess);

  /* Step 4: Compute sum of light components */
  vec3 light_color = light_params[0] +
    light_params[1] * n_dot_l +
    light_params[2] * blinn;
  light_color = clamp(light_color, 0.0f, 1.0f);

  /* Step 5: Blend light color and original color */
  vec3 color_sum =
    clamp((light_color + new_color)/2.0f, 0.0f, 1.0f);
  out_color = vec4(color_sum, 1.0);
}
```

9.5.5 Depth Testing

After the fragment shader computes a color for a fragment, the application performs a depth test to determine if the fragment should be discarded. In the ch09_cubes module, the `CubesView` configures each value in the depth buffer to occupy 16 bits. Inside the `CubesRenderer`, the `onSurfaceCreated` method enables the depth buffer by calling `glEnable` with `GL_DEPTH_TEST`.

The depth test discards fragments whose depth exceeds a given value. That is, a fragment passes the test if its depth is less than the value. For this reason, the onSurfaceCreated method calls glDepthFunc with GL_LESS.

The onSurfaceCreated method also calls glClearDepthf to identify an initial value for the depth buffer's values. But the depth buffer isn't updated until the onDrawFrame method, which calls glClear with GL_COLOR_BUFFER_BIT and GL_DEPTH_BUFFER_BIT.

When this executes, it fills the color buffer with the color identified by glClearColor. It also fills the depth buffer with the value identified by glDepthFunc.

9.6 Drawing the Cube

Much of the code in the CubesRenderer class is similar to the code in Chapter 8's FourTrianglesRenderer class. But there's one major difference: the CubesRenderer draws its vertices by calling glDrawElementsInstanced while preceding applications used glDrawArrays and glDrawArraysInstanced.

It's important to understand the difference between the glDrawArrays* methods and the glDrawElements* methods. The first part of this section explains this difference and the second part presents the topic of primitive restart.

9.6.1 Indexed Rendering

In Chapter 7, the ch07_triangle module rendered a triangle containing three vertices. Because the model was so simple, the application transferred the vertices to the GPU and called glDrawArrays, which told the GPU to draw each vertex in the given order.

For complex models, it's usually a bad idea to draw vertices in order. This is because many vertices may be reused and because vertices may need to be oriented in a specific way for the purposes of polygon culling. For this reason, many applications provide an array of index values that identify the order in which vertices should be drawn.

To tell the GPU to select vertices by index, the application needs to call glDrawElements or one of its variants. For example, the CubesRenderer starts the rendering process with the following code:

```
GLES32.glDrawElementsInstanced(GLES32.GL_TRIANGLE_STRIP, 24,
  GLES32.GL_UNSIGNED_BYTE, indexBuffer, 3);
```

This tells the GPU to draw 24 vertices and combine them into triangle primitives. Vertices should be selected according to the index values in the `indexBuffer` and each index value is an unsigned byte. The last argument tells the GPU to draw three instances.

To clarify the differences between the `glDrawArrays*` and `glDrawElements*` methods, Table 9.3 presents the different variants available for both methods.

Table 9.3

glDrawArrays and glDrawElements Methods

Methods	Description
`glDrawArrays(int mode, int first, int count)`	Draws count vertices in the given order, starting with first
`glDrawArraysInstanced(int mode, int first, int count, int instanceCount)`	Draws instanceCount instances, where each instance contains count vertices in the given order, starting with first
`glDrawArraysIndirect(int mode, long indirect)`	Draws vertices in order using parameters given in an indirect buffer
`glDrawElements(int mode, int count, int type, Buffer indices)`	Draws vertices by selecting count indices of the given type
`glDrawElementsInstanced(int mode, int count, int type, Buffer indices, int instanceCount)`	Draws instanceCount instances, where each instance is drawn by selecting count indices of the given type
`glDrawElementsIndirect(int mode, long indirect)`	Draws vertices by index using parameters given in an indirect buffer
`glDrawElementsBaseVertex(int mode, int count, int type, Buffer indices, int basevertex)`	Draws vertices by selecting count indices of the given type starting from the basevertex index
`glDrawElementsInstancedBaseVertex( int mode, int count, int type, Buffer indices, int instanceCount, int basevertex)`	Draws instanceCount instances, where each instance is drawn by selecting count indices of the given type starting from the basevertex index

`glDrawArrays` accesses vertices in the order in which they're provided and `glDrawArraysInstanced` draws multiple instances of the vertices. The `glDrawArraysIndirect` method is similar to `glDrawArrays`, but the number of vertices and the first vertex to be drawn are provided to the GPU in a separate buffer.

Indirect rendering provides a minor performance gain. The main advantage is that the parameters (first vertex and number of vertices) don't need to be known in advance. They can be computed dynamically by compute/geometry shaders.

As mentioned earlier, glDrawElements selects vertices using the index values in an NIO Buffer. The type argument identifies the data type of the index values, and may be set to GL_UNSIGNED_BYTE, GL_UNSIGNED_SHORT, or GL_UNSIGNED_INT. It's important to note that the count argument identifies the number of indices provided in the Buffer, not the number of vertices.

glDrawElementsInstanced is similar to glDrawElements, but draws multiple instances of the vertices. glDrawElementsIndirect is similar to glDrawElementsInstanced, but provides its parameters in a structure referenced by the last argument.

The last two methods in the table end with BaseVertex. In both methods, the last argument identifies an offset to be applied to the indices read from the Buffer. This can be useful when an application needs to access the same block of vertex data with multiple calls to glDrawElements*.

9.6.2 Primitive Restart

Drawing a cube presents a minor problem. OpenGL ES doesn't provide a primitive for quadrilaterals, so each face must be drawn as a pair of triangles. Each new triangle is connected to two preceding vertices, so after one face is drawn, there's no easy way to draw a triangle on a perpendicular face.

One solution is to execute a glDraw* method six times, one for each face. In this manner, the triangles in one face will always be distinct from the triangles in another.

Another method is to insert extra vertices so that triangles between faces will have zero area. These are called degenerate triangles, and this method usually provides better performance than calling glDraw* multiple times.

As of OpenGL ES 3.0, a third option is available called *primitive restart*. This uses a special index value that tells the GPU to restart drawing primitives. When the GPU receives a primitive restart index, the vertex identified by the next index will be drawn as if it was the first vertex, and won't be connected to preceding primitives.

To see how this works, it helps to look at the declaration of the indexData array in the CubesRenderer class:

```
private static final byte[] indexData = {
  0, 1, 3, 2, (byte)0xff,
  7, 6, 4, 5, (byte)0xff,
  11, 10, 8, 9, (byte)0xff,
  12, 13, 15, 14, (byte)0xff,
  19, 18, 16, 17, (byte)0xff,
  20, 21, 23, 22, (byte)0xff};
```

The primitive mode is set to GL_TRIANGLE_STRIP, which means the first three vertices form a triangle, and the fourth vertex forms a second triangle connected to the first. In this case, the first rendered triangle is formed from the first (0), second (1), and fourth (3) vertices.

After drawing each face, the 0xff value tells the GPU to restart the process of drawing primitives. For example, the primitives formed from the vertices on the second line (starting with Index 7) won't be connected to the primitives formed from the vertices on the first line (starting with Index 0).

The value of 0xff is the primitive restart value because it's the largest possible value for the index type (byte). If indexData contained shorts instead of bytes, the 0xffff value would tell the GPU to restart drawing primitives.

Primitive restart isn't enabled by default. To enable this feature, the application must call glEnable with GL_PRIMITIVE_RESTART_FIXED_INDEX. When this is called, the largest possible index value will be interpreted as a primitive restart value.

9.7 Summary

Virtual reality gamers expect immersive experiences with real-world lighting and textures. This is commonplace in many applications, but it's not easy to program. Developers need to consider the viewing region, the user's orientation, light sources, and the material properties of the model's objects. There's a lot of math and it's not easy.

Thankfully, Android and the Google VR SDK provide classes that simplify coding. The Matrix class provides methods that initialize view matrices and the Eye class provides methods for perspective matrices. When multiplying these matrices, remember that order is important: A * B does not equal B * A.

The Blinn-Phong Lighting Model is a vital tool in the field of 3-D app development. Whether you're reflecting moonlight off of a bat wing or laser light off of an alien mothership, it's crucial to keep track of all the vectors involved. That is, applications need to be aware of the user's point of view, the direction to the light source, and the normal vector pointing outward from the surface.

Chapter 10

Textures and Text

In preceding chapters, all of the example code has assigned solid colors to surfaces—one rectangle is blue, one triangle is red, and so on. But objects in the real world have texture. That is, the appearance of their surfaces depends on the material. A brown cardboard box looks markedly different than a brown rug, even if they have the same shade of brown.

To account for this in virtual reality, applications assign images to surfaces instead of solid colors. The image data is stored in structures called *textures*, and OpenGL provides a wide range of methods for creating and configuring textures. The first section of this chapter presents these methods and demonstrates how Android bitmaps can be converted into OpenGL textures.

Textures are particularly important for applications that need to display text. Rather than draw every line of every character, applications generally extract characters from textures. This chapter presents two methods of drawing text by accessing textures.

The first method involves pre-generating a bitmap containing all the desired characters. This bitmap is called a texture atlas, and it can be easily customized with other texture content. The disadvantage is that the size and font of the characters is fixed. An application may shrink or expand these characters, but the quality will suffer.

The second method involves programmatically generating a texture to draw a specific portion of text. An Android application can print a string to a `Canvas`, convert the `Canvas` to a bitmap, and convert the bitmap to an OpenGL texture. The main advantage is that the size and font of the characters can be determined at runtime. The main disadvantage is that accessing the `Canvas` in code can require a significant amount of processing time.

10.1 Textures

Chapter 8 explained how fragment shaders assign colors to fragments and Chapter 9 explained how the Blinn-Phong Model computes colors mathematically. But in many applications, fragment shaders select colors from images. That is, the fragment shader reads (or *samples*) pixel data from an image and assigns the color to its fragment. The image data used in this process is stored in objects called *textures*.

Applying a texture to a surface is like putting up wallpaper. In both cases, blank surfaces are made more appealing by attaching decorative images. In both cases, the corners of the pattern must be carefully matched to the corners of the surface. It's also important to make sure that the pattern is oriented correctly.

But textures are easier to work with than wallpaper because there's no need to do any measuring. OpenGL will stretch or shrink the texture as needed. And if a texture needs to be reduced in size, you can tell OpenGL to use a miniaturized version of the texture called a *mipmap*.

The goal of this section is to explain how to apply textures in Android-GLES applications. The first part of the section presents the code needed to initialize a texture and pass it to the fragment shader. The second part explains how the fragment shader can read color data from the texture and use it to set a fragment's color. The section ends with example code that demonstrates how textures are used in practice.

10.1.1 Initializing and Configuring Textures

To initialize a texture and make it available to a fragment shader, an application needs to perform four steps:

1. Create a numeric descriptor for the texture
2. Make a texture unit active
3. Bind the texture to a target
4. Configure the texture and associate it with data

OpenGL ES doesn't provide specific data types for textures. Instead, each texture is identified by a number. An application can operate on a texture by binding its number to a target. Only one texture can be bound to a target at a time, and once a texture is bound, all operations involving the target are performed on the bound texture.

In an Android app, textures are initialized and configured using methods of `GLES32` and `GLUtils`. Table 10.1 lists nine methods in the order in which they're usually called.

Table 10.1
Texture Processing Methods

Method	Description
`glGenTextures(int num, IntBuffer textures)/ glGenTextures(int num, int[] textures, int offset)`	Initialize texture descriptors
`glActiveTexture(int texture)`	Make a texture unit active
`glBindTexture(int target, int texture)`	Associate a texture with a target
`glPixelStorei(int param, int value)`	Configure how the pixel data should be loaded and stored
`glTexParameteri(int target, int param, int value)`	Configure how the pixel data should be used
`GLUtils.texImage2D( int target, int level, Bitmap bmp, int border)`	Associate image data with the texture
`glDeleteTextures(int num, IntBuffer textures)/ glDeleteTextures(int num, int[] textures, int offset)`	Delete textures corresponding to descriptors

The first method, `glGenTextures`, generates a set of descriptors that can be used to uniquely identify textures. The first argument determines how many descriptors are generated. The descriptors can be placed in an `IntBuffer` or in an `int` array.

OpenGL can only process a limited number of textures at a time. Each texture processing capability is called a *texture unit*, and each texture unit is represented by an ID starting with `GL_TEXTURE0`. To make a texture unit active, an application needs to call `glActiveTexture` with the desired ID.

For example, the following code makes the third texture unit active:

```
GLES32.glActiveTexture(GL_TEXTURE0 + 2);
```

Once a texture unit is active, all subsequent texture changes will affect that unit. If an application needs to access N textures in a fragment shader at the same time, it should call `glActiveTexture` N times. In most applications, fragment shaders only access one texture at a time, so there's only one call to `glActiveTexture`.

When dealing with OpenGL textures, a *target* identifies the manner in which a texture will be used. Each target is identified by a constant defined in the GLES32 class. Possible target values include GL_TEXTURE_2D, GL_TEXTURE_2D_MULTISAMPLE, GL_TEXTURE_2D_MULTISAMPLE_ARRAY, GL_TEXTURE_3D, GL_TEXTURE_2D_ARRAY, GL_TEXTURE_CUBE_MAP, GL_TEXTURE_CUBE_MAP_ARRAY, and GL_TEXTURE_BUFFER.

The glBindTexture method associates one of the descriptors obtained from glGenTextures with a target. For example, the following code binds the second descriptor in the textures array with the GL_TEXTURE_2D target:

```
GLES32.glBindTexture(textures[1], GLES32.GL_TEXTURE_2D);
```

Only one texture descriptor can be bound to a target at a given time. In this case, any further operations involving the GL_TEXTURE_2D target will affect the texture represented by the textures[1] descriptor.

The glPixelStorei function identifies how pixel data should be loaded and stored. This associates a loading/storage parameter with an integer value. Table 10.2 lists the different parameters available.

Table 10.2

Loading/Storage Parameters of glPixelStorei

Parameter	Description
GL_UNPACK_ROW_LENGTH	The number of pixels per row when loading
GL_UNPACK_IMAGE_HEIGHT	The number of rows (if greater than 0)
GL_UNPACK_SKIP_ROWS	The number of rows to skip before loading
GL_UNPACK_SKIP_PIXELS	The number of pixels to skip before loading
GL_UNPACK_SKIP_IMAGES	The number of images to skip before loading
GL_UNPACK_ALIGNMENT	Byte alignment for loading each row (1, 2, 4, or 8)
GL_PACK_ROW_LENGTH	The number of pixels per row when storing
GL_PACK_SKIP_ROWS	The number of rows to skip before storing
GL_PACK_SKIP_PIXELS	The number of pixels to skip before storing
GL_PACK_ALIGNMENT	Byte alignment for storing each row (1, 2, 4, or 8)

The six parameters starting with GL_UNPACK identify how pixels should be unpacked from memory. For example, GL_UNPACK_ROW_LENGTH specifies the number of pixels in a row. If an image contains 128 pixels per row, this can be indicated with the following code:

```
GLES32.glPixelStorei(GLES32.GL_UNPACK_ROW_LENGTH, 128);
```

The four parameters starting with GL_PACK identify how pixels should be packed into memory. For example, GL_PACK_ALIGNMENT specifies the byte boundaries that should be employed when storing rows. The default value is 4.

glTexParameteri is similar to glPixelStorei, but instead of identifying how the image data should be loaded and stored, it configures how a texture should be displayed. Table 10.3 lists the parameter names accepted by glTexParameteri.

Table 10.3

Texture Display Parameters of glTexParameteri

Parameter	Characteristic
GL_TEXTURE_MIN_FILTER	The interpolation method used for minimization
GL_TEXTURE_MAG_FILTER	The interpolation method used for enlargement
GL_TEXTURE_WRAP_S	How the texture should be displayed in the s-direction at coordinates beyond its dimensions
GL_TEXTURE_WRAP_T	How the texture should be displayed in the t-direction at coordinates beyond its dimensions
GL_TEXTURE_WRAP_R	How the texture should be displayed in the r-direction at coordinates beyond its dimensions
GL_TEXTURE_MIN_LOD	The texture's lowest mipmap level
GL_TEXTURE_MAX_LOD	The texture's highest mipmap level
GL_TEXTURE_BASE_LEVEL	The index of the lowest-defined mipmap level
GL_TEXTURE_MAX_LEVEL	The index of the highest-defined mipmap level
GL_TEXTURE_SWIZZLE_R	Sets the value of the texel's R component
GL_TEXTURE_SWIZZLE_G	Sets the value of the texel's G component
GL_TEXTURE_SWIZZLE_B	Sets the value of the texel's B component
GL_TEXTURE_SWIZZLE_A	Sets the value of the texel's A component
GL_DEPTH_STENCIL_TEXTURE_MODE	How to read data from depth/stencil textures
GL_TEXTUER_COMPARE_MODE	Texture comparison mode for depth textures
GL_TEXTURE_COMPARE_FUNC	The comparison used in the depth texture test

The following discussion presents most of these parameters by dividing them into three categories: filtering modes, external coordinates, and level of detail. The topics of texture swizzling and texture-based depth testing are beyond the scope of this book.

Filtering Modes

Fragment shaders use floating-point coordinates to identify what point of a texture should be sampled. If a point lies between multiple texture elements, or *texels*, the shader has two options. It can read data from the texel whose center is nearest the point or it can compute a weighted sum of the surrounding texels. These options are represented by two constants:

- `GL_NEAREST` — select data from the texel whose center is nearest
- `GL_LINEAR` — compute a weighted average of surrounding texels

These constants identify *filtering modes*. The second mode reads data using a process called *bilinear interpolation*. To understand how this works, suppose that the point P lies between four neighboring texels: A, B, C, and D. Figure 10.1 shows what this looks like.

To identify P's location relative to the surrounding texels, we use two values, t_1 and t_2. These are called *interpolation parameters* and range from 0 to 1. If t_1 and t_2 both equal 1, P coincides with the center of D. If t_1 and t_2 both equal 0, P coincides with the center of A.

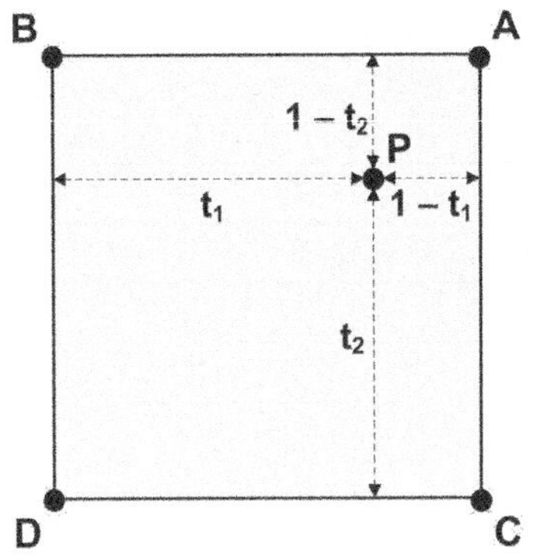

Figure 10.1 Bilinear Interpolation

In this figure, P is closest to A. Therefore, if the filtering mode is set to `GL_FILTER_NEAREST`, the color of P will be set equal to that of A. But if the filtering mode is set to `GL_FILTER_LINEAR`, P's color will be computed using the following equation:

$$
\begin{aligned}
Color(P) = {} & t_1 \times t_2 \times Color(A) \\
& + (1 - t_1) \times t_2 \times Color(B) \\
& + t_1 \times (1 - t_2) \times Color(C) \\
& + (1 - t_1) \times (1 - t_2) \times Color(D)
\end{aligned}
$$

An application can set the filter mode by calling glTexParameteri with the parameter name set to GL_TEXTURE_MIN_FILTER or GL_TEXTURE_MAG_FILTER. The GL_TEXTURE_MIN_FILTER parameter is used when the rendering surface is smaller than the texture. GL_TEXTURE_MAG_FILTER is used when the rendering surface is larger than the texture.

For example, the following code specifies that bilinear interpolation should be employed whenever a two-dimensional texture needs to be minified:

```
GLES32.glTexParameteri(GLES32.GL_TEXTURE_2D,
  GLES32.GL_TEXTURE_MIN_FILTER, GLES32.GL_LINEAR);
```

GL_LINEAR and GL_NEAREST are the only filtering modes that can be associated with the GL_TEXTURE_MAG_FILTER parameter. But the GL_TEXTURE_MIN_FILTER parameter can be associated with four additional modes:

- GL_NEAREST_MIPMAP_NEAREST — Chooses the nearest mipmap and sets the filtering mode to GL_NEAREST
- GL_LINEAR_MIPMAP_NEAREST — Chooses the nearest mipmap and sets the filtering mode to GL_LINEAR
- GL_NEAREST_MIPMAP_LINEAR — Finds the two closest mipmaps, selects the nearest value on each mipmap, and takes the weighted average of both values
- GL_LINEAR_MIPMAP_LINEAR — Finds the two closest mipmaps, uses bilinear interpolation to select values from the two mipmaps, and takes the weighted average of both values

Mipmap levels can be thought of as a third dimension. When bilinear filtering is combined with mipmap linear filtering, the result is called *trilinear filtering*.

External Coordinates

If a shader tries to read data beyond a texture's boundary, a question arises regarding what value should be returned. An application can configure this by setting values for GL_TEXTURE_WRAP_S, GL_TEXTURE_WRAP_T, and GL_TEXTURE_WRAP_R. In texture space, the (s, t, r) axes correspond to the (x, y, z) axes in regular space. glTexParameteri can assign each of these parameters to one of four values:

- GL_REPEAT — In-range coordinates are extended beyond the texture. If the maximum dimension is N, an out-of-range texel X is set to the texel at X mod N
- GL_MIRRORED_REPEAT — Texels beyond the texture are set to the reflections of the corresponding in-range texels

- GL_CLAMP_TO_EDGE — Texels beyond the texture are set to the texels at the texture's edge
- GL_CLAMP_TO_BORDER — Texels beyond the texture are set to a border color

The images in Figure 10.2 show what happens when a shader reads texels outside of the texture's boundaries. In each case, the coordinates run from –0.25 to 1.25.

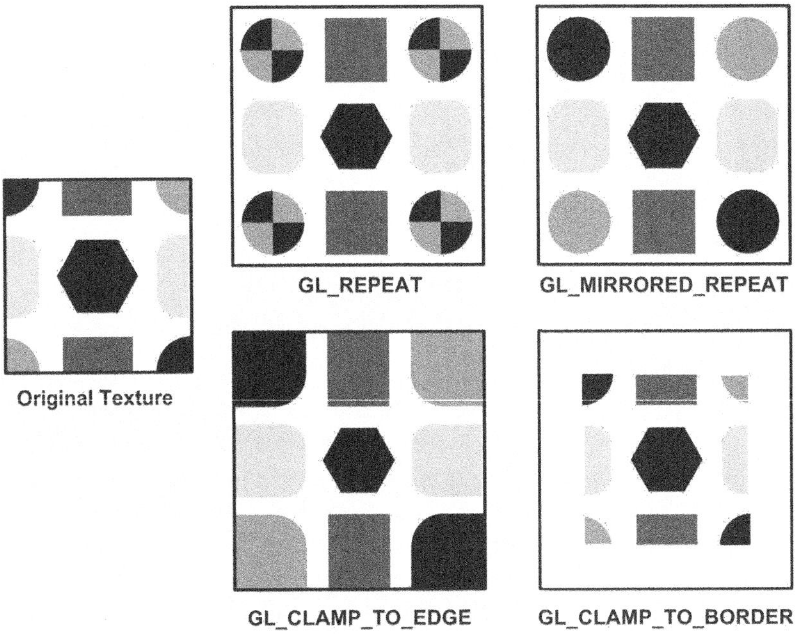

Figure 10.2 Texture Wrap Results

In the figure, the GL_SAMPLER_ADDRESS_MODE_CLAMP_TO_BORDER example sets the border color to opaque white. In code, this can be configured by calling glTexParameterfv. This is similar to glTexParameteri, but instead of setting a parameter equal to an integer, it sets the parameter to a FloatBuffer. To set the border color, the parameter name should be set to GL_TEXTURE_BORDER_COLOR and the FloatBuffer should contain the color's components.

The following code shows how this works. In this case, colorBuffer contains four floats that identify the color's R, G, B, and A components.

```
GLES32.glTexParameterfv(GLES32.GL_TEXTURE_2D,
  GLES32.GL_TEXTURE_BORDER_COLOR, colorBuffer);
```

Level of Detail and Mipmapping

As a viewer moves away from a texture, the texture's resolution should decrease. One way to accomplish this is by reading fewer samples from the texture. This is referred to as a level of detail (LOD) method. An application can specify the minimum LOD by calling `glTexParameteri` with the `GL_TEXTURE_MIN_LOD` parameter and the maximum LOD with the `GL_TEXTURE_MAX_LOD` parameter.

A common LOD method is to add mipmap levels to a texture, where each level's image has a lower resolution than the one preceding it. That is, the Level 0 image has the highest resolution, the Level 1 image has the next highest, and so on. An application can set the minimum mipmap level by calling `glTexParameteri` with the `GL_TEXTURE_BASE_LEVEL` parameter and the maximum mipmap level with the `GL_TEXTURE_MAX_LEVEL` parameter.

10.1.2 Associating Textures with Image Data

After a texture's properties have been configured, an application can call `glTexImage2D` to associate the texture with image data. The `GLES32` method is given as follows:

```
glTexImage2D(int target, int level, int internalformat, int width,
      int height, int border, int format, int type, Buffer pixels)
```

With nine arguments, this method is difficult to use. In particular, the `internalformat`, `format`, and `type` arguments are hard to set. `internalformat` identifies the components of the image's texels, `format` identifies how the components are arranged, and `type` identifies the data type of each component.

To simplify coding, Android provides a class named `GLUtils`. This contains a method named `texImage2D` that performs the same operation as `glTexImage2D`. The difference is that `texImage2D` only needs four arguments:

```
texImage2D(int target, int level, Bitmap bitmap, int border)
```

This method examines the `Bitmap` and determines the `internalformat`, `format`, and `type` arguments automatically. The `level` argument identifies the mipmap level and the `border` argument should always be set to `0`.

To demonstrate how this is used, the following code associates the texture bound to the `GL_TEXTURE_2D` with a `Bitmap` named bmp:

```
GLUtils.texImage2D(GLES32.GL_TEXTURE_2D, 0, bmp, 0);
```

10.1.3 Sampling Textures in the Fragment Shader

As discussed in Chapter 8, the main job of a fragment shader is to assign colors to fragments. One method is to read color data from a texture. Given this role, you might expect the OpenGL Shading Language (GLSL) to have data types for textures. But that's not the case.

Instead, GLSL provides sampler data types and a series of functions that read texel data. This discussion explains both topics and demonstrates how these data types and functions can be accessed in a shader.

Sampler Data Types

The preceding discussion explained how to create textures and associate them with targets. To access data from a texture, a fragment shader needs to access a variable whose type corresponds to the texture's target. Table 10.4 lists these data types and their corresponding targets.

Table 10.4

GLSL Sampler Data Types (Abridged)

Sampler Data Type	Texture Target
`sampler2D`	`GL_TEXTURE_2D`
`sampler3D`	`GL_TEXTURE_3D`
`sampler2DArray`	`GL_TEXTURE_2D_ARRAY`
`samplerCube`	`GL_TEXTURE_CUBE_MAP`
`samplerCubeShadow`	`GL_TEXTURE_CUBE_MAP`
`sampler2DArrayShadow`	`GL_TEXTURE_2D_ARRAY`

An example will clarify how a sampler can be declared in a fragment shader. Suppose that the application binds a texture to `GL_TEXTURE_2D`. A shader can access the sampler with the following declaration:

```
uniform sampler2D tex_sampler;
```

As shown in Table 10.4, GLSL doesn't support a data type named `sampler`. But if a shader declares a variable named `sampler`, this will result in an incomprehensible error. Be sure not to use `sampler` as a variable name.

Texture Functions

GLSL provides functions that enable shaders to read from textures using samplers. Table 10.5 lists six of them.

Table 10.5

Texture Functions (Abridged)

Function	Description
`texture(sampler_t s, coord_t point, [, float bias])`	Sample the texture at the given point
`textureOffset(sampler_t s, coord_t point, int_coord_t offset, [, float bias])`	Sample the texture at the given point, with an offset added to the (u, v, w) coordinates
`textureLod(sampler_t s, coord_t point, float lod)`	Sample the texture at the given point with the specified level of detail
`texelFetch(sampler_t s, int_coord_t point [, float lod])`	Sample the texture at the point with the given (u, v, w) coordinates
`texelFetchOffset(sampler_t s, int_coord_t point, int lod)`	Sample the texture at the given point
`textureSize(sampler_t s, int lod)`	Identifies the size of the texture at the given level of detail

In each of these functions, the first argument must be set to one of the sampler data types listed in Table 10.4. The `coord_t` type identifies a suitable data type for the coordinates. This would be a `vec2` for two-dimensional textures and a `vec3` for three-dimensional textures. The `int_coord_t` type identifies a data type in which the coordinates are given as integers.

Of these functions, the first is the most important. `texture` accepts a sampler and a set of coordinates, and returns the texel data at the given point in the texture. In most cases, the result is a `vec4` containing color information. The following code shows how this function can be used:

```
vec4 tex_color = texture(tex_sampler, tex_coords);
```

`texture` accepts an optional third argument that adds a bias to the level of detail. Similarly, the third argument of `textureLod` function identifies the desired level of detail.

texelFetch provides texel information at a specific point in u-v-w space. In this case, the coordinates are given as integers that lie between 0 and the maximum extent in the given dimension. As an example, the following code returns the color of the texel at the position (30, 40) with the level of detail set to 2:

```
ivec2 coords = ivec2(30, 40);
vec4 color = texelFetch(tex_sampler, coords, 2);
```

textureOffset and texelFetchOffset are similar to texture and texelFetch, but their second argument provides an offset to the coordinates. This offset must be as an integer, and in the case of textureOffset, the offset is applied after the coordinates have been converted into u-v-w space.

10.2 Example Application – Simple Texture

The ch10_simpletexture module demonstrates how textures can be created and accessed in an Android application. This creates a two-dimensional rectangle and covers it with a two-dimensional texture. This discussion presents the code in the SimpleTextureRenderer class and the module's fragment shader.

10.2.1 The SimpleTextureRenderer Class

Most of the code in the SimpleTextureRenderer is similar to code from previous examples. The only difference is the initTexture method, which is called inside the onSurfaceCreated method. This generates a texture descriptor and configures the texture's properties. Listing 10.1 presents the code of initTexture.

Listing 10.1: ch10_simpletexture/src/main/java/.../SimpleTextureRenderer.java

```
void initTexture() {

  // Generate a texture descriptor
  textureIDs = new int[1];
  GLES32.glGenTextures(1, textureIDs, 0);

  // Make the first texture unit active
  GLES32.glActiveTexture(GLES32.GL_TEXTURE0);
```

Listing 10.1: ch10_simpletexture/src/main/java/.../SimpleTextureRenderer.java (Continued)

```
    // Bind the first texture descriptor to its target
    GLES32.glBindTexture(GLES32.GL_TEXTURE_2D, textureIDs[0]);

    // Set texture parameters
    GLES32.glTexParameteri(GLES32.GL_TEXTURE_2D,
      GLES32.GL_TEXTURE_WRAP_S, GLES32.GL_REPEAT);
    GLES32.glTexParameteri(GLES32.GL_TEXTURE_2D,
      GLES32.GL_TEXTURE_WRAP_T, GLES32.GL_REPEAT);

    // Set filter modes
    GLES32.glTexParameteri(GLES32.GL_TEXTURE_2D,
      GLES32.GL_TEXTURE_MIN_FILTER, GLES32.GL_LINEAR);
    GLES32.glTexParameteri(GLES32.GL_TEXTURE_2D,
      GLES32.GL_TEXTURE_MAG_FILTER, GLES32.GL_LINEAR);

    // Read pixel data and associate it with texture
    GLUtils.texImage2D(GLES32.GL_TEXTURE_2D, 0, bitmap, 0);
}
```

`initTexture` starts by generating a texture descriptor with `glGenTextures`. This descriptor is stored in the single-element `textureIDs` array. Next, `initTexture` calls `glActiveTexture` to the first texture unit active. Then it calls `glBindTexture` to associate the descriptor (`textureIDs[0]`) with the `GL_TEXTURE_2D` target.

`initTexture` calls `glTexParameteri` four times to configure the texture bound to the `GL_TEXTURE_2D` target. The first two calls configure the texture to repeat texels when a sampler reads data beyond the texture's boundaries. The next two calls configure the sampler to use bilinear interpolation when reading data from the texture.

The last line of `initTexture` calls `GLUtils.texImage2D` to associate the texture with image data. This reads the data from a `Bitmap` that was created in the constructor using the `BitmapFactory.decodeResource` method discussed in Chapter 4. In this case, the `Bitmap` was created from the smiley.png resource in the module's src/main/res/drawable folder.

To destroy the texture object, the `SimpleTextureRenderer` calls `glDeleteTextures` in the `onRendererShutdown` method.

10.2.2 The SimpleTextureRenderer Fragment Shader

The fragment shader in the ch10_simpletexture module provides a basic demonstration of how a fragment's color can be read from a texture. This declares a `sampler2D` variable and accesses it through the `texture` method. Listing 10.2 presents the shader's code.

Listing 10.2: ch10_simpletexture/src/main/assets/simpletexture.frag

```
#version 300 es

uniform sampler2D texSampler;

in vec2 new_texcoords;
out vec4 out_color;

void main() {

  // Read the texture color at the given coordinates
  vec3 color = vec3(texture(texSampler, new_texcoords));

  out_color = vec4(color, 1.0);
}
```

`texSampler` is declared as a `uniform`, but the application doesn't need to access it with `glGetUniformLocation` or `glGetUniform*`. Because the sampler's type is `sampler2D`, it will be associated with the texture bound to the `GL_TEXTURE_2D` target.

This shader receives texture coordinates, `new_texcoords`, from the vertex shader. These are provided as attribute data, which means that each vertex needs its own texture coordinates.

10.3 Displaying Text

When it comes to displaying text in a Daydream app, two approaches are available. First, the `GvrView` can overlay a `TextView` from the Android API. This is flexible and easy to code, but mixing Android views with OpenGL rendering can dramatically degrade performance.

A second approach involves drawing characters as objects in the graphical model. This provides better performance but takes time to code. There are many methods of drawing characters in an Android-GLES app, and this section focuses on two:

1. Combine the characters into a single texture called a *texture atlas*. Use coordinates to display each character separately.
2. Write text on a `Canvas`, convert the `Canvas` to a `Bitmap`, and display the `Bitmap` as a texture.

Chapter 16 presents a third method, which generates textures using the FreeType toolset. But that method requires the Android NDK, not the SDK.

10.3.1 Texture Atlas

Today, most fonts are provided in TrueType Font (TTF) format. This identifies character shapes using geometric features like line segments and Bézier curves. As a result, TTF characters can be scaled and rotated without affecting the quality of the display.

Displaying TTF fonts in OpenGL requires a significant amount of code and processing time, so many developers combine characters from a TTF font into a bitmap and create a texture atlas from the bitmap.

To generate the texture atlas for the ch10_textdemo module, I downloaded Google's Droid Sans font from fonts.google.com and downloaded Andreas Jonsson's Bitmap Generator from http://www.angelcode.com/products/bmfont. Figure 10.3 shows what the resulting texture atlas looks like.

Figure 10.3 Texture Atlas for Droid Sans

Most texture atlases only include characters of a given size. In this case, the characters are meant to be printed on 32-pixel lines. Characters can be enlarged or reduced, but for acceptable results, it's important to enable bilinear filtering.

In addition to generating a texture atlas, the Bitmap Generator creates a file that provides information about the characters. Each line of the text file starts with a special descriptor: `info`, `common`, `page`, `chars`, or `char`. Only one line starts with `common`, and for the Droid Sans example, this line is given as follows:

```
common lineHeight=32 base=26 scaleW=256 scaleH=256 pages=1
       packed=0 alphaChnl=1 redChnl=0 greenChnl=0 blueChnl=0
```

The fields in the `common` line define characteristics that apply to the entire texture and all of the font's characters. There are ten fields in total:

1. `lineHeight` — the height of each line in pixels
2. `base` — offset of the baseline from the top edge
3. `scaleW` — the width of the entire texture
4. `scaleH` — the height of the entire texture
5. `pages` — the number of pages in the atlas
6. `packed` — identifies if monochrome characters have been packed
7. `alphaChnl` — Content of the alpha channel
8. `redChnl` — Content of the red channel
9. `greenChnl` — Content of the green channel
10. `blueChnl` — Content of the blue channel

For the example texture atlas, the `lineHeight` field indicates that characters are intended to be printed in 32-pixel lines. The baseline is 26 pixels below the top edge. The dimensions of the atlas are 256-by-256 and only one page is available.

Most of the lines in the file start with `char`, which means they provide information about a single character. One `char` line in the Droid Sans font file is given as follows:

```
char id=112 x=131 y=77 width=13 height=21 xoffset=2 yoffset=11
     xadvance=16 page=0 chnl=15
```

Each `char` line defines ten fields:

1. `id` — the ASCII code of the character
2. `x` — the x-coordinate of the character's upper-left corner in the image
3. `y` — the y-coordinate of the character's upper-left corner in the image
4. `width` — the character's width
5. `height` — the character's height
6. `xoffset` — distance from the current position to the start of the character
7. `yoffset` — vertical offset to be applied when printing the character
8. `xadvance` — distance from the current position to the end of the character space
9. `page` — the page containing the texture
10. `chnl` — channel containing data (1 = blue, 2 = green, 4 = red, 8 = alpha, 15 = all)

The character corresponding to ASCII code 113 is `p`, so the example `char` line presents the properties of that letter. Figure 10.4 depicts the dimensions of the line and the character.

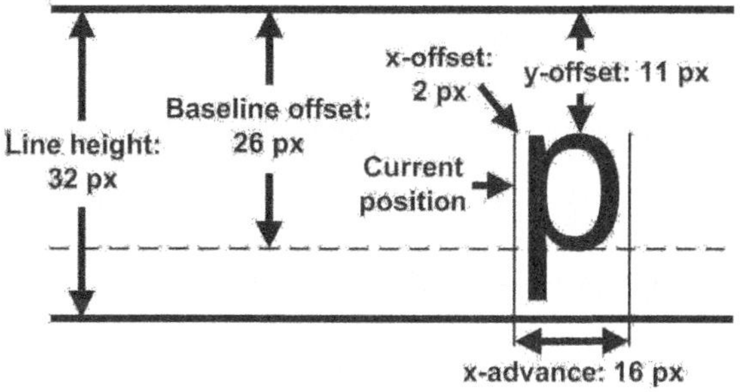

Figure 10.4 Line and Character Dimensions

The figure illustrates the difference between the `xoffset` and `xadvance`. Both identify the horizontal distance from the current position. `xoffset` specifies the distance from the current position to where the character should be displayed. `xadvance` indicates the distance from the initial current position to the next current position.

In the ch10_textdemo module, the application accesses the characteristics of a texture atlas using a class called `TextureAtlas`. Its definition is given as follows:

```
class TextureAtlas {
  short lineHeight;
  short baselineOffset;
  short scaleW, scaleH;
  short numChars;
  HashMap<Integer, TextureChar> charMap;
};
```

This contains all of the information about the font and its characters. This class assumes that the texture atlas fits on a single page.

Many fonts don't provide characters for every possible ASCII code. For example, Droid Sans doesn't contain any characters for Codes 0–31 or 127-159. For this reason, the `TextureAtlas` stores its characters in a `HashMap` instead of an array. This `HashMap` associates each character's ASCII code with a `TextureChar` that contains the character's information.

The `HashMap` contains a `TextureChar` for each char line in the generated font file. The following code shows how the `TextureChar` can be defined.

```
class TextureChar {
  float x, y;
  float width, height;
  float xoffset, yoffset, xadvance;
};
```

Each of these dimensions is given as a `float` that is computed by dividing the dimension by the corresponding dimension of the bitmap size. This simplifies the process of computing the texture coordinates needed to extract the character from the atlas.

For example, the following code obtains a `TextureChar` for the letter `p`. Then it uses the dimensions of the `TextureChar` to determine four pairs of texture coordinates:

```
TextureChar pChar = atlas.charMap.get(113);
cornerA.x = pChar.x;
cornerA.y = pChar.y;
cornerB.x = pChar.x;
cornerB.y = pChar.y + pChar.height;
cornerC.x = pChar.x + pChar.width;
cornerC.x = pChar.y + pChar.height;
cornerD.x = pChar.x + pChar.width;
cornerD.x = pChar.y;
```

In addition to computing the texture coordinates needed to extract a character from the atlas, the application needs to compute vertex coordinates for the rectangle containing the character. This can be accomplished by obtaining the character's dimensions and scaling them appropriately for the display.

10.3.2 Canvas to Bitmap to Texture

This book has discussed many Android classes related to graphics, such as `Drawable`, `ImageView`, and `GvrView`. But the `Canvas` class hasn't been mentioned. This is because `Canvas`es are usually used for custom drawing and VR apps rely on OpenGL-based views for drawing.

But in addition to drawing shapes, a `Canvas` can be used to write text to a `Bitmap`. In my code, this process consists of four steps:

1. Create and configure a `Paint` instance.
2. Create a `Bitmap` with the desired dimensions and format.
3. Create and configure a `Canvas` from the `Bitmap`.
4. Call `drawText` to print text to the `Bitmap` using the `Paint` instance.

After these four steps are accomplished, the `Bitmap` will contain the desired text. The `Bitmap` can be converted to a texture using the `GLUtils.texImage2D` method discussed earlier.

Creating and Configuring a Paint Instance

The methods of the `Canvas` class make it possible to draw shapes, fill colors, and display text. The last argument of each method is a `Paint` instance that defines how the operation should be performed.

The `Paint` class provides a number of methods for configuring `Canvas` operations. Table 10.6 lists 16 of these methods, focusing on those that display text.

Table 10.6

Paint Configuration Methods (Abridged)

Method	Description
`setAntiAlias(boolean anti)`	Specifies whether antialiasing should be used
`setColor(int color)`	Sets the color to be applied
`setElegantTextHeight( boolean height)`	Increases text height to display elegant text (such as when starting a book or chapter)
`setFakeBoldText(boolean fbt)`	Specifies whether normal text should be drawn in a fake boldface
`setFontFeatureSettings( String settings)`	Sets CSS-based font settings
`setLetterSpacing(float spacing)`	Sets spacing between letters
`setStrikeThruText( boolean strikeThruText)`	Prints text with a line through the center
`setStyle(Paint.Style style)`	Identifies if text should be filled and/or stroked
`setSubpixelText(boolean subpixelText)`	Improves text resolution using subpixel rendering
`setTextAlign(Paint.Align align)`	Specifies text alignment
`setTextLocale(Locale locale)`	Identifies locale to set text display properties
`setTextScaleX(float scaleX)`	Specifies horizontal scale factor
`setTextSize(float size)`	Sets text size
`setTextSkewX(float skewx)`	Specifies horizontal skew factor
`setTypeface(Typeface typeface)`	Sets the typeface used to display text
`setUnderlineText(boolean und)`	Specifies whether text should be underlined

Most of these methods are easy to understand, but `setColor`, `setStyle`, and `setTypeface` deserve explanation. As its name implies, `setColor` sets the color of all draw operations performed by the `Paint` instance. The color must be given as an integer, and this is usually provided in one of two forms:

- Hexadecimal — Combine RGBA components into one hexadecimal value, such as `0xff00ffff` for magenta (ff – red, 00 – green, ff – blue, ff – alpha)
- `Color` member — Field of the `Color` class, such as `Color.RED`, `Color.GREEN`, `Color.BLUE`, `Color.BLACK`, `Color.WHITE`, `Color.GRAY`, `Color.YELLOW`, or `Color.MAGENTA`

`setStyle` identifies whether the drawing operation will be filled, stroked, or filled and stroked. This accepts three values: `Paint.Style.FILL`, `Paint.Style.STROKE`, and `Paint.Style.FILL_AND_STROKE`. The default style is `Paint.Style.FILL`.

The `Paint` class doesn't provide any methods for setting the font, but `setTypeface` makes it possible to control how the text is printed. This accepts a value of the `Typeface` class or a combination thereof:

- `DEFAULT` — Regular text without boldface or monospace
- `DEFAULT_BOLD` — Regular text in boldface
- `MONOSPACE` — Regular text in monospace
- `SANS_SERIF` — The default sans serif font
- `SERIF` — The default serif font

For example, the following code creates a `Paint` instance and configures it to display bold, blue, anti-aliased text at a size of 32:

```
Paint paint = new Paint();
paint.setTypeface(Typeface.DEFAULT_BOLD);
paint.setColor(Color.BLUE);
paint.setAntiAlias(true);
paint.setTextSize(32);
```

The `Paint` class also provides an important method called `measureText`. This accepts a `String` and returns the pixel width of the `String`'s text when drawn by the `Paint` instance. The following code demonstrates how this can be used:

```
float textWidth = paint.measureText("Hello there!");
```

Create a Bitmap

After creating a Paint instance, an application needs to create a Bitmap to hold the desired text. Chapter 4 presented a number of ways to create Bitmaps using methods of the Bitmap and BitmapFactory classes. If an application needs a blank Bitmap, it can call Bitmap.createBitmap, whose signature is given as follows:

```
createBitmap(int width, int height, Bitmap.Config config)
```

The config argument identifies the format of the Bitmap's pixels, and can be set to Bitmap.Config.ALPHA_8, Bitmap.Config.RGB_565, or Bitmap.Config.ARGB_8888. If the application associates the Bitmap with an OpenGL texture with texImage2D, the method will take care of the pixel format conversion.

If the sole purpose of the Bitmap is to print text, the height argument can be safely set to the height of the text. The width argument can be set by calling the measureText method of the Paint instance discussed earlier.

Create and Configure a Canvas

A Canvas represents a drawing and the Canvas class provides a constructor that accepts a Bitmap to store the drawing's content. For example, the following code creates a new Canvas from an existing Bitmap named bmp:

```
Canvas c = new Canvas(bmp);
```

Most methods of the Canvas class perform localized drawing operations. But an application can set the background color with drawRGB or drawARGB. Both methods accept integers identifying the RGB or ARGB components.

Drawing Text

After creating a Paint instance and a Canvas instance, an application can draw text using the drawText method of the Canvas class:

```
drawText(String text, float x, float y, Paint paint)
```

The first argument identifies the text to be displayed. The second and third arguments specify where the text should be positioned in the Canvas. The last argument identifies the Paint instance whose properties determine how the text will be displayed.

10.4 Example Application – Text Demo

The ch10_textdemo module demonstrates how OpenGL textures can be created using a `Bitmap` generated from a texture atlas and a `Bitmap` generated from a `Canvas`. Figure 10.5 shows what the resulting text looks like for both methods.

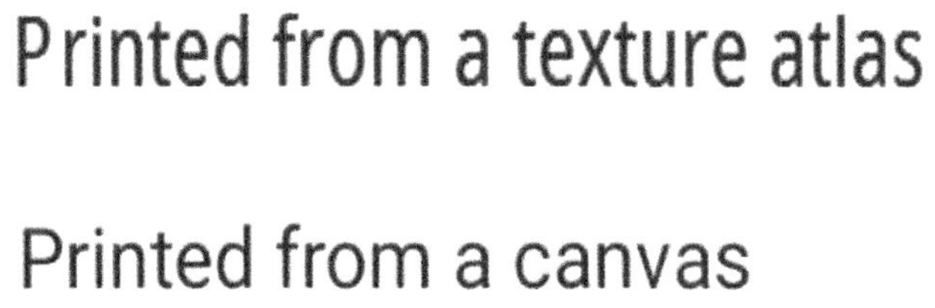

Figure 10.5 Text from a Texture Atlas and Canvas

Both methods produce readable text, but the `Canvas` text is cleaner. Also, if you look at the spacing between the first two letters, you'll see that the `Canvas` text does a better job of adjusting the spaces between characters. This is called *kerning*, which is a topic of obsession for many graphic artists.

Given these results, we can draw some basic conclusions. If you know in advance what text should be displayed, you're probably better off using a `Canvas`. But if text needs to be determined dynamically, it's probably better to use a texture atlas instead of generating new `Canvas` and `Bitmap` instances.

If you look through the code in the project's `TextDemoRenderer` class, you'll see that it takes much more code to work with the texture atlas than the `Canvas`. With the texture atlas, each character requires four vertex coordinate pairs (x, y), four texture coordinate pairs (u, v), and four index values.

The `TextDemoRenderer` constructor calls `AtlasUtils.readAtlas` to obtain a `TextureAtlas` structure representing the characters in the Droid Sans texture atlas. As discussed earlier, this structure contains the top-level geometric information for the texture atlas and a `HashMap` containing `TextureChar` structures. Each `TextureChar` stores the geometric information for a single character in the atlas, including its position, dimensions, and offsets.

After obtaining the `TextureAtlas`, the `TextDemoRenderer` calls `generateDataFromAtlas`. This iterates through the characters in the desired string and sets values for the vertex coordinates and texture coordinates. Listing 10.3 presents the code for this method.

Listing 10.3: ch10_textdemo/src/main/java/.../TextDemoRenderer.java (Abridged)

```
void generateDataFromAtlas(TextureAtlas atlas) {

  // Determine scaling factor
  float intendedHeight =
    (float)atlas.lineHeight/(float)atlas.scaleH;
  float actualHeight =
    java.lang.Math.abs(atlasVertexData[5] - atlasVertexData[1]);
  float scale = actualHeight/intendedHeight;

  // Set character positions
  float currentX = atlasVertexData[0];
  float top = atlasVertexData[5];
  TextureChar currentChar;

  for(int i=0; i<ATLAS_MSG.length(); i++) {
    currentChar = atlas.charMap.get((int)ATLAS_MSG.charAt(i));

    // Set texture coordinates
    atlasVertexData[16*i+2] = currentChar.x;
    atlasVertexData[16*i+3] = currentChar.y + currentChar.height;
    atlasVertexData[16*i+6] = currentChar.x;
    atlasVertexData[16*i+7] = currentChar.y;
    atlasVertexData[16*i+10] = currentChar.x + currentChar.width;
    atlasVertexData[16*i+11] = currentChar.y+ currentChar.height;
    atlasVertexData[16*i+14] = currentChar.x + currentChar.width;
    atlasVertexData[16*i+15] = currentChar.y;

    // Set vertex coordinates
    if(i != 0) {
      atlasVertexData[16*i] =
        currentX + currentChar.xoffset * scale;
      atlasVertexData[16*i+1] = atlasVertexData[1];
      atlasVertexData[16*i+4] = atlasVertexData[16*i];
      atlasVertexData[16*i+5] = top - currentChar.yoffset*scale;
    } else {
      atlasVertexData[5] -= currentChar.yoffset * scale;
    }
    atlasVertexData[16*i+8] =
      atlasVertexData[16*i] + currentChar.width * scale;
    atlasVertexData[16*i+9] = atlasVertexData[1];
    atlasVertexData[16*i+12] = atlasVertexData[16*i+8];
    atlasVertexData[16*i+13] = top - currentChar.yoffset * scale;

    // Update current horizontal position
    currentX += currentChar.xadvance * scale;
  }
}
```

The method starts by computing a scale factor for the character's dimensions. This is obtained by dividing the intended height of the character (the height in the `TextureChar` structure) by the desired height set by the application. This scale factor is applied to the character's `xoffset`, `yoffset`, and `xadvance` fields.

Most of this method is occupied by a loop that iterates once for each character in the text to be printed. With each iteration, the method sets values for four texture coordinate pairs and four vertex coordinate pairs. To determine vertex coordinates, the loop updates a value called `currentX`, which represents the current position in the text. At the end of each iteration, the application adds the scaled `xadvance` value to determine the next current position.

After processing the texture atlas data, the application creates a `Bitmap` containing text drawn in a `Canvas`. This is accomplished with the following code:

```
// Create Paint object and determine text width
Paint paint = new Paint();
paint.setColor(Color.BLACK);
paint.setAntiAlias(true);
paint.setTextSize(32);
int textWidth =
  java.lang.Math.round(paint.measureText(CANVAS_MSG));

// Create Bitmap to store text
canvasBitmap =
  Bitmap.createBitmap(textWidth, 33, Bitmap.Config.ARGB_8888);

// Create the Canvas for drawing characters
Canvas canvas = new Canvas(canvasBitmap);
canvas.drawARGB(255, 255, 255, 255);
canvas.drawText(CANVAS_MSG, 0.0f, 32.0f, paint);
```

This code starts by creating a `Paint` object that prints black, anti-aliased text at a height of 32 pixels. Then it creates a `Bitmap` whose format is set to `ARGB_8888` and a `Canvas` whose background color is set to white. The last line uses the `Paint` instance to draw the message inside the `Canvas`.

The renderer's `onSurfaceCreated` method calls `initTextures`, which creates textures from the two `Bitmaps`. This allocates two texture descriptors and binds both to the `GL_TEXTURE_2D` target. The `GLUtils.texImage2D` method is called twice to associate the `Bitmaps` with their descriptors. Listing 10.4 presents the code.

In both cases, we want the device to use bilinear interpolation when resizing the textures. This is accomplished by calling `glTexParameteri` with the `GL_TEXTURE_MIN_FILTER` and `GL_TEXTURE_MAG_FILTER` parameters set to `GL_LINEAR`.

Listing 10.4: ch10_textdemo/src/main/java/.../TextDemoRenderer.java (Abridged)

```
void initTextures() {

  // Generate a texture descriptor
  textureIDs = new int[2];
  GLES32.glGenTextures(2, textureIDs, 0);

  // Make the first texture unit active
  GLES32.glActiveTexture(GLES32.GL_TEXTURE0);

  // Bind the first texture descriptor to its target
  GLES32.glBindTexture(GLES32.GL_TEXTURE_2D, textureIDs[0]);

  // Set texture parameters
  GLES32.glTexParameteri(GLES32.GL_TEXTURE_2D,
    GLES32.GL_TEXTURE_MIN_FILTER, GLES32.GL_LINEAR);
  GLES32.glTexParameteri(GLES32.GL_TEXTURE_2D,
    GLES32.GL_TEXTURE_MAG_FILTER, GLES32.GL_LINEAR);

  // Read pixel data and associate it with texture
  GLUtils.texImage2D(GLES32.GL_TEXTURE_2D, 0, atlasBitmap, 0);

  // Bind the second texture descriptor to its target
  GLES32.glBindTexture(GLES32.GL_TEXTURE_2D, textureIDs[1]);

  // Set texture parameters
  GLES32.glTexParameteri(GLES32.GL_TEXTURE_2D,
    GLES32.GL_TEXTURE_MIN_FILTER, GLES32.GL_LINEAR);
  GLES32.glTexParameteri(GLES32.GL_TEXTURE_2D,
    GLES32.GL_TEXTURE_MAG_FILTER, GLES32.GL_LINEAR);

  // Read pixel data and associate it with texture
  GLUtils.texImage2D(GLES32.GL_TEXTURE_2D, 0, canvasBitmap, 0);
}
```

The code in the rest of the application is similar to code presented in preceding chapters. One difference is that the application provides the vertex shader with a vertical scaling value. This ensures that the text characters will be scaled properly for the display.

The renderer's `onRendererShutdown`'s method deallocates the textures by destroying their descriptors. This is accomplished by `glDeleteTextures`, which accepts the number of descriptors to be destroyed and the array containing the descriptors.

10.5 Summary

In computer games and virtual reality applications, it's common to apply textures to every surface in the model. Therefore, it's vitally important to understand how textures can be created and configured in code. The first part of this chapter discussed the `GLES32` methods that make this possible.

The process of extracting texel data from a texture is called *sampling*, and applications can configure the sampling process in a number of ways. A texture's filtering mode determines what value should be returned when the sampling point lies between texels. Similarly, an application can specify what value should be returned when the sampling point lies outside the boundaries of the texture.

The second half of this chapter discussed the topic of text. There are a number of ways to draw text in OpenGL ES applications, and this chapter has looked at two: generating a texture atlas and drawing text from a `Canvas`. Texture atlases are ideal when an application's text may change over the course of its execution. Drawing text from a `Canvas` is ideal when an application knows in advance what text should be displayed.

Chapter 11

Advanced OpenGL ES Development

When I first started working with OpenGL, my applications ran in *immediate mode*. In this mode, the CPU transfers data to the GPU in tiny packets—one triplet of vertex coordinates, then one triplet of color components, and so on. The code was easy to understand, but because of the constant transfers of small amounts of data, the performance was awful.

Over the years, OpenGL has supported automating the data transfer and sending the data in larger and larger packages. The use of `glVertexAttribPointer` is a major improvement on the days when I sent data between `glBegin` and `glEnd`.

OpenGL's support for larger transfer packages has evolved further, and today's programs store data in buffer objects, which include vertex buffer objects (VBOs), uniform buffer objects (UBOs), and index buffer objects (IBOs). These may seem confusing at first, but once you see how they streamline CPU-GPU transfers, you'll use them in all your applications.

Unlike buffer objects, vertex array objects (VAOs) don't store data. Instead, they store the relationships between a VBO and its attributes. If an application requires multiple VBOs and programs, VAOs make it easy to switch between states to ensure that the correct data will be sent to the GPU.

The last part of this chapter introduces framebuffer objects, or FBOs. FBOs make it possible to render graphics into a custom memory region instead of drawing graphics to the screen. Once you understand how FBOs work, you'll be able to access a number of high-level graphics features, such as rendering graphics to a texture. To demonstrate this, the example module presented in this chapter draws a triangle onto a texture and displays the texture in the graphical window.

11.1 Vertex Buffer Objects (VBOs)

The example code in preceding chapters has transferred rendering data to the GPU with every frame. This is suitable when an application's data changes with every frame, but if data is intended to remain constant, this mode of rendering requires an unacceptable amount of time and processing.

OpenGL provides an alternative that makes use of vertex buffer objects, or VBOs. This allocates GPU memory to hold attribute data (vertex coordinates, colors, and so on) so that the data isn't constantly transferred with each frame. From this chapter onward, the example code will store vertex data in VBOs.

Working with VBOs is like working with textures, but there are no texture units involved. First, the application generates one or more numeric descriptors. Then it makes one descriptor active and configures the VBO through this descriptor.

Table 11.1 lists the `GLES32` methods that make this possible. As we'll see, some of these methods can be used to configure different types of buffer objects besides VBOs.

Table 11.1

Vertex Buffer Object (VBO) Methods

Method	Description
`glGenBuffers(int num, IntBuffer buffers)/ glGenBuffers(int n, int[] buffers, int offset)`	Generates buffer descriptors in an IntBuffer or an array
`glBindBuffer(int target, int desc)`	Binds the descriptor to a target
`glBufferData(int target, int size, Buffer data, int usage)`	Allocates device memory for the VBO
`glMapBufferRange(int target, int offset, int len, int access)`	Returns a Buffer to contain the data to be passed to the GPU
`glUnmapBuffer(int target)`	Unmaps the Buffer from the VBO's data store
`glDeleteBuffers(int num, IntBuffer buffers)/ glDeleteBuffers(int n, int[] buffers, int offset)`	Deletes VBOs from an IntBuffer or an array

A good way to understand these methods is to compare them with the texture methods discussed in Chapter 10. For example, the following code creates a texture descriptor, binds it to a target, associates it with a `Bitmap`, and deletes the descriptor.

```
int[] textureIDs = new int[1];
GLES32.glGenTextures(1, textureIDs, 0);
GLES32.glBindTexture(GLES32.GL_TEXTURE_2D, textureIDs[0]);
GLUtils.texImage2D(GLES32.GL_TEXTURE_2D, 0, bitmap, 0);
...
GLES32.glDeleteTextures(1, textureIDs, 0);
```

Working with VBOs uses similar code. For example, the following code generates a VBO descriptor, binds it to a target, allocates 8k of memory, maps the content of `dataArray` to the buffer, terminates the mapping, and deletes the descriptor:

```
int[] vboIDs = new int[1];
GLES32.glGenBuffers(1, vboIDs, 0);

GLES32.glBindBuffer(GLES32.GL_ARRAY_BUFFER, vboIDs[0]);

GLES32.glBufferData(GLES32.GL_ARRAY_BUFFER, 8192, null,
                    GLES32.GL_DYNAMIC_DRAW);

ByteBuffer buff = (ByteBuffer)GLES32.glMapBufferRange(
   GLES32.GL_ARRAY_BUFFER, 0, 8192, GLES32.GL_MAP_WRITE_BIT);

buff.order(ByteOrder.nativeOrder());
buff.put(dataArray);

GLES32.glUnmapBuffer(GLES32.GL_ARRAY_BUFFER);
GLES32.glDeleteBuffers(1, vboIDs, 0);
```

The first difference involves the nature of the target. While textures can be bound to targets like `GL_TEXTURE_2D`, a VBO descriptor must be bound to `GL_ARRAY_BUFFER`. A later section will discuss other targets of `glBindBuffer`, which include `GL_UNIFORM_BUFFER` and `GL_ELEMENT_ARRAY_BUFFER`.

When accessing textures, `texImage2D` takes care of allocating the texture's memory and initializing its data. `glBufferData` is capable of performing both tasks, but for performance reasons, this book's code only uses it for memory allocation. This is accomplished by setting the second argument of `glBufferData` equal to the number of bytes to be allocated and the third argument to `null`.

The fourth argument of `glBufferData` tells the system how the buffer's data is intended to be accessed. This accepts one of the nine values listed in Table 11.2.

Table 11.2

glBufferData Usage Identifiers

Value	Description
GL_STATIC_DRAW	Data is intended for drawing–it will be modified once and used frequently
GL_STATIC_READ	Data is intended to be read from the renderer–it will be modified once and used frequently
GL_STATIC_COPY	Data is intended to be read from the renderer and used for drawing–it will be modified once and used frequently
GL_DYNAMIC_DRAW	Data is intended for drawing–it will be modified repeatedly and used frequently
GL_DYNAMIC_READ	Data is intended to be read from the renderer–it will be modified repeatedly and used frequently
GL_DYNAMIC_COPY	Data is intended to be read from the renderer and used for drawing–it will be modified repeatedly and used frequently
GL_STREAM_DRAW	Data is intended for drawing–it will be updated frequently (once per frame)
GL_STREAM_READ	Data is intended to be read from the renderer–it will be updated frequently (once per frame)
GL_STREAM_COPY	Data is intended to be read from the renderer and used for drawing–it will be updated frequently (once per frame)

Each value identifies the intended direction of the buffer's data and the frequency of its usage. `DRAW` implies that that data will be written from the CPU to the GPU, `READ` implies that the data will be read from the GPU, and `COPY` implies that data is intended to be read from the GPU and used for drawing purposes. `STATIC` implies that the data will change rarely but be used frequently, `DYNAMIC` implies that the data will be read and written frequently, and `STREAM` implies that the data will be updated after each use.

For example, the following code allocates memory for a 16k buffer whose data will be drawn frequently:

```
GLES32.glBufferData(GLES32.GL_ARRAY_BUFFER, 16384, null,
                    GLES32.GL_DYNAMIC_DRAW);
```

After the buffer is allocated, the application can write to it by calling two methods: `glMapBufferRange` and `glUnmapBuffer`. One advantage of using `glMapBufferRange` is that the data transfer can be performed asynchronously. Another advantage is that it can write to a portion of the VBO instead of the entire object.

The fourth argument of glMapBufferRange configures the VBO's data transfer. This can be set to one of the six values listed in Table 11.3 or a combination thereof.

Table 11.3

glMapBufferRange Access Identifiers

Value	Description
GL_MAP_READ_BIT	The Buffer may be used to read VBO data
GL_MAP_WRITE_BIT	The Buffer may be used to write VBO data
GL_MAP_INVALIDATE_RANGE_BIT	The previous content of the given range may be discarded (not usable with GL_MAP_READ_BIT)
GL_MAP_INVALIDATE_BUFFER_BIT	The previous content of the VBO may be discarded (not usable with GL_MAP_READ_BIT)
GL_MAP_FLUSH_EXPLICIT_BIT	One or more subranges may be modified (can only be used with GL_MAP_WRITE_BIT)
GL_MAP_UNSYNCHRONIZED_BIT	glMapBufferRange should return without waiting for the GPU

The GL_MAP_INVALIDATE_BUFFER_BIT value is helpful for applications that need to stream data to the GPU. This is because the VBO's previous content will be invalidated each time the application writes to it.

By default, glMapBufferRange forces the CPU to wait for the GPU to finish processing. But if GL_MAP_UNSYNCHRONIZED_BIT is set, the data transfer will be performed asynchronously. This frees the CPU to perform other tasks.

The following code demonstrates how glMapBufferRange can be used in practice. It obtains a mapped Buffer, initializes its content, and then removes the mapping.

```
ByteBuffer buff = (ByteBuffer) GLES32.glMapBufferRange(
  GLES32.GL_ARRAY_BUFFER, 0, 16382, GLES32.GL_MAP_WRITE_BIT |
  GLES32.GL_MAP_UNSYNCHRONIZED_BIT);
buff.order(ByteOrder.nativeOrder());
buff.put(dataArray);
boolean status = GLES32.glUnmapBuffer(GLES32.GL_ARRAY_BUFFER);
```

Android's documentation for GLES32 states that glMapBufferRange returns a Buffer. In practice, the method returns a direct ByteBuffer that can be used like a regular ByteBuffer.

glUnmapBuffer must be called before the VBO's data can be processed. This returns a boolean that identifies whether the unmapping completed successfully.

11.2 Vertex Array Objects (VAOs)

After a VBO has been created, the application needs to identify how its data should be provided to the vertex shader. Chapter 7 explained how this can be accomplished by obtaining the index of a vertex shader variable and associating data with the index. The following code shows how this works:

```
int coordIndex = GLES32.glGetAttribLocation(program, "in_coords");

GLES32.glEnableVertexAttribArray(coordIndex);

GLES32.glVertexAttribPointer(coordIndex, 2, GLES32.GL_FLOAT,
                             false, 20, vertexBuffer);
```

If a model contains different types of graphics, the application may need to execute multiple shaders. This means that `glEnableVertexAttribArray` and `glVertexAttribPointer` must be invoked during rendering for each attribute in each vertex shader. This can take a significant amount of time.

To reduce the processing burden, OpenGL provides a mechanism that stores how data is associated with shader attributes. This is called a *vertex array object*, or VAO. A VAO stores all of the associations needed to access the data in a VBO.

Like VBOs, VAOs are accessed through numeric descriptors. Unlike VBOs, VAOs are not bound to targets. Table 11.4 lists the basic methods involved.

Table 11.4

Vertex Array Object (VAO) Methods

Method	Description
`glGenVertexArrays(int num, IntBuffer buffers)/ glGenVertexArrays(int num, int[] buffers, int offset)`	Generates array descriptors in an IntBuffer or an array
`glBindVertexArray(int desc)`	Makes the VAO active
`glDeleteVertexArrays(int num, IntBuffer buffers)/ glDeleteVertexArrays(int num, int[] buffers, int offset)`	Deletes VAOs from an IntBuffer or an array

The first two functions, `glGenVertexArrays` and `glBindVertexArray`, work like the `glGenBuffers` and `glBindBuffer` methods discussed earlier. `glGenVertexArrays` initializes an array of unique descriptors. This is shown in the following code.

```
// Allocate descriptor
int[] vao = new int[1];

// Generate a descriptor
GLES32.glGenVertexArrays(1, vao, 0);

// Make the VAO active
GLES32.glBindVertexArray(vao[0]);
```

`glBindVertexArray` doesn't bind the VAO to a target. Instead, it makes the VAO active, which means that following operations will be associated with the given VAO. These operations include binding a VBO, setting a VBO's data, and associating the VBO's data with shader attributes. This is shown in the following code.

```
// Make the VAO active
GLES32.glBindVertexArray(vao[0]);

// Bind a VBO
GLES32.glBindBuffer(GLES32.GL_ARRAY_BUFFER, vbos[0]);

// Allocate memory for the VBO
GLES32.glBufferData(GLES32.GL_ARRAY_BUFFER,
  dataArray.length, null, GL_DYNAMIC_DRAW);

// Associate VBO with the content of dataArray
ByteBuffer buff = (ByteBuffer) GLES32.glMapBufferRange(
  GLES32.GL_ARRAY_BUFFER, 0, 16382, GLES32.GL_MAP_WRITE_BIT |
  GLES32.GL_MAP_UNSYNCHRONIZED_BIT);
buff.order(ByteOrder.nativeOrder());
buff.put(dataArray);
GLES32.glUnmapBuffer(GLES32.GL_ARRAY_BUFFER);

// Identify portion of VBO to be associated with in_coords
int coordIndex = GLES32.glGetAttribLocation(program, "in_coords");
GLES32.glEnableVertexAttribArray(coordIndex);
GLES32.glVertexAttribPointer(coordIndex, 2, GLES32.GL_FLOAT,
                             false, 20, 0);
```

Because of `glBindVertexArray`, the VAO is associated with the VBO and its attribute bindings. Note that the last argument of `glVertexAttribPointer` is set to an offset into the VBO, not the buffer containing the data.

This may seem like a lot of work, but VAOs simplify the code needed to draw vertices. Suppose the `vaos` array contains three VAO descriptors and each descriptor has one or more associated VBOs with shader attributes. The following code draws the content of each of the three VAOs:

```
GLES32.glBindVertexArray(vaos[0]);
GLES32.glDrawArrays(GLES32.GL_TRIANGLE_STRIP, 0, num_points_a);

GLES32.glBindVertexArray(vaos[1]);
GLES32.glDrawArrays(GLES32.GL_TRIANGLE_STRIP, 0, num_points_b);

GLES32.glBindVertexArray(vaos[2]);
GLES32.glDrawArrays(GLES32.GL_TRIANGLE_STRIP, 0, num_points_c);
```

`glDrawArrays` isn't the only method that can be used to draw the content of a VAO. Any `glDraw*` method can be used. If the VAO has an associated index buffer object, a method like `glDrawElements` will access the indices when drawing the model.

11.3 More Buffer Objects

In addition to vertex buffer objects, OpenGL supports additional types of buffer objects that store data intended for the GPU. This section introduces uniform buffer objects (UBOs), index buffer objects (IBOs), and framebuffer objects (FBOs).

11.3.1 Uniform Buffer Objects (UBOs)

If a shader needs multiple uniform variables, it's more efficient for the application to package the data in a UBO than to call `glUniform*` multiple times. Another advantage is that one UBO can be associated with multiple programs.

In code, working with UBOs is a lot like working with VBOs. The process consists of five familiar steps:

1. Create one or more buffer object descriptors by calling `glGenBuffers`.
2. Associate a descriptor with the `GL_UNIFORM_BUFFER` target by calling `glBindBuffer`.
3. Allocate memory for the UBO by calling `glBufferData`.
4. Set the UBO's data.
5. When they're no longer needed, delete the descriptors with `glDestroyBuffers`.

For example, suppose an application needs to pass matrices to a vertex shader and they're stored in an array called `matrixArray`. The following code configures the UBO:

```
int[] ubo = new int[1];
GLES32.glGenBuffers(1, ubo, 0);
GLES32.glBindBuffer(GLES32.GL_UNIFORM_BUFFER, ubo);
GLES32.glBufferData(GLES32.GL_UNIFORM_BUFFER, matrixSize, null,
  GLES32.GL_DYNAMIC_DRAW);
ByteBuffer buff = (ByteBuffer)GLES32.glMapBufferRange(
  GLES32.GL_UNIFORM_BUFFER, 0, matrixSize,
  GLES32.GL_MAP_WRITE_BIT | GLES32.GL_MAP_UNSYNCHRONIZED_BIT);
buff.order(ByteOrder.nativeOrder());
buff.asFloatBuffer().put(matrixArray);
GLES32.glUnmapBuffer(GLES32.GL_UNIFORM_BUFFER);
```

In my experiments, `glMapBufferRange` executes slowly for uniform buffers when it works at all. For this reason, I prefer to set uniform buffer data with `glBufferSubData`.

To access data in a UBO, a shader needs to declare a *uniform block*, also called an *interface block*. This may contain multiple variable declarations. For example, the following block declaration defines three matrices:

```
uniform matrix_block {
  mat4 model_view_matrix;
  mat4 projection_matrix;
  mat4 inv_matrix;
};
```

To associate uniform blocks like `matrix_block` with data, an application needs to perform three steps:

1. Obtain the location of the uniform block.
2. Set a binding point that represents the UBO.
3. Associate the binding point with the location of the uniform block.

Just as `glGetUniformLocation` returns the location of a uniform variable, `glGetUniformBlockIndex` returns the location of a uniform block.

```
glGetUniformBlockIndex(int program, String block_name)
```

As an example, the following code returns the location of `matrix_block`:

```
int loc = GLES32.glGetUniformBlockIndex(prog, "matrix_block");
```

A UBO can be associated with multiple programs. Therefore, if the UBO's data changes, every shader will receive updated data. Each association between a UBO and a program must be made separately, and each can be identified by a *binding point*. To establish a binding point, an application needs to call `glBindBufferBase`:

```
glBindBufferBase(int target, int binding_point, int descriptor)
```

For example, suppose an application needs to associate the `ubo` descriptor with the `trans_matrices` uniform block in `prog1` and the `new_matrices` block in `prog2`. The application can associate `ubo` with both blocks by setting two binding points. This is shown in the following code:

```
int loc1 = GLES32.glGetUniformBlockIndex(prog1, "trans_matrices");
GLES32.glBindBufferBase(GLES32.GL_UNIFORM_BUFFER, 0, ubo);
GLES32.glUniformBlockBinding(prog1, loc1, 0);

int loc2 = GLES32.glGetUniformBlockIndex(prog2, "new_matrices");
GLES32.glBindBufferBase(GLES32.GL_UNIFORM_BUFFER, 1, ubo);
GLES32.glUniformBlockBinding(prog2, loc2, 1);
```

As shown, `glUniformBlockBinding` establishes the connection between the program, the block index, and the binding point. In this code, the first binding point has a value of `0` and the second has a value of `1`.

11.3.2 Index Buffer Objects (IBOs)

Up to this point, applications have provided indices for vertex drawing by setting the last argument of `glDrawElements` to an NIO buffer. But `GLES32` provides a second `glDrawElements` method whose last argument is an integer that serves as an offset. For example, the following code sets the offset to 0:

```
GLES32.glDrawElements(GLES32.GL_TRIANGLE_STRIP, 4,
                      GLES32.GL_UNSIGNED_BYTE, 0);
```

This offset identifies the first byte that should be accessed from a buffer object containing indices. This buffer object is referred to as an index buffer object (IBO) or an element buffer object (EBO).

An IBO can be created and configured using the same methods as used for a VBO. The only difference is that the descriptor needs to be bound to `GL_ELEMENT_ARRAY_BUFFER` instead of `GL_ARRAY_BUFFER`. This is shown in the following code.

```
int[] ibo = new int[1];
GLES32.glGenBuffers(1, ibo, 0);
GLES32.glBindBuffer(GLES32.GL_ELEMENT_ARRAY_BUFFER, ibo);
GLES32.glBufferData(GLES32.GL_ELEMENT_ARRAY_BUFFER,
  indexArray.length, null, GLES32.GL_DYNAMIC_DRAW);

ByteBuffer buff = (ByteBuffer)GLES32.glMapBufferRange(
  GLES32.GL_ELEMENT_ARRAY_BUFFER, 0, indexArray.length,
  GLES32.GL_MAP_WRITE_BIT | GLES32.GL_MAP_UNSYNCHRONIZED_BIT);
buff.order(ByteOrder.nativeOrder());
buff.put(indexArray);

GLES32.glUnmapBuffer(GLES32.ELEMENT_ARRAY_BUFFER);
```

After an IBO has been configured, draw commands will access the active IBO whenever indices are needed. An application can change the active IBO by calling `glBindBuffer` with the `ELEMENT_ARRAY_BUFFER` target and a new descriptor.

IBOs can also be associated with the vertex array objects (VAOs) discussed earlier. When a VAO is made active with `glBindVertexArray`, its IBO will also be made active.

11.3.3 Framebuffer Objects (FBOs)

As discussed in Chapter 7, the graphics rendering pipline resembles an assembly line, and the last stage updates a framebuffer. A framebuffer is a container of two-dimensional memory buffers such as color buffers, a depth/stencil buffer, and an accumulation buffer. After the fragment shader executes, the content of one of the color buffers will be updated and displayed in the viewport.

An application can create custom framebuffers, which are represented by framebuffer objects, or FBOs. These are more complex than the other objects we've looked at, and their main purpose isn't to improve performance. Instead, FBOs make it possible to display special effects. For example, a later section demonstrates how FBOs enable applications to draw graphics on textures.

This discussion explains how to create FBOs and associate them with data buffers. The last part of the discussion explains how to associate an FBO's buffer with texture data.

Basic FBO Operations

The code needed to create and configure an FBO is essentially similar to the code we've looked at earlier. But the methods have slightly different names. The creation method is `glGenFramebuffers` instead of `glGenBuffers`. The method for binding an FBO is `glBindFramebuffers` instead of `glBindBuffer`. Table 11.5 lists the signatures of these methods.

Table 11.5
Basic Framebuffer Object (FBO) Methods

Method	Description
`glGenFramebuffers(int num, IntBuffer buffers)/ glGenFramebuffers(int num, int[] buffers, int offset)`	Generate framebuffer descriptors in an IntBuffer or an array
`glBindFramebuffer(int target, int descriptor)`	Bind the FBO descriptor to a target
`glDeleteFramebuffers(int num, IntBuffer buffers)/ glDeleteFramebuffers(int num, int[] buffers, int offset)`	Delete FBOs from an IntBuffer or an array

Like VBO descriptors, an FBO descriptor must be bound to a target before it can be used. The first argument of `glBindFramebuffer` can be set to one of three values:

- `GL_DRAW_FRAMEBUFFER` — The data is intended to be displayed
- `GL_READ_FRAMEBUFFER` — The data is intended to be read by the application
- `GL_FRAMEBUFFER` — The FBO's data is intended to be displayed or read by the application

`glBindFramebuffer` identifies which framebuffer should be used for rendering. That is, when an FBO has been bound to `GL_FRAMEBUFFER`, the FBO's framebuffer will be affected by draw operations instead of the default framebuffer. The following code shows how this works.

```
int[] fbos = new int[1];
GLES32.glGenFramebuffers(1, fbos, 0);
GLES32.glBindFramebuffer(GLES32.GL_FRAMEBUFFER, fbos[0]);
```

To return to regular rendering, an application needs to remove the FBO's binding. This can be accomplished by setting the second argument of `glBindFrameBuffer` to 0:

```
GLES32.glBindFramebuffer(GLES32.GL_FRAMEBUFFER, 0);
```

After an FBO has been bound, the application can associate it with memory buffers. This association is made possible through *attachments*, which will be discussed next.

Attachments

Before an FBO can hold data, it needs to have one or more memory buffers associated with it. Each memory buffer is called an *attachment* and an application can add an attachment to one of an FBO's *attachment points*. Each attachment point is identified by a numeric value:

- `GL_COLOR_ATTACHMENTi` — The FBO receives image data (`i` can be at least 0–7)
- `GL_DEPTH_ATTACHMENT` — The FBO receives depth values
- `GL_STENCIL_ATTACHMENT` — The FBO receives stencil values
- `GL_DEPTH_STENCIL_ATTACHMENT` — The FBO receives combined depth/stencil values

An application can attach one of two types of data to an attachment point: a texture or a renderbuffer. A renderbuffer resembles a texture, but may be faster to process because it's not intended to be used as a texture. This discussion focuses on attaching textures to FBOs, and this can be accomplished with `glFramebufferTexture`:

```
glFramebufferTexture(int fbo_target, int attachment_point,
                     int texture_id, int level)
```

The first argument sets the FBO target and the second identifies the FBO's attachment point. The third argument identifies the texture to be attached and the last argument sets the mipmap level of the attached texture.

FBO Rendering

If an FBO has been bound to `GL_DRAW_FRAMEBUFFER` or `GL_FRAMEBUFFER` and it has a color attachment, it can serve as a rendering target. That is, the color attachment can receive pixels from the fragment shader that can be displayed in the viewport.

The `glDrawBuffers` method identifies which of the FBO's attachments should receive rendering results. Its signature is given as follows:

```
glDrawBuffers(int num, IntBuffer attachment_points)
```

The first argument identifies how many attachments should be targeted. The second argument is a buffer that contains the attachment points to which the targeted attachments are bound. In other words, the `IntBuffer` should contain `num` attachment point identifiers.

11.4 Example Application – Render to Texture

The ch11_rendertexture application draws a triangle on a texture and then displays the texture. In effect, it combines the ch07_triangle module and the ch10_simpletexture module.

From a developer's perspective, the ch11_rendertexture marks an important turning point. First of all, it uses four of the objects discussed in this chapter: vertex buffer objects (VBOs), vertex array objects (VAOs), index buffer objects (IBOs), and framebuffer objects (FBOs). Second, because there are two drawing operations involved, the project requires two sets of shaders, two sets of attribute data, and two `glDraw*` calls.

In the `RenderTextureRenderer` class, `onSurfaceCreated` calls four important methods:

1. `initFramebuffer` — Creates the FBO and attaches a texture
2. `initTriangleData` — Creates a VAO/VBO to store the triangle-drawing data
3. `initRenderData` — Creates a VAO/VBO to store the texture-drawing data
4. `renderToTexture` — Draws the triangle on the FBO's texture

To explain how the project works, this section discusses the code in the `initFramebuffer`, `initTriangleData`, and `renderToTexture` methods.

11.4.1 Initializing the Framebuffer

The `initFramebuffer` method demonstrates how FBOs can be created and how a texture can be attached to an FBO's attachment point. Listing 11.1 presents the code.

Listing 11.1: ch11_rendertexture/src/main/java/../RenderTextureRenderer.java

```
void initFramebuffer() {

  // Enable texture processing
  GLES32.glEnable(GLES32.GL_TEXTURE_2D);

  // Make the first texture unit active
  GLES32.glActiveTexture(GLES32.GL_TEXTURE0);

  // Generate framebuffer
  GLES32.glGenFramebuffers(1, fbos, 0);
  GLES32.glBindFramebuffer(GLES32.GL_FRAMEBUFFER, fbos[0]);
```

Listing 11.1: ch11_rendertexture/src/main/java/../RenderTextureRenderer.java

```
    // Generate a texture descriptor
    GLES32.glGenTextures(1, texIDs, 0);
    GLES32.glBindTexture(GLES32.GL_TEXTURE_2D, texIDs[0]);

    // Set texture parameters
    GLES32.glTexParameteri(GLES32.GL_TEXTURE_2D,
      GLES32.GL_TEXTURE_MIN_FILTER, GLES32.GL_LINEAR);
    GLES32.glTexParameteri(GLES32.GL_TEXTURE_2D,
      GLES32.GL_TEXTURE_MAG_FILTER, GLES32.GL_LINEAR);

    // Read pixel data and associate it with texture
    GLES32.glTexImage2D(GLES32.GL_TEXTURE_2D, 0, GLES32.GL_RGBA,
      800, 800, 0, GLES32.GL_RGBA, GLES32.GL_UNSIGNED_BYTE, null);

    GLES32.glFramebufferTexture(GLES32.GL_FRAMEBUFFER,
      GLES32.GL_COLOR_ATTACHMENT0, texIDs[0], 0);

    // Identify the attachment point
    int[] attachmentPoints = new int[1];
    attachmentPoints[0] = GLES32.GL_COLOR_ATTACHMENT0;
    ByteBuffer tempBuffer =
      ByteBuffer.allocateDirect(attachmentPoints.length * 4);
    tempBuffer.order(ByteOrder.nativeOrder());
    IntBuffer pointsBuffer = tempBuffer.asIntBuffer();
    pointsBuffer.put(attachmentPoints);
    pointsBuffer.rewind();
    GLES32.glDrawBuffers(1, pointsBuffer);

    // Remove the binding
    GLES32.glBindFramebuffer(GLES32.GL_FRAMEBUFFER, 0);
}
```

This code starts by generating an FBO descriptor and binding it to the `GL_FRAMEBUFFER` target. Then it generates a texture descriptor, binds it to `GL_TEXTURE_2D`, and configures the texture's properties. This method calls `glTexImage2D` instead of `GLUtils.texImage2D` because the texture is empty.

The `glFramebufferTexture` method associates the texture with the `GL_COLOR_ATTACHMENT0` attachment point. Then `glDrawBuffers` receives an `IntBuffer` that identifies that the `GL_COLOR_ATTACHMENT0` attachment will be the rendering target.

Because `GL_COLOR_ATTACHMENT0` is the rendering surface, the fragment shader needs to associate its `out_color` variable with `GL_COLOR_ATTACHMENT0`. This can be accomplished by preceding the variable's declaration with `layout(location=0)`.

11.4.2 Storing Drawing Data

The `initTriangleData` method configures a VAO to hold all the information needed to draw a triangle. This information includes a VBO containing the vertex data (coordinates and colors) and the associations between the VBO's content and the variables of the vertex shader.

Listing 11.2 presents the code of `initTriangleData`. The method begins by binding the first VAO. This ensures that succeeding operations will affect the VAO.

Listing 11.2: ch11_rendertexture/src/main/java/../RenderTextureRenderer.java

```
void initTriangleData() {

  // Bind the VAO
  GLES32.glBindVertexArray(vaos[0]);

  // Configure the VBO
  GLES32.glBindBuffer(GLES32.GL_ARRAY_BUFFER, vbos[0]);
  int dataSize = triangleData.length * 4;
  GLES32.glBufferData(GLES32.GL_ARRAY_BUFFER,
    dataSize, null, GLES32.GL_DYNAMIC_DRAW);
  ByteBuffer buff = (ByteBuffer)GLES32.glMapBufferRange(
    GLES32.GL_ARRAY_BUFFER, 0, dataSize,
    GLES32.GL_MAP_WRITE_BIT | GLES32.GL_MAP_UNSYNCHRONIZED_BIT);
  buff.order(ByteOrder.nativeOrder());
  FloatBuffer tmpBuffer = buff.asFloatBuffer();
  tmpBuffer.put(triangleData);
  GLES32.glUnmapBuffer(GLES32.GL_ARRAY_BUFFER);

  // Associate coordinate data with in_coords
  int coordIndex =
    GLES32.glGetAttribLocation(programs[0], "in_coords");
  GLES32.glEnableVertexAttribArray(coordIndex);
  GLES32.glVertexAttribPointer(coordIndex, 2,
    GLES32.GL_FLOAT, false, 20, 0);

  // Associate color data with in_colors
  int colorIndex =
    GLES32.glGetAttribLocation(programs[0], "in_color");
  GLES32.glEnableVertexAttribArray(colorIndex);
  GLES32.glVertexAttribPointer(colorIndex, 3,
    GLES32.GL_FLOAT, false, 20, 2 * 4);

  // Bind the VAO
  GLES32.glBindVertexArray(0);
}
```

After binding the VAO, the method binds a VBO and allocates its memory by calling `glBufferData`. In this case, the VBO needs to store the `float`s in the `triangleData` array. For this reason, the second argument of `glBufferData` is set to `triangleData.length * 4`.

To write the content of `triangleData` to the VBO, the method calls `glMapBufferRange` and `glUnmapBuffer`. `glMapBufferRange` provides a `Buffer` that can be cast to a `ByteBuffer` that can be converted into a `FloatBuffer`. The `GL_MAP_UNSYNCHRONIZED_BIT` flag indicates that the write operation should be performed asynchronously. After the data is written, the VBO map is closed by calling `glUnmapBuffer`.

After configuring the VBO, the code associates two shader variables, `in_coords` and `in_color`, with portions of the VBO's data. This uses the same three functions as in previous applications (`glGetAttribLocation`, `glEnableVertexAttribArray`, and `glVertexAttribPointer`), but there's one important difference. The last argument of `glVertexAttribPointer` is an integer, not a buffer. The integer identifies a byte offset into the VBO.

For example, consider the following code:

```
GLES32.glVertexAttribPointer(colorIndex, 3, GLES32.GL_FLOAT,
  false, 20, 2 * 4);
```

The last argument is `8`, which indicates that the initial data for the shader variable corresponding to `colorIndex` can be accessed eight bytes into the VBO.

The last line of `initTriangleData` calls `glBindVertexArray` with the argument set to `0`. This unbinds the VAO, but doesn't erase its associated data. When the VAO's data is needed, the application can call `glBindVertexArray` with the VAO's descriptor.

11.4.3 Drawing the Triangle

After configuring the FBO and the VAO, the application can draw a triangle on the FBO's associated texture. This is accomplished by the `renderToTexture` method, whose code is presented in Listing 11.3.

The method starts by binding the FBO configured in `initFramebuffer` and the VAO configured in `initTriangleData`. This ensures that draw operations will target the FBO and will use the data associated with the VAO. In addition, the method calls `glUseProgram` to identify which program's shaders should be executed by the draw operation.

Listing 11.3: ch11_rendertexture/src/main/java/../RenderTextureRenderer.java

```
void renderToTexture() {

  // Set the FBO
  GLES32.glBindFramebuffer(GLES32.GL_FRAMEBUFFER, fbos[0]);

  // Bind the VAO and program
  GLES32.glBindVertexArray(vaos[0]);
  GLES32.glUseProgram(programs[0]);

  // Configure draw operation
  GLES32.glViewport(0, 0, 800, 800);
  GLES32.glLineWidth(10);
  GLES32.glClearColor(0.8f, 0.8f, 0.8f, 1.0f);
  GLES32.glClear(GLES32.GL_COLOR_BUFFER_BIT);

  // Draw the triangle
  GLES32.glDrawArrays(GLES32.GL_LINE_LOOP, 0, 3);

  // Unbind the FBO and VAO
  GLES32.glBindFramebuffer(GLES32.GL_FRAMEBUFFER, 0);
  GLES32.glBindVertexArray(0);
}
```

The `glViewport` method is important because it identifies the rendering region. In this case, `glViewport` configures the rendering to occupy the entire 800-by-800 pixel texture.

The method calls `glDrawArrays` to actually draw the triangle. Because the custom FBO is bound, the rendering will be performed on the FBO's texture, not the default framebuffer.

After the drawing is performed, the method unbinds the FBO and VBO. By unbinding the FBO, the method ensures that future draw operations will target the default framebuffer.

11.5 Summary

Since its initial release in the early 1990s, OpenGL has evolved in many ways. OpenGL didn't support shaders until 2004, and even then, it only supported vertex and fragment shaders. Today, developers can take advantage of six different types of programmable routines for the GPU.

OpenGL has also improved the manner in which data is passed to the GPU. Initially, graphical data was transferred in small packets. But modern OpenGL applications package data in large buffer objects, such as vertex buffer objects (VBOs), uniform buffer objects (UBOs), and index buffer objects (IBOs).

Most of this chapter has been devoted to explaining how these buffer objects are used. In most cases, the process involves allocating descriptors, binding a descriptor to a target, and invoking methods that configure the bound buffer object. VBOs and IBOs can be created and configured with nearly identical code, but VBOs must be bound to `GL_ARRAY_BUFFER` and IBOs must be bound to `GL_ELEMENT_ARRAY_BUFFER`.

The last part of the chapter discussed the fascinating topic of framebuffer objects (FBOs). FBOs make it possible to render graphics to a memory region instead of to the display screen. This enables a number of special effects, including render-to-texture and shadow mapping.

Chapter 12

Accessing the Daydream Controller

Up to this point, all of the example applications have focused on drawing graphics. But Daydream applications also need to receive data from the controller. In effect, the controller serves as a three-dimensional mouse.

The Google VR SDK makes it simple to connect to the controller and access its data. The first class to know is `ControllerManager`, whose `EventListener` interface provides information about software compatibility and notifies applications when the user recenters the controller.

The most important role of the `ControllerManager` is to provide an instance of the second important class, `Controller`. This `Controller` instance serves as a software representation of the physical controller. `Controller` has a nested `EventListener` class that provides information about the controller's physical state and the state of its connection to the Android device.

After an application obtains a `Controller` instance, reading the controller's data is straightforward. But there's a catch—the controller's orientation is provided as a quaternion. Quaternions are convenient in many theoretical respects, but the mathematics of multiplying them is complex. But if you want to know where the controller is pointing, it's crucial to have a basic familiarity with quaternions.

The last part of the chapter presents an application that uses the Google VR SDK to determine which object is being pointed to by the controller. To accomplish this, the application accesses a `ControllerManager` and obtains a `Controller` instance representing the controller. Then it reads the controller's orientation and performs the quaternion operations needed to determine where the controller's vector intersects the drawing plane.

12.1 The Controller Hardware

At the time of this writing, the Google Daydream package contains a handheld controller that communicates with the device using Bluetooth Low Energy (BLE). The controller has a touchpad and two buttons: an App button and a Home button. Figure 12.1 shows what it looks like.

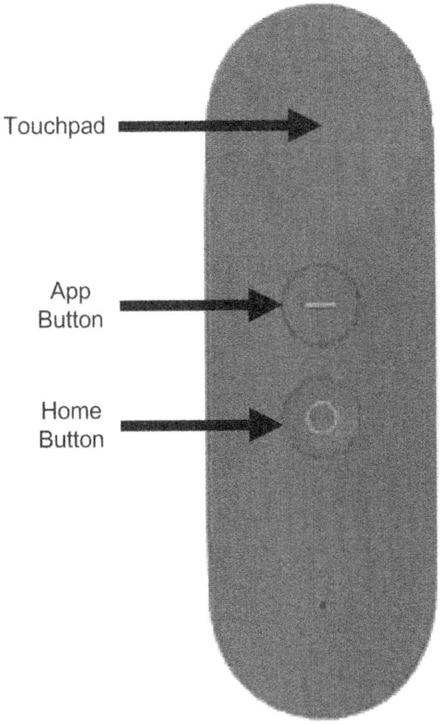

Figure 12.1 The Daydream Controller

The touchpad can function like a computer's mouse. That is, applications can receive both click events and motion events. In addition, applications can identify the location of the click event on the touchpad.

Applications can receive and process App button events without restriction, but the Home button is intended for recentering the controller. As Chapter 17 will make clear, the Daydream requirements specify that applications should not interfere with the recentering process.

12.2 ControllerManager and Controller

The Google VR SDK provides an Android archive named sdk-controller-*x*-*y*-*z*.aar. This contains two important classes that provide access to the Daydream controller: `ControllerManager` and `Controller`. This section explains what these classes accomplish and the next section presents an application that uses them to read and display data from the controller.

The goal of accessing the controller is to receive events such as the pressing of the App key or a click on the touchpad. To make this possible, the `Controller` class defines a nested class named `EventListener` and the `ControllerManager` class defines an *interface* named `EventListener`. It's important not to confuse the two.

12.2.1 ControllerManager

The `ControllerManager` manages the device's connection to the controller. To be specific, it accesses the VR service running on the device and monitors a controller's operational state.

In code, this singleton serves two purposes. First, it provides an `EventListener` interface that receives events related to the controller's status. Second, it provides access to a `Controller` object representing the connected controller.

An application can access a `ControllerManager` by calling its constructor, whose signature is given as follows:

```
ControllerManager(Context context,
                  ControllerManager.EventListener listener)
```

The second argument is an object that implements the `ControllerManager`'s `EventListener` interface. This will be discussed next.

The ControllerManager.EventListener Interface

The `ControllerManager.EventListener` interface declares two methods that provide information about the state of the Daydream controller:

- `onApiStatusChanged(int code)` — Provides the operational status of the controller
- `onRecentered()` — Called when the user recenters the controller's orientation

The first method makes it possible to handle controller errors. The integer provided by the method can take one of seven values listed in Table 12.1.

Table 12.1
ApiStatus Codes

Values	Description
OK	No error has occurred
ERROR_UNSUPPORTED_API	The device doesn't support the controller
ERROR_UNAVAILABLE	The required VR service isn't present
ERROR_SERVICE_OBSOLETE	The VR service is too old to interface the controller
ERROR_CLIENT_OBSOLETE	The controller is too old to interface the VR service
ERROR_NOT_AUTHORIZED	The app hasn't received permission to access the controller
ERROR_MALFUNCTION	The VR service isn't functioning properly

These errors relate to the underlying capability of connecting to the controller, and do not reflect the state of any current connection. The `onApiStatusChanged` method may be called at any time, so it's a good idea to add code that tells users about any issues with the VR service and controller.

As mentioned earlier, a user can recenter the controller by holding down the Home button. When this takes place, the `EventListener`'s `onRecenter` method will be called. This allows the application to make any necessary adjustments to its model or the graphical rendering.

Obtaining a Controller

To access a Daydream controller, an application needs to obtain a `Controller` instance that represents the controller. This is accomplished by calling the `ControllerManager`'s `getController` method, which returns a `Controller` object.

After the connection is made, a `Controller` provides its position and orientation in a continuous stream of Bluetooth data. To conserve power, an application can control when it receives data by calling the `start` and `stop` methods of the `ControllerManager`. When `start` is called, the device will read the Bluetooth data coming from the controller. In general, `start` is called in an activity's `onStart` lifecycle method.

Just as `start` tells the device to listen for controller data, the `ControllerManager`'s `stop` method halts the listening process. This is frequently called inside the activity's `onStop` lifecycle method. In this manner, halting the application halts the operations that read data from the controller.

12.2.2 Controller

After the application calls `getController` to obtain a `Controller` and calls `start` to initiate the listening process, an application can receive data from the controller device. This involves three steps:

1. Call the `Controller`'s `update` method to request data.
2. Define a subclass of `Controller.EventListener` to receive data.
3. Call `setEventListener` to associate the `EventListener` with the `Controller`.

The first step is simple. The `Controller`'s `update` method has no arguments and no return value. It tells the `Controller` instance to update its state by reading data from the controller. For the second step, the application needs to define a subclass of `Controller.EventListener`.

The Controller.EventListener Class

The `Controller.EventListener` class defines two methods:

- `onUpdate()` — Called when the `Controller`'s physical state changes
- `onConnectionStateChanged(int code)` — Called when the `Controller`'s connection status changes

An example will clarify the difference between these methods. If the user presses the App key or changes the controller's orientation, `onUpdate` will be called. If the device loses its connection to the controller, `onConnectionStateChanged` will be called.

When `onUpdate` is called, the controller's physical state can be accessed through the `Controller`'s fields. Table 12.2 lists eleven of these fields along with their data types.

Table 12.2

Controller Fields

Field	Data Type	Description
`position`	`float[]`	The controller's position
`batteryLevelBucket`	`int`	The level of the controller's battery
`appButtonState`	`boolean`	Whether the App button is currently pressed
`homeButtonState`	`boolean`	Whether the Home button is currently pressed
`clickButtonState`	`boolean`	Whether the Click button is currently pressed

isTouching	boolean	Whether the user is currently touching the touchpad
touch	PointF	Location on the touchpad touched by the user
timestamp	long	Time when the last update occurred
volumeDown ButtonState	boolean	Whether the user is currently holding the Volume Down button
volumeUp ButtonState	boolean	Whether the user is currently holding the Volume Up button
orientation	Orientation	The controller's angular orientation

Most of these fields are self-explanatory. `appButtonState` is true when the App button is pressed and `timestamp` identifies the time when the last update took place.

The last field, `orientation`, is particularly important. This is an `Orientation` that provides the controller's orientation in a structure called a *quaternion*. Quaternions are frequently used to represent rotations and a later section will discuss them in detail.

Connection State

In addition to reading a controller's physical state, an application can access a controller's connection state through the integer code provided by the `onConnectionStateChanged` method of the `Controller.EventListener`.

This code can take one of the four values of the `Controller.ConnectionStates` enumerated type. Table 12.3 lists these values and provides a description of each.

Table 12.3

Connection State Codes

Values	Description
SCANNING	The device is scanning for controllers
CONNECTING	The device is in the process of connecting to a controller
CONNECTED	The device has connected to a controller
DISCONNECTED	The device is not connected to the controller

The values of the `ConnectionStates` type identify the state of the device, which starts in the `DISCONNECTED` state. The `Controller` is in the `SCANNING` mode when the device starts searching for a controller and it enters the `CONNECTED` mode when the connection has been made. The device can only connect to one controller at a time.

An example will clarify how a controller's connection state can be monitored. The following code creates a subclass of `Controller.EventListener` and uses a `switch-case` statement to respond to changes in the connection's state.

```
class ExampleListener extends Controller.EventListener {

  public void onConnectionStateChanged(int state) {
    switch(state) {
      case ConnectionStates.CONNECTED:
        ...
        break;
      case ConnectionStates.DISCONNECTED:
        ...
        break;
    }
  }
}
```

The next section provides a full example that connects to a controller and monitors the controller's physical state and connection state.

12.3 Example Application – Controller Reader

The ch12_controllerreader module demonstrates how the Daydream controller can be accessed in code. It doesn't display any graphics, but instead prints aspects of the controller's state. Figure 12.2 shows what the application looks like.

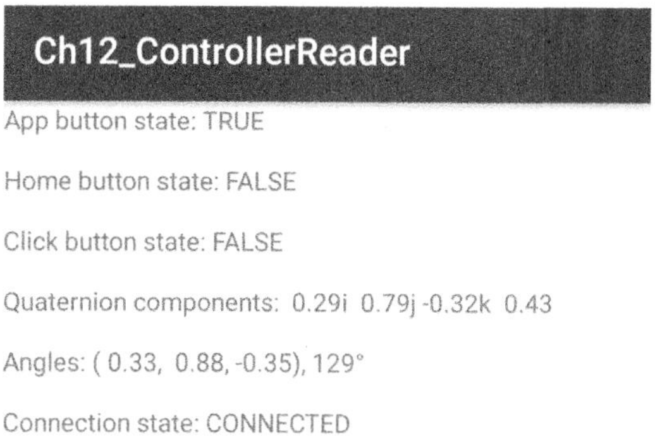

Figure 12.2 The Ch12_ControllerReader Application

As shown, the application displays information about the controller's state:

1. The state of the controller's buttons (`TRUE` if pressed, `FALSE` if not)
2. The controller's orientation, using quaternion components and angles
3. The controller's connection state, which can be `DISCONNECTED`, `SCANNING`, `CONNECTING`, or `CONNECTED`

The code in the ch12_controllerreader module doesn't use the `GvrActivity` or `GvrView` classes. But VR Mode must be enabled so that Google's VR Services will be able to connect to the controller. To provide the `ControllerManager` and `Controller` classes, the module's build file must access the sdk-controller AAR in addition to sdk-base and sdk-common.

Listing 12.1 presents the code in the `ControllerReaderActivity` class. When the activity is created, it accesses a `ControllerManager` and calls `getController` to obtain a `Controller` instance. Then it associates the `Controller` with a `ControllerListener` that will respond to the controller's events.

This application handles `Controller` events, but ignores `ControllerManager` events. This is why the methods of the `ControllerManagerListener` class are empty.

Listing 12.1: ch12_controllerreader/src/main/java/.../ControllerReaderActivity.java

```
public class ControllerReaderActivity extends Activity {

  private Controller controller;
  private ControllerManager manager;

  // Display results from controller
  static class ControllerHandler extends Handler {
    TextView textView;
    CharSequence[] labels;

    ControllerHandler(TextView tv, CharSequence[] strArray) {
      textView = tv;
      labels = strArray;
    }

    public void handleMessage(Message msg) {
      StringBuilder sb = new StringBuilder();
      Bundle b = msg.getData();

      // App button state
      sb.append(labels[0]).append(": ").
        append(b.getString("APP_MSG")).append("\n\n");
```

Listing 12.1: ch12_controllerreader/src/main/java/.../ControllerReaderActivity.java (Continued)

```
        // Home button state
        sb.append(labels[1]).append(": ").
          append(b.getString("HOME_MSG")).append("\n\n");

        // Click button state
        sb.append(labels[2]).append(": ").
          append(b.getString("CLICK_MSG")).append("\n\n");

        // Orientation as a quaternion
        sb.append(labels[3]).append(": ").
          append(b.getString("QUATERNION_MSG")).append("\n\n");

        // Orientation as a set of angles
        sb.append(labels[4]).append(": ").
          append(b.getString("ANGLE_MSG")).append("\n\n");

        // Connection state
        sb.append(labels[5]).append(": ").
          append(b.getString("CONNECTION_MSG")).append("\n\n");

        // Update textview
        textView.setText(sb.toString());
      }
    }

  public void onCreate(Bundle savedInstanceState) {

      super.onCreate(savedInstanceState);
      setContentView(R.layout.main_layout);

      // Turn on VR mode
      AndroidCompat.setVrModeEnabled(this, true);

      // Access the controller manager
      manager = new ControllerManager(this,
        new ControllerManagerListener());

      // Create the handler
      ControllerHandler handler = new ControllerHandler(
        (TextView)findViewById(R.id.tv), new CharSequence[] {
         getText(R.string.app_msg), getText(R.string.home_msg),
         getText(R.string.click_msg),
         getText(R.string.quaternion_msg),
         getText(R.string.angle_msg),
         getText(R.string.connection_msg)
      });
```

Listing 12.1: ch12_controllerreader/src/main/java/.../ControllerReaderActivity.java (Continued)

```
    // Configure the controller
    ControllerListener listener =
      new ControllerListener(handler);
    controller = manager.getController();
    controller.setEventListener(listener);
    listener.setController(controller);
  }

  @Override
  protected void onStart() {
    super.onStart();
    manager.start();
    controller.update();
  }

  @Override
  protected void onStop() {
    manager.stop();
    super.onStop();
  }

  // Handle ControllerManager events
  private class ControllerManagerListener
    implements ControllerManager.EventListener {

    public void onApiStatusChanged(int i) {}

    public void onRecentered() {}
  }
}
```

When `onStart` is called, the activity calls the `ControllerManager`'s `start` method and the `Controller`'s `update` method. This initiates the process of reading state information from the controller. When the information is available, the `onUpdate` method of the `Controller`'s `EventListener` will be called.

The activity receives the controller's state information through its `Handler`. As discussed in Chapter 5, a `Handler` makes it possible to transfer data from a child thread to the UI thread. In this case, the `ControllerHandler` accesses the controller's information through a `Message` containing a series of strings. The `Handler` uses these strings to update the activity's `TextView`.

Listing 12.2 presents the code of the `EventListener` associated with the `Controller`. This implements the `Runnable` interface, and when the listener's `update` method is called, the code in the `run` method executes in a different thread. The `run` method accesses the activity's `Handler` and configures a `Message`.

Listing 12.2: ch12_controllerreader/src/main/java/.../ControllerListener.java

```
class ControllerListener extends Controller.EventListener
  implements Runnable {

  private Handler handler;
  private Controller controller;
  private int connectionCode = ConnectionStates.DISCONNECTED;

  ControllerListener(Handler h) {
    handler = h;
  }

  void setController(Controller c) {
    controller = c;
  }

  @Override
  public void onConnectionStateChanged(int state) {
    connectionCode = state;
    handler.post(this);
  }

  @Override
  public void onUpdate() {
    handler.post(this);
  }

  @Override
  public void run() {

    // Configure a Message for the UI thread
    Message msg = Message.obtain(handler);

    // Create a Bundle to hold the message data
    Bundle b = msg.getData();

    b.putString("APP_MSG",
      controller.appButtonState ? "TRUE" : "FALSE");

    b.putString("HOME_MSG",
      controller.homeButtonState ? "TRUE" : "FALSE");

    b.putString("CLICK_MSG",
      controller.clickButtonState ? "TRUE" : "FALSE");

    b.putString("QUATERNION_MSG",
      controller.orientation.toString());
```

Listing 12.2: ch12_controllerreader/src/main/java/.../ControllerListener.java (Continued)

```
        b.putString("ANGLE_MSG",
          controller.orientation.toAxisAngleString());

        switch(connectionCode) {

          // Respond when the controller is disconnected
          case ConnectionStates.DISCONNECTED:
            b.putString("CONNECTION_MSG", "DISCONNECTED");
            break;

          // Respond when the device is searching for the controller
          case ConnectionStates.SCANNING:
            b.putString("CONNECTION_MSG", "SCANNING");
            break;

          // Respond when the device is in the process of connecting
          case ConnectionStates.CONNECTING:
            b.putString("CONNECTION_MSG", "CONNECTING");
            break;

          // Respond when the device has created the connection
          case ConnectionStates.CONNECTED:
            b.putString("CONNECTION_MSG", "CONNECTED");
            break;
        }

        // Send message to UI thread
        handler.sendMessage(msg);

        // Access the controller again
        controller.update();
      }
    }
```

The listener receives the activity's `Handler` in its constructor. When the controller's state changes, the `onUpdate` and `onConnectionStateChanged` methods call the `Handler`'s `post` method. This executes the code in the `run` method, which creates a `Message` and configures its `Bundle` with the controller's state information.

The last line of the `run` method invokes the controller's `update` method, which launches a new read operation. In this manner, the activity receives data from the controller in an infinite loop.

12.4 Controller Targeting

When developing Daydream apps, it's critical to keep track of where the controller is pointing. The preceding discussion mentioned that this information is provided by the `orientation` field of the `Controller` instance. But the discussion didn't mention how this field can be accessed.

The hard part of working with the `Controller` is that the orientation's data is provided as a *quaternion*. Quaternions have a number of advantages over rotation matrices, but the main disadvantage is that they're difficult to understand. This section explains what quaternions are and then shows how they can be used to determine where the controller is pointing.

12.4.1 Overview of Quaternions

In the late eighteenth century, a surveyor named Caspar Wessel made a major mathematical discovery: if a pair of 2-dimensional coordinates are multiplied in a certain way, the resulting point has an angle equal to the sum of the angles of the original coordinates. This may not sound impressive, but Wessel's multiplication provides an easy way to rotate a point in two dimenions.

An example will demonstrate how this works. To rotate (a, b) through an angle β, find the point with unit length and angle β, and multiply the two coordinates using Wessel's method: if the second point is at (x, y), the rotation of (a, b) is located at (ax – by, ay + bx). This is shown in Figure 12.3.

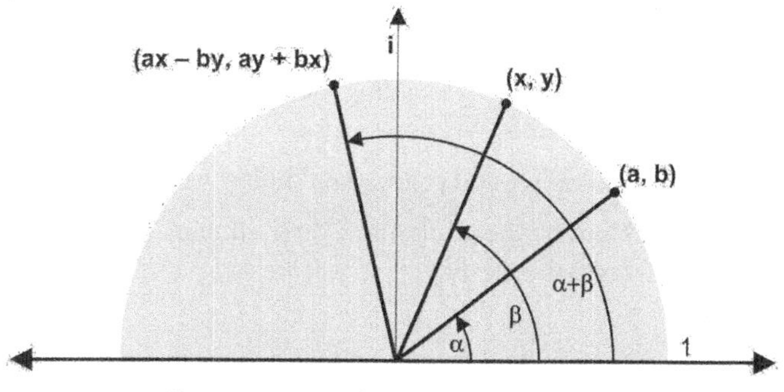

Figure 12.3 Two-Dimensional Rotation

The vertical axis in the figure is labeled i, and coordinates in this space are commonly identified as x + **i**y. The **i** stands for 'imaginary' because $i = \sqrt{-1}$.

In general, to rotate (x, y) by angle β, (x, y) must be multiplied by cos(β) + **i** sin(β). For example, to rotate (3, 7) by 30°, the coordinates of the rotated point can be obtained by computing {3cos(30°) – 7sin(30°), 3sin(30°) + 7cos(30°)}, which equals (–0.9, 7.56).

Nearly 50 years after Wessel's discovery, William Hamilton devised a similar method for rotating coordinates in three dimensions. But instead of using x + **i**y, he conceived of a four-element structure, w + **i**x + **j**y + **k**z, where **i**, **j**, and **k** all equal $\sqrt{-1}$ but point in different directions. Hamilton called this new structure a quaternion.

As mentioned earlier, cos(β) + **i** sin(β) represents a rotation in two dimensions. The expression for three-dimensional rotation is similar. To rotate through an angle of β around an axis whose vector components are (a, b, c), the quaternion equals cos(β/2) + **i**[a sin(β/2)] + **j**[b sin(β/2)] + **k**[c sin(β/2)].

If multiple rotations need to be combined, multiplying quaternions requires less time and effort than multiplying rotation matrices. For example, if x equals a + **i**b + **j**c + **k**d and y equals p + **i**q + **j**r + **k**s, the product of x and y is given as:

$$xy = (ap - bq - cr - ds) + \mathbf{i}(aq + bp - cs + dr) + \mathbf{j}(ar + bs + cp - dq) + \mathbf{k}(as - br + cq + dp)$$

Now for the hard part. The process of rotating a point or vector using a quaternion is much more complicated than regular matrix-vector multiplication. If p is the point to be rotated and q is the rotation quaternion, the resulting point p' can be obtained by computing p' = qpq'.

This is called the *Hamilton product* and q' is called the *conjugate* of q. The general method of computing this product requires four steps:

1. Replace p with a quaternion whose real term is set to zero. That is, if p = (x, y, z), replace p with the quaternion 0 + **i**x + **j**y + **k**z.
2. Compute q' by negating the imaginary terms of q. That is, if q = w + **i**x + **j**y + **k**z, set q' equal to w – **i**x – **j**y – **k**z.
3. Multiply q and p, and then multiply that product by q'.
4. Convert the result into a three-dimensional value by extracting the imaginary terms from the product.

Computing this product requires a significant amount of effort and this discussion won't present a general example. However, the following discussion explains how the Hamilton product can be used to determine the direction of the Daydream controller.

12.4.2 Quaternions and Controller Orientation

An earlier discussion explained how to obtain a `Controller` instance representing the user's controller. This provides an `orientation` field that has four `float` fields named `w`, `x`, `y`, and `z`. These values define a quaternion whose terms equal $w + \mathbf{i}x + \mathbf{j}y + \mathbf{k}z$.

To identify where the controller is pointing, an application needs to find the Hamilton product of the quaternion and the controller's previous direction. Hamilton products are difficult to understand, so many applications convert the quaternion to a rotation matrix and use traditional matrix-vector multiplication instead. This approach is adopted by the ndk-controllerpaint project provided in the Google VR NDK.

But in my opinion, there's a much more efficient method. When the user centers the controller, its direction is always taken to be the –z direction. That is, the pointing vector is always (0, 0, –*distance*), where *distance* identifies the default distance used for painting. The ndk-controllerpaint project sets this default vector to (0, 0, –200), and this book will adopt this as well.

Because the pointing vector has only one non-zero term, the Hamilton product is simple to compute. If q is given as (w, x, y, z) and p is given as (0, 0, 0, –d), the product qp is given as follows:

$$qp = zd + \mathbf{i}yd - \mathbf{j}xd - \mathbf{k}wd$$

To compute the Hamilton product, qp must be multiplied by q', which equals (w, –x, –y, –z). The full expression for the Hamilton product is given as:

$$qpq' = (dwz + dxy - dxy - dwz) + \mathbf{i}(-dxz + dwy - dxz + dwy) + \mathbf{j}(-dyz - dyz - dwx - dwx) + \mathbf{k}(-dz^2 + dy^2 + dx^2 - dw^2)$$

The first term equals zero, as it should. Using basic algebra, the expression can be simplified in the following way:

$$qpq' = \mathbf{i}(2dwy - 2dxz) + \mathbf{j}(-2dwx - 2dyz) + \mathbf{k}[-dw^2 + dx^2 + dy^2 - dz^2)]$$

Each term in the expression contains d, so it can be separated from the final result:

$$qpq' = d\{\mathbf{i}(2wy - 2xz) + \mathbf{j}(-2wx - 2yz) + \mathbf{k}(-w^2 + x^2 + y^2 - z^2)\}$$

Therefore, the vector identifying the controller's direction is given as follows:

$$\text{vector} = [d(2wy - 2xz), d(-2wx - 2yz), d(-w^2 + x^2 + y^2 - z^2)]$$

This is certainly easier to compute than converting a quaternion into a 4-by-4 matrix and performing matrix-vector multiplication. It should be clear that the precise value of d isn't important—it's a scaling factor for the controller's pointing vector.

12.4.3 Pick Selection

After computing the controller's direction, the next step is to determine if the controller is pointing at an object in the model. This is called *pick selection* or just *picking*.

Many methods have been devised for pick selection, and most assume that the pick operation is performed with a mouse. These methods generally start by converting the screen coordinates of the click into a vector pointing into the model. Then they find the nearest object touched by the vector.

For Daydream apps, pick selection is more involved. To determine which object the user is pointing at, the application needs to construct a ray starting from (0, 0, 0) and pointing in the controller's direction. If the components of the controller's direction are (a, b, c), this ray can be expressed mathematically as (at, bt, ct).

For fine-grained pick selection, an application can test individual triangles to see whether the ray intersects one. This requires advanced vector mathematics, and I wrote an article about the process at https://www.codeproject.com/Articles/625787/Pick-Selection-with-OpenGL-and-OpenCL.

For this discussion, we'll assume that the application knows the desired depth of the objects that can be selected. If we call this depth D, the pick selection process can be performed in four steps:

1. Compute the controller's direction vector using the method described earlier.
2. Transform this vector so that it points inside the viewing region. We'll denote the transformed vector as (a, b, c) and the expression for the ray as (at, bt, ct).
3. At the desired depth, ct will equal D. Therefore, the desired t equals D/c. This means x = aD/c and y = bD/c at the desired depth.
4. Of the objects at the given depth, find the one that occupies the point (aD/c, bD/c).

In practice, I've found that the signs of x and y need to be inverted to match the controller's angle. The following section discusses how this process can be implemented.

12.5 Example Application – Targeting

The ch12_targeting application shows how an application can use the `Controller`'s quaternion to determine what the user is pointing at. The application draws sixteen white squares and a red dot representing the controller. When the dot moves onto one of the squares, the square's color changes to blue.

Figure 12.4 gives an idea of what this looks like.

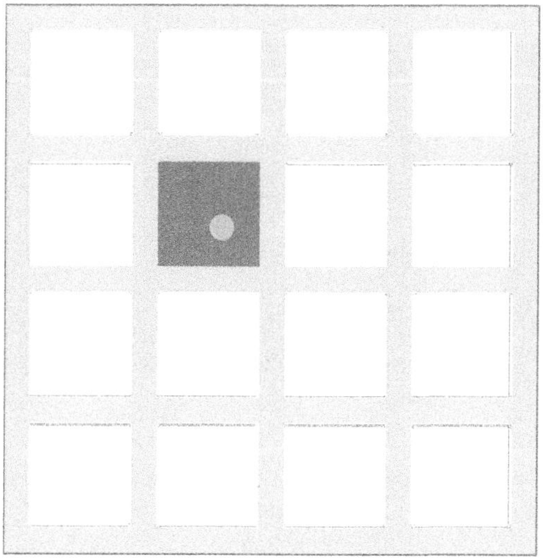

Figure 12.4 The Ch12_Targeting Application

The application creates two vertex array objects—one for drawing the sixteen squares and one for drawing the controller's dot. The first VAO is generated and configured in the `initSquareData` method of the `TargetingRenderer` class. The second is generated and configured in the `initPointerData` method.

To monitor the controller's state, the `TargetingActivity` creates an instance of the `ControllerListener`. This class extends `Controller.EventListener` and implements `Runnable` and `ControllerManager.EventListener`.

The operation of the `ControllerListener` resembles that of the listener in the ch12_controllerreader project discussed earlier. That is, its `run` method accesses the controller's state and places the data in a `Message` to be posted to a `Handler`. In this case, the only required state information is the controller's connection state and orientation. The following code shows how this is packaged.

```
public void run() {

  // Configure a Message for the UI thread
  Message msg = Message.obtain(handler);
  Bundle b = msg.getData();

  // Store quaternion components
  float[] quaternion = {controller.orientation.w,
    controller.orientation.x, controller.orientation.y,
    controller.orientation.z};
  b.putFloatArray("QUAT", quaternion);

  // Store connection state
  switch(connectionCode) {
    case ConnectionStates.DISCONNECTED:
      b.putString("CONNECTION_MSG", "DISCONNECTED");
      break;
    case ConnectionStates.SCANNING:
      b.putString("CONNECTION_MSG", "SCANNING");
      break;
    case ConnectionStates.CONNECTING:
      b.putString("CONNECTION_MSG", "CONNECTING");
      break;
    case ConnectionStates.CONNECTED:
      b.putString("CONNECTION_MSG", "CONNECTED");
      break;
  }

  // Send message to UI thread
  handler.sendMessage(msg);

  // Access the controller again
  controller.update();
}
```

Every time the listener sends the message, it calls the controller's `update` method. This restarts the process of obtaining the controller's state information.

The `TargetingRenderer` defines a `Handler` subclass that receives the listener's `Message`. Its definition is given as follows:

```
static private class ControllerHandler extends Handler {
  public void handleMessage(Message msg) {
    Bundle b = msg.getData();
    connected =
      b.getString("CONNECTION_MSG", "").equals("CONNECTED");
    quat = b.getFloatArray("QUAT");
  }
}
```

As shown, the connection's state is stored in the `connected` variable and the quaternion components are stored in the `quat` array. These values are accessed in the `TargetingRenderer`'s `onNewFrame` method, which is called every time a new frame needs to be drawn. Listing 12.3 presents the code.

Listing 12.3: ch12_targeting/src/main/java/.../TargetingRenderer.java

```
public void onNewFrame(HeadTransform headTransform) {

  // Determine where the controller is pointing
  float tmp = (quat[0] * quat[0]) - (quat[1] * quat[1]) -
    (quat[2] * quat[2]) + (quat[3] * quat[3]);
  target[0] = (2.0f * (quat[0] * quat[2]) -
    (2 * quat[1] * quat[3])) * (SQUARE_DEPTH / tmp);
  target[1] = (-2.0f * (quat[0] * quat[1]) -
    (2 * quat[2] * quat[3])) * (SQUARE_DEPTH / tmp);

  // Update the UBO with the target information
  targetBuffer.put(target);
  targetBuffer.rewind();
  GLES32.glBindBuffer(GLES32.GL_UNIFORM_BUFFER, ubos[1]);
  GLES32.glBufferSubData(GLES32.GL_UNIFORM_BUFFER,
    0, target.length * 4, targetBuffer);

  // Determine which square is selected
  selectedSquare = -1;
  for(int i=0; i<offsets.length; i+=2) {
    if((target[0] > (offsets[i] - 0.2f)) &&
       (target[0] < (offsets[i] + 0.2f)) &&
       (target[1] > (offsets[i+1] - 0.2f)) &&
       (target[1] < (offsets[i+1] + 0.2f))) {
      selectedSquare = i/2;
      break;
    }
  }

  // Update the UBO with the selected square
  selectBuffer.put(selectedSquare);
  selectBuffer.rewind();
  GLES32.glBindBuffer(GLES32.GL_UNIFORM_BUFFER, ubos[0]);
  GLES32.glBufferSubData(GLES32.GL_UNIFORM_BUFFER,
    (offsets.length + mvpMatrix.length) * 4, 4, selectBuffer);

  // Initialize the view matrix
  Matrix.setLookAtM(headMatrix, 0, 0.0f, 0.0f, 0.01f,
      0.0f, 0.0f, 0.0f, 0.0f, 1.0f, 0.0f);
}
```

By computing the Hamilton product, this code determines the (x, y) coordinates of the pointer's ray at the given depth. These are stored in the `target` array, which is used to update a uniform buffer object (UBO) that identifies where the pointer's dot should be drawn.

After determining where the dot should be drawn, `onNewFrame` determines whether the dot's location falls on one of the squares. If so, the `selectedSquare` variable is set to the square's index. This variable is associated with the portion of the UBO that identifies which square should be drawn blue.

The vertex shader receives the application's `selectedSquare` variable through the `selected_index` field of the uniform block named `ubo`. As shown in Listing 12.4, the shader compares `selected_index` to the `gl_InstanceID`. If the two values are equal, the instance's color is set to blue.

Listing 12.4: ch12_targeting/src/main/assets/square.vert

```
// Attribute data
in  vec3 in_coords;
out vec3 new_color;

// Uniform buffer object
uniform ubo {
  mat4 trans_matrix;
  vec2 target;
  vec2 offset[16];
  int selected_index;
};

void main(void) {

  // Rotate the incoming vertex
  vec4 new_coords = vec4(in_coords, 1.0);

  // Apply the offset and the transformation
  new_coords.xy += offset[gl_InstanceID];
  new_coords = trans_matrix * new_coords;

  // Set the output coordinates
  gl_Position = new_coords;

  // Set the outgoing color
  new_color = vec3(1.0, 1.0, 1.0);
  if(selected_index == gl_InstanceID) {
    new_color = vec3(0.0, 0.0, 1.0);
  }
}
```

12.6 Summary

Accessing the controller is a fundamental capability expected of Daydream apps. The controller's orientation identifies the part of the model that the viewer is interested in. When the user clicks one of the controller's buttons, the application should be able to interpret the event and respond appropriately.

The two classes that make controller access possible are `ControllerManager` and `Controller`. The `ControllerManager` handles the overall controller access and provides information about version compatibility. Its `getController` method provides a `Controller` representing the Daydream controller. After a connection is established, the `Controller`'s `update` method is called when new data is available.

The most difficult aspect of working with the Daydream controller involves determining where the controller is pointing. The controller provides its orientation in a quaternion, which means that applications need to compute a Hamilton product in order to rotate a vector by the quaternion. Thankfully, if the vector is pointing in the negative z direction, the product is relatively easy to compute.

Chapter 13

Spatial Audio, Panoramas, and Video

This book has covered most of the classes and features of the Google VR SDK. But three capabilities haven't been mentioned—spatial audio, panoramas, and video. The goal of this chapter is to explore these features and look at the classes that enable applications to take advantage of their functionality.

For most Android apps, the most advanced audio feature is stereo playback, which produces sounds from two sources. But the Google VR SDK provides a class called `GvrAudioEngine`, which supports audio containing up to 16 sources. Each source can be assigned its own position, volume, and attenuation model. The first section of this chapter presents the methods that create and configure these sources. Then we'll look at an example app that demonstrates how they're used.

Most Daydream apps rely on a `GvrView` to display their content, but the Google VR SDK provides two other views: `VrPanoramaView` and `VrVideoView`. The first class displays panoramic images and the second class displays video. Both are subclasses of `VrWidgetView`, whose methods make it possible to configure how the VR views are displayed.

A `VrPanoramaView` loads panoramic image data from a bitmap. If the bitmap consists of two vertically-stacked images, the view will be able to display the image in stereo mode. That is, the top image will be displayed for the left eye and the bottom image will be displayed for the right eye. The view will only display a portion of the image at a time, so viewers can explore the scene by touching and dragging the view's content.

A `VrVideoView` loads video data from an MP4, WebM, Ogg, AAC, or Http Live Streaming (HLS) source. The view's methods make it possible to play, pause, or seek, and the view can be associated with a listener to monitor playback events.

13.1 Playing Audio

The Google VR SDK contains an Android archive named sdk-audio-*x*-*y*-*z*.aar. This provides an important class named `GvrAudioEngine`. The methods of this class make it possible to read audio data from a file and configure how the sounds should be received by the listener.

The basic process of playing audio in a VR app consists of three steps:

1. Create a `GvrAudioEngine` instance by invoking its constructor with the desired audio mode.
2. Obtain and configure an audio source.
3. Call `playSound` to play audio from a given source.

In the first step, the `GvrAudioEngine` constructor requires a value that identifies the engine's rendering mode. This determines what features are available for configuring the properties of the audio, and can be set to one of three values:

- `STEREO_PANNING` — Renders sound in stereo, without regard to head position
- `BINAURAL_LOW_QUALITY` — Renders sound from up to eight virtual sources
- `BINAURAL_HIGH_QUALITY` — Renders sound from up to sixteen virtual sources

The `GvrAudioEngine` can access audio data from a number of different file types, including WAVs, MP3s, and MP4s. It's important to be aware of the audio's content. That is, you should know whether the source contains monophonic sound (one sound channel), stereophonic sound (two or more sound channels without locations), or Ambisonic sound (multiple channels with locations).

The audio content determines which rendering mode can be employed. Monophonic (mono) sources can be used in any of the three modes. Stereophonic (stereo) sources can only be used in the `STEREO_PANNING` mode. Ambisonic sound can be used with the `BINAURAL_LOW_QUALITY` or `BINAURAL_HIGH_QUALITY` modes.

This discussion won't explore the theory related to spatial audio or Ambisonic sound. Instead, we'll focus on the methods of the `GvrAudioEngine` class. The section starts by explaining the methods needed to play non-spatialized audio. Then it presents the methods that make it possible to play spatial audio from multiple mono sources. Then we'll examine the methods for working with Ambisonic sound.

13.1.1 Non-Spatialized Audio

If an application's audio should remain constant regardless of the headset's orientation, the `GvrAudioEngine`'s rendering mode should be set to `STEREO_PANNING`. Despite the name, the audio can be provided as both mono and stereo. In this mode, the headset behaves like a regular pair of headphones.

The `GvrAudioEngine` makes it easy to play audio in this mode. The entire process consists of four steps:

1. Create a `GvrAudioEngine` instance.
2. Invoke `preloadSoundFile` to load audio data from the mono/stereo file.
3. Call `createStereoSound` to obtain an identifier for the sound source.
4. Play the audio by calling `playSound` with the identifier.

In the third step, `createStereoSound` returns an integer that uniquely identifies the source of the audio data. This identifier is required by the `playSound` method, whose signature is given as follows:

```
playSound(int sourceId, boolean loop)
```

The second argument specifies whether the audio should be played in a continuous loop. If this is set to false, the audio will only be played once.

If sound.wav contains regular mono/stereo sound, the following code will load the file's audio data and play the audio in a loop:

```
GvrAudioEngine engine = new GvrAudioEngine(this,
  GvrAudioEngine.RenderingMode.STEREO_PANNING);
engine.preloadSoundFile("sound.wav");
int sound_id = createStereoSound("sound.wav");
playSound(sound_id, true);
```

As shown, the `preloadSoundFile` and `createStereoSound` methods both require the name of the audio file. The integer returned by `createStereoSound` can be used in methods like `playSound`, `pauseSound`, and `resumeSound`. The identifier is destroyed when the audio playback stops.

This code calls the `GvrAudioEngine` constructor with the `STEREO_PANNING` value. However, if a `GvrAudioEngine` has been created with `BINAURAL_LOW_QUALITY` or `BINAURAL_HIGH_QUALITY`, it can still be used to play non-spatialized audio using the steps listed above.

13.1.2 Spatial Audio from Monophonic Sources

Spatial audio is one of the most impressive effects in a VR application. Nothing immerses the user in a virtual world like hearing sounds coming from different locations. If the rendering mode is set to `BINAURAL_LOW_QUALITY`, an application can set up to eight sounds. If set to `BINAURAL_HIGH_QUALITY`, up to sixteen sounds can be set.

The process of playing spatial audio is essentially similar to playing non-spatial audio. The main difference is the amount of configuration. In general, working with spatial sound consists of eight steps:

1. Obtain a `GvrAudioEngine` instance.
2. Invoke `preloadSoundFile` to load audio data.
3. For each sound source, call `createSoundObject` to obtain an identifier.
4. For each sound source, call `setSoundObjectPosition` to position the sound source in the virtual world.
5. (Optional) Configure a virtual room surrounding the user.
6. (Optional) Specify how the music's volume decreases over distance.
7. As the user's head turns, call `setHeadPosition` and/or `setHeadRotation` to identify the state of the user's headset.
8. For each sound source, call `playSound` to play its audio.

In the third step, it's important to note that `createSoundObject` requires the audio source to be monophonic. After an identifier is received for an audio source, the source's position can be set with the `setSoundObjectPosition` method, whose signature is given as follows:

```
setSoundObjectPosition(int soundId, float x, float y, float z)
```

The (x, y, z) coordinates are given in *world coordinates*. Chapter 9 introduced the topic of world coordinates and explained how model transformations are used to convert from object coordinates to world coordinates.

The `GvrAudioEngine` doesn't monitor the user's headset, so the application needs to update the engine when the headset's position or rotation changes. This can be accomplished with two methods:

- `setHeadPosition(float x, float y, float z)` — Identifies the position of the user's head in world coordinates
- `setHeadRotation(float x, float y, float z, float w)` — Identifies the orientation of the user's head using quaternion components

The arguments of these methods can be obtained by accessing the `HeadTransform` object provided by the `GvrView`'s `onNewFrame` method. For example, the quaternion components required by `setHeadRotation` can be obtained by calling the `HeadTransform`'s `getQuaternion` method.

Sound in a Virtual Room

If the virtual world consists of an enclosed area, the audio can be configured to resemble sound bouncing off the room's walls. Configuring this in code requires three steps:

1. Enable the room model by calling `enableRoom` with its argument set to `true`.
2. Specify the room's characteristics by calling `setRoomProperties`.
3. Control how sound travels in the room by calling `setRoomReverbAdjustments`.

In the second step, an application can control the size of the room and the wall materials with the `setRoomProperties` method:

```
setRoomProperties(float sizeX, float sizeY, float sizeZ,
  int wallMaterial, int ceilingMaterial, int floorMaterial)
```

The first three arguments specify the room's width, height, and depth. The last three arguments identify the materials used in the room's walls, ceiling, and floor. In each case, the value identifies a material defined in the `MaterialName` enumerated type. Table 13.1 lists the different values available.

Table 13.1

Values of the MaterialName Type

ACOUSTIC_CEILING_TILES	GLASS_THIN	PLYWOOD_PANEL
BRICK_BARE	GRASS	SHEET_ROCK
BRICK_PAINTED	LINOLEUM_ON_CONCRETE	POLISHED_CONCRETE_OR_TILE
CONCRETE_BLOCK_COARSE	MARBLE	TRANSPARENT
CONCRETE_BLOCK_PAINTED	METAL	WATER_OR_ICE_SURFACE
CURTAIN_HEAVY	PARQUET_ON_CONCRETE	WOOD_CEILING
FIBER_GLASS_INSULATION	PLASTER_ROUGH	WOOD_PANEL
GLASS_THICK	PLASTER_SMOOTH	

The choice of material determines how sound reverberates in the room. For example, if the room's dimensions are small and the wall material is set to `MaterialName.METAL`, the user will clearly hear sounds echo off the walls. If the wall material is set to `MaterialName.TRANSPARENT`, the user won't hear any echoes from the walls.

An application can further customize how sound travels in a room by calling `setRoomReverbAdjustments`:

```
setRoomReverbAdjustments(float gain, float timeAdjust,
                         float brightnessAdjust)
```

The `gain` argument serves as a weighting for the reverberation value. The volume will be decreased if `gain` is between 0.0 and 1.0, and increased if `gain` is set to a value greater than 1.0.

If the room has many walls, the reverberation will last longer. An application can't configure the number of walls, but the `timeAdjust` argument specifies how long the reverberation should last. The length of time will be decreased if `timeAdjust` is between 0.0 and 1.0, and increased if `timeAdjust` is greater than 1.0.

The third argument, `brightnessAdjust`, affects the frequencies of the sounds reverberating in the room. A value between 0.0 and 1.0 will emphasize low frequencies and a value greater than 1.0 will emphasize high frequencies.

To demonstrate how these methods can be used, the following code configures a virtual room with heavy curtains on the walls, plywood flooring, and a wooden ceiling. The time length of the reverberation is doubled.

```
engine.enableRoom(true);
engine.setRoomProperties(20.0f, 10.0f, 15.0f,
  MaterialName.HEAVY_CURTAINS, MaterialName.WOOD_CEILING,
  MaterialName.PLYWOOD_PANEL);
engine.setRoomReverbAdjustments(1.0f, 2.0f, 1.0f);
```

None of the example code in this book creates room-like environments. But if I intended to code a haunted-house game, I would certainly use this feature.

Setting the Attenuation Model

In addition to setting the positions of sound sources, an application can specify how the perceived loudness decreases (or *attenuates*) as the viewer gets further away from the source. This can be configured with the `setSoundObjectDistanceRolloffModel` method, whose signature is given as follows:

```
setSoundObjectDistanceRolloffModel(int soundId,
  int rolloffModel, float minDistance, float maxDistance)
```

The first argument identifies a sound source and the second argument identifies the mathematical relationship to be used when computing how the sound is attenuated in space. This must be set to one of the three values in the `DistanceRolloffModel` enumerated type:

- `LINEAR` — Loudness will decrease linearly as the viewer moves away from the sound source
- `LOGARITHMIC` — Loudness will decrease logarthmically as the viewer moves away from the sound source
- `NONE` — No attenuation model will be employed

The third and fourth arguments identify the minimum and maximum distances for which the attenuation model should be applied. That is, if the viewer's distance from the sound source is d, the attenuation will be applied if d is between `minDistance` and `maxDistance`.

13.1.3 Spatial Audio from an Ambisonic Source

In the 1970s, the UK's National Research Development Corporation developed the Ambisonics technology for storing sound. Like regular stereophonic sound, Ambisonics can store audio from multiple channels. Unlike stereo sound, Ambisonics also stores the directions of the different sources. Put another way, an Ambisonic audio source has been pre-spatialized, so there's no need to set source positions manually.

The mathematics behind the Ambisonics technology is complex but the code needed to work with Ambisonics sources is straightforward. There's no need to call `preloadSoundFile`, so the process consists of four steps:

1. Obtain a `GvrAudioEngine` instance.
2. Call `createSoundfield` to obtain an identifier.
3. When needed, call `setSoundfieldRotation` to rotate the direction of the Ambisonics sound.
4. Call `playSound` to play its audio.

Like the `createSoundObject` method discussed earlier, `createSoundfield` accepts a file name and returns an identifier for the audio source. Note that the audio source must have four audio channels.

An Ambisonic source can't be assigned a position with setSoundObjectPosition, but its orientation can be set with setSoundfieldRotation, whose signature is given as follows:

```
setSoundfieldRotation(int soundId,
  float x, float y, float z, float w)
```

The x, y, z, and w arguments identify the components of the quaternion that represents the desired rotation. These values can be obtained by calling the getQuaternion method of the HeadTransform provided by onNewFrame.

13.1.4 Additional Methods

The GvrAudioEngine class provides a number of other methods in addition to those discussed earlier. Table 13.2 lists seven of these methods and provides a description of each.

Table 13.2

Additional Methods of the GvrAudioEngine

Method	Description
update()	Called to update the audio engine's state
pauseSound(int sourceId)	Pauses audio from the given source
resumeSound(int sourceId)	Resumes audio from the given source
pause()	Pauses audio from all sources
resume()	Resumes audio from all sources
setSoundVolume(int sourceId, float volume)	Specifies the desired volume for the given audio source
isSoundPlaying(int sourceId)	Identifies whether audio is playing from the given source

The update method alerts the engine that an aspect of its state needs to be updated. As a result, the engine will execute background operations outside of the audio thread. This is frequently called to update the engine after the headset's position or orientation changes.

Just as playSound plays the audio for a given source, pauseSound pauses playing for a given source. After a source's playing has been paused, it can be resumed with resumeSound.

pause and resume are similar to pauseSound and resumeSound, but they affect all of the application's sound sources. It's a good idea to pause the application's sound when the activity pauses and resume playing when the activity resumes. For this reason, pause is commonly called in the activity's onPause method and resume is commonly called in onResume.

An application can control the volume of a sound source with setSoundVolume. This accepts a source ID and a float value between 0.0 (mute) and 1.0 (maximum volume).

13.2 Example Application – Audio Player

The ch13_audioplayer module not only shows how audio can be played in a Daydream application, but demonstrates many other capabilities discussed in previous chapters:

- Displaying text by creating a texture from a Canvas
- Controller targeting
- Retrieving data from child threads using Handlers
- Vertex buffer objects (VBOs), vertex array objects (VAOs), uniform buffer objects (UBOs), and index buffer objects (IBOs)

The player's user interface consists of three buttons that pause, play, and stop the audio playback. Above the buttons, a text message identifies the player's state. Figure 13.1 shows what the user interface looks like.

Figure 13.1 The ch13_audioplayer Application

The AudioPlayerRenderer constructor initializes audio playback by creating the GvrAudioEngine and setting its volume and position. Listing 13.1 presents the code.

Listing 13.1: ch13_audioplayer/src/main/java/.../AudioPlayerRenderer.java (Constructor)

```
AudioPlayerRenderer(Context ctx, GvrAudioEngine e) {

  context = ctx;
  engine = e;

  // Initialize objects and programs
  vaos = new int[NUM_VAOS];
  vbos = new int[NUM_VBOS];
  ibos = new int[NUM_IBOS];
  tids = new int[NUM_TEXTURES];
  ubos = new int[NUM_UBOS];
  programs = new int[NUM_PROGRAMS];

  // Initialize other structures
  quat = new float[4];
  headMatrix = new float[16];
  viewMatrix = new float[16];
  mvpMatrix = new float[16];

  // Create Bitmap for buttons
  final BitmapFactory.Options options =
    new BitmapFactory.Options();
  options.inScaled = false;
  buttonBitmap = BitmapFactory.decodeResource(
    ctx.getResources(), R.drawable.buttons, options);

  // Initialize audio playing
  engine.preloadSoundFile(AUDIO_FILE);
  sourceId = engine.createSoundObject(AUDIO_FILE);
  engine.setSoundObjectPosition(sourceId, 0.0f, 0.0f, 5.0f);
  engine.setSoundVolume(sourceId, 0.5f);

  // Create buffer for matrix data
  ByteBuffer tempBuffer =
    ByteBuffer.allocateDirect(mvpMatrix.length * 4);
  tempBuffer.order(ByteOrder.nativeOrder());
  mvpBuffer = tempBuffer.asFloatBuffer();
  mvpBuffer.rewind();

  // Store offset data in buffer
  tempBuffer =
    ByteBuffer.allocateDirect(buttonOffsets.length * 4);
  tempBuffer.order(ByteOrder.nativeOrder());
  offsetBuffer = tempBuffer.asFloatBuffer();
  offsetBuffer.put(buttonOffsets);
  offsetBuffer.rewind();
```

Listing 13.1: ch13_audioplayer/src/main/java/.../AudioPlayerRenderer.java (Constructor)

```
  // Create buffer to store target
  target = new float[2];
  target[0] = 0.0f; target[1] = 0.0f;
  tempBuffer =
      ByteBuffer.allocateDirect(target.length * 4);
  tempBuffer.order(ByteOrder.nativeOrder());
  targetBuffer = tempBuffer.asFloatBuffer();
  targetBuffer.put(target);
  targetBuffer.rewind();

  // Create buffer to store selected index
  tempBuffer = ByteBuffer.allocateDirect(4);
  tempBuffer.order(ByteOrder.nativeOrder());
  selectBuffer = tempBuffer.asIntBuffer();

  // Initialize text canvas
  initTextCanvas();
}
```

This code creates a sound object from a file named harp.wav. Then it sets the object's position to (0, 0, 5) and its volume to 0.5.

As the headset moves, the application updates the audio engine to maintain its position relative to the user. This is accomplished by obtaining the quaternion for the `HeadTransform` provided by `onNewFrame`. Listing 13.2 presents the method's code.

Listing 13.2: ch13_audioplayer/src/main/java/.../AudioPlayerRenderer.java (onNewFrame)

```
public void onNewFrame(HeadTransform headTransform) {

  GLES32.glActiveTexture(GLES32.GL_TEXTURE0);

  // Determine where the controller is pointing
  float tmp = (quat[0] * quat[0]) - (quat[1] * quat[1]) -
    (quat[2] * quat[2]) + (quat[3] * quat[3]);
  target[0] = (2.0f * (quat[0] * quat[2]) -
    (2 * quat[1] * quat[3])) * (DRAW_DEPTH / tmp);
  target[1] = (-2.0f * (quat[0] * quat[1]) -
    (2 * quat[2] * quat[3])) * (DRAW_DEPTH / tmp);

  // Update the UBO with the target information
  targetBuffer.put(target);
  targetBuffer.rewind();
  GLES32.glBindBuffer(GLES32.GL_UNIFORM_BUFFER, ubos[0]);
  GLES32.glBufferSubData(GLES32.GL_UNIFORM_BUFFER,
      mvpMatrix.length * 4, target.length * 4, targetBuffer);
```

Listing 13.2: ch13_audioplayer/src/main/java/.../AudioPlayerRenderer.java (onNewFrame)

```
// Determine which square is selected
boolean changed = false;
int oldSelectedButton = selectedButton;
if(buttonDown) {

  for(int i=0; i < buttonOffsets.length; i+=2) {
    if((target[0] > (buttonOffsets[i] - 0.2f)) &&
      (target[0] < (buttonOffsets[i] + 0.2f)) &&
      (target[1] > (buttonOffsets[i+1] - 0.2f)) &&
      (target[1] < (buttonOffsets[i+1] + 0.2f))) {
        if(selectedButton != i/2) {
          selectedButton = i/2;
          changed = true;
        }
        break;
    }
  }
}

// Update audio state
if(changed) {
  switch (selectedButton) {

    case 0:  // Pause button
      if (engine.isSoundPlaying(sourceId)) {
        engine.pauseSound(sourceId);
      }
      firstVertex = 8;
      break;

    case 1: // Play button
      if((oldSelectedButton == 0) ||
          (oldSelectedButton == 2)) {
        engine.resumeSound(sourceId);

      }
      else engine.playSound(sourceId, true);
      firstVertex = 4;
      break;

    case 2: // Stop button
      engine.pauseSound(sourceId);
      firstVertex = 12;
      break;

    default: break;
  }
}
```

Listing 13.2: ch13_audioplayer/src/main/java/.../AudioPlayerRenderer.java (onNewFrame)

```
  // Update the UBO with the selected square
  selectBuffer.put(selectedButton);
  selectBuffer.rewind();
  GLES32.glBufferSubData(GLES32.GL_UNIFORM_BUFFER,
    (mvpMatrix.length + target.length + buttonOffsets.length)
    * 4, 4, selectBuffer);

  // Initialize the view matrix
  Matrix.setLookAtM(headMatrix, 0, 0.0f, 0.0f, 0.01f,
      0.0f, 0.0f, 0.0f, 0.0f, 1.0f, 0.0f);

  // Update the audio engine
  float[] headQuat = new float[4];
  headTransform.getQuaternion(headQuat, 0);
  engine.setHeadRotation(headQuat[0], headQuat[1],
    headQuat[2], headQuat[3]);
  engine.update();
}
```

As shown, the application obtains the quaternion identifying the controller's orientation and computes the (x, y) coordinates of the controller's vector at the drawing depth. With this information, it determines whether the user clicked on one of the player's buttons.

If the user clicked on a button different than the one previously active, the application will change the audio state. That is, if the Pause button was pressed, the application will pause playback by calling the `pauseSound` method of the `GvrAudioEngine`. If the Play button was pressed, the application will call `resumeSound` or `playSound`.

It may seem strange that pressing the Stop button causes the application to invoke `pauseSound` instead of `stopSound`. But there's a good reason for this. `stopSound` destroys the sound object created in the constructor. Rather than recreate and reconfigure the sound object, it's easier to call `pauseSound`.

The last portion of `onNewFrame` updates the audio engine when the headet's orientation changes. This process consists of four steps:

1. Create a four-element array to store the headset's quaternion.
2. Call the `getQuaternion` method of the `HeadTransform` to populate the array with the quaternion's components.
3. Call the `GvrAudioEngine`'s `setHeadRotation` method with the four components of the quaternion provided by `getQuaternion`.
4. Call the `GvrAudioEngine`'s `update` method to update the state of the audio engine.

13.3 Panoramas and Video

Chapter 3 explained that `Views` define the content of an `Activity`'s window. If a VR application displays graphics using the Google VR SDK, it will generally use a `GvrView`. Chapter 14 will explain how the `GLSurfaceViews` are used by applications based on the Google VR NDK.

In addition to `GvrView`, the Google VR SDK provides two more view classes that can be accessed by applications: `VrPanoramaView` and `VrVideoView`. Both are easy to use, but there are two points to keep in mind:

- Unlike `GvrViews`, these views are usually associated with regular `Activity` subclasses instead of `GvrActivity` subclasses.
- To access these classes, build.gradle must include sdk-panowidget-*x.y.z*.aar or sdk-videowidget-*x.y.z*.aar.

`VrPanoramaView` and `VrVideoView` are both subclasses of `VrWidgetView`, which provides general methods for configuring VR views. Figure 13.2 illustrates the inheritance hierarchy.

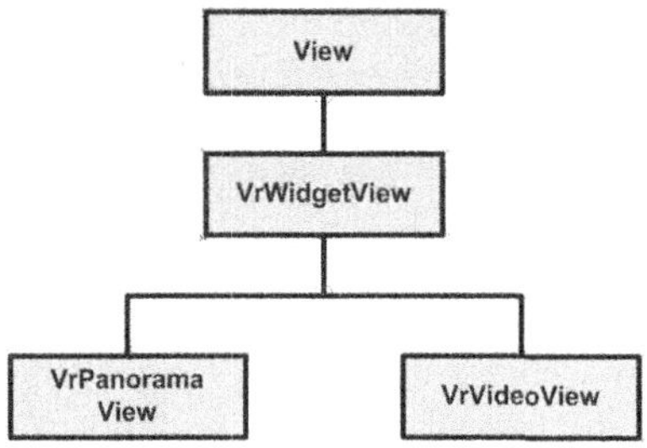

Figure 13.2 The VrWidgetView Class Hierarchy

The goal of this section is to explore these classes and explain how they can be used in applications. We'll look at the `VrWidgetView` class followed by the `VrEventListener` class. Then we'll look at the `VrPanoramaView` and the `VrVideoView`.

13.3.1 VrWidgetView

The `VrWidgetView` class is abstract, so it can't be inserted directly into an application. But its methods make it possible to configure the properties of its concrete subclasses. Table 13.3 lists these methods and provides a description of each.

Table 13.3
VrWidgetView Methods

Method	Description
getDisplayMode()/ setDisplayMode(int mode)	Gets/sets the view's display mode, which determines its behavior in the window
pauseRendering()	Pauses the view's display/playback
resumeRendering()	Resumes the view's display/playback
shutdown()	Ends rendering and releases resources
setFullscreenButtonEnabled(boolean enabled)	Identifies whether the view should display a fullscreen button (default: true)
setStereoModeButtonEnabled(boolean enabled)	Identifies whether the view should display a button to launch stereo mode (default: true)
setInfoButtonEnabled(boolean enabled)	Identifies whether the view should display an info button (default: true)
setTouchTrackingEnabled(boolean enabled)	Identifies whether the user can explore the view by touching and dragging (default: true)
setTransitionViewEnabled(boolean enabled)	Identifies whether the application should display a window for connecting the device to a headset
getHeadRotation(float[] yawAndPitch)	Provides the orientation of the user's headset

Unlike GvrViews, VrWidgetViews do not necessarily occupy the entire window. The view's behavior can be set by calling setDisplayMode with one of three values:

1. EMBEDDED — the view is inserted into the application's layout and doesn't occupy the entire screen
2. FULLSCREEN_MONO — the view occupies the entire window and isn't displayed in stereoscopic mode
3. FULLSCREEN_STEREO — the view occupies the entire window and is displayed in stereoscopic mode

The stereo mode for a VrWidgetView is similar to that for a GvrView. That is, the view's content is drawn twice—once for each eye.

The operating state of a VrWidgetView can be controlled by calling pauseRendering, resumeRendering, and shutdown. In general, these methods are invoked in the corresponding Activity lifecycle methods: onPause, onResume, and onDestroy.

If a `VrWidgetView` isn't launched in stereo mode, the view will display three buttons by default:

- A fullscreen button in the lower right increases the view's size so that it occupies the entire screen.
- A stereo mode button in the lower right changes the rendering from monoscopic to stereoscopic.
- An info button opens up an information window.

These buttons can be disabled using three of the methods listed in Table 13.1. That is, calling `setFullscreenButtonEnabled` with an argument of false disables the fullscreen button, calling `setStereoModeButtonEnabled` with an argument of false disables the stereo mode button, and calling `setInfoButtonEnabled` with an argument of false disables the info button.

To provide an immersive effect despite monoscopic rendering, `VrWidgetViews` don't display their entire content in the view's rectangle. Instead, the user can explore the view by touching and dragging. This is called *touch tracking*, and this behavior can be disabled by calling `setTouchTrackingEnabled` with a value of false.

If a `VrWidgetView` is launched in stereo mode, a window will appear asking the user to place the device in a compatible headset. After the connection is made, `getHeadRotation` returns the headset's orientation. This method populates a `float` array with two values: the headset's rotation angle in the y-axis and its rotation angle in the x-axis. Both values are given in degrees.

13.3.2 VrEventListener

As will be shown in later discussions, instances of `VrPanoramaView` and `VrVideoView` can have listeners attached to them whose methods are called in response to different events. These listeners are subclasses of `VrEventListener`, whose inheritance hierachy is depicted in Figure 13.3.

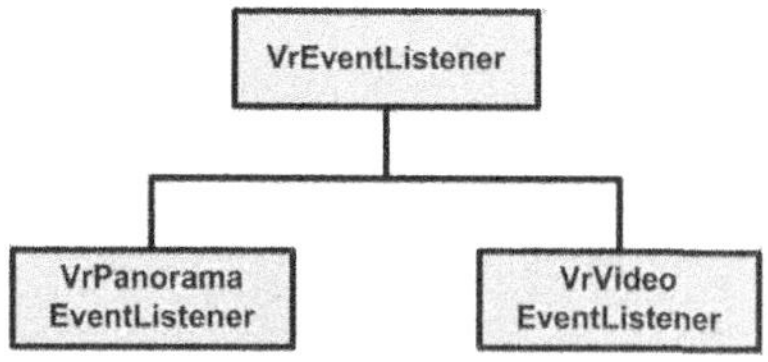

Figure 13.3 The VrEventListener Class Hierarchy

An application can respond to view events by associating a `VrEventListener` with a view and adding code to the appropriate method. Table 13.4 lists the four methods available.

Table 13.4

VrEventListener Methods

Method	Description
`onLoadSuccess()`	Called when the resource is successfully loaded
`onLoadError( String errorMessage)`	Called if the application fails to load the resource
`onClick()`	Called when the user clicks (touches) the view
`onDisplayModeChanged( int displayMode)`	Called when the view's display mode changes

`VrPanoramaViews` and `VrVideoViews` define their appearance by loading resources. That is, `VrPanoramaViews` load images and `VrVideoViews` load videos. If one of these views has an attached listener, the listener's `onLoadSuccess` method will be called if the resource is loaded successfully and its `onLoadError` method will be called if the loading operation failed.

If the view isn't launched in stereo mode, an application can respond to touch events by adding code to the listener's `onClick` method. Similarly, if the user changes the display mode, the listener's `onDisplayModeChanged` method will provide the new display mode.

13.3.3 VrPanoramaView

The word panorama stems from the roots *pan* (all) and *horama* (see). A panoramic image is expected to display not just part of a scene, but all 360° of a complete scene. In the Google VR SDK, a `VrPanoramaView` is a view that displays a panoramic image.

To provide an immersive effect, the view only displays part of the panoramic image at a time. If the view isn't displayed in stereo mode, a user can explore the scene by touching and dragging parts of the view.

As with an `ImageView`, a `VrPanoramaView`'s content is assigned by loading pixel data from a `Bitmap`. This is accomplished by the `loadImageFromBitmap` method, whose signature is given as follows:

```
loadImageFromBitmap(Bitmap bitmap, VrPanoramaView.Options options)
```

The `Bitmap`'s pixel data must be provided in the `ARGB_8888` or `RGB_565` format. Chapter 4 explained the different `BitmapFactory` methods that create a `Bitmap` from an image file.

If a panoramic image is intended to be displayed in stereo mode, it should contain two identically-sized images stacked on top of one another. An application can specify this with the second argument of `loadImageFromBitmap`. This must be set to a `VrPanoramaView.Options` whose `inputType` field can be set to one of two values:

- `TYPE_MONO` — the `Bitmap` contains a single panorama image
- `TYPE_STEREO_OVER_UNDER` — the `Bitmap` contains two vertically-stacked panorama images

The `loadImageFromBitmap` method returns immediately. An application can execute code when the loading is finished by associating the `VrPanoramaView` with a `VrPanoramaEventListener`. `VrPanoramaEventListener` is a subclass of the `VrEventListener` class discussed earlier.

An application can associate a `VrPanoramaView` with a `VrPanoramaEventListener` by calling the view's `setEventListener` method:

```
boolean setEventListener(VrPanoramaEventListener listener)
```

The `VrPanoramaEventListener` class has one method, `isLoadSuccessful`. This returns a `boolean` that identifies if the view's `Bitmap` was loaded successfully. The following code accesses a `VrPanoramaView` from a layout resource, loads its `Bitmap`, and associates the view with an anonymous `VrPanoramaEventListener`:

```
VrPanoramaView panoView =
  (VrPanoramaView)findViewById(R.id.panoview);

VrPanoramaView.Options opts = new VrPanoramaView.Options();
opts.inputType = VrPanoramaView.Options.TYPE_STEREO_OVER_UNDER;
panoView.loadImageFromBitmap(bmp, opts);

panoView.setEventListener(new VrPanoramaEventListener() {

  public void onLoadSuccess() { ... }

  public void onLoadError(String error) { ... }
});
```

Panoramic images become important when submitting Daydream apps for publication. Chapter 17 will discuss this further.

13.3.4 VrVideoView

One exciting capability of Daydream apps is the ability to play video in stereoscopic mode. This not only provides a wide-range viewing screen, but also enables real 3-D video display. To support this, the Google VR SDK provides the `VrVideoView` class.

The `VrVideoView` class is similar to the `VrPanoramaView` class in many respects. One important difference is that, instead of loading a `Bitmap` with `loadImageFromBitmap`, a `VrVideoView` can load video using one of two methods:

- `loadVideo(Uri uri, VrVideoView.Options opts)` — loads video from the given Uniform Resource Identifier (URI)
- `loadVideoFromAsset(String file, VrVideoView.Options opts)` — loads video from the given asset file

The second argument of both methods is a `VrVideoView.Options` that identifies the video's format and the nature of the display. This class has two fields:

- `inputFormat` — Identifies the video's format, and may be set to `FORMAT_DEFAULT` for MP4, WebM, Ogg, and AAC videos, or `FORMAT_HLS` for HTTP Live Streaming
- `inputType` — Identifies the type of display, and may be set to `TYPE_MONO` for a monoscopic display or `TYPE_STEREO_OVER_UNDER` for stereo display.

Once the video has been loaded, the application can play or pause the video, or skip ahead a given time. Table 13.5 lists the methods that make this possible.

Table 13.5

VrVideoView Methods

Method	Description
`playVideo()`	Plays the loaded video
`pauseVideo()`	Pauses the loaded video
`getCurrentPosition()`	Returns the current video position
`seekTo(long millis)`	Skips ahead to the given position
`getDuration()`	Returns the duration of the video in milliseconds
`setVolume(float volume)`	Sets the volume of the video's sound (0.0 to 1.0)
`pauseRendering()`	Pauses video rendering and playback
`setEventListener( VrVideoEventListener eventListener)`	Associates the view with an event listener

As the video plays, the view keeps track of the position in milliseconds. This position can be obtained with `getCurrentPosition` and it can be set with `seekTo`. `getDuration` provides the total length of the video in milliseconds.

The `setVolume` method accepts a value between 0.0 (mute) and 1.0 (maximum volume). The default value is 1.0.

The `VrVideoView`'s `pauseRendering` method overrides the pauseRendering method of the `VrWidgetView` class. The difference is that, in addition to pausing the view's rendering, the `VrVideoView`'s `pauseRendering` method also pauses the video playback.

The last method in the table, `setEventListener`, associates a `VrVideoEventListener` with the `VrVideoView`. The `VrVideoEventListener` class is a subclass of the `VrEventListener` class discussed earlier, and it provides two event-handling methods of its own:

- `onNewFrame()` — Called as each new video frame is played
- `onCompletion()` — Called when the video playback is complete

As an example, the following code accesses a `VrVideoView` from a layout resource and loads video from an asset file named video.mp4. When the loading is complete, the view starts playing the video. When the playback is finished, the view sets the position to the video's start.

```
VrVideoView videoView = (VrVideoView)findViewById(R.id.videoview);

VrVideoView.Options opts = new VrVideoView.Options();
opts.inputFormat = VrVideoView.Options.FORMAT_DEFAULT;
opts.inputType = VrVideoView.Options.TYPE_STEREO_OVER_UNDER;
videoView.loadImageFromBitmap("video.mp4", opts);

videoView.setEventListener(new VrVideoEventListener() {

  public void onLoadSuccess() {
    videoView.playVideo();
  }

  public void onCompletion() {
    videoView.seekTo(0);
  }
});
```

This chapter doesn't provide a complete example that demonstrates video playback. However, the code is straightforward and the Google VR SDK contains a module named sdk-simplevideowidget that shows how this view can be used.

13.4 Summary

Spatial audio is one of the most impressive effects in VR applications, and the first part of this chapter explained how it can be used. The process is simple: create an instance of `GvrAudioEngine`, load an audio resource, assign a position, and play the sound. The `GvrAudioEngine` can be configured to play monophonic, stereophonic, or Ambisonic audio, but if an application needs to set positions of multiple sources, each audio source must be monosonic.

The rest of the chapter explored the `VrPanoramaView` and `VrVideoView` classes. These views make it possible to display images and video in VR applications. To be specific, `VrPanoramaView`s display panoramic images by loading bitmaps and `VrVideoView`s display video by loading content from a URI or video file. Unlike `GvrView`s, which are intended only for stereo display, these views can display their content in mono or stereo mode. They can also be associated with regular Android `Activity` windows.

Chapter 14

Introduction to the Google VR Native Development Kit (NDK)

High-speed graphical rendering is a critical priority for virtual reality applications. For every frame, VR applications have to draw the model twice—once for each eye—and if the frame rate isn't high enough, users develop nausea.

One method of improving performance is to employ native code. While Java bytecode executes on a virtual machine, native code runs directly on the processor. This usually results in faster execution.

To assist with native development of VR apps, Google provides the Google VR Native Development Kit (NDK). This provides Java classes and C/C++ files that developers can use to add native code to Daydream projects. This chapter's goal is to introduce the NDK and explore its features.

The first part of the chapter looks at two important Java classes: `GvrLayout` and `GLSurfaceView`. The `GvrLayout` manages the appearance of an activity's window and its methods make it possible to configure the window's behavior.

The `GvrLayout` delegates the actual drawing responsibilities to a `GLSurfaceView`. As its name implies, this view makes it possible to access OpenGL ES rendering. In particular, it assigns its rendering tasks to a `GLSurfaceView.Renderer` instance.

In an NDK app, the `GLSurfaceView.Renderer` performs its rendering by calling native methods. These native methods access C/C++ functions through the Java Native Interface (JNI). The later sections of this chapter discuss the JNI in detail, including its many data types and built-in functions.

The last part of the chapter explains how Android Studio can be configured to build native modules. This discussion presents the CMake tool, which Android Studio uses to compile C/C++ code into native libraries.

14.1 Installing the NDK

The Google VR NDK is provided as part of the Google VR SDK, but the files aren't immediately available. The NDK's files need to be extracted using the gradlew tool discussed in Chapter 2. This requires two steps:

1. Change to the SDK's top-level directory.
2. At a command line, execute `./gradlew :extractNdk`

After gradlew completes, a folder named jni will appear in the SDK's libraries directory. This contains directories representing different architectures. At the time of this writing, all Daydream devices are based on 32-bit ARM processors, so the folder we're interested in is armeabi-v7a.

This folder contains two libraries: libgvr.so and libgvr_audio.so. These provide the C++ classes and functions that will be explored in this chapter and later chapters.

The declarations of these classes and functions can be found in the NDK's header files. The four files are gvr.h, gvr_audio.h, gvr_controller.h, and gvr_types.h, and they're located in the SDK's libraries/headers/vr/gvr/capi/include directory.

In the DreamBookVR project, the ch14_blankscreen, ch15_spinningtexture, and ch16_mediaplayer modules require NDK files to be inserted into the module folders:

- The libgvr.so library must be copied to the src/main/jniLibs/armeabi-v7a folder in each of the three modules. libgvr_audio.so must be included for ch16_mediaplayer.
- The libraries/headers/vr directory must be copied to the src/main/jni folder in each of the three modules.

Once these steps are performed, the modules can be included in the DreamBookVR project by uncommenting the last three lines in the settings.gradle file. Note that the ch16_mediaplayer module won't compile without the FreeType library and its headers.

14.2 GvrLayout

An NDK application contains a regular `Activity` that delegates its presentation to a `GvrLayout`. This `GvrLayout` doesn't directly control its appearance. Instead, it wraps around a concrete view called a *presentation view*. If the application performs graphical rendering, the `GvrLayout`'s presentation view should be set to a `GLSurfaceView`.

The methods of the `GvrLayout` provide access to features needed for VR processing. Table 14.1 lists these methods and provides a description of each.

Table 14.1
GvrLayout Methods

Method	Description
`onPause()`	Called when the parent activity is paused
`onResume()`	Called when the parent activity is resumed
`onTouchEvent(MotionEvent event)`	Responds when the user touches the screen
`shutdown()`	Destroys the layout and frees its resources
`setPresentationView(View view)`	Assigns a view to define the layout's appearance
`isPresenting()`	Identifies if the layout has an associated presentation view
`addPresentationListener( GvrLayout.PresentationListener pl)`	Assigns a listener to handle presentation events
`setFixedPresentationSurfaceSize( int w, int h)`	Configures the dimensions of the layout's presentation view
`setAsyncReprojectionEnabled( boolean enabled)`	Enables asynchronous reprojection in the layout
`enableAsyncReprojectionVideoSurface( GvrLayout.ExternalSurfaceListener listener, Handler handler, boolean useProtectedBuffers)`	Enables a video surface for asynchronous reprojection
`getAsyncReprojectionVideoSurface()`	Returns the video surface used for asynchronous projection
`getAsyncReprojectionVideoSurfaceId()`	Returns the ID of the video surface used for asynchronous projection
`getGvrApi()`	Returns the layout's GvrApi instance
`getUiLayout()`	Returns the layout's GvrUiLayout

To present these methods, this section divides them into four categories: event handling, presentation, asynchronous reprojection, and VR access.

14.2.1 Event/Lifecycle Methods

The first four methods in Table 14.1 relate to the `GvrLayout`'s lifecycle and event handling. The `onPause` and `onResume` methods serve the same purpose as the `onPause` and `onResume` methods of the `Activity` class. That is, they tell the `GvrLayout` to pause or resume its processing. Each of these methods should be invoked in the corresponding method of the layout's activity.

The next method, `onTouchEvent`, responds when the user touches the device's screen. This method provides a `MotionEvent` that contains information about the event such as its coordinates and time interval.

Unlike most Java objects, a `GvrLayout` should be explicitly destroyed in code. This is accomplished with `shutdown`, which shuts down the `GvrLayout` and frees its resources. This should be called in the `onDestroy` method of the `GvrLayout`'s activity.

14.2.2 Presentation Methods

The next four methods in the table relate to the `GvrLayout`'s appearance. The first method, `setPresentationView`, assigns a `View` instance to define the layout's presentation. After a view has been assocated, the `isPresenting` method will return true.

Users may execute VR applications on an external display, such as a computer monitor. An application can access the new display by calling `addPresentationListener`, which associates the `GvrLayout` with an object that implements the `PresentationListener` interface. This interface defines two methods:

- `onPresentationStarted(Display display)` — Called when the presentation view has connected to an external display
- `onPresentationStopped()` — Called when the presentation view has disconnected from an external display and connects to a default display

The `Display` provided by `onPresentationStarted` represents the external display. This provides information about the display's characteristics, such as its dimensions, refresh rate, VSYNC offset time, and support for high-dynamic range (HDR) rendering.

In most VR applications, the `GvrLayout`'s presentation view will occupy all of the layout's space, which is usually the entire screen. But the `setFixedPresentationSurfaceSize` method makes it possible to assign a fixed height and width for the surface.

14.2.3 Asynchronous Reprojection

Motion-to-photon latency is the time between the headset's motion and the display of a new frame. To keep this as low as possible, a device can transform an existing frame and redisplay the result in a separate thread. This is called asynchronous reprojection, also called asynchronous spacewarp (ASW) by users and developers of the Oculus Rift.

A Google VR application can enable asynchronous reprojection by calling `setAsyncReprojectionEnabled` with its argument set to `true`. An application can receive events related to asynchronous reprojection by calling `enableAsyncReprojectionVideoSurface`. This accepts an object that implements the `ExternalSurfaceListener` interface, which defines two event-handling methods:

- `onSurfaceAvailable(Surface surface)` — Called when an external `Surface` becomes available for rendering
- `onFrameAvailable()` — Called when a new frame is available on the external `Surface`

After calling `enableAsyncReprojectionVideoSurface`, an application can access the `Surface` managed by the reprojection thread by calling `getAsyncReprojectionVideoSurface`. The application can also call `getAsyncReprojectionVideoSurfaceId` to obtain an identifier for the surface. Interacting with `Surface` objects is beyond the scope of this book.

14.2.4 Accessing VR Capabilities

While the Google VR SDK provides many capabilities automatically, the NDK forces developers to access many features manually. For example, in an SDK application, the head transformation matrix can be accessed by the `HeadTransform` in the `GvrView`'s `onNewFrame` method. These and other classes aren't provided in the NDK, but applications can access this information through a `GvrApi` instance.

This `GvrApi` instance can be obtained through the `GvrLayout`'s `getGvrApi` method. This has a large number of methods that provide low-level access to Android's rendering features. The most important `GvrApi` method is `getNativeGvrContext`. This doesn't accept any arguments and returns a `long` that serves as a pointer (!) to a native `GvrApi` instance that can be accessed in C/C++ code. The next chapter will discuss this native `GvrApi` in detail.

The `GvrLayout` also provides a method named `getUiLayout`, which provides a `UiLayout` instance. The methods of this class configure the window's behavior, but the same result can be accomplished in C/C++.

14.3 GLSurfaceViews and Renderers

A view sets the appearance of a rectangle in an activity's window. For most views, this appearance is determined mainly by the `View` subclass. A `TextView` displays text, an `ImageView` displays an image, and so on.

`SurfaceViews` are different. A `SurfaceView` doesn't have a predetermined appearance, but instead gives the developer complete control over the rectangle. Every `SurfaceView` provides access to a `Canvas` that lets you draw simple two-dimensional shapes like lines and circles. Chapter 10 explained how `Canvas` instances can be used to display text in graphical applications.

As VR developers, our main interest is three-dimensional rendering. For this reason, this section focuses on a subclass of `SurfaceView` called `GLSurfaceView`. This view makes it possible to add OpenGL-based rendering to an application.

The actual rendering operations are performed by an object associated with the `GLSurfaceView` called a `GLSurfaceView.Renderer`. This section discusses both classes and their methods.

14.3.1 GLSurfaceView

`GLSurfaceViews` make it possible for NDK applications to perform 3-D rendering. In general, an `Activity` will create a new `GLSurfaceView`, configure its behavior, and call `setPresentationView` to associate the view with the `GvrLayout`.

The code in the `GLSurfaceView` subclass doesn't perform any graphical rendering on its own. Instead, it has three main purposes:

1. Configure the rendering process and the renderer
2. (Optional) Communicate with the renderer
3. (Optional) Set up debugging

This discussion presents the `GLSurfaceView` methods that make these operations possible.

Configure the Rendering Process

Before any rendering is performed, the constructor of the `GLSurfaceView` subclass needs to specify how the view's rendering should be performed. This can be accomplished by calling the eight methods listed in Table 14.2.

Table 14.2

GLSurfaceView Configuration Methods

Method	Description
`setEGLConfigChooser( int redBits, int greenBits, int blueBits, int alphaBits, int depthBits, int stencilBits)`	Specifies the sizes of the components in the pixels to be rendered
`setEGLContextClientVersion( int version)`	Sets the version of OpenGL ES to be accessed by the application
`setRenderer( GLSurfaceView.Renderer renderer)`	Identifies the object to manage the view's rendering
`setRenderMode(int renderMode)`	Specifies how frequently the view's rendering should be performed
`setPreserveEGLContextOnPause( boolean preserveOnPause)`	Identifies whether the application should release the context after a pause
`setEGLContextFactory( GLSurfaceView. EGLContextFactory factory)`	Provides a custom object to create the application's EGL context
`setEGLWindowSurfaceFactory( GLSurfaceView. EGLWindowSurfaceFactory factory)`	Provides a custom object to create the application's EGL surface
`setGLWrapper( GLSurfaceView.GLWrapper glWrapper)`	Provides a custom object to serve as the bridge between Java and OpenGL ES

The first three methods are the most important. `setEGLConfigChooser` identifies what components should be present in the rendered pixels and how many bits should be assigned per component.

For example, the following function call specifies that the red, green, blue, and alpha components should occupy eight bits each:

```
setEGLConfigChooser(8, 8, 8, 8, 0, 0);
```

The `depthBits` and `stencilBits` arguments become important when the application needs to perform depth and/or stencil testing. Depth and stencil testing were discussed in Chapter 9 for the Google VR SDK. For NDK apps, the testing process is nearly identical.

The setEGLContextClientVersion method identifies the version of OpenGL ES that the application intends to access. At the time of this writing, devices must support at least OpenGL ES 3.2 to execute Daydream apps properly. An application can configure this by calling setEGLContextClientVersion with the argument set to 3.

The setRenderer method identifies a GLSurfaceView.Renderer that should perform the application's rendering. This object is very important, and the GLSurfaceView.Renderer class will be discussed shortly.

The last four methods in Table 14.2 are optional. setRenderMode identifies how frequently the view should be redrawn. Its argument can be set to one of two values:

- RENDERMODE_CONTINUOUSLY — Render the view's content in a continuous loop
- RENDERMODE_WHEN_DIRTY — Render the view's content when the view is created, or when the requestRender method is called

A graphical application stores its rendering state data in a special data object called an EGL context. When an application is paused, its default behavior is to release the context so that other graphical applications can use it. But if the argument of setPreserveEGLContextOnPause is set to true, the application will continue to hold exclusive access to the context.

The last three methods in the table are rarely used. setEGLContextFactory identifies a custom EGLContextFactory that should be used to create the application's EGL context. Similarly, setEGLWindowSurfaceFactory identifies a custom EGLWindowSurfaceFactory that should be used to create the interface between EGL and the underlying window. setGLWrapper accepts a GLWrapper to serve as the interface between Java and OpenGL.

Communicate with the Renderer

An application's rendering is performed in a separate thread than its main thread. This makes it difficult to transfer data to and from the renderer. Nevertheless, a view may need to update the renderer's data or receive data. This communication is made possible through the queueEvent method:

```
queueEvent(Runnable r)
```

As discussed in Chapter 5, a Runnable defines an operation to be carried out in a separate thread. In this case, the Runnable's operation is performed in the rendering thread. In general, a GLSurfaceView calls queueEvent in response to an external event, and its Runnable invokes a method of the GLSurfaceView.Renderer that was registered by the setRenderer method.

Setting Up Debugging

Errors in graphical applications are particularly frustrating because of the difficulty of communicating with the GPU. By default, Android apps don't provide any debugging information related to graphical rendering. This can be changed by calling the `setDebugFlags` method of the `GLSurfaceView` class. This accepts an integer that can be set to one or more of the following values:

- `DEBUG_CHECK_GL_ERROR` — Throw an exception whenever an OpenGL ES call produces an error
- `DEBUG_LOG_GL_CALLS` — Log a message for each OpenGLGL ES call at the verbose level

For example, if an application intends to receive debugging information, the `GLSurfaceView` should be configured with code similar to the following:

```
setDebugFlags(DEBUG_CHECK_GL_ERROR | DEBUG_LOG_GL_CALLS);
```

During development and functional testing, it's a good idea to acquire as much debugging information as possible. When it comes time for release or performance measuring, be sure to remove any calls to `setDebugFlags`.

14.3.2 GLSurfaceView.Renderer

When coding graphical apps, most of the work is spent configuring the `Renderer` specified in the `GLSurfaceView`'s `setRenderer` method. As its name implies, this object performs the application's rendering. For this reason, this object is frequently referred to as "the renderer class" or just "the renderer."

To implement `GLSurfaceView.Renderer`, the renderer class must provide code for three methods that are invoked during the rendering process. For improved performance, the operations performed by these methods are frequently coded in C/C++ instead of Java. The three methods are given as follows:

1. `onSurfaceCreated(GL10 gl, EGLConfig config)` — Called when the rendering surface is initialized
2. `onSurfaceChanged(GL10 gl, int width, int height)` — Called when the rendering surface is moved or resized
3. `onDrawFrame(GL10 gl)` — Called to perform draw operations for a frame before it's drawn

Each of these functions provides a `GL10` object that doesn't serve a useful purpose. Similarly, I've never used the `EGLConfig` provided in `onSurfaceCreated`.

As NDK developers, our job is to add code to these three methods. The following section presents a simple project that demonstrates how this can be accomplished.

14.4 Example Application – Blank Screen

Because of the C/C++ code, NDK projects are more complex than their SDK counterparts. Therefore, before delving into the details of native code, I'd like to present a simple module that demonstrates how the NDK can be used. The ch14_blankscreen module, which simply displays a blank screen, is a good place to start.

To structure the files in ch14_blankscreen and the other NDK modules, I've adopted conventions established by Google. Each project has the following characteristics:

- The module's Java files are placed in the src/main/java directory.
- The module's C/C++ files are placed in the src/main/jni directory.
- The external native libraries required by the module, such as libgvr.so, must be placed in the src/main/jniLibs directory.
- The module's top-level directory and the src/main/jni directory both contain a file called CMakeLists.txt. This is required by the CMake utility, which will be discussed toward the end of the chapter.

The acronym JNI stands for the Java Native Interface, which makes it possible for Java methods to invoke C/C++ functions, and vice-versa. Being familiar with the JNI is crucial in NDK development, and the topic will be explored shortly.

This section looks at the `BlankScreenActivity` class of the ch14_blankscreen module. This demonstrates how a `GvrLayout`, `GLSurfaceView`, and `GLSurfaceView.Renderer` can work together.

The `BlankScreenActivity` sets the application's overall appearance and behavior. To accomplish this, it performs five important operations:

1. Loads the native library containing compiled C++ code.
2. Configures the behavior of the application's window.
3. Creates a `GvrLayout` to manage the activity's appearance.
4. Creates a `GLSurfaceView` and associates it with the `GvrLayout`.
5. Creates a `GLSurfaceView.Renderer` and associates it with `the GLSurfaceView`.

Listing 14.1 presents the code for the `BlankScreenActivity`. In later NDK projects, activities will be defined using similar code.

Listing 14.1: ch14_blankscreen/src/main/java/.../BlankScreenActivity.java

```
public class BlankScreenActivity extends Activity {

  private GvrLayout gvrLayout;
  private long nativeInst;

  // Load the blankscreen library
  static {
    System.loadLibrary("blankscreen");
  }

  public void onCreate(Bundle savedInstanceState) {
    super.onCreate(savedInstanceState);

    // Set window properties
    setImmersiveSticky();
    getWindow()
      .getDecorView()
      .setOnSystemUiVisibilityChangeListener(
        new View.OnSystemUiVisibilityChangeListener() {

          @Override
          public void onSystemUiVisibilityChange(int visibility){
            if((visibility & View.SYSTEM_UI_FLAG_FULLSCREEN)==0){
              setImmersiveSticky();
            }
          }
        });

    // Set the layout
    gvrLayout = new GvrLayout(this);

    // Set sustained performance mode
    AndroidCompat.setVrModeEnabled(this, true);
    if (gvrLayout.setAsyncReprojectionEnabled(true)) {
      AndroidCompat.setSustainedPerformanceMode(this, true);
    }

    // Configure the layout's view
    GLSurfaceView glSurfaceView = new GLSurfaceView(this);
    glSurfaceView.setEGLContextClientVersion(3);
    glSurfaceView.setEGLConfigChooser(8, 8, 8, 8, 0, 0);
    glSurfaceView.setPreserveEGLContextOnPause(true);
    gvrLayout.setPresentationView(glSurfaceView);
    setContentView(gvrLayout);
```

Listing 14.1: ch14_blankscreen/src/main/java/.../BlankScreenActivity.java (Continued)

```
    // Set the renderer
    glSurfaceView.setRenderer(new GLSurfaceView.Renderer() {
      public void onSurfaceCreated(GL10 gl, EGLConfig config) {
        nativeOnSurfaceCreated(nativeInst);
      }
      public void onSurfaceChanged(GL10 gl, int w, int h) {}
      public void onDrawFrame(GL10 gl) {
        nativeOnDrawFrame(nativeInst);
      }
    });

    // Access the native renderer
    nativeInst = createRenderer(gvrLayout.getGvrApi().
      getNativeGvrContext());
  }

  // Respond when the activity is paused
  protected void onPause() {
    super.onPause();
    nativeOnPause(nativeInst);
    gvrLayout.onPause();
  }

  // Respond when the activity is resumed
  protected void onResume() {
    super.onResume();
    nativeOnResume(nativeInst);
    gvrLayout.onResume();
  }

  // Respond when the activity is destroyed
  protected void onDestroy() {
    super.onDestroy();
    gvrLayout.shutdown();
    nativeOnDestroy(nativeInst);
  }

  private void setImmersiveSticky() {
    getWindow()
      .getDecorView()
      .setSystemUiVisibility(
        View.SYSTEM_UI_FLAG_LAYOUT_STABLE
          | View.SYSTEM_UI_FLAG_LAYOUT_HIDE_NAVIGATION
          | View.SYSTEM_UI_FLAG_LAYOUT_FULLSCREEN
          | View.SYSTEM_UI_FLAG_HIDE_NAVIGATION
          | View.SYSTEM_UI_FLAG_FULLSCREEN
          | View.SYSTEM_UI_FLAG_IMMERSIVE_STICKY);
  }
```

Listing 14.1: ch14_blankscreen/src/main/java/.../BlankScreenActivity.java (Continued)

```
  // Native methods
  private native long createRenderer(long nativeInst);
  private native void nativeOnSurfaceCreated(long nativeInst);
  private native long nativeOnDrawFrame(long nativeInst);
  private native void nativeOnPause(long nativeInst);
  private native void nativeOnResume(long nativeInst);
  private native void nativeOnDestroy(long nativeInst);
}
```

Much of this code should look familiar. But before the activity's `onCreate` method is called, the activity loads a native library with the following method call:

```
static {
  System.loadLibrary("blankscreen");
}
```

No matter what operating system you use for development, the target system is Android, which is a variant of Linux. Therefore, when dealing with native libraries, you need to understand Linux's naming conventions. Linux shared library files are named `lib`*`name`*`.so`, where *`name`* is the library's name and `so` stands for *shared object*.

In the example code, the argument of `System.loadLibrary` is `blankscreen`. This is the library's name but not the name of the file. The name of the library file is libblankscreen.so, and when `System.loadLibrary` executes, the application loads the native code from libblankscreen.so.

When `onCreate` is called, the activity starts by setting the window's characteristics. This includes hiding the navigation bar and executing the application in immersive mode. In this mode, the application occupies all of the screen's area. The activity also enables the sustained performance mode and VR mode.

Next, the activity creates a `GvrLayout` and a `GLSurfaceView`. The `GLSurfaceView` is configured to access OpenGL 3.2 commands and to use eight bits for the pixels' red, green, blue, and alpha components. After creating the `GLSurfaceView`, the activity associates it with the `GvrLayout` by calling the layout's `setPresentationView` method.

After creating the `GLSurfaceView`, the activity calls `setRenderer` to associate the view with an anonymous `GLSurfaceView.Renderer`. The renderer's `onSurfaceCreated` method calls a native method named `nativeOnSurfaceCreated`. Similarly, the renderer's `onDrawFrame` method calls a native method named `nativeOnDrawFrame`.

The onCreate method ends with the following code:

```
nativeInst = createRenderer(gvrLayout.getGvrApi().
  getNativeGvrContext());
```

createRenderer is a native method that accepts a GvrContext. As mentioned earlier, this isn't a traditional Java object, but a long that serves as a pointer to a native GvrApi instance. This GvrApi instance enables the native code to access features of the Google VR NDK, and this will be discussed later in the chapter.

The last lines of BlankScreenActivity declare the native methods invoked in the class. These declarations don't contain any Java code, but serve as Java handles to functions coded in C/C++. The next section explains how the Java Native Interface makes this Java-C/C++ interaction possible.

14.5 The Java Native Interface

The Java Native Interface, or JNI, serves as a bridge between Java code and C/C++ code. The discussion in this section won't discuss all of its features, but concentrates on the JNI's data types and built-in functions.

The JNI scares many Java programmers because of the strange data types and the complexity of generating the specially-formatted C/C++ code. Thankfully, Android Studio simplifies the process of working with the JNI, so I'll start by discussing this first.

14.5.1 Generating C/C++ Functions with Android Studio

In general, the process of coding a Java application that calls C/C++ functions requires six steps:

1. In the Java code, call System.loadLibrary with the name of the library.
2. For each native function to be called, declare a corresponding method in the Java code. These are *native methods*, and each declaration must contain the native modifier.
3. Generate a C/C++ function declaration for each native method in Step 2.
4. Add C/C++ code to the function declarations generated in Step 3.
5. Compile the C/C++ functions into a dynamic library (*.so on Linux).
6. Execute the Java application.

In this process, the Java code must be written before the C/C++ code. This is because the signatures of the C/C++ functions must be specially formatted in order to be accessible to Java.

For the first step, the discussion of the ch14_blankscreen project explained how a Java class can load a native library using `System.loadLibrary`. The second step is also straightforward—a native method must be preceded by the `native` modifier and must have no associated Java code.

In the third step, a C/C++ function declaration must be generated for each native method in the Java code. Android Studio makes this easy. For example, suppose a Java class contains the following native method declaration:

```
public native String getMessage(int x, float y);
```

If there is no C/C++ function already defined, Android Studio will print the method name, `getMessage`, in red. To generate a C/C++ function declaration, click on the method name and select the first option in the context menu. Figure 14.1 shows what the context menu option looks like.

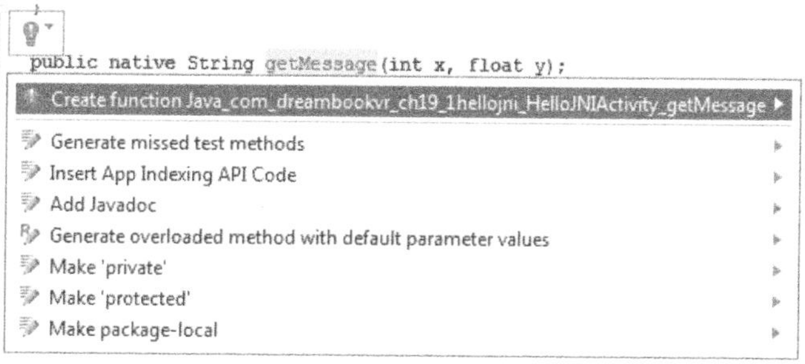

Figure 14.1 Generating C/C++ Code for a Native Method

When the option is selected, Android Studio automatically inserts code into a file called *name*.c in the module's jni directory, where *name* is the name of the library accessed with `System.loadLibrary`. If the Java class calls `System.loadLibrary(hello)`, Android Studio will insert the generated code in jni/hello.c.

Inside the generated code, the function names and data types are completely unlike anything you'd normally encounter in C, C++, or Java. To see what I mean, consider the following native method declaration:

```
public native String getMessage(int x, float y);
```

In jni/*name*.c, the C code generated for this native method takes the following form:

```
JNIEXPORT jstring JNICALL
  Java_com_dreambookvr_example_ExampleActivity_getMessage(
    JNIEnv *env, jobject instance, jint x, jfloat y) {

  return (*env)->NewStringUTF(env, returnValue);
}
```

Though ugly, this is a valid C function and its name follows the standard JNI convention. That is, it starts with `Java` followed by the package name separated by underscores (`com_dreambookvr_example`). The last part of the function's name consists of the name of the class followed by the name of the method (`ExampleActivity_getMessage`).

This book focuses on C++ coding instead of C. Therefore, in the example projects, the code generated by Android Studio will be copied from jni/*name*.c to jni/*name*.cpp. After copying the code, three changes must be made:

- The type of the second argument must be changed from `jobject` to `jclass`.
- The code must be surrounded by `extern "C"` to ensure that the function's name isn't mangled during compilation.
- When calling JNI's built-in functions, the first argument (a `JNIEnv*`) must be removed and the `(env*)->` notation must be changed to `env->`.

As a result of these changes, the C++ code in jni/*name*.cpp takes the following form:

```
extern "C" {

  JNIEXPORT jstring JNICALL
    Java_com_dreambookvr_example_ExampleActivity_getMessage(
      JNIEnv *env, jclass clazz, jint x, jfloat y) {

    return env->NewStringUTF(returnValue);
  }
}
```

It's important to see how the data types in the generated function relate to the Java data types. The native method returns a `String` and the C++ function returns a `jstring`. The arguments of the native method are an `int` and `float`, and the arguments of the C++ function are a `JNIEnv*`, a `jclass`, a `jint`, and a `jfloat`. These data types are specific to JNI, and before proceeding further, it's important to be familiar with the different types available.

In the ch14_blankscreen project, the src/main/jni folder contains three C++ files: blankscreen.cpp, blankscreen_renderer.cpp, and blankscreen_renderer.h. The generated C++ functions are in blankscreen.cpp, and they access the `BlankScreenRenderer` class declared in blankscreen_renderer.h and defined in blankscreen_renderer.cpp. This code will be discussed further at the end of this section.

14.5.2 Data Types

Dealing with JNI's data types, structures, and functions is a large part of the reason why Java developers hate accessing native code. JNI's `jint` and `jfloat` types correspond to C's `int` and `float` types, but many of the data types aren't as simple. Table 14.3 lists twelve of JNI's basic types, along with their equivalents in Java and C/C++.

Table 14.3

Basic JNI Data Types

JNI Type	Java Type	C/C++ Type
`void`	`void`	`void`
`jboolean`	`boolean`	`--`
`byte`	`byte`	`byte`
`jchar`	`--`	`unsigned short`
`jshort`	`short`	`short`
`jint`	`int`	`int`
`jlong`	`long`	`long`
`jfloat`	`float`	`float`
`jdouble`	`double`	`double`
`jstring`	`String`	`--`
`jobject`	`Object`	`--`
`jclass`	`Class`	`--`

JNI's `jchar` type occupies two bytes because it represents a Unicode character instead of an 8-bit character. There's no equivalent type in Java because Java doesn't support unsigned 16-bit integers.

The `jstring` type doesn't correspond to the traditional `char*` or `const char*` types in C/C++. This means `printf` can't be called to display the content of a `jstring`. Because of this incompatibility, JNI provides built-in functions for processing `jstrings`. The following discussion introduces these and other functions.

14.5.3 Built-in Functions

The first argument of every JNI function is a pointer to a `JNIEnv`, which provides access to JNI's built-in functions. For example, `GetStringUTFChars` converts a `jstring` to a `const char*`, and the following code shows how it can be called:

```
const char* newstr = env->GetStringUTFChars(...)
```

This discussion won't present all of JNI's built-in functions, but will explore the functions that fall into three categories: buffer transmission, string handling, and calling Java methods.

Buffer Transmission

In addition to the primitive data types listed in Table 14.3, JNI supports transfering data to and from native code using Java arrays. But when arrays are used, the data is (commonly) copied from the application's heap to an accessible memory location. For large amounts of data, this can require a significant amount of time.

Applications can avoid the memory copy by passing data in direct NIO buffers, which were introduced in Chapter 7. Table 14.4 lists the three JNI functions that receive and process NIO buffers.

Table 14.4

Buffer Functions

Function	Description
`GetDirectBufferAddress(jobject buf)`	Returns the address of the data stored in an NIO buffer
`GetDirectBufferCapacity(jobject buf)`	Returns a jlong identifying the number of elements in the NIO buffer
`NewDirectByteBuffer(void* data, jlong capacity)`	Creates a new ByteBuffer to pass data from native code

The first function, `GetDirectBufferAddress`, accepts an NIO buffer and returns a `void` pointer to the start of the buffer's data. This pointer can be cast to any data type, so in essence, this function makes it possible to convert Java NIO Buffers to C/C++ arrays.

The second function, `GetDirectBufferCapacity`, identifies how many elements are in the NIO buffer. This provides the same value as the `capacity` method of the NIO `Buffer` class.

The following code demonstrates how GetDirectBufferCapacity and GetDirectBufferAddress can be used. In this case, the function accepts a FloatBuffer as a jobject named buff:

```
// Get the number of floats in the buffer
long numFloats = env->GetDirectBufferCapacity(buff);

// Access the buffer memory with a float pointer
float* array = (float*)env->GetDirectBufferAddress(buff);

// Iterate through the elements
float sum = 0.0;
for(int i=0; i<numFloats; i++) {
  sum += array[i];
}
```

The last function in the table, NewDirectByteBuffer, makes it possible to create a direct ByteBuffer that can be transferred to a Java class. The buffer's capacity is set by the capacity argument and its data is set with the data argument.

String Handling

If an application needs to handle strings, native code can access the std::string class and all its functions. The problem is that JNI passes and receives character data in the form of jstrings whose characters occupy 16 bits each.

To enable transfer of characters, the JNI provides functions that convert character data to and from jstrings. Table 14.5 lists these functions and provides a description of each.

Table 14.5

String Handling Functions

Function	Description
GetStringUTFChars(jstring str, jboolean *isCopy)	Returns a const char* for a jstring that can be used in C/C++ functions
NewStringUTF(const char* chars)	Returns a jstring formed from a const char*
ReleaseStringUTFChars(jstring str, const char* chars)	Tells the JVM that the character buffer can be deallocated
GetStringUTFLength(jstring str)	Returns the number of 8-bit characters in the jstring

`GetStringUTFRegion(jstring str, jsize start, jsize length, char* buffer)`	Translates a given range of a jstring into a buffer of modified UTF-8 characters
`GetStringChars(jstring str, jboolean *isCopy)`	Returns a const jchar* for a given jstring
`NewString(const jchar* chars)`	Returns a jstring containing the characters
`ReleaseStringChars(jstring str, const jchar* chars)`	Tells the JVM that the character buffer can be deallocated
`GetStringLength(jstring str)`	Returns the number of jchars in the jstring
`GetStringRegion(jstring str, jsize start, jsize length, jchar* buffer)`	Translates a given range of a jstring into a buffer of jchars

The first five functions have `UTF` (Unicode Transformation Format) in their names. This indicates that characters are encoded according to the *modified* UTF-8 standard. This is similar to the standard format used for C `char`s, but there are important differences. One significant difference is that modified UTF-8 doesn't support the NULL character.

To access character data in the standard UTF-8 format, it's recommended to use the last five functions, which rely on UTF-16LE (little endian) or UTF-16BE (big endian) encoding. These characters (`jchar`s) can be converted into `std::wstring`s, which can be converted into regular `std::string`s.

The following code shows how this works. It converts a `jstring` named `jstr` into an array of `jchar`s, and then converts the array to a `std::wstring`. Then it converts the `std::wstring` to a `std::string`, modifies the string, and converts the string to an array of regular `char`s. The last line returns a `jstring` formed from the `char` array.

```
// Convert the jstring to a wstring
const jchar* jchars = env->GetStringChars(jstr, NULL);
jsize length = env->GetStringLength(jstr);
std::wstring wstr;
wstr.assign(jchars, jchars + length);

// Convert the wstring to a string
std::wstring_convert<std::codecvt_utf8<wchar_t>> converter;
std::string str = converter.to_bytes(wstr);

// Process the string and obtain its bytes
str += " there!";
const char* chars = str.c_str();

// Return a jstring containing the bytes of the processed string
return env->NewStringUTF(chars);
```

The second argument of GetStringUTFChars and GetStringChars is a jboolean pointer that identifies if the read operation completed successfully. If the operation was successful, the argument will point to a value of JNI_TRUE. If not, the argument will point to a value of JNI_FALSE.

Invoking Java Methods

In addition to enabling Java classes to call native methods, JNI makes it possible for native code to call Java methods. The functions can be difficult to understand because there are separate functions for calling instance methods versus static methods and different functions for different return values. Table 14.6 lists the signatures of these functions.

Table 14.6

Java Method Invocation Functions

Function	Description
FindClass(const char* class_name)	Returns a jclass corresponding to the class name
GetMethodID(jclass clazz, const char *name, const char *sig)	Returns a unique identifier for a Java method
Call<type>Method(jobject obj, jmethodID methodID, ...)	Invokes the instance method with the given ID
Call<type>MethodA(jobject obj, jmethodID methodID, const jvalue *args)	Invokes the instance method with the given ID
Call<type>MethodV(jobject obj, jmethodID methodID, va_list args)	Invokes the instance method with the given ID
CallStatic<type>Method(jobject obj, jmethodID methodID, ...)	Invokes the static method with the given ID
CallStatic<type>MethodA(jobject obj, jmethodID methodID, const jvalue *args)	Invokes the static method with the given ID
CallStatic<type>MethodV(jobject obj, jmethodID methodID, va_list args)	Invokes the static method with the given ID
CallNonvirtual<type>Method(jobject obj, jmethodID methodID, ...)	Invokes the nonvirtual method with the given ID
CallNonvirtual<type>MethodA(jobject obj, jmethodID methodID, const jvalue *args)	Invokes the nonvirtual method with the given ID
CallNonvirtual<type>MethodV(jobject obj, jmethodID methodID, va_list args)	Invokes the nonvirtual method with the given ID

The first function, `FindClass`, accepts the name of the class that provides the method. It returns a `jclass` that can be used in the second function, `GetMethodID`, which returns a `jmethodID` for the specific method. The following code demonstrates how these functions can be used to obtain an ID for a method named `getValue` in a class named `com.dreambookvr.ExampleActivity`.

```
// Get a jclass representing the ExampleActivity class
jclass cls = env->FindClass("com/dreambookvr/ExampleActivity");

// Get a jmethodID representing the getValue method
jmethodID id = env->GetMethodID(cls, "getValue", "()I");
```

This code is straightforward to understand except for the last argument of `GetMethodID`. This argument identifies the data types of the method's arguments and return value. This ensures that `GetMethodID` will return a unique ID even if the class has multiple methods with the same name.

The last argument of `GetMethodID` has two parts. The first part identifies the types of the method's arguments inside parentheses. The second part, which follows the parentheses, identifies the type of the method's return value. In the above code, the method of interest doesn't accept any arguments and returns an `int`. The `int` type is abbreviated with `I`, and Table 14.7 lists other abbreviations.

Table 14.7

JNI Data Type Abbreviations

Java Data Type	JNI Abbreviation
`void`	`V`
`boolean`	`Z`
`byte`	`B`
`char`	`C`
`short`	`S`
`int`	`I`
`long`	`J`
`float`	`F`
`double`	`D`
type`[]`	`[ type_abbreviation`
`com.example.MyClass`	`Lcom/example/class`

This notation can be difficult to understand at first, so it helps to look at examples of how different methods are represented:

- float addFloats(float a, float b) — (FF)F
- void setName(String name) — (Ljava/lang/String)V
- int arrayLength(int[] intArray) — ([I)I
- int bufferCapacity(ByteBuffer buff) — (Ljava/nio/ByteBuffer;)I

After obtaining a jmethodID for a given method, an application can call one of the Call* methods in Table 14.6. In the table, each of the method names contains <type>, which identifies the type of the method's return value. This can be set to Void, Boolean, Byte, Char, Short, Int, Long, Float, Double, or Object.

If the desired method is an instance method of the class invoking the native code, the native code should call Call<type>Method, Call<type>MethodA, or Call<type>MethodV. The difference between these three functions involves how the method's arguments are provided.

- Call<type>Method — Method arguments are provided separated by commas following the jmethodID argument
- Call<type>MethodA — Method arguments are referenced by a pointer following the jmethodID argument
- Call<type>MethodV — Method arguments are provided in a va_list following the jmethodID argument

An example will clarify how Call<type>Method is used. Suppose that native code needs to call a Java method named addFloats in the ExampleActivity class. The following code invokes the method with the two arguments set to 3.0 and 5.0:

```
jclass classID =
  env->FindClass("com/dreambookvr/ExampleActivity");

jmethodID methodID =
  env->GetMethodID(classID, "addFloats", "(FF)F");

float sum = env->CallFloatMethod(clazz, methodID, 3.0, 5.0);
```

This code uses CallFloatMethod because the return value of addFloats is a float. If addFloats is a static method, the native code would call CallStaticFloatMethod instead. Both functions accept the same arguments, and in both cases, the first argument identifies the class (clazz) invoking the native code.

The `CallNonvirtual<type>Method` functions in Table 14.6 are similar to the `Call<type>Method` functions in that they both invoke instance methods. The difference is that the `Call<type>Method` functions can only invoke methods of the class of the object invoking the native code. The `CallNonvirtual<type>Method` functions can invoke methods of whatever class provided the `jmethodID`.

14.5.4 Rendering a Blank Screen

At this point, you should have a basic understanding of how the JNI works. Now let's look at the JNI code in the ch14_blankscreen project. The generated code (modified for C++) can be found in the blankscreen.cpp source file, and Listing 14.2 shows what it looks like.

Listing 14.2: ch14_blankscreen/src/main/jni/blankscreen.cpp

```
JNIEXPORT jlong JNICALL
Java_com_dreambookvr_ch14_1blankscreen_BlankScreenActivity_
  createRenderer(JNIEnv *env, jclass cls, jlong context) {

  // Accept the GvrContext and return the native instance
  BlankScreenRenderer *renderer = new BlankScreenRenderer(
    reinterpret_cast<gvr_context*>(context));
  return reinterpret_cast<intptr_t>(renderer);
}

JNIEXPORT void JNICALL
Java_com_dreambookvr_ch14_1blankscreen_BlankScreenActivity_
  nativeOnSurfaceCreated(JNIEnv *env, jclass cls, jlong renderer)
{

  // Call the OnSurfaceCreated function of the native instance
  reinterpret_cast<BlankScreenRenderer *>
    (renderer)->OnSurfaceCreated();
}

JNIEXPORT void JNICALL
Java_com_dreambookvr_ch14_1blankscreen_BlankScreenActivity_
  nativeOnDrawFrame(JNIEnv *env, jclass cls, jlong renderer) {

  // Call the OnDrawFrame function of the native instance
  reinterpret_cast<BlankScreenRenderer *>
    (renderer)->OnDrawFrame();
}
```

Listing 14.2: ch14_blankscreen/src/main/jni/blankscreen.cpp (Continued)

```
JNIEXPORT void JNICALL
Java_com_dreambookvr_ch14_1blankscreen_BlankScreenActivity_
  nativeOnResume(JNIEnv *env, jclass cls, jlong renderer) {

  // Call the OnResume function of the native instance
  reinterpret_cast<BlankScreenRenderer *>(renderer)->OnResume();
}

JNIEXPORT void JNICALL
Java_com_dreambookvr_ch14_1blankscreen_BlankScreenActivity_
  nativeOnPause(JNIEnv *env, jclass cls, jlong renderer) {

  // Call the OnPause function of the native instance
  reinterpret_cast<BlankScreenRenderer *>(renderer)->OnPause();
}

JNIEXPORT void JNICALL
Java_com_dreambookvr_ch14_1blankscreen_BlankScreenActivity_
  nativeOnDestroy(JNIEnv *env, jclass cls, jlong renderer) {

  // Delete the native instance
  delete reinterpret_cast<BlankScreenRenderer *>(renderer);
}
```

The first function in Listing 14.2 is particularly important. It corresponds to the native `createRenderer` method called at the end of the activity's `onCreate` method. This accepts a pointer (`jlong`) to a `gvr_context` structure that the native code will use to access features of the Google VR NDK.

The first function creates a new `BlankScreenRenderer` instance, which we'll look at shortly. The function provides the instance's pointer as its return value, and the activity passes the pointer to all of the other functions in blankscreen.cpp.

For example, when the application needs to draw a frame, it calls the `onDrawFrame` method of the activity's `GLSurfaceView`. In the `BlankScreenActivity`, `onDrawFrame` calls the native method `nativeOnDrawFrame` and passes it a `jlong` that points to the `BlankScreenRenderer` instance.

Similarly, when the application closes, it calls the activity's `onDestroy` method. In the `BlankScreenActivity`, `onDestroy` calls the native method `nativeOnDestroy` and passes it a `jlong` that points to the `BlankScreenRenderer` instance. As shown, `nativeOnDestroy` deletes the `BlankScreenRenderer`.

In essence, the code in blankscreen.cpp serves as a bridge between the Java class and the `BlankScreenRenderer` class. Listing 14.3 presents the class definition in full.

Listing 14.3: ch14_blankscreen/src/main/jni/blankscreen_renderer.cpp

```
BlankScreenRenderer::BlankScreenRenderer(gvr_context*
gvrContext): gvrApi(gvr::GvrApi::WrapNonOwned(gvrContext)) {}

BlankScreenRenderer::~BlankScreenRenderer() {}

// Called when the surface is created
void BlankScreenRenderer::OnSurfaceCreated() {

  // Initialize OpenGL processing
  gvrApi->InitializeGl();

  // Print a message to the log
  __android_log_write(ANDROID_LOG_INFO, "BlankScreenRenderer",
    "Creating the surface");
}

// Called to draw a frame
void BlankScreenRenderer::OnDrawFrame() {}

// Called when the activity is paused
void BlankScreenRenderer::OnPause() {}

// Called when the activity is resumed
void BlankScreenRenderer::OnResume() {}
```

There are three important points to notice about this code:

1. The constructor receives a pointer to a `gvr_context` and uses it to obtain a pointer to a `GvrApi` instance.
2. When the surface is created, the `OnSurfaceCreated` function calls the `GvrApi`'s `InitializeGl` function.
3. The `OnSurfaceCreated` function also prints a message to the log by calling the `__android_log_print` function.

The `GvrApi` class, declared in gvr.h, plays a central role in NDK development. This is because its functions make it possible to access the capabilities of Android and Google VR. For example, one function returns the rotation matrix that identifies the headset's orientation. Another provides access to the user's preferences. Chapter 15 will discuss the `GvrApi`'s methods in greater detail.

The `GvrApi` is essentially a C++ wrapper for a `gvr_context`. In an NDK app, this structure is obtained by accessing a `GvrLayout` and calling `getGvrApi().getNativeGvrContext()`. Because the structure is obtained externally, we say that the `gvr_context` structure isn't owned by the `GvrApi`.

Because the `gvr_context` isn't owned, the application needs to call the `GvrApi`'s `WrapNonOwned` function to obtain a pointer to a new `GvrApi` instance. In Listing 14.3, the constructor calls `WrapNonOwned` during its initialization to set the `gvrApi` variable equal to the `GvrApi` pointer.

The `InitializeGl` function creates the data structures needed to render OpenGL graphics. For this reason, `InitializeGl` must be called before any graphical rendering can be performed. Chapter 15 will explain how OpenGL ES can be accessed in native code.

The `__android_log_write` function is one of the helpful functions declared in the log.h header of the Android NDK. The four logging functions are given as follows:

- `__android_log_write(int priority, const char *tag, const char *text)` — Logs a message at the given priority
- `__android_log_print(int priority, const char *tag, const char *fmt, ...)` — Logs formatted text at the given priority
- `__android_log_vprint(int priority, const char *tag, const char *fmt, va_list ap)` — Logs formatted text at the given priority whose parameters are given in a `va_list`
- `__android_log_assert(const char *cond, const char *tag, const char *fmt, ...)` — Logs an assertion failure and raises SIGTRAP

The first argument of these functions identifies the priority of the logging message. This can be set to a number of values, including `ANDROID_LOG_VERBOSE`, `ANDROID_LOG_DEBUG`, `ANDROID_LOG_INFO`, `ANDROID_LOG_WARN`, `ANDROID_LOG_ERROR`, and `ANDROID_LOG_FATAL`. The second argument is a tag name that can be used to identify the logged message

As an example, the following code logs an error message containing the status code returned by `glGetError`:

```
int error = glGetError();

__android_log_print(ANDROID_LOG_ERROR, "Example",
    "Error detected, status code: %d", error);
```

To access these logging functions, the build process must link the liblog.so library into the application. Configuring the building of native code can be a complex process because of the number of required tools and configuration files. The next section discusses this process.

14.6 Gradle and the NDK

As discussed in Chapter 2, Android Studio relies on Gradle to build Android projects. Every project has a build.gradle file for the project-level settings and each module as a build.gradle file for module-level settings.

Android Studio supports building NDK modules in addition to modules based on the SDK. In this book's NDK modules, each build.gradle file contains the following configuration:

1. In the main `android` element, the `defaultConfig` contains an `ndk` element that identifies the target processor architecture.
2. In the main `android` element, the `defaultConfig` contains an `externalNativeBuild` element that identifies the desired build tool.
3. The main `android` element contains another `externalNativeBuild` element that specifies the path of the build file.

A Gradle file may provide settings for multiple processor architectures by including multiple elements inside `productFlavors`. But at the time of this writing, the only devices that support Daydream development are 32-bit ARM processors. Every executable and library for a 32-bit ARM processor must follow a specific application binary interface (ABI) whose designation is `armeabi-v7a`. The following code shows how this can be specified in build.gradle:

```
android {
  ...
  defaultConfig {
    ...
    ndk {
      abiFilters 'armeabi-v7a'
    }
  }
}
```

The Android NDK and the Google VR NDK both provide libraries and code for multiple ABIs. This designation tells Android Studio which ABI should be used when building the project.

When I started working with the NDK, native code was compiled with the GNU C compiler (gcc) and the build process was managed using Makefiles. But things have changed. At the time of this writing, the default compiler is Clang and the recommended build management tool is CMake.

An application can specify the build tool by adding an `externalNativeBuild` element to build.gradle. The following code shows how this can be configured:

```
android {
  ...
  defaultConfig {
    externalNativeBuild {
      cmake {
        arguments '-DANDROID_PLATFORM=android-24',
                  '-DANDROID_TOOLCHAIN=clang',
                  '-DANDROID_STL=gnustl_static'
      }
    }
  }
}
```

This indicates that Gradle should call on CMake to build the module's native code. It also provides three arguments that should be set as part of the CMake build process. Table 14.8 lists ten arguments that can be set in the `arguments` field:

Table 14.8

CMake Arguments in Gradle

Argument	Description
ANDROID_TOOLCHAIN	The compiler to be used (`gcc` or `clang`)
ANDROID_PLATFORM	The name of the target Android platform
ANDROID_STL	The Standard Template Library (STL) that should be used when building C++ code
ANDROID_PIE	Whether to use position-independent executables (set to ON by default for platforms greater than android-16)
ANDROID_CPP_FEATURES	Enables features for building C++ code (`rtti` and `exceptions`)
ANDROID_ALLOW_UNDEFINED_SYMBOLS	Specifies whether to throw an error if an undefined reference is encountered - `TRUE` or `FALSE` (default)
ANDROID_ARM_MODE	The format of the generated binary (`arm` or `thumb`)
ANDROID_ARM_NEON	Specifies whether the build should support NEON instructions - `TRUE` or `FALSE` (default)
ANDROID_DISABLE_RELRO	Specifies whether to enable read-only relocations
ANDROID_DISABLE_FORMAT_STRING_CHECKS	Identifies whether an error should be thrown when a printf is used with a non-constant format string

The Google VR documentation recommends setting the target Android platform to `android-24` and the build toolchain to `clang`. The `ANDROID_STL` argument is important for projects containing C++ code because it determines which library should be included in the application's linking step.

All of the NDK projects in this book contain C++ code, so the value associated with `ANDROID_STL` determines which C++ features can be accessed in code. At the time of this writing, CMake builds can use one of the six values listed in Table 14.9:

Table 14.9

STL Library Values

Property Value	Size	Notes
`stlport_static`	7,660 KB	No restrictions on distributing binaries
`stlport_shared`	3,593 KB	Recommended instead of the static version
`gnustl_static`	10,554 KB	Released under GPL v3
`gnustl_shared`	5,517 KB	Released under GPL v3
`c++_static`	6,093 KB	Not considered stable
`c++_shared`	654 KB	Not considered stable

The first two options identify the STLport library, which places no restrictions on distributing binaries. The next two options involve the GNU Standard Template Library (STL), or libstdc++-v3. This is released under the GPL, but an exemption exists for compiled binaries. The last two options relate to the LLVM libc++. This provides C++11 by default but RTTI support and exceptions must be specifically enabled.

As mentioned earlier, a project's native code is compiled into a shared library (*.so). If an application needs to link multiple shared libraries to an STL library, one of the shared options (`*_shared`) should be selected. If multiple libraries are linked to a static library, errors may result due to the duplication of global variables.

The NDK documentation states that libc++ isn't stable, and points out that applications may crash when exceptions are thrown. But in my experience, libc++ has given me less trouble than libstdc++. Also, libc++ has C++11 enabled by default. Therefore, even though `gnustl_static` is the default setting, the NDK projects in this book set `ANDROID_STL` to `c++_static`.

In addition to specifying the build tool and its arguments, the build.gradle file needs to identify the build file. This can be accomplished by adding an `externalNativeBuild` element to the file's `android` element. For CMake builds, `externalNativeBuild` should contain a `cmake` element that sets path equal to `CMakeLists.txt`. The next section explains why CMakeLists.txt is so important.

14.7 CMake

If you look through the ch14_blankscreen module, you'll see that it contains two CMakeLists.txt files: one in the top-level directory and one in the src/main/jni directory. The module's build.gradle file identifies the first CMakeLists.txt file with the following element:

```
externalNativeBuild {
  cmake {
    path 'CMakeLists.txt'
  }
}
```

The two CMakeLists.txt files tell CMake how to build the native library loaded by the `BlankScreenActivity` class (libblankscreen.so). The goal of this section is to present CMake in sufficient depth to enable you to understand these files and customize them for your own NDK projects. To start with, there are two fundamental facts to know:

1. When CMake runs, it looks for a CMakeLists.txt file and executes its commands.
2. CMake commands resemble C functions, but have no return values or semicolons. Arguments of a command are separated by spaces, not commas.

For example, the first commands in CMakeLists.txt usually identify the project's name and the required version of CMake. The first operation is accomplished with the `project` command, which accepts the project name. The second operation is accomplished with `cmake_minimum_required`, which accepts at least two arguments: the name `VERSION` and a value that identifies the minimum acceptable CMake version.

The following code shows how these commands are used in CMakeLists.txt:

```
project(BlankScreen)
cmake_minimum_required(VERSION 3.4.0)
```

The full set of commands can be found at https://cmake.org. The discussion in this section focuses on four aspects of CMake:

- Build commands — commands needed to build targets from dependencies
- Variables — storing values for use in commands
- File operations — commands that access and modify files
- Functions — split complex builds into modular subroutines

This section explores each of these topics. Then we'll look at the two CMakeLists.txt files in the ch14_blankscreen module.

14.7.1 Build Commands

The most important CMake commands to know are those directly involved in building code. In CMake's terminology, the file produced by a build is a *target*. The build process may require compile options, header files, and libraries. Table 14.10 presents nine CMake commands that configure how a target should be built.

Table 14.10

Build Commands (Abridged)

Command	Description
add_executable(target sources...)	Define an executable target
add_library(target STATIC|SHARED|MODULE sources...)	Define a library target
target_compile_options(target INTERFACE|PUBLIC|PRIVATE options...)	Set compile options to be used when the target is compiled
target_include_directories(target <INTERFACE|PUBLIC|PRIVATE dirs...)	Identify directories containing header files to be included when building the target
target_link_libraries(target items...)	Link one or more libraries when building the target
add_compile_options(options...)	Set compile options for all targets
include_directories(dirs...)	Set include directories for all targets
link_directories(dirs...)	Set library directories for all targets
link_libraries(libs...)	Identify libraries to be linked into all targets

The first two commands, add_executable and add_library, identify the targets that need to be built. For both commands, the first argument is the name of the target and the last argument identifies one or more source files to be compiled for the build. These file names must be separated by spaces—CMake doesn't have specific notation for an array of names.

If the target is a library, CMake needs to know what type of library should be built. For this reason, `add_library` must include `STATIC`, `SHARED`, or `MODULE`. For native Android builds, the goal is always to create a shared library, so `add_library` will contain `SHARED`. This is shown in the following build command, taken from the CMakeLists.txt file in the ch14_blankscreen module:

```
add_library(blankscreen SHARED blankscreen.cpp
            blankscreen_renderer.cpp)
```

When setting the name of a CMake target, there's no need to provide the suffix. For Android projects, CMake knows the target should be a Linux shared library (*.so).

The next three commands in the table constrain how builds should be performed. These commands are target-specific and the first argument identifies the target to be built. `target_compile_options` sets compile options, `target_include_directories` identifies folders containing header files, and `target_link_libraries` identifies libraries that should be linked to the target.

In the `target_compile_options` and `target_include_directories` commands, each item may be preceded with `INTERFACE`, `PUBLIC`, or `PRIVATE`. These designations are important for targets that are intended to be reused, such as libraries:

- `PRIVATE` — the constraints apply to the library target, but not to targets that use the library
- `INTERFACE` — the constraints apply to targets that use the library, but not to the library target
- `PUBLIC` — the constraints apply to the library and targets that use the library

CMake doesn't have a command specifically for setting linker options. However, `target_link_libraries` can be used for this purpose by replacing library names with options.

The following code defines a simple library build. Specifically, `add_library` specifies the target name, `example`, and the required source files, a.cpp and b.cpp. `target_compile_options` states that the compiler should take advantage of C++11 features and `target_link_libraries` tells the linker to link a library named liblog.so into the build.

```
add_library(example SHARED a.cpp b.cpp)

target_compile_options(example PRIVATE -std=c++11)

target_link_libraries(example log)
```

The last four commands, add_compile_options, include_directories, link_directories, and link_libraries, are not target specific. Their constraints apply to all target builds following the command. When possible, it's safer to use target-specific commands instead of general-purpose commands.

14.7.2 Variables

Like most build tools, CMake makes it possible to associate a variable with one or more values. A variable can be defined with the set command, and the following code shows how it's used:

```
set(name, value)
```

Here, name identifies the variable to be created and *value* identifies the variable's data, which can be a string or a list of strings. As a simple example, the following code sets a variable named SRC_FILES to a list containing "a.cpp" and "b.cpp". Then it uses SRC_FILES in an add_library command:

```
set(SRC_FILES a.cpp b.cpp)

add_library(example SHARED ${SRC_FILES})
```

As shown, the value of a CMake variable can be referenced by surrounding its name with ${...}. Variables can be evaluated inside a string, so if MAIN_DIR is set to "android/main", the string "${MAIN_DIR}/src" will equal "android/main/src".

In addition to user-defined variables, CMake commands can access predefined variables that identify aspects of the CMake environment. Table 14.11 lists nine of these variables.

Table 14.11

Predefined Variables

Variable	Description
CMAKE_SOURCE_DIR	The directory containing the top-level CMakeLists.txt file
LIBRARY_OUTPUT_PATH	The directory where CMake should store library targets
CMAKE_INCLUDE_PATH	The search path CMake uses to find header files
CMAKE_LIBRARY_PATH	The search path CMake uses to find library files

CMAKE_C_FLAGS/ CMAKE_CXX_FLAGS	Flags to be used when compiling C/C++ code
CMAKE_CXX_FLAGS_DEBUG	Flags for compiling a debug build from C++ code
CMAKE_CXX_FLAGS_RELEASE	Flags for compiling a release build from C++ code
CMAKE_SHARED_LINKER_ FLAGS	Flags to be used when building shared libraries
$ENV{*env_name*}	Accesses an environment variable on the computer

Most of these variables are easy to understand, but the last variable deserves attention. If *env_name* is an environment variable on the user's system, the variable's value can be returned by accessing `$ENV{`*env_name*`}`. For example, CMake can access the system's `PATH` variable with `$ENV{PATH}`.

14.7.3 File Operations

CMake can perform many other operations than just compiling and linking targets. It provides commands for reading, writing, copying, and finding files. Table 14.12 lists six of these commands and provides a description of each.

Table 14.12

File Operation Commands

Command	Description
`file(READ|WRITE|APPEND fileName content|variable)`	Opens a file and reads, writes, or appends content
`configure_file(in_file out_file [COPYONLY] [ESCAPE_QUOTES] [NEWLINE_STYLE [UNIX|DOS|WIN32|LF|CRLF]])`	Copy an input file to an output file with zero or more modifications
`find_file(VAR fileName [paths...])`	Find a file and store its directory to a variable
`find_path(VAR pathName [paths...])`	Find a path and store its directory to a variable
`find_library(VAR libName [paths...])`	Find a library and store its directory to a variable
`find_program(VAR programName [paths...])`	Find a program and store its directory to a variable

The file command makes it possible to read text, write text, or append text to a file. If the first argument is set to WRITE or APPEND, the command will create the file if it doesn't exist. For example, the following command writes "ABC" to text.txt, creating the file if it doesn't already exist.

```
file(WRITE text.txt ABC)
```

If the first argument is set to READ, file will read the file's content and associate it with the variable name given as the third argument. As an example, the following code stores the content of text.txt to a variable named VAR and displays the variable's content:

```
file(READ new.txt VAR)
message(${VAR})
```

The configure_file command makes a copy of a file. If COPYONLY is inserted, the output file will contain the same content as the input file. If not, the command will make the following changes before producing the output file:

- If the input file contains variable expressions like ${VAR}, the output file will substitute the variable's value.
- If ESCAPE_QUOTES is inserted, quote characters will be preceded by an escape character (\).
- If NEWLINE_STYLE is set, every line will terminate with the desired newline character. If UNIX or LF is given, this will be \n. If WIN32, this will be \r\n.

The last four commands in the table search for a specific path or type of file. If the search is successful, the directory will be stored in the variable given as the first argument. This is particularly helpful when searching for a library to be linked into the target. For example, the following code searches for a library named libexample and places its path in the LIB_PATH variable if it succeeds:

```
find_library(LIB_PATH example)
```

During the search process, CMake looks through paths identified by its environment variables. Depending on the type of file, these variables may include CMAKE_LIBRARY_PATH, CMAKE_INCLUDE_PATH, and CMAKE_FRAMEWORK_PATH. CMake will also look through system environment variables, such as the computer's PATH variable.

Each find command can identify search paths by adding arguments to the command. If the search fails, the variable will be set to *VAR*-NOTFOUND, where *VAR* is the name of the variable.

14.7.4 Functions

For complex builds, it helps to divide CMake commands into subroutines. For this reason, CMake makes it possible to define functions. A CMake function bears a slight resemblance to a C function in that both require the `function` keyword and contain a parameter list in parentheses. But there are important differences:

- The name of a CMake function is the first parameter in the parameter list.
- In CMake, a function block starts with `function` and ends with `endfunction(name)`, where *name* is the function's name.
- The `ARGC` variable contains the number of function arguments. `ARGV` contains the list of arguments.
- CMake functions have no return value.

An example will clarify how these functions can be defined. The following code defines a simple function whose argument identifies a file. The function copies the file's content to output.txt and then prints a message.

```
function(copyFile fileName)
  configure_file(${fileName} output.txt COPYONLY)
  message("Copied ${fileName}")
endfunction(copyFile)
```

The function's name is given by the first argument, `copyFile`. Therefore, to copy input.txt to output.txt, this function should be invoked with `copyFile(input.txt)`.

14.7.5 CMake in NDK Projects

If a project's files are distributed across multiple directories, the accepted convention is to have one CMakeLists.txt file in a top-level directory and other CMakeLists.txt files in every subdirectory containing source files. The ch14_blankscreen module adopts this convention and Listing 14.4 presents the content of its top-level CMakeLists.txt file.

Listing 14.4: ch14_blankscreen/CMakeLists.txt

```
project(BlankScreen)
cmake_minimum_required(VERSION 3.4.1)

# Execute CMake in a subdirectory
add_subdirectory(src/main/jni)
```

The `project` and `cmake_minimum_required` commands were discussed earlier, but `add_subdirectory` is new. This accepts a path (absolute or relative) of a subdirectory to include in the build. Put another way, this command tells CMake to execute the commands in the directory's CMakeLists.txt file.

In this case, `add_subdirectory` tells CMake to look in the src/main/jni directory. Listing 14.5 presents the content of this file.

Listing 14.5: ch14_blankscreen/src/main/jni/CMakeLists.txt

```
# Identify the directory containing the Google VR libraries
link_directories(${PROJECT_SOURCE_DIR}/src/main/jniLibs/armeabi-
v7a)

# Identify the target library and the source code
add_library(blankscreen SHARED blankscreen.cpp
            blankscreen_renderer.cpp)

# Enable C++11 processing
target_compile_options(blankscreen PRIVATE -std=c++11)

# Tell CMake to look for header files in the current directory
include_directories(.)

# Identify libraries to be linked into the build
target_link_libraries(blankscreen # target name
                      gvr         # provides GvrApi code
                      log         # provides logging methods
                      EGL)        # enables graphical rendering
```

This build file accomplishes four main tasks:

1. It tells CMake to build libblankscreen.so from the source files blankscreen.cpp and blankscreen_renderer.cpp.
2. It enables C++11 processing by adding the `-std=c++11` flag to the compiler options.
3. It tells CMake to start looking for header files in the current directory. The Google VR headers are in the vr/gvr/capi/include folder because that's where they expect to find one another.
4. It identifies three required libraries: libgvr.so, liblog.so, and libEGL.so.

This general structure will be used to build the native libraries in every example project of this book. The main difference is that advanced projects require additional libraries and header files.

14.8 Summary

Make no mistake—native development of Android applications is difficult. In addition to knowing the Android API, you have to be familiar with the Java Native Interface (JNI), Gradle, C/C++, and CMake. But for many VR applications, the improved performance is worth the investment of effort.

Like regular Android apps, an NDK app contains an `Activity` that uses a view to define its appearance. In an NDK app, the `Activity` sets its content to a `GvrLayout` that delegates drawing operations to a `GLSurfaceView`. The `GLSurfaceView` configures the rendering process but doesn't actually render any graphics on its own. Instead, it calls on a `GLSurfaceView.Renderer` to perform its drawing operations.

In NDK apps, the `GLSurfaceView.Renderer` performs its rendering by calling native methods. These native methods invoke C/C++ functions through the Java Native Interface (JNI). This chapter has discussed the process of generating C/C++ function declarations with the JNI, and we also looked at many of the JNI's data types and built-in functions.

Android Studio can build NDK modules if the build.gradle file is configured properly. This configuration involves specifying the desired Android platform, toolchain, and build management tool. This book's example code uses Clang as the toolchain and CMake as the build management tool. The last part of the chapter explained how CMake commands can be defined in CMakeLists.txt files.

Chapter 15

Swap Chains and Native Rendering

Chapter 14 introduced the Google VR NDK and presented a basic module that demonstrated how the Java and native code work together. This chapter goes further and explains how graphical rendering can be performed in native code. More specifically, we'll look at drawing graphics by calling OpenGL ES functions directly instead of accessing them through `GLES32`.

Before an application can render graphics, it needs to perform a series of tasks to obtain a frame for rendering. The first task involves creating `BufferSpec` instances that specify properties of the desired frame. The next task is to create a swap chain, which serves as a container of the buffers. The last task is to associate a frame with a buffer so that it can receive the results of rendering.

After acquiring a frame, an application can draw graphics by calling OpenGL ES functions. For a VR application, one of the first responsibilities is to set the viewport for each eye. Then the application needs to set a stencil region to make sure that the rendering for one viewport doesn't affect the other.

Another responsibility involves transforming vertices according to the orientations of the headset and the user's eyes. The transformation matrices are provided by the `GvrApi` class, which is defined in gvr.h. Once the application obtains these matrices, it can construct the same modelview and perspective matrices as discussed in Chapter 9.

The last part of the chapter explains how direct OpenGL ES calls differ from the `GLES32` calls discussed in earlier chapters. Two major differences are the lack of NIO buffers and OpenGL-specific data types. To demonstrate how OpenGL ES calls can be performed in practice, the last section presents a native VR application that displays a spinning triangle.

15.1 Obtaining Frames from a Swap Chain

The preceding chapter presented the ch14_blankscreen module and explained how native code can use a `gvr_context` to obtain a `GvrApi` instance. The example code demonstrated how the `GvrApi`'s `initializeGl` method can be called to initialize resources required for graphical rendering.

It would be nice if we could call OpenGL ES functions immediately after `initializeGl`, but NDK applications need to perform pre-rendering tasks. To be specific, an application needs to perform three steps before it can start drawing graphics:

1. Create and configure a `SwapChain`.
2. Acquire a `Frame` from the `SwapChain`
3. Associate the `Frame` with a buffer

This section explains how these steps can be accomplished. After a `Frame` has been acquired from a `SwapChain` and associated with a buffer, the application can call OpenGL ES functions to draw graphics.

15.1.1 Creating the Swap Chain

Chapter 11 discussed the topic of framebuffers and explained how they can be accessed in OpenGL ES applications. A framebuffer is really a container of memory buffers, and NDK applications access these buffers through a container called a *swap chain*.

In code, swap chains are represented by `SwapChain` instances. Just as an `int[]` contains a series of integers, a `SwapChain` contains a series of `Frame`s. Before an application can perform any rendering, it needs to acquire a `Frame` from the `SwapChain`.

An application can obtain a `Swapchain` instance by calling `CreateSwapChain`:

```
CreateSwapChain(const std::vector<BufferSpec>& specs)
```

The argument is a vector of `BufferSpec` objects. Each `BufferSpec` defines properties of a rendering surface.

`BufferSpec`s can be created through the `GvrApi`'s `CreateBufferSpec` function. To configure a `BufferSpec`'s properties, an application needs to call functions of the `BufferSpec` class. Table 15.1 lists seven of these functions.

Table 15.1
BufferSpec Functions

Function	Description
`GetSamples()/` `SetSamples(int num_samples)`	The number of samples taken per pixel

`GetSize()/`
`SetSize(Sizei size)/`
`SetSize(int width, int height)`
	The size of the buffer in pixels

`SetColorFormat(ColorFormat format)`	The format of the buffer's pixels
`SetDepthStencilFormat(` `DepthStencilFormat format)`	The format of the depth/stencil buffer's values

These functions determine the number of pixels that will be rendered in the framebuffer and the content of each pixel. The following discussion explains what these functions accomplish and how they're used.

Sampling and the Frame Size

Most Android apps execute with maximum resolution. But for VR applications, the gvr.h header file recommends against using maximum pixel dimensions: "this is probably too large for most applications to use as a render target size. Applications should scale this value to be appropriate to their graphical load."

To scale the size appropriately, an application needs to configure a `BufferSpec` to occupy a reduced space. This requires three steps:

1. Determine the maximum pixel dimensions.
2. Call `SetSamples` to tell the device to compute N samples per pixel.
3. Call `SetSize` with the maximum pixel size scaled by N.

Step 1 can be performed by calling the `GetMaximumEffectiveRenderTargetSize` function of the `GvrApi`. This returns a `Sizei` structure whose `width` and `height` fields define the maximum dimensions of the rendering surface.

Chapter 9 explained how the rendering pipeline converts vertices into pixels. After assembling primitives from vertices, the renderer can use multisampling to ensure that each polygon will be drawn with smooth edges. In NDK code, an application can set the number of samples with the `SetSamples` function. If this is set to 0 or 1, multisampling will be disabled. In general, this is set to a power of 2.

For the third step, an application needs to scale the maximum pixel size by 1/N, where N is the number of samples. To accomplish this, the maximum pixel height and width should be divided by √N. That is, if the renderer computes two samples per pixel, the width and height should be divided by √2. If the renderer computes four samples per pixel, the width and height should be divided by 2.

The following code shows how this works in practice. It creates a `BufferSpec`, configures four samples per pixel, determines the maximum framebuffer dimensions, and sets the frame's size to half of the maximum dimensions:

```
gvr::Sizei max = gvrApi->GetMaximumEffectiveRenderTargetSize();
std::vector<gvr::BufferSpec> specs;
specs.push_back(gvrApi->CreateBufferSpec());
specs[0].SetSamples(4);
specs[0].SetSize(max.width/2, max.height/2);
```

The Google VR NDK doesn't support creating individual `BufferSpec` instances. As shown in the code, a `BufferSpec` can be configured after it's added to a vector.

Color Format and Depth Stencil Format

In addition to setting the buffer's size and sampling, a `BufferSpec` can specify a buffer's color format and depth/stencil format. The color format determines the content of the rendered pixels, and the argument of `SetColorFormat` must be set to one of two values:

- `GVR_COLOR_FORMAT_RGBA_8888` — Each pixel contains red, green, blue, and alpha components, and each component occupies eight bits
- `GVR_COLOR_FORMAT_RGB_565` — Each pixel contains red, green, and blue components, with red occupying five bits, green occupying six bits, and blue occupying five bits

Chapter 9 explained how OpenGL ES makes it possible to perform depth testing, which uses values in a depth buffer to test whether vertices should be discarded. An application can configure the nature of the depth buffer's values by calling `SetDepthStencilFormat`, whose argument must be set to one of seven values:

- `GVR_DEPTH_STENCIL_FORMAT_NONE` — No depth/stencil testing will be performed
- `GVR_DEPTH_STENCIL_FORMAT_DEPTH_16` — Each depth buffer value is a 16-bit integer
- `GVR_DEPTH_STENCIL_FORMAT_DEPTH_24` — Each depth buffer value is a 24-bit integer

- GVR_DEPTH_STENCIL_FORMAT_DEPTH_32_F — Each depth buffer value is a 32-bit floating-point value
- GVR_DEPTH_STENCIL_FORMAT_DEPTH_24_STENCIL_8 — Each depth buffer value is a 24-bit integer and each stencil value is an 8-bit integer
- GVR_DEPTH_STENCIL_FORMAT_DEPTH_32_F_STENCIL_8 — Each depth buffer value is a 32-bit floating-point value and each stencil value is an 8-bit integer
- GVR_DEPTH_STENCIL_FORMAT_STENCIL_8 — Each stencil value is an 8-bit integer

The last three formats set aside bits in each depth buffer value to be used for stencil testing. Each fragment has a stencil value that is usually configured by the fragment shader. A stencil test compares the fragment's stencil value with the stencil value in the depth buffer and discards the fragment if the test fails.

15.1.2 Obtaining Frames from the Swap Chain

After using a vector of BufferSpecs to create a SwapChain, the next step is to acquire a Frame. This is made possible by the SwapChain's AcquireFrame function. Table 15.2 lists this function and others provided by the SwapChain class.

Table 15.2
SwapChain Functions

Function	Description
GetBufferCount()	Returns the number of buffers contained in the swap chain
GetBufferSize(int32_t index)	Returns the size of the buffer
ResizeBuffer(int32_t index, Sizei size)	Updates the size of the buffer
AcquireFrame()	Provides the available frame

In looking at these functions, it's important to understand the difference between a frame and the buffer. In the Google VR NDK, a frame may have multiple buffers associated with it, though only one buffer will be bound at a time.

The properties of these buffers are (theoretically) determined by the BufferSpecs used to create the SwapChain. GetBufferCount identifies the number of buffers, GetBufferSize identifies the size of a buffer, and ResizeBuffer updates the size of a buffer.

The last function in the table is the most important. `AcquireFrame` returns a `Frame` that the application can use as a rendering surface. The function makes no guarantee when the `Frame` will be available or in what order it will be provided.

15.1.3 Associating a Frame with a Buffer

Before a `Frame` can be used as a rendering target, it must be associated with a buffer. An application can create this association by calling the `Frame`'s `BindBuffer` function, which accepts the index of the `BufferSpec` that defines the buffer's properties.

To demonstrate how this works, the following code creates a `SwapChain` with two `BufferSpec`s. Then it obtains a `Frame` and binds it to the second buffer.

```
void XYZRenderer::OnSurfaceCreated() {

  // Create the vector
  std::vector<gvr::BufferSpec> specs;

  // Configure the first BufferSpec
  specs.push_back(gvrApi->CreateBufferSpec());
  specs[0].SetColorFormat(...);
  specs[0].SetDepthStencilFormat(...);
  specs[0].SetSize(...);
  specs[0].SetSamples(...);

  // Configure the second BufferSpec
  specs.push_back(gvrApi->CreateBufferSpec());
  specs[1].SetColorFormat(...);
  specs[1].SetDepthStencilFormat(...);
  specs[1].SetSize(...);
  specs[1].SetSamples(...);

  // Create the swap chain
  swapChain = gvrApi->CreateSwapChain(specs);
}

void XYZRenderer::OnDrawFrame() {

  // Acquire the frame
  gvr::Frame frame = swapChain.AcquireFrame();

  // Bind the frame to the second buffer spec
  frame.BindBuffer(1);

  // Perform draw operations
  ...
}
```

The Frame's association with a buffer can be removed by calling the unbind function. Table 15.3 lists BindBuffer, Unbind, and other functions of the Frame class.

Table 15.3

Frame Functions

Function	Description
BindBuffer(int index)	Associates the frame with the given buffer
Unbind()	Removes the frame's association with its buffer
GetFramebufferObject(int index)	Returns an ID for the given framebuffer object (FBO)
Submit(const BufferViewportList& list, const Mat4f& headMatrix)	Submits a frame for display

Chapter 11 explained how framebuffer objects (FBOs) enable an application to render to a texture. The glGenFramebuffers function generates IDs for FBOs, and the same ID can be obtained with the GetFramebufferObject function of the Frame class.

The last function, Submit, is called after the application has performed its draw operations and has unbound the Frame from its buffer. Submit tells the device that the Frame's graphics are ready to be displayed.

The first argument of Submit is a BufferViewportList, which identifies the BufferViewports to be used in the display process. The next section will explain what BufferViewports are and how they can be configured in code.

Chapter 6 introduced the SDK's HeadTransform object, whose getHeadView method provides the transformation matrix needed to convert world coordinates to head coordinates. The second argument of Submit is a matrix that performs the same operation, and a later section will discuss the Mat4f type and the manner in which this transformation matrix can be obtained.

15.2 Buffer Viewports and Lists

In OpenGL development, a *viewport* is the region of the frame that should be used for drawing. Many graphical applications define a single viewport that occupies all of the available space. An application can configure the size and location of a viewport by calling glViewport.

A VR application needs to draw two viewports—one for each eye. The Google VR NDK makes it possible to configure these viewports by creating `BufferViewports`. To be useful, these `BufferViewports` must be placed in a `BufferViewportList`, which is the first argument of the `Frame`'s `Submit` function.

15.2.1 Buffer Viewports

An application can create a `BufferViewport` by calling the `CreateBufferViewport` function of the `GvrApi` instance. To configure how the viewport is drawn, the application needs to call the `BufferViewport`'s functions. Table 15.4 lists twelve of these functions and provides a description of each.

Table 15.4

BufferViewport Functions

Function	Description
`GetSourceFov()` / `SetSourceFov(const Rectf& fov)`	Access the viewport's field of view
`GetSourceUv()` / `SetSourceUv(const Rectf& fov)`	Access the viewport's position and location
`GetTargetEye()` / `SetTargetEye(Eye eye)`	Identify which eye will be looking at the viewport
`GetSourceBufferIndex()` / `SetSourceBufferIndex(int index)`	Associate the buffer viewport with one of the buffer specs used to create the swap chain
`GetExternalSurfaceId()` / `SetExternalSurfaceId(int id)`	Access the identifier of the external surface
`GetReprojection()` / `SetReprojection( gvr_reprojection reprojection)`	Access whether the viewport's display should make use of asynchronous reprojection

The first method, `SetSourceFov`, accepts a `Rectf` that defines the desired field of view for the `BufferViewport`. This `Rectf` contains angles (in degrees) corresponding to the planes that bound the viewing region (`left`, `right`, `bottom`, `top`).

The `SetSourceUv` method also accepts a `Rectf`, but its fields define the location and position of the region to be drawn. Each field is a `float` between 0.0 and 1.0, where 0.0 represents the leftmost or bottommost position. For example, the following code sets the viewport for the right-half of the plane, from (0.5, 0.0) to (1.0, 1.0):

```
bufferViewport.SetSourceUv({0.5f, 1.0f, 0.0f, 1.0f});
```

To apply distortion correctly, the system needs to know whether the viewport will be viewed by the left eye or right eye. An application can identify this with `SetTargetEye`, which accepts one of two values, `GVR_LEFT_EYE` or `GVR_RIGHT_EYE`. For example, the following code indicates that `bufferViewport` is intended to be viewed by the right eye:

```
bufferViewport.SetTargetEye(GVR_RIGHT_EYE);
```

An earlier discussion explained how the `BindBuffer` function associates a `Frame` with a buffer. Every `BufferViewport` also needs to be associated with a buffer, and this is made possible through the `SetSourceBufferIndex` function. This accepts the index of the `BufferSpec` that identifies the buffer's properties. For example, the following code associates the `BufferViewport` with the second `BufferSpec` in the vector used to create the application's `SwapChain`:

```
bufferViewport.SetSourceBufferIndex(1);
```

The last function in the table, `SetReprojection`, identifies whether asynchronous reprojection should be employed when displaying in the viewport. As discussed earlier, this process transforms and redisplays an existing frame to account for the user's movement. `SetReprojection` accepts one of two values: `GVR_REPROJECTION_NONE` or `GVR_REPROJECTION_FULL`.

15.2.2 Buffer Viewport Lists

Before `BufferViewport`s can be used in the drawing process, an application must place them in a `BufferViewportList` and provide this list as the first argument of the `Frame`'s `Submit` function. A `BufferViewportList` instance can be created with `CreateEmptyBufferViewportList`, as demonstrated in the following code:

```
gvr::BufferViewportList list =
  gvr->CreateEmptyBufferViewportList();
```

After creating the `BufferViewportList`, an application can add a `BufferViewport` to the list by calling `SetBufferViewport`. This accepts an index for the element and a `BufferViewport` to be placed in the list. For example, the following code inserts `viewport` into the list at the second position:

```
list.SetBufferViewport(1, viewport);
```

Similarly, an application can access the `BufferViewport` at a given index by calling `GetBufferViewport`. Table 15.5 lists this and other methods of the `BufferViewportList` class.

Table 15.5

BufferViewportList Functions

Function	Description
`SetBufferViewport(size_t index, const BufferViewport& port)`	Inserts the BufferViewport into the list at the given index
`GetBufferViewport(size_t index, BufferViewport* port)`	Returns the BufferViewport at the given index
`GetSize()`	Returns the number of BufferViewports
`SetToScreenBufferViewports()`	Inserts undistorted BufferViewports corresponding to the screen's configuration
`SetToRecommendedBufferViewports()`	Inserts recommended BufferViewports with distortion correction

The last two methods make it possible to automatically initialize the content of a `BufferViewportList`. `SetToScreenBufferViewports` initializes the list with `BufferViewports` without distortion correction. `SetToRecommendedBufferViewports` initializes the list with `BufferViewports` with suitable distortion correction for the viewer.

I tested the `SetToRecommendedBufferViewports` function on my Google Pixel and examined the initialized list. The function adds two `BufferViewports` to the list: one for the left eye and one for the right eye. The characteristics of the left `BufferViewport` are given as follows:

- UV coordinates: `left: 0.0, right: 0.5, bottom: 0.0, top: 1.0`
- Field of view: `left: -1.469070, right: 50.494850, bottom: 50.494850, top: 60.0`
- Reprojection: `GVR_REPROJECTION_FULL`

The characteristics of the right `BufferViewport` are as follows:

- UV coordinates: `left: 0.5, right: 1.0, bottom: 0.0, top: 1.0`
- Field of view: `left: 50.494869, right: -1.469075, bottom: 50.494850, top: 60.0`
- Reprojection: `GVR_REPROJECTION_FULL`

For both `BufferViewports`, the source buffer index is 0. Therefore, if both viewports are intended to display the same rendering, the application can safely initialize the `BufferViewportList` with `SetToRecommendedBufferViewports`.

15.3 Tracking and Transformations

At this point, you should understand what transformation matrices are and why they're so critical in graphical applications. In SDK projects, these matrices are represented by instances of the `Matrix` class, which was discussed in Chapter 8.

NDK applications can't access the `Matrix` class without complex JNI calls, but they can use the `Mat4f` type. This is defined in gvr_types.h with the following code:

```
typedef struct gvr_mat4f {
  float m[4][4];
} gvr_mat4f;

typedef gvr_mat4f Mat4f;
```

The `GvrApi` has functions that provide `Mat4f`s that identify the orientation of the user's headset and the transformations needed for the eyes. The first part of this section explains how to obtain these matrices.

Unfortunately, the NDK doesn't provide functions for generating `Mat4f` transformation matrices or performing math operations. For this reason, I've coded my own functions in a class called `MatrixUtils`. The second part of this section discusses them and their usage in code.

15.3.1 Head Tracking

No matter which way the user faces, the headset's orientation must define the –z direction of the rendering space. Monitoring this orientation is called head tracking, and the Google VR SDK provides the headset's orientation through the `HeadTransform` of the `StereoRenderer`'s `onNewFrame` method.

The Google VR NDK doesn't have a `HeadTransform` or a `StereoRenderer`, but the `GvrApi` provides the same information through its functions. Table 15.6 lists the functions involved in NDK head tracking.

Table 15.6

Head Tracking Functions

Function	Description
`GetHeadSpaceFromStartSpaceRotation( ClockTimePoint time)`	Returns a Mat4f identifying the headset's orientation
`GetTimePointNow()`	Returns a ClockTimePoint representing the current time
`PauseTracking()`	Halts head tracking
`ResumeTracking()`	Resumes head tracking
`ApplyNeckModel( const Mat4f& headOrientation, float factor)`	Use a neck model to update the head orientation

The primary function to know is `GetHeadSpaceFromStartSpaceRotation`, which returns a `Mat4f` identifying the headset's *future* orientation. This future time is set by the function's argument. By setting the future time, an application can account for the headset's processing delay.

In code, an application can set the desired future time by updating the `ClockTimePoint` returned by `GetTimePointNow`. This structure has a single field, `monotonic_system_time_nanos`, that provides the same value returned by Android's `System.nanoTime()` method.

Google's example code sets the headset's processing delay to 50 milliseconds, and this book adopts the same value. The following code shows how this can be used to obtain the headset's orientation:

```
// Determine the current time
gvr::ClockTimePoint time = gvr::GvrApi::GetTimePointNow();

// Add a 50ms delay
time.monotonic_system_time_nanos += 50000000;

// Determine the headset's future orientation
gvr::Mat4f headMatrix =
  gvrApi->GetHeadSpaceFromStartSpaceRotation(time);
```

By default, the device starts monitoring the headset's orientation as soon as a VR application starts. But when an activity pauses, it's a good idea to pause the head tracking. This is accomplished with `PauseTracking`, and when the activity resumes, the application should call `ResumeTracking`.

Just as the headset's orientation determines the –z direction, the headset's position determines the origin of the rendering space. But there's a problem—the axis of the headset's rotation is the user's neck, not the headset's position. To account for this, the NDK makes it possible to apply a neck model by calling the `ApplyNeckModel` function.

The second argument of `ApplyNeckModel` determines how much of the neck model should be applied. A value of 0.0 disables the neck model and a value of 1.0 applies it in full. The example code in this book always applies the neck model in full.

15.3.2 Eye Transformations

Every Daydream app needs to create one viewport for each eye. The model displayed in each viewport needs to be transformed slightly to enable stereoscopic vision. In an SDK app, the transformation matrix can be obtained through the `StereoRenderer`'s `onDrawEye` method.

In an NDK app, the transformation matrix for a given eye can be obtained through the `GvrApi`'s `GetEyeFromHeadMatrix` function, whose signature is given as follows:

```
gvr::Mat4f GetEyeFromHeadMatrix(Eye eye)
```

The function's argument identifies whether the transformation matrix should be returned for the left eye or right eye. This can be set to one of two values: `GVR_LEFT_EYE` or `GVR_RIGHT_EYE`. The following code shows how this can be used:

```
gvr::Mat4f leftEye = gvrApi->GetEyeFromHeadMatrix(GVR_LEFT_EYE);
```

After an application has obtained transformation matrices for the headset's orientation and a given eye, it needs to multiply them together to obtain the view matrix. At the time of this writing, the Google VR NDK doesn't provide any functions that multiply `Mat4f`s. The following discussion presents the C++ class I wrote to perform matrix multiplication and other operations.

15.3.3 The MatrixUtils Class

If you look in the src/main/jni directory of the ch15_spinningtexture module, you'll notice two new source files, matrixutils.cpp and matrixutils.h. These files provide a `MatrixUtils` class whose functions make it possible to generate `Mat4f` matrices and multiply them together. As listed in Table 15.7, their signatures are somewhat similar to those of the methods of the `Matrix` class discussed in Chapter 8.

Table 15.7
MatrixUtils Functions

Functions	Description
`translateM(float x, float y, float z)`	Returns a transformation matrix that translates by (x, y, z)
`rotateM(float angle, float x, float y, float z)`	Returns a matrix that rotates by the given angle about the axis (x, y, z)
`scaleM(float x, float y, float z)`	Returns a transformation matrix that scales by factors x, y, and z
`multiplyMM(gvr::Mat4f matA, gvr::Mat4f matB)`	Returns the product of matrices matA and matB

These functions are straightforward to understand and use. The `angle` argument in `rotateM` must be given in degrees and it represents the amount of rotation in counterclockwise direction.

Keep in mind that order is important when performing matrix multiplication. Therefore, `multiplyMM(A, B)` will usually not equal `multiplyMM(B, A)`.

15.3.4 Obtaining View Matrices

At this point, you should understand how to obtain the transformation matrices for the headset's orientation and both eyes. In general, these matrices need to be computed every time `OnDrawFrame` is called. This method obtains a view matrix for each eye by multiplying each eye matrix by the head matrix. The following code demonstrates this:

```
// Determine the headset's future orientation
gvr::ClockTimePoint time = gvr::GvrApi::GetTimePointNow();
time.monotonic_system_time_nanos += 50000000;
gvr::Mat4f headMatrix =
  gvrApi->GetHeadSpaceFromStartSpaceRotation(time);

// Obtain view matrices
gvr::Mat4f leftView = MatrixUtils::matrixMM(
  gvrApi->GetEyeFromHeadMatrix(GVR_LEFT_EYE), headMatrix);
gvr::Mat4f rightView = MatrixUtils::matrixMM(
  gvrApi->GetEyeFromHeadMatrix(GVR_RIGHT_EYE), headMatrix);
```

After the view matrices have been computed, an application can pass them to the vertex shader. The code in the Ch15_spinningtexture module shows how this can be done, and the last section of this chapter discusses the module in detail.

15.4 OpenGL Rendering in Native Code

Chapter 7 introduced the `GLES32` object and its methods for performing graphical operations with OpenGL ES. In native code, the `GLES32` is unnecessary because you can call OpenGL ES functions directly. This means you can draw vertices by calling `glDrawArrays` or `glDrawElements` instead of `GLES32.glDrawArrays` or `GLES32.glDrawElements`.

This is just one of many advantages of accessing OpenGL ES in native code. Other advantages include:

1. Improved performance and control of rendering operations
2. No need for NIO buffers—applications can specify data using regular C/C++ arrays
3. Access features from C++11, such as smart pointers and type inference
4. Take advantage of single-instruction multiple data (SIMD) toolsets like NEON
5. Link native libraries into the application, such as libpng and libfreetype
6. Access OpenGL ES extensions that provide additional capabilities

In my opinion, the last two points are particularly important. Chapter 16 will explain how to access extensions of the OpenGL ES standard and display text using the FreeType library.

Unfortunately, accessing OpenGL ES in native code also presents disadvantages that make graphical development challenging. This chapter has already explained the need for frames, swap chains, and buffer viewports, which aren't used in SDK applications. Other disadvantages include the following:

1. Dealing with the Java Native Interface (JNI), with its strange functions and data types
2. Can't (easily) access Java features like `GLUtils`, `Bitmaps`, `Canvas` instances, and the `Matrix` class
3. Pointer usage requires constant concern over memory leaks and overruns
4. Working with OpenGL-specific data types
5. Defining rendering operations for both eyes

This section discusses the last two disadvantages. The first part discusses OpenGL's data types and the second part explains how to configure rendering operations for both eyes.

15.4.1 OpenGL ES Data Types

Rather than rely on existing C/C++ data types and their processor-dependent bit lengths, OpenGL ES provides its own set of data types. Table 15.8 lists each data type with its prefix and description.

Table 15.8

OpenGL ES Data Types

Data Type	Abbreviation	Description
`GLbyte`	`b`	Signed (two's-complement) byte
`GLubyte`	`ub`	Unsigned byte
`GLboolean`	`ub`	Unsigned byte for storing boolean values
`GLshort`	`s`	Signed (two's-complement) short integer
`GLushort`	`us`	Unsigned short integer
`GLsizei`	`i`	Signed integer for defining dimensions
`GLint`	`i`	Signed (two's-complement) integer
`GLuint`	`ui`	Unsigned integer
`GLenum`	`ui`	Unsigned integer for enumerated values
`GLbitfield`	`ui`	Unsigned integer to hold binary values
`GLfloat`	`f`	Single-precision floating-point value
`GLclampf`	`f`	Single-precision floating-point value between 0.0 and 1.0
`GLdouble`	`d`	Double-precision floating-point value
`GLclampd`	`d`	Double-precision floating-point value between 0.0 and 1.0

The majority of these types closely resemble their C/C++ counterparts in usage and bit width. In most cases, they can be cast to C/C++ data types without error. The `GLclampf` and `GLclampd` data types only hold values between zero and one. They are commonly used to enter color values with floating-point numbers.

The names of many OpenGL ES functions are determined by the data types they operate on, and this makes it important to understand the abbreviations in the second column. For example, `glUniform2f` ends with `f`, which means it accepts `GLfloat` arguments. `glUniform2ui` ends with `ui`, which means it only accepts `GLuint` arguments.

15.4.2 Eye Rendering

Chapter 6 introduced the `StereoRenderer` and its `onDrawEye` method. Every draw operation in `onDrawEye` will be executed twice for every frame.

The `GLSurfaceView.Renderer` doesn't have an `onDrawEye` method, so the eye rendering needs to be performed manually. This requires three steps:

1. Define the viewport and scissor region to contain the rendering.
2. Compute the transformation matrix for the eye and pass it to the shader.
3. Perform draw operations.

A viewport is a portion of the window that serves as the canvas for drawing operations. In OpenGL, this region is defined with the `glViewport` function:

```
glViewport(GLint x, GLint y, GLsizei width, GLsizei height)
```

Every VR application needs to configure two viewports. To obtain the arguments of `glViewport`, an application can access the content of the `BufferViewportList` discussed earlier in the chapter.

If `SetToRecommendedBufferViewports` is called, this list will contain two `BufferViewports`. Each viewport stores normalized coordinates (between 0.0 and 1.0) for its rendering region. In general, the viewport for the left eye occupies the left side of the window and the viewport for the right eye occupies the right side of the window.

An earlier discussion explained how to configure the framebuffer's size using the `BufferSpec` discussed earlier. If this size is denoted `renderSize`, the following code sets the viewport based on the `BufferViewport` named `buffViewport`:

```
const gvr::Rectf& rect = vport.GetSourceUv();
int left = (int)(rect.left * renderSize.width);
int bottom = (int)(rect.bottom * renderSize.height);
int width =
  (int)((rect.right - rect.left) * renderSize.width);
int height =
  (int)((rect.top - rect.bottom) * renderSize.height);
glViewport(left, bottom, width, height);
glScissor(left, bottom, width, height);
```

The last line of code calls `glScissor`, and this is an important function to know. The region set by `glViewport` affects drawing operations (`glDraw*`), but it doesn't affect operations such as `glClear`. To ensure that `glClear` only affects a specific region, an application needs to define the region with `glScissor`.

```
glScissor(GLint x, GLint y, GLsizei width, GLsizei height)
```

glScissor accepts the same arguments as glViewport. In Daydream applications, the two functions should be called with identical values. If your application appears to be drawing only one eye region, it's a good idea to make sure that glScissor is being called correctly.

To enable scissor regions, an application needs to call glEnable and set its argument to GL_SCISSOR_TEST:

```
glEnable(GL_SCISSOR_TEST);
```

After defining an eye region with glViewport and glScissor, the application needs to compute the transformation matrix needed to draw vertices in the region. This can be accompished with the GvrApi's GetHeadSpaceFromStartSpaceRotation and GetEyeFromHeadMatrix functions discussed earlier.

Transformation matrices don't change from vertex to vertex, so they should be passed as part of uniform blocks. The following code computes the model-view-projection matrix by multiplying the eye matrix, head matrix, and projection matrix.

```
// Compute the view matrix for the given eye
gvr::Mat4f viewMatrix = MatrixUtils::MultiplyMM(
  gvrApi->GetEyeFromHeadMatrix(eye), headMatrix);

// Compute the projection matrix from the BufferViewport
gvr::Mat4f projMatrix =
  MatrixUtils::Perspective(vport.GetSourceFov(), near, far);

// Compute the MVP matrix and take the transpose
gvr::Mat4f mvpMatrix = MatrixUtils::Transpose(
  MatrixUtils::MultiplyMM(projMatrix, viewMatrix));

// Bind the first uniform buffer object
glBindBuffer(GL_UNIFORM_BUFFER, ubos[0]);

// Pass the matrix data to the shader
glBufferSubData(GL_UNIFORM_BUFFER, 0,
  sizeof(gvr::Mat4f), (GLvoid*)mvpMatrix.m);
```

In this code, the application passes the transpose of the MVP matrix to the shader. This is because the application operates on matrices in row-major order but OpenGL requires matrix elements to be arranged in column-major order.

15.5 Accessing Assets

Before proceeding further, it's important to know how native code can access files in the assets folder. In Java, an activity can open asset files with the following code:

```
InputStream stream = Context.getAssets().open("shader.vert");
```

In native code, the process is more involved. To access an asset in C/C++, an application needs to perform at least six steps:

1. In the Java activity, pass the `AssetManager` to a native method.
2. In the JNI-generated function, receive the activity's `AssetManager` as a `jobject`.
3. In native code, call `AAssetManager_fromJava` to convert the `jobject` to a pointer to an `AAssetManager`.
4. Call `AAssetManager_open` with the `AAssetManager` pointer to obtain a pointer to an `AAsset`.
5. Call `AAsset_getBuffer` to obtain a pointer to the asset's data or call `AAsset_read` to read a portion of the asset's data.
6. Call `AAssetManager_close` to free the asset's resources.

The `AAssetManager_fromJava` function is declared in asset_manager_jni.h, which includes the asset_manager.h header. Any native code that needs to access assets should include asset_manager_jni.h.

To see how the second and third steps can be implemented, I recommend looking at the spinningtexture.cpp file in the ch15_spinningtexture module. The first JNI function is given as follows:

```
JNIEXPORT jlong JNICALL
Java_com_dreambookvr_ch15_1spinningtexture_
  SpinningTextureActivity_createRenderer(
    JNIEnv *env, jclass cls, jobject asset_mgr, jlong context) {

  // Create a new renderer instance
  SpinningTextureRenderer *renderer =
    new SpinningTextureRenderer(
      AAssetManager_fromJava(env, asset_mgr),
      reinterpret_cast<gvr_context*>(context));

  return reinterpret_cast<intptr_t>(renderer);
}
```

The JNI function receives the activity's AssetManager as a jobject. But before passing it to the constructor, it calls AAssetManager_fromJava to convert the jobject to a pointer to an AAssetManager.

Once the AAssetManager is available, the native code can access assets using the functions declared in asset_manager.h. Table 15.9 lists eight of these functions.

Table 15.9

Native AssetManager Functions

Functions	Description
AAssetManager_open(AAssetManager* mgr, const char* filename, int mode)	Opens the asset file and returns an AAsset
AAsset_getLength(AAsset* asset)	Returns the size in bytes of the asset's data
AAsset_getBuffer(AAsset* asset)	Returns a pointer to the asset's data
AAsset_read(AAsset* asset, void* buffer, size_t count)	Attempts to read the given number of bytes into the buffer
AAsset_seek(AAsset* asset, off_t offset, int whence)	Move to the given offset in the asset's data
Asset_getRemainingLength(AAsset* asset)	Returns the amount of data that can be read from the current position
AAsset_openFileDescriptor(AAsset* asset, off_t* outStart, off_t* outLength)	Returns a file descriptor that represents the asset file
AAsset_close(AAsset* asset)	Free resources associated with the asset

The last argument of AAssetManager_open identifies the mode used to access the asset's data. This can be set to one of three values:

- AASSET_MODE_RANDOM — Read the asset's data in a random-access fashion
- AASSET_MODE_BUFFER — Read the asset's data as one large buffer
- AASSET_MODE_STREAMING — Read the asset's data as a stream

When reading from a text file, it's a good idea to get the file's size first and call AAsset_read to read the given number of bytes. Otherwise, the lack of a null character may result in spurious characters added to the end of the text. The following code shows how an application can read data from an asset file named example.txt:

```
// Open asset file
AAsset* asset = AAssetManager_open(assetManager,
                "example.txt", AASSET_MODE_BUFFER);

// Determine the size of the asset file
int length = (int)(AAsset_getLength(asset));

// Read the asset data into a string
std::string str;
str.reserve(length);
AAsset_read(asset, &str[0], length);

// Write string to log
__android_log_print(ANDROID_LOG_INFO, "ExampleTag",
                    "File content: %s", str.c_str());

// Free the asset's resources
AAsset_close(asset);
```

In addition to the functions listed in Table 15.9, the NDK also provides functions for reading through directories in the project's assets folder. These are declared and described in the asset_manager.h header file.

15.6 Example Application – Spinning Texture

The ch15_spinningtexture application may not look impressive—it rotates a square covered with a basic texture. It's importance lies in the fact that its rendering is performed with native code. That is, the code configures its own swap chains, frames, and eye regions, calls OpenGL ES functions directly, and reads the module's asset files by accessing an `AAssetManager`.

The module's overall structure is similar to the module discussed in the preceding chapter. A regular `Activity` loads native code with `System.loadLibrary`, delegates its appearance to a `GLSurfaceView`, and calls the native methods in the methods of the view's renderer. In this case, the `SpinningTextureActivity` invokes its native methods through functions of the libspinningtexture.so library.

As given in the CMakeLists.txt file, this native library is built from four source files: spinningtexture.cpp, spinningtexture_renderer.cpp, shaderutils.cpp, and matrixutils.cpp. The spinningtexture.cpp file contains the JNI functions that correspond to the activity's native methods. The spinningtexture_renderer.h header declares the `SpinningTextureRenderer` class and the class's code is provided in spinningtexture_renderer.cpp.

This discussion focuses on three of the `SpinningTextureRenderer`'s functions. `OnSurfaceCreated` is called when the surface is created, `OnDrawFrame` is called when a new frame needs to be drawn, and `RenderEye` is called to draw both eye regions.

15.6.1 OnSurfaceCreated

The `OnSurfaceCreated` function initializes the application's graphical capabilities and configures the framebuffer. Listing 15.1 presents its code.

Listing 15.1: ch15_spinningtexture/src/main/jni/spinningtexture_renderer.cpp

```
void SpinningTextureRenderer::OnSurfaceCreated() {

  // Initialize OpenGL processing
  gvrApi->InitializeGl();
  InitShader();
  InitBuffers();
  InitTexture();
  glEnable(GL_SCISSOR_TEST);

  // Determine the rendering size
  gvr::Sizei maxSize =
    gvrApi->GetMaximumEffectiveRenderTargetSize();
  renderSize.width = maxSize.width/2;
  renderSize.height = maxSize.height/2;

  // Define a BufferSpec
  std::vector<gvr::BufferSpec> specs;
  specs.push_back(gvrApi->CreateBufferSpec());
  specs[0].SetSize(renderSize);
  specs[0].SetColorFormat(GVR_COLOR_FORMAT_RGBA_8888);
  specs[0].SetDepthStencilFormat(
    GVR_DEPTH_STENCIL_FORMAT_DEPTH_16);
  specs[0].SetSamples(4);

  // Create the swap chain
  swapChain.reset(
    new gvr::SwapChain(gvrApi->CreateSwapChain(specs)));

  // Create the buffer viewport list
  viewports.reset(new gvr::BufferViewportList(
    gvrApi->CreateEmptyBufferViewportList()));

  ready = true;
}
```

This function starts by initializing OpenGL processing by calling `InitializeGL`. Then it loads and compiles the shaders (`InitShader`), creates a vertex array object and vertex buffer object (`InitBuffers`), and loads texture data (`InitTexture`). Lastly, it enables the scissor region by calling `glEnable`.

Next, `OnSurfaceCreated` determines an appropriate size for the rendering region. To accomplish this, it obtains the maximum size and divides the width and height by 2.

To configure the framebuffer, `OnSurfaceCreated` creates a `BufferSpec` and sets its size to the desired size computed earler. It also sets the format of the framebuffer's color attachment and depth/stencil attachment. To make up for the reduced framebuffer size, the `SetSamples` function configures the `BufferSpec` to take four samples per pixel.

The last part of `OnSurfaceCreated` creates a `SwapChain` from the configured `BufferSpec`. Then it creates an empty `BufferViewportList` whose content will be set during the `OnDrawFrame` function.

15.6.2 OnDrawFrame

The `OnDrawFrame` function is called before each frame is drawn. Its job is to configure a `Frame` instance and submit it for rendering. To do this, it defines the content of the `BufferViewportList` created earlier, initializes transformation matrices, and calls the functions that render graphics in the eye regions. Listing 15.2 presents the function's code.

Listing 15.2: ch15_spinningtexture/src/main/jni/spinningtexture_renderer.cpp

```
void SpinningTextureRenderer::OnDrawFrame() {

  gvr::Sizei size =
    gvrApi->GetMaximumEffectiveRenderTargetSize();
  size.width = size.width/2;
  size.height = size.height/2;
  if(renderSize.width != size.width ||
     renderSize.height != size.height) {
    swapChain->ResizeBuffer(0, size);
    renderSize = size;
  }

  // Initialize the buffer viewport list
  viewports->SetToRecommendedBufferViewports();

  // Set the rotation
  angle += 0.1f;
  rotMatrix = MatrixUtils::RotateM(angle, 0.0f, 0.0f, -1.0f);
```

Listing 15.2: ch15_spinningtexture/src/main/jni/spinningtexture_renderer.cpp

```
  // Determine the headset's future orientation
  gvr::ClockTimePoint time = gvr::GvrApi::GetTimePointNow();
  time.monotonic_system_time_nanos += 50000000;
  gvr::Mat4f initMatrix =
    gvrApi->GetHeadSpaceFromStartSpaceRotation(time);
  headMatrix = gvrApi->ApplyNeckModel(initMatrix, 1.0);

  // Acquire the frame and bind it
  gvr::Frame frame = swapChain->AcquireFrame();
  frame.BindBuffer(0);

  // Set VAO, texture, and program
  glBindVertexArray(vaos[0]);
  glBindBuffer(GL_UNIFORM_BUFFER, ubos[0]);
  glBindTexture(GL_TEXTURE_2D, tids[0]);

  // Set the clear color
  glClearColor(1.0f, 1.0f, 1.0f, 1.0f);
  viewports->GetBufferViewport(0, &buffViewport);
  RenderEye(GVR_LEFT_EYE, buffViewport);
  viewports->GetBufferViewport(1, &buffViewport);
  RenderEye(GVR_RIGHT_EYE, buffViewport);

  glBindVertexArray(0);

  // Unbind the frame
  frame.Unbind();

  // Submit the frame
  frame.Submit(*viewports, headMatrix);
}
```

Instead of configuring the `BufferViewports` directly, the function calls `SetToRecommendedBufferViewports`. As discussed earlier, this creates two `BufferViewports` that are specifically configured to display VR graphics in the eye regions.

Next, `OnDrawFrame` obtains an initial transformation matrix representing the headset's orientation. It calls `GetHeadSpaceFromStartSpaceRotation` with a delay set to 50 milliseconds. Then it calls `ApplyNeckModel` to transform the matrix in accordance with the full neck model.

The `AcquireFrame` function provides the `Frame` object that will receive the application's drawing. After the `Frame` is bound, all rendering operations will affect its content.

After binding OpenGL objects, `OnDrawFrame` accesses the two `BufferViewports` in the `BufferViewportList`. For each `BufferViewport`, it calls `RenderEye` to execute rendering operations for the corresponding eye region. After the drawing is complete, `OnDrawFrame` unbinds the `Frame` and submits it for display.

15.6.3 RenderEye

`RenderEye` accepts two arguments: a value identifying the eye region (`GVR_LEFT_EYE` or `GVR_RIGHT_EYE`) and a `BufferViewport` that provides information about the region. With this information, the function configures the viewport and scissor region. Listing 15.3 presents the code of the `RenderEye` function.

Listing 15.3: ch15_spinningtexture/src/main/jni/spinningtexture_renderer.cpp

```
void SpinningTextureRenderer::RenderEye(gvr::Eye eye,
  const gvr::BufferViewport& vport) {

  // Set the viewport and scissor
  const gvr::Rectf& rect = vport.GetSourceUv();
  int left = (int)(rect.left * renderSize.width);
  int bottom = (int)(rect.bottom * renderSize.height);
  int width = (int)((rect.right - rect.left) * renderSize.width);
  int height = (int)((rect.top - rect.bottom)*renderSize.height);
  glViewport(left, bottom, width, height);
  glScissor(left, bottom, width, height);
  glClear(GL_COLOR_BUFFER_BIT | GL_DEPTH_BUFFER_BIT);

  // Compute the MVP matrix
  gvr::Mat4f viewMatrix = MatrixUtils::MultiplyMM(
    gvrApi->GetEyeFromHeadMatrix(eye), headMatrix);
  gvr::Mat4f projMatrix =
    MatrixUtils::Perspective(vport.GetSourceFov(), near, far);
  gvr::Mat4f mvpMatrix =
    MatrixUtils::MultiplyMM(projMatrix, viewMatrix);
  gvr::Mat4f lastMatrix = MatrixUtils::Transpose(
    MatrixUtils::MultiplyMM(mvpMatrix, rotMatrix));

  // Pass MVP matrix to shader
  glBufferSubData(GL_UNIFORM_BUFFER, 0,
    sizeof(gvr::Mat4f), (GLvoid*)lastMatrix.m);

  // Draw the square
  glDrawElements(GL_TRIANGLE_STRIP, 4, GL_UNSIGNED_BYTE, 0);
}
```

To ensure that drawing and clear operations only affect the eye region, `RenderEye` calls `glViewport` and `glScissor` with the region's boundaries. Afterward, the function performs a series of matrix operations to obtain the final transformation matrix:

1. Obtains a view matrix by multiplying the head matrix computed in `OnDrawFrame` by the eye matrix provided by `GetEyeFromHeadMatrix`.
2. Determines the eye region's field of view by calling the `BufferViewport`'s `GetSourceFov` function.
3. Obtains a projection matrix for the eye region by calling the `Perspective` function of the `MatrixUtils` class with the region's field of view.
4. Obtains the model-view-projection matrix by multiplying the projection matrix by the view matrix and the rotation matrix.
5. Calls the `Transpose` function to arrange the matrix's elements in column-major order instead of row-major order.

After performing these steps, `RenderEye` calls `glBufferSubData` to transfer the matrix to the currently-bound uniform buffer object. The last step is to call `glDrawElements`, which draws the square in the eye region.

15.7 Summary

The gvr.h header file defines a set of C++ classes that enable applications to render graphics to a frame. The first class to know is `BufferSpec`, which identifies properties of a desired frame, such as the size and pixel format. The second class to know is `SwapChain`, which is a container class for buffers. The last class to know is `Frame`, which represents a rendering surface. Once an application has bound a `Frame` to a buffer and acquired the `Frame`, it can start rendering graphics.

To display graphics properly, an application needs to know the orientation of the headset and the user's eyes. The Google VR NDK provides these transformation matrices through the `GvrApi` class. Unfortunately, the Google VR NDK doesn't provide functions for operating on these matrices. For this reason, I've added a class called `MatrixUtils` to this book's NDK modules.

NDK programming is difficult in many respects, but I prefer to call OpenGL ES functions directly instead of accessing them through the `GLES32` object. It's much easier to provide data in C/C++ arrays instead of NIO buffers. And although many Java programmers hate pointers, I'd rather use them to reference memory than Java arrays with offsets.

One more difficulty in NDK development involves accessing asset files. To access assets in native code, the activity needs to pass its `AssetManager` to a native method. The corresponding C/C++ function will receive this as an `AAssetManager` instance. Then it can obtain an `AAsset` by calling `AAssetManager_open` and read from the `AAsset` by calling `AAsset_read`.

Chapter 16

Advanced NDK Development

This chapter discusses four topics that NDK developers should be familiar with when coding Daydream apps:

1. Accessing the Daydream controller
2. Spatial and non-spatial audio
3. OpenGL ES extensions
4. The FreeType library for generating text

The first topic is similar to that discussed in Chapter 12. The NDK makes controller access possible by providing two classes in gvr_controller.h: `ControllerApi` and `ControllerState`. A `ControllerApi` instance manages general communication between the Android device and Daydream controllers. A `ControllerState` instance provides state information about a specific controller.

The process of accessing audio in an NDK app is nearly identical to that of accessing audio in an SDK app. In both cases, an application needs to create audio sources and configure each source with a position and volume. The main difference is that the NDK's central class is `AudioApi` instead of `GvrAudioEngine`.

The last two topics are unique to this chapter. OpenGL ES extensions make it possible to access capabilities beyond those defined in the specification. This chapter introduces three new capabilities: persistent data mapping, debugging, and texture compression.

The last topic demonstrates how native libraries can be linked into NDK applications. The FreeType library enables applications to draw text by generating texture atlases dynamically. This chapter presents a full application that demonstrates the library's usage.

16.1 Accessing the Controller

Chapter 12 explained how the Google VR SDK enables applications to access the state of the Daydream's controller. As a quick review, the process involves obtaining a `Controller` from a `ControllerManager` and associating it with a suitable listener.

The NDK's gvr_controller.h header declares two classes that perform similar roles to the `ControllerManager` and `Controller`. The `ControllerApi` class manages access to a Daydream controller and the `ControllerState` class provides information about the controller's state. This section discusses both classes and then shows how they can be used in practice.

16.1.1 The ControllerApi Class

The `ControllerApi` constructor can be called without arguments. After a new instance is available, an application can call a number of methods, including the following three:

1. `Init(int options)` — Initializes the controller and configures its operation with the given options
2. `Pause()` — Pauses controller tracking
3. `Resume()` — Resumes controller tracking

After `Init` is called, the application can use the `ControllerApi` to receive updates from the `ControllerState` instance. The argument of `Init` specifies the type of state information that the application intends to read. This can be set to one or more of the following values:

- `GVR_CONTROLLER_ENABLE_ORIENTATION` — the controller's orientation should be provided
- `GVR_CONTROLLER_ENABLE_TOUCH` — touchpad data should be reported
- `GVR_CONTROLLER_ENABLE_GYRO` — gyroscope data should be reported
- `GVR_CONTROLLER_ENABLE_ACCEL` — accelerometer data should be reported
- `GVR_CONTROLLER_ENABLE_GESTURES` — gesture data should be reported
- `GVR_CONTROLLER_ENABLE_POSE_PREDICTION` — pose prediction data should be reported

The static `DefaultOptions` function returns an integer identifying the default controller settings. The following code shows how it can be used:

```
gvr::ControllerApi controllerApi = new gvr::ControllerApi();
controllerAPI->Init(gvr::ControllerApi::DefaultOptions());
```

The `DefaultOptions` value is a bitfield containing `GVR_CONTROLLER_ENABLE_ORIENTATION`, `GVR_CONTROLLER_ENABLE_TOUCH`, and `GVR_CONTROLLER_ENABLE_POSE_PREDICTION`.

`Init` is usually called in the `GLSurfaceView`'s `OnSurfaceCreated` function. Similarly, `Pause` should be called when the activity pauses and `Resume` should be called when the activity resumes.

16.1.2 The ControllerState Class

After the `ControllerApi` instance has been created and initialized, an application can access a `ControllerState` instance to read information from the Daydream controller. Table 16.1 lists the functions that provide the controller's state information.

Table 16.1

ControllerState Functions

Function	Description
`Update(ControllerApi& api)`	Read data from the controller
`GetApiStatus()`	Returns information about the controller's API support
`GetGyro()`	Returns a vector identifying the gyroscope's setting
`GetAccel()`	Returns a vector identifying the accelerometer's state
`GetOrientation()`	Returns a quaternion identifying the controller's orientation
`IsTouching()`	Identifies whether the user is touching the touchpad
`GetTouchPos()`	Identifies the coordinates of the user's touch on the touchpad
`GetTouchDown()`	Identifies if the user just started touching the touchpad
`GetTouchUp()`	Identifies if the user just stopped touching the touchpad
`GetRecentered()`	Identifies whether the controller was recently recentered
`GetButtonState( ControllerButton button)`	Identifies whether the given button is currently pressed

`GetButtonDown( ControllerButton button)`	Identifies whether the given button was recently pressed
`GetButtonUp( ControllerButton button)`	Identifies whether the given button was recently released
`GetLastOrientation Timestamp()`	Returns the timestamp when the last orientation event was received
`GetLastGyroTimestamp()`	Returns the timestamp when the last gyro event was received
`GetLastAccelTimestamp()`	Returns the timestamp when the last accelerometer event was received
`GetLastTouchTimestamp()`	Returns the timestamp when the last touch event was received
`GetLastButtonTimestamp()`	Returns the timestamp when the last button event was received
`GetConnectionState()`	Returns information about the controller's connection

It's important to understand the difference between the `ControllerState`'s `Update` function and the `onUpdate` method of the `Controller.EventListener` class discussed in Chapter 12. The `onUpdate` method is called automatically when the controller's data is available. For this reason, SDK applications receive controller data in a separate thread.

In contrast, an NDK application calls `Update` when it wants the most recent data from the controller. This accepts a `ControllerApi` instance, and once `Update` has been called, the application can access the controller's state using the other functions in Table 16.1. No second thread is needed.

The `GetApiStatus` provides a value that describes the state of the software running on the controller. There are seven possible values:

- `GVR_CONTROLLER_API_OK` — the device/controller software is working properly
- `GVR_CONTROLLER_API_UNSUPPORTED` — the device doesn't support the software running on the controller
- `GVR_CONTROLLER_API_NOT_AUTHORIZED` — the app isn't authorized to access the controller service
- `GVR_CONTROLLER_API_UNAVAILABLE` — the VR service isn't available
- `GVR_CONTROLLER_API_SERVICE_OBSOLETE` — the VR service is too old
- `GVR_CONTROLLER_API_CLIENT_OBSOLETE` — the VR service is too new
- `GVR_CONTROLLER_API_MALFUNCTION` — the VR service isn't functioning properly

Unlike the SDK's classes, the NDK's `ControllerState` provides direct access to the controller's gyroscope readings. The gyroscope measures the controller's angular velocity in radians per second. The three `float` fields of the `gvr_vec3f` returned by `GetGyro` identify the angular speed around the controller's axes:

- `x` — angular speed about the axis pointing to the right of the controller
- `y` — angular speed about the axis pointing perpendicular to the controller's top
- `z` — angular speed about the axis pointing along the controller's body, with the +z direction pointing away from the touchpad

Figure 16.1 clarifies how these axes are oriented. Note that the y-axis is intended to be drawn perpendicular to the controller's surface.

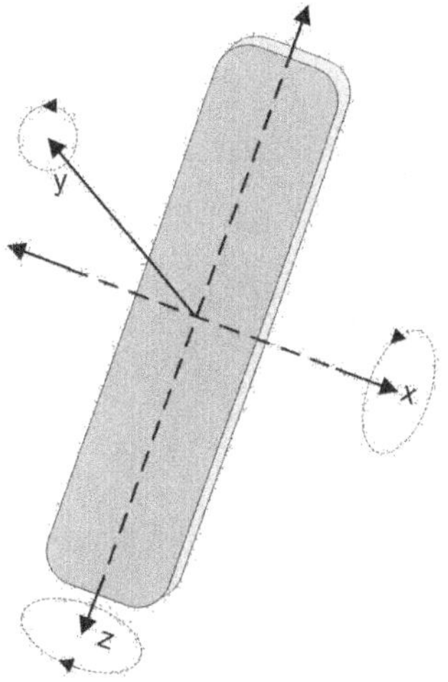

Figure 16.1 Rotation Axes of the Controller's Gyroscope

Like `GetGyro`, `GetAccel` also returns a `gvr_vec3f` structure. In this case, the fields identify the controller's acceleration in the x, y, and z planes depicted in Figure 16.1. The components of the acceleration are given in meters per second squared (m/s^2). Therefore, if the controller lies motionless on a surface, the y component will equal 9.8 because the surface is pushing upward on the controller to counteract gravity.

The `getOrientation` function identifies the controller's angular orientation. The orientation is provided in a `gvr_quatf` structure, which contains the components of the rotation's quaternion: `qx`, `qy`, `qz`, and `qw`. Chapter 12 provided an overview of quaternions and explained how they can be used to determine where a controller is pointing. When accessing these values, keep in mind that `qw` identifies the real part of the quaternion and `qx`, `qy`, and `qz` are the imaginary parts.

The GetButtonState, GetButtonDown, and GetButtonUp functions each accept a ControllerButton that specifies which button is being examined. This can be set to one of six values:

- GVR_CONTROLLER_BUTTON_CLICK — The touchpad
- GVR_CONTROLLER_BUTTON_HOME — The home button
- GVR_CONTROLLER_BUTTON_APP — The app button
- GVR_CONTROLLER_BUTTON_VOLUME_UP — The volume up button
- GVR_CONTROLLER_BUTTON_VOLUME_DOWN — The volume down button
- GVR_CONTROLLER_BUTTON_NONE — No button

The last function in the table, GetConnectionState, returns a value that identifies the state of the device's Bluetooth connection to the controller. This can be set to one of four values:

- GVR_CONTROLLER_DISCONNECTED — No connection
- GVR_CONTROLLER_SCANNING — The device is searching for a connection
- GVR_CONTROLLER_CONNECTING — The device is in the process of connecting to the controller
- GVR_CONTROLLER_CONNECTED — The device has connected to the controller

To show how a ControllerState can be used, the following code calls Update and determines the controller's position if it's connected.

```
controllerState.Update(controllerApi);
if(controllerState.GetConnectionState() ==
    GVR_CONTROLLER_CONNECTED) {

  gvr_quatf q = controllerState.GetOrientation();
  float tmp =
    (q.qw * q.qw) - (q.qx * q.qx) - (q.qy * q.qy) + (q.qz * q.qz);
  target[0] =
    (2.0f * q.qw * q.qy - 2.0f * q.qx * q.qz) * (DEPTH / tmp);
  target[1] =
    (-2.0f * q.qw * q.qx - 2.0f * q.qy * q.qz) * (DEPTH / tmp);
}
```

The ch16_mediaplayer module uses similar code to determine if the controller is pointing at one of the player's three buttons. The last section of this chapter discusses the module's code in detail.

16.2 Accessing Audio

Chapter 13 explained how the Google VR SDK makes it possible to play audio in Daydream applications. The audio can be spatial or non-spatial (stereo), and the spatial audio can be defined using one or more virtual sources or a single Ambisonic source. Each virtual source needs to be assigned a position in space.

The NDK provides the same capabilities through the `AudioApi` class declared in the gvr_audio.h header. This section explains how the `AudioApi` functions make it possible to play stereo and spatial audio in NDK applications.

Table 16.2

AudioApi Functions

Function	Description
`Init(JNIEnv* env, jobject context, jobject loader, AudioRenderingMode mode)`	Initializes the audio processing capability
`Pause()`	Pauses the audio engine
`Resume()`	Resumes the audio engine
`Update()`	Execute background operations outside of the audio thread
`PreloadSoundfile(const std::string& file)`	Starts loading audio file into memory
`UnloadSoundfile(const std::string& file)`	Unloads an audio file from memory
`EnableStereoSpeakerMode(bool enable)`	Enables the stereo speaker mode
`CreateStereoSound(const std::string& file)`	Returns an ID for the stereo sound data in the given file
`CreateSoundObject(const std::string& file)`	Returns an ID for the monophonic sound data in the given file
`CreateSoundField(const std::string& file)`	Returns an ID for the Ambisonic sound data in the given file
`PlaySound(AudioSourceId id, bool looping)`	Plays the sound with the given ID
`PauseSound(AudioSourceId id)`	Pauses the sound with the given ID
`ResumeSound(AudioSourceId id)`	Resumes the sound with the given ID

`StopSound(AudioSourceId id)`	Stops the sound with the given ID
`IsSoundPlaying(AudioSourceId id)`	Identifies whether the sound with the given ID is currently playing
`SetSoundVolume(AudioSourceId id, float volume)`	Sets the volume of the given sound
`SetSoundObjectPosition( AudioSourceId id, float x, float y, float z)`	Set the position of a monophonic sound source
`SetSoundObjectDistanceRolloffModel( AudioSourceId id, gvr_audio_distance_rolloff_type model, float min_distance, float max_distance)`	Set the rolloff model for a monophonic sound source
`SetSoundfieldRotation( AudioSourceId id, const Quatf& rotation)`	Set the rotation parameter for an Ambisonic sound source
`SetHeadPose(const Mat4f& matrix)`	Updates the orientation of the user's headset
`EnableRoom(bool enable)`	Enables room-related audio effects
`SetRoomProperties(float size_x, float size_y, float size_z, gvr_audio_matrial_type wall, gvr_audio_matrial_type ceiling, gvr_audio_matrial_type floor)`	Specifies properties of the room's acoustics, including the materials used for its walls, ceiling, and floor
`SetRoomReverbAdjustments( float gain, float time_adjust, float brightness_adjust)`	Specifies how sound resonates in the configured room

Most of these functions are straightforward and closely resemble the methods of the `GvrAudioEngine` class discussed in Chapter 13. The `Init` function deserves special mention because of its arguments. The first argument is a `JNIEnv` pointer, which is only available in the JNI interface code. This makes it necessary to create and initialize the `AudioApi` in the JNI code, not the regular C++ code.

`Init`'s second and third arguments are both `jobjects`. The first should be set to the application's context and the third should be set to the application's classloader. An `Activity` can access the context by calling `getApplicationContext` and it can access the classloader with `getClass().getClassLoader()`.

An example will clarify how an `AudioApi` can be created. In this case, the native method that creates the renderer is named `createRenderer`:

```
native long createRenderer(long nativeContext,
  ClassLoader loader, Context context);
```

The first argument is the same `gvr_context` pointer that we've encountered earlier. The second and third arguments are new, and the following code shows how an `Activity` can call this method with suitable values:

```
long nativeInst = nativeCreateRenderer(
  getClass().getClassLoader(), this.getApplicationContext(),
  gvrLayout.getGvrApi().getNativeGvrContext());
```

The JNI interface code will receive the first argument as a `jlong` and the last two arguments as `jobjects`. If JNI associates the native method with the `nativeCreateRenderer` function, the function's code can be given as follows:

```
JNIEXPORT jlong JNICALL
nativeCreateRenderer(JNIEnv *env, jclass cls, jlong gvrContext,
  jobject loader, jobject appContext) {

  // Create a new AudioApi
  std::unique_ptr<gvr::AudioApi> audioApi(new gvr::AudioApi);

  // Initialize the AudioApi
  audioApi->Init(env, appContext, loader,
    GVR_AUDIO_RENDERING_BINAURAL_HIGH_QUALITY);

  // Create a new Renderer instance with the AudioApi
  Renderer *renderer = new Renderer(std::move(audioApi),
    reinterpret_cast<gvr_context*>(gvrContext));

  // Return a pointer to the new instance
  return reinterpret_cast<intptr_t>(renderer);
}
```

The last argument of `Init` identifies the type of audio that will be played in the application. This can be set to one of three values:

- `GVR_AUDIO_RENDERING_STEREO_PANNING` — Renders sound in stereo, without regard to head position
- `GVR_AUDIO_RENDERING_BINAURAL_LOW_QUALITY` — Renders sound from up to eight virtual sources
- `GVR_AUDIO_RENDERING_BINAURAL_HIGH_QUALITY` — Renders sound from up to sixteen virtual sources

After initializing an `AudioApi`, an application can play stereo sound, monophonic sound, or Ambisonic sound. To play regular stereo sound, an application needs to perform three steps:

1. Call `PreloadSoundFile` to load audio data from the audio file.
2. Call `CreateStereoSound` to obtain an identifier for the sound source.
3. Play the audio by calling `PlaySound` with the identifier.

In the first step, `PreloadSoundFile` automatically accesses the given audio file in the module's assets folder. This means there's no need to read the file's content with an `AssetManager`.

The process of playing spatial audio is similar to that of playing stereo, but an addition step is required:

1. Call `PreloadSoundFile` to load audio data from the audio file.
2. Call `CreateStereoSound` to obtain an identifier for the sound source.
3. Invoke `SetSoundObjectPosition` to assign a position for the sound source.
4. Play the audio by calling `PlaySound` with the identifier.

An example will clarify how these steps can be accomplished. If the `AudioApi` instance is named `audioApi`, the following code shows how an application can read and play audio contained in music.wav:

```
// Load audio from the file
audioApi->PreloadSoundfile("music.wav");

// Obtain an ID for the sound source
gvr::AudioSourceId id = audioApi->CreateSoundObject("music.wav");

// Assign a position for the sound source
audioApi->SetSoundObjectPosition(id, 0.0f, 0.0f, 5.0f);

// Play the sound
audioApi->PlaySound(id, true);
```

To render spatial audio properly, the `AudioApi` needs to know how the headset is oriented. An application can provide this information by calling `SetHeadPose` with the `Mat4f` matrix containing the headset's orientation.

`AudioApi` provides two pairs of similarly-named functions: `Pause`/`PauseSound` and `Resume`/`ResumeSound`. `Pause` and `Resume` should be called in response to changes in the activity's lifecycle.

16.3 OpenGL ES Extensions

OpenGL ES extensions provide functions and capabilities beyond those defined in the basic specification. Using these extensions can dramatically affect an application's performance. Good programmers master the core OpenGL functions; great programmers master the extensions.

This section starts by explaining what extensions are and how they can be accessed in code. Then we'll look at three useful capabilities provided by OpenGL ES extensions: persistent data mapping, debugging, and texture compression.

16.3.1 Overview

The OpenGL ES standard specifies a set of features that all compliant devices must be able to support. As hardware improves, vendors can create extensions that provide capabilities beyond those defined in the standard. Each extension must be given a name that conforms to the following structure:

```
GL_<vendor_code>_<ext_name>
```

A full list of OpenGL ES extensions can be found at https://www.khronos.org/registry/gles/#otherextspecs. For example, `GL_AMD_program_binary_Z400` is provided by AMD and `GL_NV_depth_nonlinear` is provided by Nvidia. These extensions can only be accessed when the application runs on the vendor's hardware.

Many extensions start with `GL_OES_`, which means the vendor is the OpenGL ES Working Group. These extensions are widely available, but are not required by the OpenGL ES standard. Another important set of extensions start with `GL_EXT_`, which indicates that the extension has been accepted by multiple vendors. It's safe to assume that extensions starting with `GL_OES_` and `GL_EXT_` will be available on compliant devices from different vendors.

An application can check if a given extension is available by calling `glGetString` with the argument set to `GL_EXTENSIONS`. This returns a sequence of characters identifying all of the extensions that can be accessed.

An application can access core OpenGL ES 3.x functions by including the gl3.h header. Oddly, extensions for OpenGL ES 3.x can be found in the gl2ext.h header, not gl3ext.h. Therefore, an application can access 3.x extensions with the following statements:

```
#include <GLES3/gl3.h>
#include <GLES2/gl2ext.h>
```

The Android NDK provides declarations of extension functions in the gl2ext.h header. If you look through this file, you'll see that extension functions are only available if the `GL_GLEXT_PROTOTYPES` macro is defined. For this reason, the CMakeLists.txt file in the ch16_mediaplayer module defines this macro in the `target_compile_options` command.

In many cases, applications can only access functions of extensions through function pointers. A function's pointer is provided by `eglGetProcess`, which accepts a function name and returns a pointer that references the named function. The following code shows how it can be used to obtain a pointer to the `glBufferStorageEXT` function:

```
ptr_type glBufferStorageEXT =
  (ptr_type)eglGetProcAddress("glBufferStorageEXT");
```

In this code, *`ptr_type`* identifies the type of the function pointer to be returned. Each function has its own function pointer type, and this type can be determined by looking through gl2ext.h.

For example, gl2ext.h contains the following declaration of the `glBufferStorageEXT` function:

```
typedef void (GL_APIENTRYP PFNGLBUFFERSTORAGEEXTPROC) (GLenum
target, GLsizeiptr size, const void *data, GLbitfield flags);
#ifdef GL_GLEXT_PROTOTYPES
GL_APICALL void GL_APIENTRY glBufferStorageEXT (GLenum target,
GLsizeiptr size, const void *data, GLbitfield flags);
#endif
```

Though it may be hard to read, this states that the function pointer type corresponding to `glBufferStorageEXT` is `PFNGLBUFFERSTORAGEEXTPROC`. Therefore, the application can obtain a pointer to the function with code such as the following:

```
PFNGLBUFFERSTORAGEEXTPROC glBufferStorageEXT =
(PFNGLBUFFERSTORAGEEXTPROC)eglGetProcAddress(
  "glBufferStorageEXT");
```

This section discusses a small set of OpenGL ES extensions. We'll look at the `glBufferStorageEXT` function provided by the `GL_EXT_buffer_storage` extension and the debugging functions provided by the `GL_KHR_debug` extension. The last part of the section presents the important topic of texture compression.

But before I discuss the code, I'd like to introduce an important topic in modern OpenGL programming. This is called Approaching Zero-Driver Overhead, which is commonly shortened to AZDO.

16.3.2 AZDO

At the 2014 Game Developers Conference, Cass Everitt, Graham Sellers, John McDonald, and Tim Foley gave a presentation called *Approaching Zero-Driver Overhead*. This presentation has had a dramatic impact on the graphical development community and its methodology is commonly referred to as AZDO.

The main concern of the presentation is the OpenGL driver, which manages communication between the CPU and GPU. This communication can be a major bottleneck in complex graphical applications, and the goal of the AZDO methodology is to reduce the driver's workload. To reach this goal, the presentation makes a number of recommendations, including the following:

1. Pack as many objects as possible into buffer objects, such as VBOs.
2. Use `glBufferStorage` to create and initialize buffer objects.
3. Use draw commands like `glMultiDrawElementsIndirect` to perform multiple draw operations with a single call.
4. If textures occupy too much device memory, use sparse textures to take advantage of virtual memory processing.

To the best of my knowledge, sparse textures and `glMultiDraw*` functions can't be accessed on current Android devices. But the `glBufferStorage` function is available, and the following discussion will explain how to use this important function.

16.3.3 Persistent Data Mapping

Chapter 14 explained how `glBufferData` and `glMapBufferRange` can be used to create buffer objects and associate them with data. The following code presents a typical example:

```
glBufferData(GL_ARRAY_BUFFER, dataSize, NULL, GL_DYNAMIC_DRAW);
GLfloat* vertexBuffer = (GLfloat*)glMapBufferRange(
    GL_ARRAY_BUFFER, 0, dataSize, GL_MAP_WRITE_BIT);
...
glUnmapBuffer(GL_ARRAY_BUFFER);
```

If the application needs to update the data in the buffer object, it must call `glMapBufferRange` and `glUnmapBuffer` again. This mapping and unmapping can take a considerable amount of time. It would be better if the application could call `glMapBufferRange` once and then update the buffer object's data whenever it was necessary.

The GL_EXT_buffer_storage extension provides this improvement through its glBufferStorageEXT function. Like glBufferData, this function allocates memory for a new buffer object. But if a buffer object is created with glBufferStorageEXT, it won't need to be unmapped after the initial mapping.

The signature of glBufferStorageEXT is given as follows:

```
glBufferStorageEXT(GLenum target, GLsizeiptr size,
                   const void *data, GLbitfield flags)
```

As with glBufferData, the first argument identifies the buffer object to be created. This may be set to GL_ARRAY_BUFFER for VBOs, GL_ELEMENT_ARRAY_BUFFER for IBOs, or GL_UNIFORM_BUFFER for UBOs.

The second argument identifies the size of the data to be allocated for the buffer object. This must be given in bytes. The third argument is a pointer to the data to be associated with the buffer. If this is set to NULL, the function will allocate memory for the buffer object but not initialize its data.

The flags argument determines how the data can be stored and accessed. This can be set to a combination of six values:

- GL_MAP_READ_BIT — The application intends to read from the buffer
- GL_MAP_WRITE_BIT — The application intends to write to the buffer
- GL_DYNAMIC_STORAGE_BIT — The application may update the buffer dynamically by calling glBufferSubData
- GL_MAP_CLIENT_MEMORY_BIT — The buffer's data should be stored on the client
- GL_MAP_PERSISTENT_BIT_EXT — The GPU can access the data even when the buffer object is mapped to client memory
- GL_MAP_COHERENT_BIT_EXT — Updates to the buffer's data should be immediately visible to the GPU

If glBufferStorageEXT is called with the GL_MAP_PERSISTENT_BIT_EXT flag set, the application can map the data to client memory using glMapBufferRange. After the data is mapped, the CPU and the GPU will be able to access the data. This means the application doesn't have to unmap the data with glUnmapBuffer.

Simultaneous data access can lead to synchronization issues. For example, if the GPU attempts to read from the buffer before its contents have been initialized, the results can be indeterminate. OpenGL ES makes it possible to synchronize data access using barriers and fences, but these topics lie beyond the scope of this book.

A simpler method of synchronizing access is to set GL_MAP_COHERENT_BIT_EXT. When this flag is set, any write operations to the buffer's data will be immediately visible to the GPU. The following code shows how this works in practice:

```
// Allocate memory for a VBO
glBufferStorageEXT(GL_ARRAY_BUFFER, size, NULL, GL_MAP_WRITE_BIT |
  GL_MAP_PERSISTENT_BIT_EXT | GL_MAP_COHERENT_BIT_EXT);

// Obtain a pointer to the VBO's data store
GLfloat* buffPointer = (GLfloat*)glMapBufferRange(
  GL_ARRAY_BUFFER, 0, size, GL_MAP_WRITE_BIT);
```

Because of the GL_MAP_PERSISTENT_BIT_EXT flag in glBufferStorageEXT, the application doesn't have to call glUnmapBuffer to terminate the VBO mapping. This means the application can access data through the pointer returned by glMapBufferRange whenever it needs to.

16.3.4 OpenGL Debugging

Chapter 11 explained how to obtain error messages when shaders fail to compile, but no mention has been made of general error checking. The goal of this discussion is to introduce a few different methods of receiving error notifications. During the course of this presentation, we'll explore capabilities provided by two extensions: GL_KHR_debug and GL_EXT_debug_marker.

The simplest way to receive error alerts is to call glGetError. This returns a code that identifies whether a recent OpenGL ES operation resulted in an error, and if so, the error's code. The following code shows how this can be used:

```
int code = glGetError();
__android_log_print(ANDROID_LOG_ERROR, TAG, "Error: %d", code);
```

This is helpful, but it's more efficient to enable event messaging. Then, if an event such as an error occurs, a message will be generated automatically.

Event messaging is made possible by the GL_KHR_debug extension, and at minimum, the process of using the extension consists of three steps:

1. Call glEnable with the argument set to GL_DEBUG_OUTPUT_KHR.
2. Code a function to receive event messages as they're generated.
3. Call glDebugMessageCallbackKHR to identify the function from Step 2.

In Step 2, the function that receives messages must return `void` and accept seven specific arguments. The required order of these arguments is as follows:

- `source` — a `GLenum` that identifies the source (`GL_DEBUG_SOURCE_API_KHR`, `GL_DEBUG_SOURCE_WINDOW_SYSTEM_KHR`, `GL_DEBUG_SOURCE_SHADER_COMPILER_KHR`, `GL_DEBUG_SOURCE_THIRD_PARTY_KHR`, `GL_DEBUG_SOURCE_APPLICATION_KHR`, or `GL_DEBUG_SOURCE_OTHER_KHR`)
- `type` — a `GLenum` that identifies the type (`GL_DEBUG_TYPE_ERROR_KHR`, `GL_DEBUG_TYPE_DEPRECATED_BEHAVIOR_KHR`, `GL_DEBUG_TYPE_UNDEFINED_BEHAVIOR_KHR`, `GL_DEBUG_TYPE_PORTABILITY_KHR`, `GL_DEBUG_TYPE_PERFORMANCE_KHR`, `GL_DEBUG_TYPE_MARKER_KHR`, `GL_DEBUG_TYPE_PUSH_GROUP_KHR`, `GL_DEBUG_TYPE_POP_GROUP_KHR`, `GL_DEBUG_TYPE_OTHER_KHR`)
- `id` — a `GLuint` that serves as the message's ID
- `severity` — a `GLenum` that identifies the severity (`GL_DEBUG_SEVERITY_HIGH_KHR`, `GL_DEBUG_SEVERITY_MEDIUM_KHR`, `GL_DEBUG_SEVERITY_LOW_KHR`, or `GL_DEBUG_SEVERITY_NOTIFICATION_KHR`)
- `size` — a `GLsizei` that identifies the message's length
- `message` — a `const GLchar*` containing the message's text
- `userParam` — a `void*` containing user-specified data

The callback's last argument is provided through the second argument of `glDebugMessageCallbackKHR`. For example, the following code specifies that the `handleMessage` function should receive event messages and that its `userParam` argument should point to a value of 10:

```
int data = 10;
glDebugMessageCallbackKHR(handleMessage, &data);
```

This code demonstrates how `handleMessage` can be implemented.

```
void handleMessage(GLenum source, GLenum type, GLuint id,
  GLenum severity, GLsizei length, const GLchar* msg,
  const void* userData) {
  std::string sevMsg, typeMsg;

  // Process message severity
  switch(severity) {
    case GL_DEBUG_SEVERITY_HIGH_KHR:
      sevMsg = "High"; break;
    case GL_DEBUG_SEVERITY_MEDIUM_KHR:
      sevMsg = "Medium"; break;
```

```
    case GL_DEBUG_SEVERITY_LOW_KHR:
      sevMsg = "Low"; break;
    case GL_DEBUG_SEVERITY_NOTIFICATION_KHR:
      sevMsg = "Notification"; break;
    default:
      sevMsg = "Default";
  }

  // Process message type
  switch(type) {
    case GL_DEBUG_TYPE_ERROR_KHR:
      typeMsg = "error"; break;
    case GL_DEBUG_TYPE_DEPRECATED_BEHAVIOR_KHR:
      typeMsg = "deprecated behavior"; break;
    case GL_DEBUG_TYPE_UNDEFINED_BEHAVIOR_KHR:
      typeMsg = "undefined behavior"; break;
    case GL_DEBUG_TYPE_PORTABILITY_KHR:
      typeMsg = "portability"; break;
    case GL_DEBUG_TYPE_PERFORMANCE_KHR:
      typeMsg = "performance"; break;
    case GL_DEBUG_TYPE_MARKER_KHR:
      typeMsg = "marker"; break;
    case GL_DEBUG_TYPE_PUSH_GROUP_KHR:
      typeMsg = "push group"; break;
    case GL_DEBUG_TYPE_POP_GROUP_KHR:
      typeMsg = "pop group"; break;
    default:
      typeMsg = "default";
  }

  // Display the message
  __android_log_print(ANDROID_LOG_INFO, TAG,
    "%s priority %s message: %s (data: %d)",
    sevMsg.data(), typeMsg.data(), msg, (*(int*)userData));
}
```

An application can generate messages by calling `glDebugMessageInsertKHR`. This accepts eight arguments and their types correspond to those of the first eight arguments of `glDebugMessageCallbackKHR`. The following code shows how this can be used:

```
std::string msg = "Big problem";
glDebugMessageInsertKHR(GL_DEBUG_SOURCE_THIRD_PARTY_KHR,
  GL_DEBUG_TYPE_ERROR_KHR, 0, GL_DEBUG_SEVERITY_MEDIUM_KHR,
  msg.length(), msg.data());
```

The functions of `GL_KHR_debug` don't need to be accessed through function pointers. This is common for all extensions provided by the Khronos Group (`GL_KHR`).

16.3.5 Texture Compression

In this book's example applications, every texture's color data has consisted of eight bits for red, green, and blue components. This format is simple to work with, but textures requiring 24 bits per texel require a significant amount of time to transfer to the GPU.

To reduce the transfer time, OpenGL supports texture compression. An application can create a texture from compressed image data by calling the `glCompressedTexImage2D` function, whose signature is given as follows:

```
glCompressedTexImage2D(GLenum target, GLint level,
  GLenum internalformat, GLsizei width, GLsizei height,
  GLint border, GLsizei imageSize, const GLvoid* data)
```

The `internalFormat` argument identifies how the image data (data) is compressed. This discussion looks at two popular methods: Ericsson Texture Compression (ETC) and Advanced Scalable Texture Compression (ASTC). The last part of the discussion looks at tools for texture compression.

Ericsson Texture Compression (ETC)

The original ETC method, denoted ETC1, makes it possible to compress 24-bit RGB textures. This method compresses 4x4 texel blocks into a 64-bit word, thereby reducing the texture size by one-sixth. This compression is *lossy*, which means it discards data, but the lost data is generally imperceptible.

The ETC1 format is supported by the vast majority of Android devices starting with Android 2.2. The Android SDK provides an executable, etc1tool.exe, that compresses images using the ETC1 method.

The second version of ETC, denoted ETC2, provides better compression and can be used to compress RGBA images in addition to RGB images. Every Android device capable of OpenGL ES 3.x rendering is guaranteed to support ETC2 compression, so there's no need to access extensions.

In code, an application identifies the texture's compression by setting the `internalFormat` argument of the `glCompressedTexImage2D` function. For ETC2 compression, this can be set to one of three values:

- `GL_COMPRESSED_RGB8_ETC2` — Eight-bit RGB data compression
- `GL_COMPRESSED_RGBA8_ETC2_EAC` — Eight-bit RGBA data compression
- `GL_COMPRESSED_RGB8_PUNCHTHROUGH_ALPHA1_ETC2` — Eight-bit RGBA data compression whose texels contain single-bit alpha values

For images with fewer components per texel, Ericsson developed the Ericsson Alpha Compression (EAC) method. This is similar to ETC2 and is also guaranteed to be available on OpenGL ES 3.x devices. To identify EAC-compressed images, an application can set one of four values as the `internalFormat` argument of `glCompressedTexImage2D`:

- `GL_COMPRESSED_R11_EAC` — each texel contains one component given as an unsigned value
- `GL_COMPRESSED_SIGNED_R11_EAC` — each texel contains one component given as a signed value
- `GL_COMPRESSED_RG11_EAC` — each texel contains two components given as unsigned values
- `GL_COMPRESSED_SIGNED_RG11_EAC` — each texel contains two components given as signed values

ETC2/EAC provides excellent compression and is guaranteed to be available on Android devices that support OpenGL ES 3.x rendering. This makes ETC2/EAC a safe option for texture compression in Daydream applications. ASTC isn't as safe, but frequently provides better compression results.

Advanced Scalable Texture Compression (ASTC)

Like ETC compression, Advanced Scalable Texture Compression (ASTC) is block-based. That is, the method involves producing one value for a block of texels. And like ETC, ASTC is lossy.

The chief advantage of ASTC over ETC is that ASTC makes it possible to customize how the compression is performed. That is, applications can specify the size of the blocks used in the compression—larger blocks mean greater compression but greater data loss.

For two-dimensional textures, possible block sizes are 4x4, 5x4, 5x5, 6x5, 6x6, 8x5, 8x6, 10x5, 10x6, 8x8, 10x8, 10x10, 12x10, and 12x12. For three-dimensional textures, possible block sizes are 3x3x3, 4x3x3, 4x4x3, 4x4x4, 5x4x4, 5x5x4, 5x5x5, 6x5x5, 6x6x5, and 6x6x6.

The `GL_OES_texture_compression_astc` extension doesn't provide any functions, but instead provides a wide range of values that can be set to the `internalFormat` argument of the `glCompressedTexImage2D` function. For 2-D textures, these values have the same general format:

```
GL_COMPRESSED_<texel_format>_ASTC_<block_size>_KHR
```

Here, <texel_format> identifies the texel content, and can be set to `RGBA` or `SRGB8_ALPHA8`. For 3-D textures, the `_KHR` at the end of the value name should be replaced with `_OES`.

For example, suppose that an application wants to create a texture from 2-D RGBA image data that has been compressed using 6x5 blocks. In this case, the `internalFormat` argument of `glCompressedTexImage2D` should be set to `GL_COMPRESSED_RGBA_ASTC_6x5_KHR`.

As another example, suppose that an application wants to create a texture from 3-D sRGB image data that has been compressed using 5x4x4 blocks. In this case, the `internalFormat` argument should be set to `GL_COMPRESSED_SRGB8_ALPHA8_ASTC_5x4x4_OES`.

Image Compression Tools

Functions like `glCompressedTexImage2D` require that image data be pre-compressed. This places the burden of compression on the developer. Thankfully, there are a number of image compression tools available for download.

As mentioned earlier, the Android SDK provides a command-line utility, etc1tool.exe, that uses the ETC1 method to compress images. For ETC2 compression, etc2comp is another command-line compression tool, and can be downloaded freely from GitHub at https://github.com/google/etc2comp.

Another popular compression tool is the Mali Android OpenGL GPU Texture Compression Tool. This is provided for free by ARM, the designer of the Mali GPU for mobile devices. The download site is http://malideveloper.arm.com/resources/tools/mali-gpu-texture-compression-tool.

This ARM tool makes it possible to compress images using the ETC1, ETC2, EAC, or ASTC methods. Unlike the other tools, this runs in a graphical user interface. The process of compressing an image is straightforward, and consists of three steps:

1. After launching the tool, go to **File** > **Open images...** and select the image(s) to be compressed.
2. In the left pane, select the image(s) to be compressed and go to **File** > **Compress selected images...** in the main menu.
3. The **Configuration options** dialog has two tabs: **ASTC** and **ETC1/ETC2**. Select the desired tab, specify how the configuration should be performed, and press **OK**.

Once the process is complete, the tool will produce a file containing the compressed image data. As an example, the ch16_mediaplayer uses ASTC with 4x4 blocks to compress its texture.

16.4 FreeType

Chapter 10 explained how to draw text using a texture atlas. The atlas was generated from a bitmap containing a font's characters. This bitmap had to be created in advance because Android doesn't provide a simple means of creating atlases dynamically.

But if the FreeType toolset is available, the application can generate dynamic texture atlases from TrueType fonts. This enables applications to display text with changing fonts and sizes without suffering degradation in quality.

One important drawback of using FreeType is that the library needs to be compiled from source code. Therefore, before delving into the code, this section explains how to obtain and build the toolset.

16.4.1 Building the FreeType Library

FreeType's main download site is http://download.savannah.gnu.org/releases/freetype. If you go there, you'll see many source code archives (*.tar.gz/*.tar.bz2) but no actual libraries (*.so). The exact process of building a library from the source code depends on your operating system, but the general method consists of four steps:

1. Download the archive containing the most recent stable source code.
2. Locate the cross-compilation tools in the Android NDK.
3. Specify which modules should be included in the FreeType library.
4. Follow FreeType's instructions to build the library for the device's processor.

For the second step, Android's cross-compilation tools are executables with names like arm-linux-androideabi-*. Every Android NDK (not the Google VR NDK) contains a set of these tools. In general, the cross-compilation tools for 32-bit ARM processors can be found at $NDK/toolchains/arm-linux-androideabi-$VERSION/prebuilt/$OS/bin, where $NDK is the top-level NDK directory, $VERSION is the toolchain version, and $OS is the operating system running on the development computer.

The third step involves identifying the features that should be included in the FreeType library. This can be accomplished by editing a header file named ftoption.h in the archive's include/freetype/config directory. This contains a series of macro definitions that represent features to be included.

To reduce the size of the target library (libfreetype.a), it's a good idea to look through ftoption.h and comment out features that shouldn't be incorporated into the build. Table 16.3 lists sixteen of the macros in ftoption.h.

Table 16.3

FreeType Configuration Macros

Function	Description
FT_CONFIG_OPTION_USE_LZW	Enables access to LZW-compressed font files
FT_CONFIG_OPTION_USE_ZLIB	Enables access to ZLIB-compressed font files
FT_CONFIG_OPTION_USE_BZIP2	Enables access to BZIP2-compressed font files
FT_CONFIG_OPTION_POSTSCRIPT_NAMES	Enables the psnames module, which converts glyph names into Unicode values
FT_CONFIG_OPTION_MAC_FONTS	Enables support for outline fonts in Mac format
FT_RENDER_POOL_SIZE	Sets the size of the render pool used by the scan-line converter
FT_CONFIG_OPTION_USE_MODULE_ERRORS	Enables module identification as part of the error reporting process
FT_CONFIG_OPTION_PIC	Ensures position-independent code
TT_CONFIG_OPTION_EMBEDDED_BITMAPS	Supports embedded bitmaps in all formats using the SFNT module (TrueType and OpenType)
TT_CONFIG_OPTION_POSTSCRIPT_NAMES	Enables loading and enumeration of glyph Postscript names in TrueType/OpenType files
TT_CONFIG_OPTION_BYTECODE_INTERPRETER	Compiles a bytecode interpreter into the TrueType driver
TT_CONFIG_OPTION_SUBPIXEL_HINTING	Sets the subpixel hunting support for the TrueType driver
AF_CONFIG_OPTION_CJK	Compiles the autofit module with support for Chinese, Japanese, and Korean
AF_CONFIG_OPTION_INDIC	Compiles the autofit module with support for Indic languages
AF_CONFIG_OPTION_USE_WARPER	Compiles the autofit module with warp hinting
TT_CONFIG_OPTION_COMPONENT_OFFSET_SCALED	Configures the TrueType loader to use Apple's definition of handling component offsets

For the fourth step, FreeType provides build instructions in the INSTALL.CROSS file in the docs folder. At the time of this writing, the build procedure consists of three steps:

1. Execute the `configure` script in the top-level directory.
2. Execute `make` to compile the source code.
3. Execute `make install` to deploy the compiled results.

It's important to note that `configure` and `make` are GNU utilities, and `configure` is a Bash script. Therefore, the build must be performed in an environment that supports Bash. For Linux and Mac OS users, this isn't an issue. But Windows users may need to install a tool like MinGW to provide a suitable environment.

The `configure` script can be invoked with options that configure the build process. Two important options are as follows:

- `host` — the processor architecture for which the build should be performed
- `prefix` — the directory to contain architecture-independent files

If `host` is set to `arm-linux-androideabi` and the directory containing the build tools is added to the system's path, configure will be able to access the toolchain. As an example, the following command installs files in the /usr/local directory:

```
./configure --host=arm-linux-androideabi --prefix=/usr/local
```

After the script completes its operation, the next step is to compile the source code by invoking the `make` command. If this completes successfully, the build results can be deployed by invoking `make install`.

To include FreeType in an NDK project, the library (libfreetype.a or libfreetype.so) should be placed in the jniLibs folder. The header files, which include ftbuild.h and the many files in the freetype directory, should be placed in the jni folder.

16.4.2 The FreeType API

Once you've added FreeType's library and headers to a project, it's easy to generate a texture atlas—load the file defining the TrueType font, generate a glyph for each character in the atlas, and combine the glyphs into a texture. On an Android system, the coding process entails five steps:

1. Call `FT_Init_FreeType` to initialize FreeType processing.
2. Access a TrueType font file as an `AAsset` and call `FT_New_Memory_Face` to create an `FT_Face` from the asset's data.
3. For each character in the atlas, call `FT_Load_Char` to obtain a glyph corresponding to the character.
4. Create a texture containing the bitmap data of each glyph.
5. Free the `FT_Face` with `FT_Done_Face` and deallocate the FreeType library with `FT_Done_FreeType`.

In Step 1, the `FT_Init_FreeType` function accepts a pointer to a `FT_Library` structure. This is the overall context for FreeType's operation and serves as the first argument of many FreeType functions.

In general, a TrueType font file defines a single font family, such as Verdana. A family may contain multiple fonts, such as Verdana Italic and Verdana Bold. In FreeType, each font is represented by an `FT_Face` structure. An application can obtain an `FT_Face` for a font file by calling `FT_New_Memory_Face`:

```
FT_New_Memory_Face(FT_Library library, const FT_Byte* fontData,
  FT_Long dataSize, FT_Long index, FT_Face *face)
```

The second argument points to the data read from a TrueType font file (*.ttf). In an NDK application, this data can be obtained by creating an `AAsset` from the font file. Chapter 15 discussed the topic of reading a module's assets in native code.

The third argument of `FT_New_Memory_Face` identifies the size of the data in bytes. The fourth argument identifies the index of the font in the font file. If the function completes successfully, the last argument points to an initialized `FT_Face`.

Before continuing, it helps to look at the fields of the `FT_Face` structure. Table 16.4 lists seven of these fields and provides a description of each.

Table 16.4

Fields of the FT_Face Structure (Abridged)

Field	Data Type	Description
`num_glyphs`	`FT_Long`	Number of glyphs in the face
`family_name`	`FT_String`	Description of the font family ("Verdana")
`style_name`	`FT_String`	Description of the font style ("Italic")
`height`	`FT_Short`	Distance between consecutive baselines
`ascender`	`FT_Short`	Distance from the top to the baseline
`glyph`	`FT_GlyphSlot`	Current active glyph
`size`	`FT_Size`	Current active size

An application can specify a desired font size by calling `FT_Set_Pixel_Sizes`. This accepts an `FT_Face`, a font width, and a font height. If the width argument is set to 0, the font width will be determined automatically. For example, if `face` is an `FT_Face`, the following code sets the font size to 32:

```
FT_Set_Pixel_Sizes(face, 0, 32);
```

An FT_Face contains multiple glyphs, but only one can be accessed through the glyph field at any time. To load a glyph according to its character, an application needs to call FT_Load_Char:

```
FT_Load_Char(FT_Face face, FT_ULong character, FT_Int32 flags)
```

The second argument identifies the desired character by its code in the current character map. If the font contains a Unicode-based character map, this map will be made current.

The third argument constrains what information is loaded for the glyph. To ensure that FreeType produces a bitmap, the third argument should be set to FT_LOAD_RENDER. For example, the following code loads glyph data for the p character, whose code is 113:

```
FT_Load_Char(face, 113, FT_LOAD_RENDER);
```

When this function completes, the glyph corresponding to p can be accessed through the face's glyph field. This field's type is an FT_GlyphSlot, which provides three important fields:

- bitmap_top — the distance from the top of the line to the baseline
- bitmap — an FT_Bitmap that contains the glyph's graphical data
- metrics — an FT_Glyph_Metrics that identifies the glyph's dimensions

The bitmap field provides a field, bitmap_rows, that identifies the height of the bitmap containing the glyph. Its buffer field points to the pixels that make up the glyph.

The metrics field provides a set of values that can be used to determine the glyph's size and its position relative to its baseline and the current cursor position. Table 16.5 lists five of the available fields.

Table 16.5

Fields of the FT_Glyph_Metrics Structure

Field	Description
width	Width of the glyph
height	Height of the glyph
horiBearingX	Horizontal distance from the cursor to the left edge of the glyph
horiBearingY	Vertical distance to the top of the glyph
horiAdvance	Horizontal distance from the cursor to the cursor following the glyph

Each of these values is provided as a long integer and each is measured in units 64 times the size of pixels. Therefore, these values must be divided by 64 to obtain corresponding pixel measurements.

Figure 16.2 clarifies how these fields are related to the character's dimensions and the baseline.

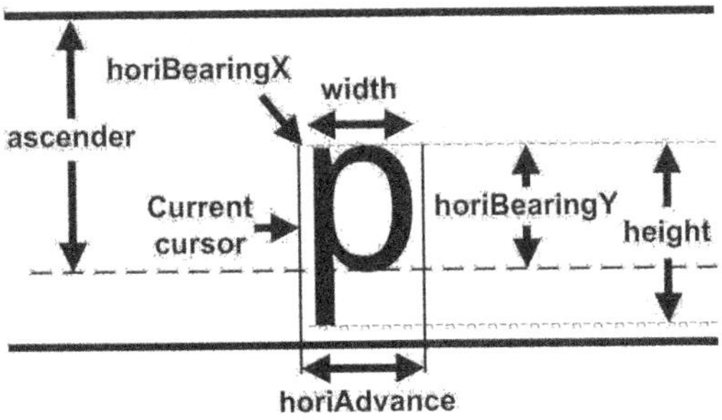

Figure 16.2 FreeType Character Dimensions

With this information, we can construct a texture atlas containing the font's glyphs. For the sake of simplicity, this atlas will contain only the glyphs of the first 128 characters, and we'll arrange them in one long horizontal sequence.

The process of creating this atlas involves three steps:

1. Determine the dimensions of the texture needed to contain the glyphs.
2. Create an uninitialized texture by calling `glTexImage2D`.
3. For each character in the atlas, add the glyph's bitmap to the texture by calling `glTexSubImage2D`.

The first step is simple. The height of the texture equals the desired line height. The width of the texture can be obtained by summing together `bitmap.width` for each glyph of interest. The following code shows how this can be implemented for characters whose codes lie between 65 and 90:

```
int textureWidth = 0;
for(unsigned int i=65; i<90; i++) {

  FT_Load_Char(face, i, FT_LOAD_RENDER);

  // Obtain the glyph metrics and add the width
  FT_Glyph_Metrics metrics = face->glyph->metrics;
  textureWidth += metrics.width/64;
}
```

If FT_Load_Char is called with the FT_LOAD_RENDER flag set, the buffer field of the glyph's FT_Bitmap will reference a bitmap containing the character image. Each pixel in the bitmap consists of a single channel. To create a texture capable of holding this bitmap, the pixel format must be set to GL_RED. This is shown in the following code:

```
glTexImage2D(GL_TEXTURE_2D, 0, GL_R8, textureWidth, size,
  0, GL_RED, GL_UNSIGNED_BYTE, 0);
```

This function allocates memory for an empty texture with a width of textureWidth and a height equal to size. To provide the texture with data, the application needs to call FT_LoadChar to load a character's bitmap and then call glTexSubImage2D to store the bitmap inside the texture. If the desired character's code is charCode, its bitmap can be inserted into a texture in the following way:

```
if(FT_Load_Char(face, charCode, FT_LOAD_RENDER) == 0) {

  // Insert the character's bitmap into the texture
  glTexSubImage2D(GL_TEXTURE_2D, 0, xcoord, 0, width, height,
    GL_RED, GL_UNSIGNED_BYTE, face->glyph->bitmap.buffer);
}
```

After all the desired characters have been added to the texture, the texture atlas is complete. The application can add characters to the model using texture coordinates, and the ch16_mediaplayer module demonstrates how this can be accomplished.

16.5 Example Application – Media Player

The ch16_mediaplayer application creates an audio player identical to the one created in the ch13_audioplayer application. The player has three buttons and a label that displays the current state. Figure 16.3 shows what the player looks like.

Figure 16.3 The ch16_mediaplayer Application

This application demonstrates six of the capabilities presented in this chapter:

1. Controller access
2. Spatial audio
3. Persistent data mapping
4. Debugging
5. Texture compression
6. Displaying text with FreeType

This section will explain how these features were implemented using native code.

16.5.1 Accessing the Controller

The ch16_mediaplayer application displays a pointer representing the controller's direction. If the user points to a button on the player and presses the App button, the player will pause, play, or stop the audio.

As discussed earlier in the chapter, controller access is made possible through two classes. A `ControllerApi` configures the controller's operation and a `ControllerState` provides information about the controller's state. In code, these objects are declared in the mediaplayer_renderer.h header:

```
std::unique_ptr<gvr::ControllerApi> controllerApi;
gvr::ControllerState controllerState;
```

The application initializes the `ControllerApi` in the `OnSurfaceCreated` method. The only state information needed is the controller's orientation, so the following code is used:

```
controllerApi.reset(new gvr::ControllerApi);
controllerApi->Init(GVR_CONTROLLER_ENABLE_ORIENTATION);
controllerApi->Resume();
```

After the `Resume` function is called, the `ControllerState` will receive orientation data from the controller. As each frame is drawn, the application checks this information and computes the (x, y) location of the pointer:

```
if(!firstFrame && controllerState.GetConnectionState()
    == GVR_CONTROLLER_CONNECTED) {
```

```
    gvr_quatf q = controllerState.GetOrientation();
    float tmp = (q.qw * q.qw) - (q.qx * q.qx) -
                (q.qy * q.qy) + (q.qz * q.qz);
    target[0] = (2.0f * q.qw * q.qy - 2.0f * q.qx * q.qz) *
                (PLAYER_DEPTH / tmp);
    target[1] = (-2.0f * q.qw * q.qx - 2.0f * q.qy * q.qz) *
                (PLAYER_DEPTH / tmp);
  } else {
    target[0] = 0.0f; target[1] = 0.0f;
  }
  if(controllerState.GetRecentered()) {
    target[0] = 0.0f; target[1] = 0.0f;
  }
```

If the controller's connection is established, this code converts the four-element quaternion into a two-dimensional array. When the user recenters the controller, the pointer's location is reset to (0, 0).

16.5.2 Spatial Audio

The application plays a sound whenever the user points to the Play button and presses the App button on the controller. All audio access is provided by an `AudioApi` instance, and as mentioned earlier, its `Init` function requires a `JNIEnv*`.

For this reason, the ch16_mediaplayer module creates and initializes the `AudioApi` in the mediaplayer.cpp source file with the following code:

```
std::unique_ptr<gvr::AudioApi> audioInst(new gvr::AudioApi);
audioInst->Init(env, appContext, loader,
    GVR_AUDIO_RENDERING_BINAURAL_LOW_QUALITY);
```

The application creates its sound object in the `OnSurfaceCreated` method with the following code:

```
audioApi->PreloadSoundfile("harp.wav");
id = audioApi->CreateSoundObject("harp.wav");
audioApi->SetSoundObjectPosition(id, 0.0f, 0.0f, 5.0f);
audioApi->SetSoundVolume(id, 0.5f);
```

The harp.wav file contains a simple harp sound. When the Play button is selected, the application executes the following code to play the sound:

```
audioApi->PlaySound(id, true);
```

16.5.3 Persistent Data Mapping

The application creates four vertex buffer objects (VBOs). Instead of allocating their memory with `glBufferData`, the application uses `glBufferStorageEXT`. This makes it possible to obtain a persistent map to the VBO data.

Before an application can call this function, it needs to access the function pointer. The type of this pointer is declared in gl2ext.h as `PFNGLBUFFERSTORAGEEXTPROC`, and the following code shows how the application obtains the pointer:

```
glBufferStorageEXT = (PFNGLBUFFERSTORAGEEXTPROC)
  eglGetProcAddress("glBufferStorageEXT");
```

After obtaining the pointer, the application can call `glBufferStorageEXT` to create vertex buffer objects:

```
glBufferStorageEXT(GL_ARRAY_BUFFER, dataSize, NULL,
  GL_MAP_WRITE_BIT | GL_MAP_PERSISTENT_BIT_EXT |
  GL_MAP_COHERENT_BIT_EXT);
```

Because the `GL_MAP_PERSISTENT_BIT_EXT` flag is set, the application can create a persistent map for the vertex buffer. Because the `GL_MAP_COHERENT_BIT_EXT` flag is set, write operations to the buffer will be immediately accessible by the GPU.

16.5.4 Debugging

The application accesses the `GL_KHR_debug` extension to respond to events. The following code enables debugging and specifies that the `handleMessage` function should be called when events occur:

```
glEnable(GL_DEBUG_OUTPUT_KHR);
glDebugMessageCallbackKHR(handleMessage, NULL);
```

`handleMessage` checks the severity and type of the incoming event. Then it logs a message that includes the message's severity, type, and content. The following statement presents the code that logs the message:

```
__android_log_print(ANDROID_LOG_INFO, TAG,
  "%s priority %s message: %s (data: %d)",
  sevMsg.data(), typeMsg.data(), msg, (*(int*)userData));
```

16.5.5 Texture Compression

The player's buttons are provided by a 300-by-200 pixel texture. If each pixel required three bytes, the image data would require 180,000 bytes. But using ASTC compression, the image's size was reduced to 60,000 bytes.

To use the compressed texture, the application reads from the buttons.astc asset using the `AAssetManager_open` function discussed in Chapter 15. Then it calls `glCompressedTexImage2D` to create the texture. The following code shows how this is accomplished:

```
AAsset* asset = AAssetManager_open(assetManager,
                    "player.astc", AASSET_MODE_BUFFER);

glCompressedTexImage2D(GL_TEXTURE_2D, 0,
  GL_COMPRESSED_RGBA_ASTC_4x4_KHR, 300, 200,
  0, 60000, AAsset_getBuffer(asset));
```

It's interesting to note that the size of the image file is 60,012 instead of 60,000. The compression process adds a 12-byte header. For this reason, you can't simply set the texture size to the file size. As I've learned from hard experience, this will give you a segmentation fault.

16.5.6 Displaying Text with FreeType

As each button is pressed, the application displays text identifying the player's state. These characters are accessed from a texture atlas created dynamically with FreeType. The application creates the atlas by calling the `CreateAtlas` function in the freetypeutils.cpp source file. Listing 16.1 presents the code of this function.

The function starts by reading data from the asset (OpenSans-Regular.ttf) and creating an `FT_Face` for the first face. Then it obtains dimensions related to the font, such as the distance from the baseline to the top and the distance from the baseline to the bottom.

The function iterates through a series of characters, with codes ranging from 32 to 128. The font may not provide characters for each of these codes, so instead of storing character data in an array, it uses an `std::map` that associates each available code with a `TextureChar` structure.

For each character, the application determines the width, height, horizontal offset, and vertical offset. It also updates a `textureWidth` value, which holds the total width of the texture atlas.

Listing 16.1: ch16_mediaplayer/src/main/java/.../freetypeutils.cpp

```
TextureAtlas FreeTypeUtils::CreateAtlas(AAssetManager* mgr,
  const char* fileName, unsigned int size) {

  FT_Library ft;
  FT_Face face;
  TextureAtlas atlas;

  // Initialize the library
  FT_Init_FreeType(&ft);

  // Load the font file
  AAsset* asset =
    AAssetManager_open(mgr, fileName, AASSET_MODE_BUFFER);

  // Access the first face
  FT_New_Memory_Face(ft, (const FT_Byte*)AAsset_getBuffer(asset),
    AAsset_getLength(asset), 0, &face);

  // Set the desired size
  FT_Set_Pixel_Sizes(face, 0, size);

  // Initialize texture atlas properties
  atlas.lineHeight = size;
  float tmp = face->ascender * size * 1.0f/face->height;
  atlas.baselineOffset = (unsigned int)std::round(tmp);
  atlas.textureWidth = 0;

  float top_to_baseline =
    floor(((float)face->ascender/
    (face->ascender - face->descender)) * size);
  float baseline_to_bottom = ceil(size - top_to_baseline);

  // Iterate through characters
  for(unsigned int i=32; i<128; i++) {

    TextureChar textChar;

    // Load the glyph data
    if(FT_Load_Char(face, i, FT_LOAD_RENDER) != 0) {
      continue;
    }

    if((face->glyph->bitmap.width > 0) &&
      (face->glyph->bitmap.rows > 0)) {

      // Obtain the glyph metrics
      FT_Glyph_Metrics metrics = face->glyph->metrics;
```

Listing 16.1: ch16_mediaplayer/src/main/java/.../freetypeutils.cpp

```
      // Set the properties of the TextureChar
      textChar.x = atlas.textureWidth;
      textChar.width = face->glyph->bitmap.width;
      textChar.height = face->glyph->bitmap.rows;
      textChar.yoffsetHigh =
        top_to_baseline - face->glyph->bitmap_top;
      textChar.yoffsetLow = baseline_to_bottom -
        (face->glyph->bitmap.rows - face->glyph->bitmap_top);
      textChar.xoffset = metrics.horiBearingX/64.0f;
      textChar.xadvance = metrics.horiAdvance/64.0f;
      atlas.charMap.emplace(i, textChar);

      // Update the texture width
      atlas.textureWidth += metrics.width/64;
    }
  }

  // Allocate and configure an uninitialized texture
  glPixelStorei(GL_UNPACK_ALIGNMENT, 1);
  glTexImage2D(GL_TEXTURE_2D, 0, GL_R8, atlas.textureWidth,
    size, 0, GL_RED, GL_UNSIGNED_BYTE, 0);
  glTexParameteri(GL_TEXTURE_2D, GL_TEXTURE_MIN_FILTER,
    GL_LINEAR);
  glTexParameteri(GL_TEXTURE_2D, GL_TEXTURE_MAG_FILTER,
    GL_LINEAR);

  // Insert characters into texture
  for(auto const& textureChar: atlas.charMap) {

    // Load the glyph data
    if(FT_Load_Char(face, textureChar.first,
      FT_LOAD_RENDER) == 0) {

      // Insert the character's bitmap into the texture
      glTexSubImage2D(GL_TEXTURE_2D, 0, textureChar.second.x, 0,
        textureChar.second.width, textureChar.second.height,
        GL_RED, GL_UNSIGNED_BYTE, face->glyph->bitmap.buffer);
    }
  }

  // Deallocate resources
  FT_Done_Face(face);
  FT_Done_FreeType(ft);
  AAsset_close(asset);

  return atlas;
}
```

After obtaining data for each of the characters, `CreateAtlas` creates a texture to hold the texture map. The height is set to the desired font height, the width is set to the total width of the atlas's characters, and the format is set to `GL_RED` because each pixel in a FreeType bitmap contains one component.

After creating the texture, `CreateAtlas` iterates through the characters a second time. For each character, it calls `glTexSubImage2D` to store the bitmap data inside of the texture. Afterward, the application deallocates resources associated with FreeType and the font asset.

16.6 Summary

NDK development may be difficult, but most graphical applications are coded in C and C++ and there's a wealth of code available. This chapter has explained how to access the FreeType library, and this is just one of many free toolsets that can be accessed in native code.

If an application needs to access a controller's state, there's no need for complex listeners or external threads. Just call the `Update` function of the `ControllerState` instance. Regarding audio, the NDK's `AudioApi` class is just as easy to work with as the SDK's `GvrAudioEngine` class.

OpenGL ES extensions are another reason to rely on native code. These extensions open up a world of new features and improved performance. This chapter discussed persistent data mapping, debugging, and texture compression, but there are many more extensions available for use.

Chapter 17

Publishing a Daydream Application

At this point, you should have a deep understanding of Daydream development and the many features expected of virtual reality applications. This chapter won't discuss any new topics in app development, but focuses instead on what to do after an app is finished. This chapter explains how to deploy Daydream apps to the Google Play Store.

Google requires that all Daydream apps behave in a certain way and maintain a consistent look and feel. The first part of this chapter discusses Google's requirements, which fall into four categories:

1. **Design** — Does the app behave like a proper VR application?
2. **Functionality** — Does the app work properly?
3. **Performance and stability** — Can the app execute at high performance without damaging the device?
4. **Publishing** — Does the app look like a proper Daydream app? Can it interact with the rest of the ecosystem?

These are more than just guidelines. Every submitted Daydream app undergoes a strict Daydream-specific review process. If the app fails to meet any of Google's criteria, the Google Play Store won't consider it suitable for Daydream operation.

The last part of the chapter walks through the process of deploying a Daydream app. The process is essentially similar to that of deploying a regular app to the Google Play Store. That is, you need to go to the Google Play Developer Console and provide graphics and information. You also need to provide guarantees regarding the app's content and assurances that the app will protect the user's data.

17.1 Design Requirements

The first set of requirements for Daydream apps relates to the features that must be supported by applications. These requirements are straightforward to understand and implement in code. Table 17.1 lists the design requirements and provides a description of each.

Table 17.1

Design Requirements

Area	ID	Description
App Design	UX-D1	User can focus on objects and read necessary text
	UX-D2	App maintains head tracking
	UX-D3	App has a stable horizon line
	UX-D4	Camera movement must be user-initiated
	UX-D5	App does not interfere with system-level recentering behavior
	UX-D6	App recenters appropriately with respect to the experience
	UX-D7	App's forward direction is consistent with the platform's global forward direction
	UX-D8	App uses a neck model
	UX-D9	App never goes to 2-D monoscopic unexpectedly
Controller Targets	UX-C1	Controller must be used as a laser pointer when clicking on UI targets
	UX-C2	App uses hand preference
	UX-C3	Scrolling through large sets of items must be done by swiping on the touchpad
	UX-C4	Cursor displays at the same depth as objects being targeted
	UX-C5	App does not interfere with system controls

The first requirement states that objects in the model must be in focus and that text must be readable. In particular, Google recommends that objects be placed more than 0.5m away from the user, with font sizes occupying at least 1.5° of the user's field of view.

To satisfy the UX-D2 requirement, applications can monitor the headset's orientation by transforming the model's vertices with the head-tracking matrix. For UX-D3 and UX-D4, the requirements specify that any change to the viewer's perspective must be initiated by the viewer.

The UX-D5 and UX-D6 requirements state that recentering should be left to the system. Recentering is performed by holding down the Home button, so this requirement asks that applications shouldn't handle button events in a way that prevents regular recentering.

The UX-D7 and UX-D8 requirements involve the model's transformation. The transformation should always be performed so that the application's forward direction (the –z direction) is determined by the headset. That is, the forward direction is always determined by the headset's orientation. This orientation should be updated using the neck model. Chapter 6 explained how to access the neck model in Java and Chapter 16 explained how to access it in C/C++.

The UX-C1 through UX-C5 requirements relate to the controller. The user should be able to interact with the app using the controller as a laser pointer. The controller's pointer should be displayed at the same depth as objects being targeted. Therefore, if objects in the model have different depths (z-values), the controller's pointer should be displayed at the same depth as the object to which it's pointing.

Regarding external controllers, Google states the following: "We won't reject apps that add additional and optional support for gamepads simply because they are playable with a gamepad. However, all apps must be fully playable with only the Daydream controller."

17.2 Functionality Requirements

The next set of requirements involve software functionality that every application is expected to support. These requirements touch on the nature of the application's SDK, the user interface, and aspects of the application's manifest. Table 17.2 lists the functionality requirements and provides a description of each.

Table 17.2

Functionality Requirements

Area	ID	Description
SDK	FN-S1	App uses a supported version of the Google VR SDK
	FN-S2	App uses Daydream API calls to transition between activities
Manifest	FN-M1	App manifest doesn't request NFC permission
	FN-M2	App manifest sets correct VR activity styles
	FN-M3	App manifest sets hardware features according to the platform(s) supported

UI	FN-UI	App hides the status bar and navigation bar while in VR
App state	FN-A1	App pauses when the user exits VR
	FN-A2	App closes from VR correctly

The first three requirements are easy to understand. NFC is required to link the device with the headset, so the app shouldn't access the capability on its own.

The fourth requirement, FN-M2, specifies that Daydream apps should use an appropriate style. As discussed in Chapter 6, this requirement can be fulfilled by setting the `android:theme` attribute in the project's manifest to `@style/VrActivityTheme`. This is defined in the sdk-common AAR.

If an activity can be launched from Daydream Home or another VR activity, the manifest's `android:enableVrMode` attribute should be set to `@string/gvr_vr_mode_component`. Like `@style/VrActivityTheme`, this is defined in the sdk-common AAR.

If an application is intended to be run solely through Daydream Home, the manifest should include the following:

```
android:enableVrMode="@string/gvr_vr_mode_component"
```

The manifest should also require that devices support certain features, such as sensors and OpenGL ES support. This is shown in the following markup:

```
<uses-feature android:glEsVersion="0x00020000"
  android:required="true" />

<uses-feature android:name="android.hardware.sensor.accelerometer"
  android:required="true"/>

<uses-feature android:name="android.hardware.sensor.gyroscope"
  android:required="true"/>

<uses-feature android:name="android.software.vr.mode"
  android:required="true"/>

<uses-feature android:name="android.hardware.vr.high_performance"
  android:required="true"/>
```

It's important to note that setting the required OpenGL ES version to 2.0 doesn't preclude the application from using features of OpenGL ES 3.x. Also, if an application is intended to execute with Daydream and Cardboard systems, the last two features are not required.

When I submitted my first app, it was rejected because of FN-UI, which requires that applications hide the status bar and navigation bar when running in VR mode. To meet this requirement, I needed to insert the following code into the activity's `onCreate` method:

```
// Set the window properties
setImmersiveSticky();
getWindow()
  .getDecorView()
  .setOnSystemUiVisibilityChangeListener(
     new View.OnSystemUiVisibilityChangeListener() {

       @Override
       public void onSystemUiVisibilityChange(int visibility) {
       if ((visibility & View.SYSTEM_UI_FLAG_FULLSCREEN) == 0) {
          setImmersiveSticky();
       }
     }
   });

private void setImmersiveSticky() {
  getWindow()
    .getDecorView()
    .setSystemUiVisibility(
       View.SYSTEM_UI_FLAG_LAYOUT_STABLE
         | View.SYSTEM_UI_FLAG_LAYOUT_HIDE_NAVIGATION
         | View.SYSTEM_UI_FLAG_LAYOUT_FULLSCREEN
         | View.SYSTEM_UI_FLAG_HIDE_NAVIGATION
         | View.SYSTEM_UI_FLAG_FULLSCREEN
         | View.SYSTEM_UI_FLAG_IMMERSIVE_STICKY);
}
```

This code ensures that the activity's window will occupy the full screen and that the navigation bar and status bar will remain hidden while the activity is running.

For NDK applications, the lifecycle methods of the activity's `GvrLayout` and `GLSurfaceView` should be called by the appropriate lifecycle methods of the surrounding activity. The following code shows what this looks like:

```
protected void onPause() {
  super.onPause();
  nativeOnPause(nativeInst);
  gvrLayout.onPause();
  glSurfaceView.onPause();
}
```

```
protected void onDestroy() {
  super.onDestroy();
  gvrLayout.shutdown();
  nativeOnDestroy(nativeInst);
}
```

With this code in place, an NDK application should have no trouble meeting the last two requirements in the table.

17.3 Performance and Stability Requirements

The third set of requirements relate to the application's performance during execution. Virtual reality apps require a significant amount of processing, so stability is a prime concern. Table 17.3 lists the requirements related to performance and stability.

Table 17.3

Performance and Stability Requirements

Area	ID	Description
Stability	PS-S1	App installs and runs without crashing
Performance	PS-P1	App loads quickly or provides VR feedback if it takes more than three seconds to load
	PS-P2	App maintains high performance
	PS-P3	App does not display a thermal warning during 30 minutes of usage
Visual Quality	PS-V1	App renders without unexpected distortion when viewed through a Daydream viewer

The first three requirements are straightforward. A Daydream app should execute without crashing, and if it takes more than three seconds to load, it should provide a message. The third requirement relates to the application's frame rate (should be high) and the delay between head movement and the change in scene (should be low). To satisfy this, applications should ensure that asynchronous reprojection is enabled if available and VR mode is enabled if available.

Graphical processing increases device temperature. If the device overheats, it will display a warning. The fourth requirement states that this warning must not appear within the first 30 minutes of an app's execution.

17.4 Publishing Requirements

The last set of requirements are the most involved. Every Daydream app must be specially packaged for the Google Play Store.

Table 17.4

Publishing Requirements

Area	ID	Description
Publishing	PB-P1	App adheres to all Google Play content policies
	PB-P2	App has a VR icon
	PB-P3	App has a 360° stereo photosphere
	PB-P4	App content matches description
	PB-P5	App is for users 13 years and older
	PB-P6	App has the correct Motion Intensity Level
	PB-P7	App must adhere to naming policy
	PB-P8	App uses correct platform terminology
	PB-P9	App does not use the Daydream logo

Regarding the first requirement, the content policies for the Google Play Store can be found at https://play.google.com/about/developer-content-policy. Gambling, violence, and deceptive/disruptive advertisements are forbidden. Apps shouldn't interfere with other apps and their content should be family-friendly. More specifically, apps should be accessible to users aged 13 and over.

To receive payment, nearly all apps must use Google Play In-app Billing. Notable exceptions include payment for physical products and for digital content that can be accessed outside of the app, such as audio files.

PB-P6 relates to the app's Motion Intensity Level, which identifies how much the user has to move. There are three possible values:

- No motion — Only head motion required, the user can execute the app while seated or standing in one position
- Moderate motion — Requires motion in at most two degrees of freedom, such as walking on a flat plane or traveling in an elevator
- Intense motion — Unlimited motion, may include flying or traveling in a vehicle, can involve extreme acceleration and deceleration

Every Daydream app must follow Google's guidelines regarding the naming policy. An application's name can't contain any of the following terms or misspellings of them:

- Daydream
- Daydream VR
- Cardboard
- Android VR
- Google VR

App descriptions should correctly distinguish between the Home button and App button. Apps should use the term *swipe* for scrolling, moving, or rotating an object with the touchpad. Apps should use the term *click* for selecting an object with the touchpad.

17.4.1 The VR Icon

Chapter 3 explained the basics of Android icons and the different sizes that should be provided. In addition, an app can have a VR icon to be displayed in Daydream Home. There are three requirements:

1. Every icon consists of two images—a foreground image and a background image
2. Each image must be 512-by-512 pixels in size and each must be submitted in PNG format.
3. The background image must be based on a mesh provided by Google.

For the last point, Google provides PSD files to help create the icon's images. They can be downloaded from https://developers.google.com/vr/downloads/stencil-examples.zip. Figure 17.1 shows what the stencil for the background image looks like.

The upper gray rectangle identifies the region where the background image content should be placed. Similarly, the content of the foreground image should be limited to this rectangle. In general, the foreground image contains the app's logo and the background image provides a colorful backdrop.

When drawing the background, make sure to fill the image to its edges. Otherwise, the image's edges may appear to flicker when displayed in Daydream Home.

The two icon files should be placed in the project's res/drawable-nodpi folder. To identify these files, the manifest needs to contain two `<meta-data>` elements inside the `<activity>` element. The first `<meta-data>` associates `com.google.android.vr.icon` with the foreground drawable and the second element associates `com.google.android.vr.icon.background` with the background drawable.

Figure 17.1 Stencil for VR Icon Background

For example, suppose that the VR icon is defined with the image files foreground.png and background.png. The project's manifest can identify them with the following markup:

```
<meta-data android:name="com.google.android.vr.icon"
           android:resource="@drawable/foreground" />

<meta-data android:name="com.google.android.vr.icon_background"
           android:resource="@drawable/background" />
```

Note that the VR icon doesn't replace the regular Android icon. This is set by inserting an `<android:icon>` element within the `<activity>`.

17.4.2 The Stereo Photosphere

To illustrate what the app's environment looks like, Requirement PB-P3 calls for a 360° stereo photosphere. A photosphere is a rectangular image that represents a spherical scene. To satisfy the requirement, this image must be 4,096-by-4,096 pixels in size and must be provided as a JPEG or PNG (preferred). The pixels must not contain alpha components.

At the time of this writing, there are no tools available for converting the user interface of a Daydream app into a photosphere. For Unity developers, eVRydayVR provides a package called 360 Panorama Capture, which is available from Unity's asset store. It's been reported that similar tools are available for Maya and Blender.

According to Google's description, "If your app contains only mono content, it's okay to use a mono image (that is, the same image in each eye) as long as the image is still in the correct stereo format." I've taken this to mean that Google will an image containing two 4,096-by-2,048 images stacked on one another. This is similar to the panorama images discussed in Chapter 13.

I've never generated a photosphere. Instead, I've stacked two 4,096-by-2,048 images to form a 4,096-by-4,096 PNG and submitted that instead. Google doesn't seem to have a problem with this.

17.5 Publishing the App

If your app satisfies all of Google's requirements, you can submit it to the Google Play Store for publication. Google makes this straightforward through the Google Play Development Console. This makes it possible for developers to manage and publish apps, and the website address is https://play.google.com/apps/publish.

Before you can access the Development Console, you need to register. This involves agreeing to Google's developer agreement and paying a $25 license fee. To complete registration, Google requires contact information, including the developer's name, email address, and phone number.

After registration, the new page will display a button entitled **Publish an Android App on Google Play**. Pressing this button will open a dialog box asking for the app's title and target language. Afterward, pressing the **Create** button will close the box.

After the box closes, the next page will ask for a great deal of information about the app, including the following:

- Title (20-30 characters)
- Short description (0-80 characters)
- Full description (0-4000 characters)
- Screenshots (2-8 screenshots required)
- 512-by-512 pixel icon
- Daydream stereoscopic image

Figure 17.2 shows what this page looks like.

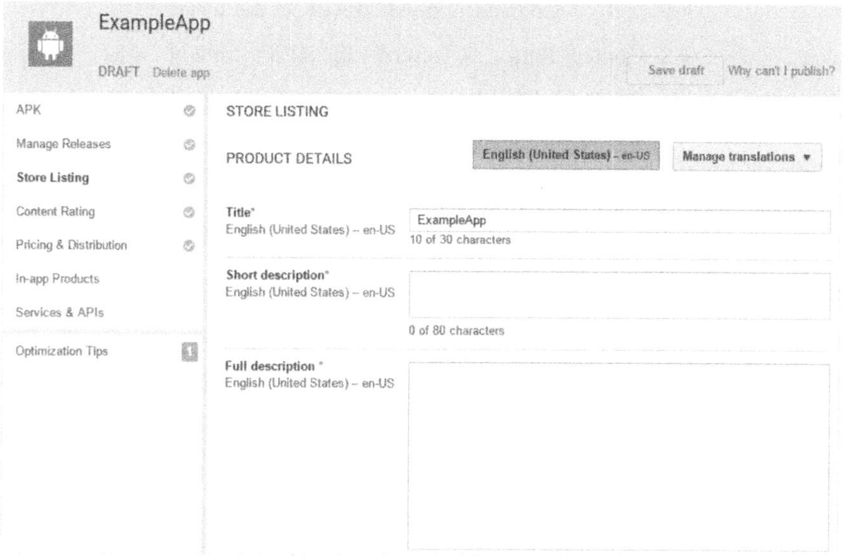

Figure 17.2 New App Publication Page

Toward the bottom of the page, there are more controls requesting information:

- Application type
- Category
- New content rating
- An associated website (optional)
- A contact email address
- A phone number (optional)

To submit the content rating, the page requires that you fill out a questionnaire. But this questionnaire can't be filled out until an APK has been uploaded.

The last portion of the page asks for an optional privacy policy URL. This URL should provide information about the app's privacy. In particular, the policy identifies how the app deals with data regarding the user and the device. This is required for apps requesting sensitive permissions or data, or apps registered in the Designed for Families program.

After filling out the page, click the **Save draft** button in the upper right. This will save the form information.

The left side of Figure 17.2 lists other pages that need to be filled out:

- APK — Upload the finished APK to the server
- Content Rating — Describe the APK's content
- Pricing & Distribution — Set the price for installing the APK

When submitting an APK, make sure that it's been digitally signed. In Android Studio, a signed APK can be constructed by going to **Build > Generate Signed APK...** in the main menu. This will ask you for information related to the keystore containing the private key that you intend to use. Google provides more information on this topic at https://developer.android.com/studio/publish/app-signing.html.

In the Pricing & Distribution page, be sure to specify that the APK is intended for Daydream. This will enable questions related to the app's distribution and motion intensity settings. As discussed earlier in the chapter, the motion levels are No Motion (just head motion), Moderate Motion (walking on a flat surface), and Intense Motion (any and all motion).

After all of the forms have been filled out, click the **Publish app** button in the upper right. It may take a few minutes for the submission to complete.

In a few hours, you'll receive an email identifying the status of the Daydream review. If the app meets the Daydream requirements discussed earlier in this chapter, the app will be considered suitable for use with the Daydream viewer. If not, you can resubmit the app for review by updating the version and republishing it.

17.6 Summary

Just as VR applications are more difficult to code than regular applications, they're also subject to more stringent requirements. Google's requirements ensure that all Daydream apps have the same basic behavior. For example, the camera is determined solely by the user's headset and the controller can select objects like a laser pointer.

This chapter has presented all of Google's current requirements for Daydream apps. If you've followed the discussion in previous chapters, they shouldn't present any serious difficulty. Just make sure the window occupies the entire screen, make sure VR mode is enabled, and make sure that the manifest contains the right configuration data.

In my opinion, the hardest requirements are PS-P2 and PS-P3, which require that apps execute at high performance without overheating the device. This can be difficult for complex graphical applications, particularly if the application plays audio and monitors the controller while rendering graphics.

If your app meets all of Google's requirements, then it's straightforward to submit it for publication. The Google Play Development Console asks for a lot of information, including titles, descriptions, and many different icons. Keep in mind that Google only accepts APKs that have been digitally signed.

The console's Pricing & Distribution page makes it possible to indicate that the app is intended for Daydream usage. If this is set, the form will enable Daydream-specific questions. In addition, the app will be subject to a Daydream-specific review process. Don't be upset if the app doesn't pass—Daydream apps are reviewed each time they're submitted for publication.

Index

F

G

H

I

J

K

L

M

N

O

P

Q

R

S

T

U

V

W

Z

Made in the USA
Middletown, DE
05 November 2026

36612685R00243